MASTER PHOTOGRAPHY

YOUR COMPLETE GUIDE TO DIGITAL PHOTOGRAPHY

TRACY MCCRACKIN

TRACY MCCRACKIN
PHOTOGRAPHY

First published by Self Published 2022

TABLE OF CONTENTS

PREFACE

Upgrade your photography game with "Master Photography"! Say goodbye to blurry and uninspiring photos as this comprehensive book will transform you into a fantastic photographer in no time. In the past, pursuing photography meant lugging around heavy and expensive equipment, making it a daunting endeavor for most. However, the digital revolution has brought forth lightweight and affordable cameras that fit in your pocket. Now, you can capture stunning images without breaking the bank or being weighed down by bulky gear. Welcome to the blissful realm of digital photography!

Whether you possess the creativity of Picasso or the experience of Ansel Adams, this content-rich book is a must-have for photographers of all levels. With 400 pages brimming with vibrant photos and helpful illustrations, it unravels the technical complexities behind photography, providing you with invaluable tools to elevate your shutter skills. Don't miss out on these digital camera tips—grab your copy now while they're still hot!

- **How to choose the best digital camera for you;**
- **Understanding various camera lenses;**
- **Understanding the exposure triangle;**
- **Stop of light and depth of field explained;**

- **How to set up your camera's settings;**
- **How to avoid camera shake;**
- **How to compose an image;**
- **How to pose and light people;**
- **How to save your photos with the right file format;**
- **Which AI imaging software to select;**
- **What is a flash, and when to use it;**
- **Which printers to buy;**
- **How to Choose the Best Photo Paper;**
- **Photography careers in today's market.**

This book is like a crash course in photography - it teaches you how to use the camera as if it were an artist's brush, creating images with its lens instead of paint. So break out that camera and venture into the world with your camera. The possibilities are endless when creativity meets technology!

To facilitate your learning experience, I have conveniently embedded affiliate links throughout my book, granting you instant access to these recommended products. While I receive a tiny commission from each sale, it contributes to my ability to provide you with valuable tutorials and instructional content in the future. Prices subject to change.

I would like to *thank* several people who helped me along the way. There's nothing like having an extraordinary partner to help you pursue your dreams. My hubby, John, was my cheering squad during the past two years of this wild writing journey.

I'm especially grateful to my dear friend Karen. Her early reading and keen feedback was so appreciated.

I'm also incredibly thankful for Phyllis, my incredible friend and comrade in travel. Her unwavering encouragement gave me the courage to pursue this book from its early beginnings - truly a blessing!

Happy Reading!

EXPERT BOOK REVIEW

"Tracy covers photography from A-Z (aperture to zoom lenses). SPECTACULAR photographs throughout illustrate the well-written text. There is so much history of photography here, that I am surprised I didn't know, or perhaps had forgotten some details during my 55 years taking photos and on production sets. From Camera Obscura to AI,-powered algorithms Tracy covers it all. Amazing illustrations throughout, with examples punctuated by Tracy's own photographs (most available for purchase on her website, using hyperlinks). The path to becoming a great photographer and cinematographer starts with the basics. Tracy offers this and so much more. For every aspiring still photographer and cinematographer, **Master Photography is a "must read."**

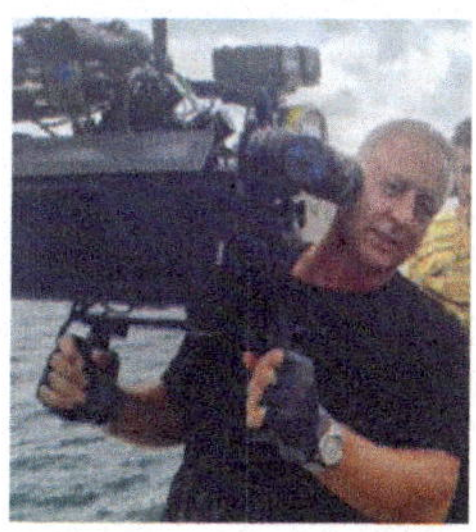

Michael Frediani is currently the Board of Governors of the Society of Camera Operators (SOC), Past President of SOC Camera Operator, Cinematographer, Director. Frediani earned his Bachelor of Arts degree in Cinema from Columbia College-Hollywood. Frediani was first elected President of the SOC in 1995 and served as Editor-in-Chief of Camera Operator magazine. Since 2004 he has been a member of the National Executive Board of International Cinematographers Guild and also edited ICG magazine. He has been chairman of both organization's Heritage and Historical committees. Frediani has been a camera operator since 1989 with over 80 film credits including 2nd unit operator on the feature films **Shattered, Hostage, and Underworld**. Frediani was elected again as SOC president in 2011. He spends a great deal of time volunteering for various projects at the SOC and teaches Camera Operators Workshops, and is a Mentor. In the past Frediani has taught seminars at NAB in Las Vegas, Dolly Grip Workshops at Local 80 in Burbank, Camera Operating at the American Film Institute, and directing actors at Rossi/Snyder Acting Studio, along with his own workshop: www.survivalonset.com.

1

HISTORY OF PHOTOGRAPHY

In order to master photography, it's crucial to grasp the technology that gave rise to modern cameras. It is not enough to simply be familiar with the mechanics of operating a camera; a deeper understanding of the scientific principles behind its functioning is essential. Photography revolves around the study of light, making it imperative to explore how light has been harnessed and evolved in creating cameras. This forms the initial lesson in your journey through this book on photography.

The history of photography spans several centuries and is marked by significant technological advancements and artistic developments. Here is a broad overview of the history of photography.

Precursors to Photography

The principles of photography can be traced back to ancient times, with the invention of the *camera obscura*, a device that projected an image onto a surface through a small hole or lens. Artists used camera obscura to trace or draw images. The first versions were in very large rooms, but over time condensed down to table-top size.

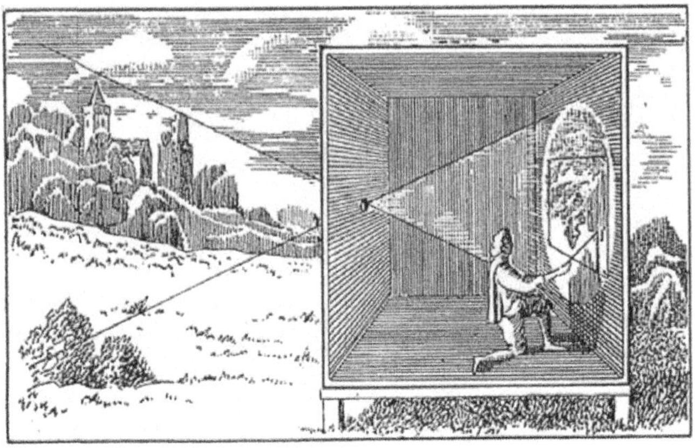

The camera obscura, meaning *"dark room"* in Latin, is an early optical device that has played a significant role in the development of visual perception and the understanding of light. It comprises a darkened chamber or box with a small hole or aperture on one side. When light passes through the aperture, an inverted image of the external scene is projected onto a surface inside the box or room.

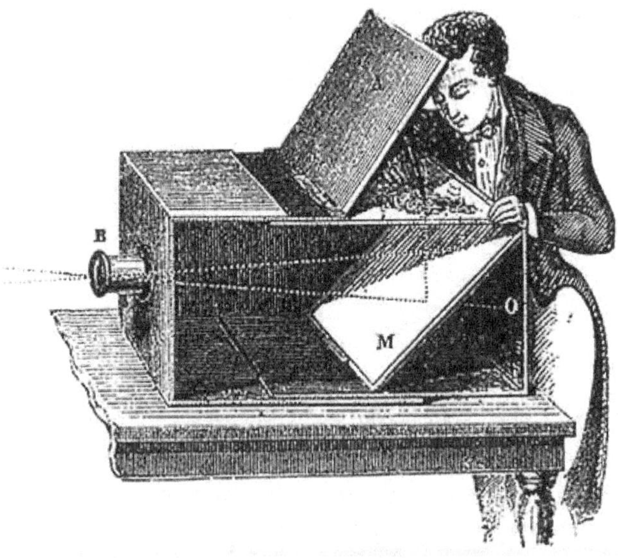

The camera obscura has been used by artists, scientists, and photographers throughout history, allowing them to study perspective, create accurate drawings, and explore the principles of optics. It served as a precursor to the invention of photography, offering a glimpse into the magic of image formation and the power of light. The camera obscura remains an intriguing testament to the ingenuity and curiosity of human beings in their quest to understand and capture the world around them.

The Invention of the Camera

In the early 19th century, inventors began experimenting with capturing permanent images using light-sensitive materials. In 1826, Nicéphore Niépce captured the *first permanent photograph* using a camera obscura and a bitumen-coated plate. One of the earliest `saved photographs (Heliograph).

Nicéphore Niépce (1765-1833) was a French inventor and pioneer in photography. He is widely recognized as one of the founding figures of photography. He is credited with creating the world's first permanent photograph using a process known as heliography. Using a bitumen-coated plate and a long exposure time, Niépce was able to create an image of the view from his window in his estate at Le Gras, France. The resulting photograph, titled "View from the Window at Le Gras," is considered the oldest surviving photograph in existence.

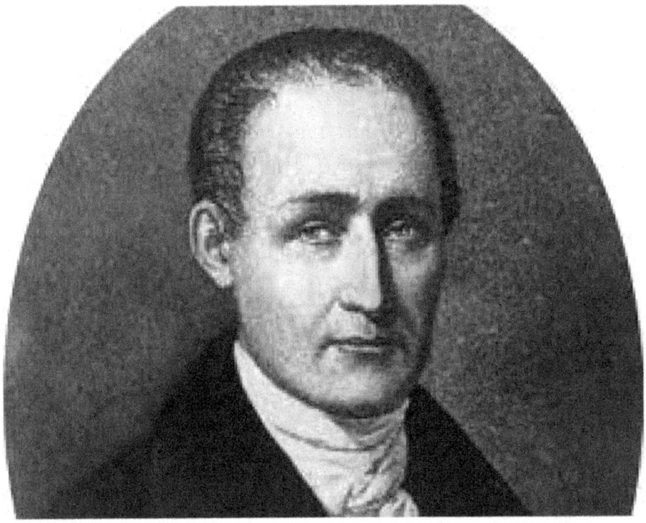

His experiments with light-sensitive materials and long exposure times paved the way for subsequent advancements in photographic processes by later inventors such as Louis Daguerre and William Henry Fox Talbot. His pioneering efforts marked the beginning of a new era, leading to the democratization and widespread accessibility of image-making that we enjoy in the modern world.

Daguerreotype

The daguerreotype is a photographic process invented by Louis-Jacques-Mandé Daguerre and announced to the public in 1839. It is one of the earliest practical methods of capturing and producing more *permanent, sharper images*.

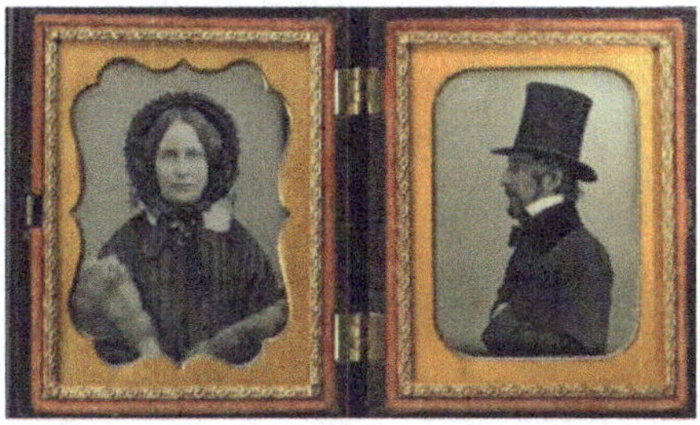

The process involved several steps. A silver-plated copper plate was polished to a mirror-like finish, creating a highly reflective surface. The plate was then sensitized by exposing it to iodine vapor, which created a light-sensitive surface of silver iodide. The sensitized plate was loaded into a camera and exposed to light, capturing the image. The exposure times could vary, ranging from several minutes to even hours, depending on the light and the subject being photographed. After the exposure, the plate was developed using mercury vapor, which caused the latent image to become visible. It became a positive image - with no negative.

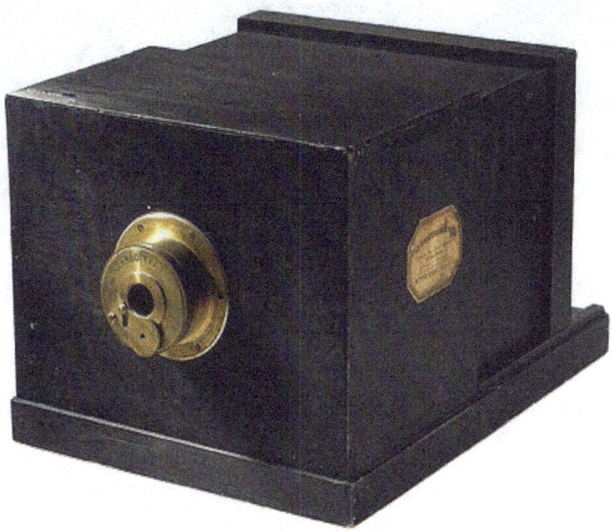

Daguerreotypes gained popularity quickly and were known for their exceptional level of detail and clarity, capturing intricate textures and delicate nuances.

However, the process had its limitations. The images were one-of-a-kind, and couldn't be reproduced. Each daguerreotype was a unique object, often housed in a protective case or frame. The process played a crucial role in the development of photography, serving as the foundation for subsequent advancements in photographic technology and processes.

Calotype and Collodion Processes

William Henry Fox Talbot developed the calotype process, which involved making a negative image on paper and producing positive prints from it. In 1851, Frederick Scott Archer introduced the wet plate collodion process, using glass plates coated with a light-sensitive emulsion. This is the 1867 Collodion Wet Plate.

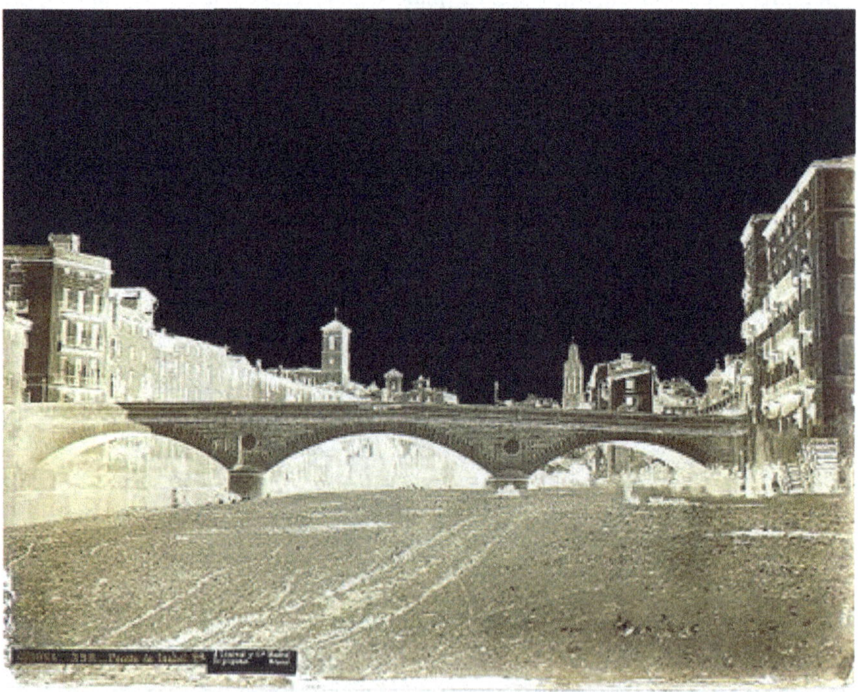

The collodion process, also known as the *wet plate collodion process*, was a photographic technique developed in the mid-19th century. It improved upon earlier processes by allowing the production of negative images on glass plates, *offering greater clarity and the potential for multiple prints.*

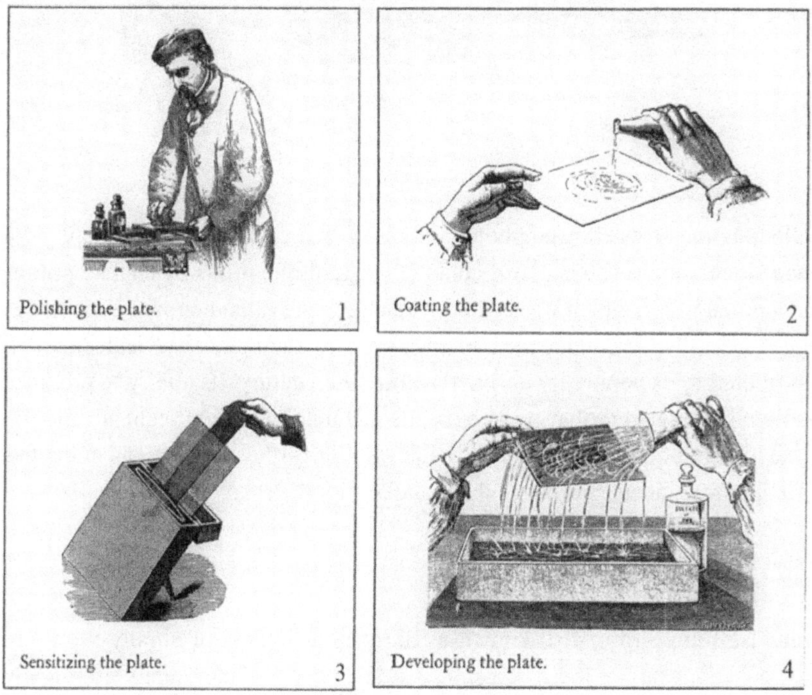

Polishing the plate. 1

Coating the plate. 2

Sensitizing the plate. 3

Developing the plate. 4

A glass plate was first coated with a solution of collodion, a syrupy mixture of cellulose nitrate dissolved in alcohol and ether. While the collodion was still wet, it was sensitized by immersing it in a bath of silver nitrate, which converted the collodion into a light-sensitive material. The sensitized plate was then exposed to a camera while still wet. The exposure times varied depending on the available light and the desired effect, but they were typically longer than with modern photographic processes. After exposure, the plate had to be developed immediately. It was typically treated with a developer containing pyrogallic acid, which transformed the exposed silver salts into metallic silver, forming a negative image.

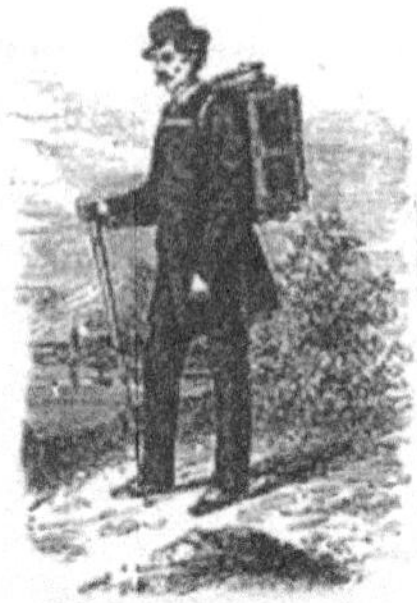

The wet-plate photographer needed a strong back if he went into the field.

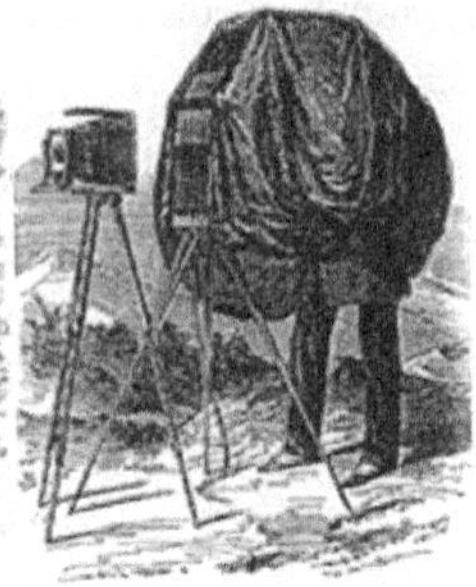

The wet-plate photographer, on the road.

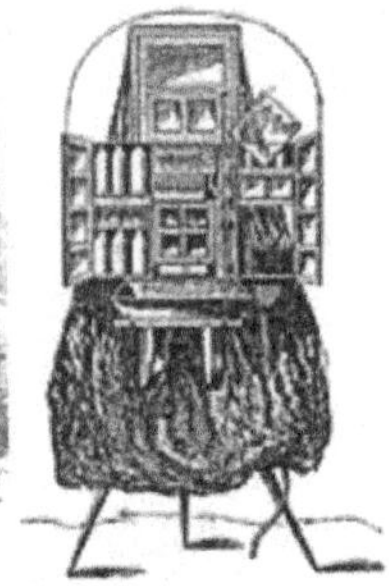

Inside the darkroom with the cover removed.

Collodion negatives allowed photographers to create sharp, detailed images with a wide tonal range. The negative could create multiple prints by contact printing on albumen paper, which was coated with egg white (albumen) and sensitized with silver salts. This made the collodion process commercially viable and contributed to its popularity during the mid-19th century. Its ability to produce high-quality negatives that could be replicated marked a significant advancement in the history of photography, paving the way for further innovations in the field. Soon, photographers could take their cameras on the road.

Development of Film

Cellulose nitrate film, also known as nitrocellulose film or simply nitrate film, was indeed created in the 19th century. It is a type of photographic film that was widely used in the early days of cinema and photography. Nitrocellulose, a highly flammable material, was used as the base for the film stock.

In the late 19th century, pioneers like George Eastman and Thomas Edison recognized the potential of cellulose nitrate for capturing moving images. Cellulose nitrate film offered several advantages, such as flexibility, transparency, and the ability to record continuous sequences of images. This breakthrough led to the development and growth of the motion picture industry.

However, one significant drawback of cellulose nitrate film was its highly flammable nature. The film stock was prone to spontaneous combustion, which could lead to dangerous fires in theaters or storage facilities. Several tragic incidents occurred due to nitrate film fires, highlighting the urgent need for safer alternatives.

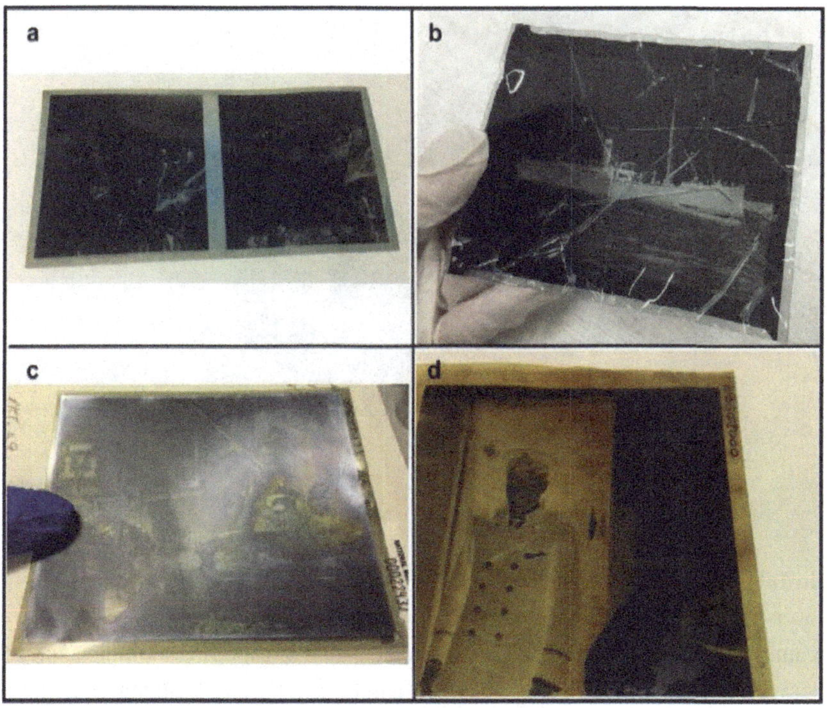

In the early 20th century, cellulose acetate film gradually replaced nitrate film as a safer alternative. Cellulose acetate, commonly known as a safety film, was less flammable and became the industry standard for many years. Nitrate film production eventually ceased in the mid-20th century because of safety concerns.

Despite the risks associated with cellulose nitrate film, its existence and development in the 19th century laid the foundation for the modern film industry. It represented a significant milestone in the history of cinema and photography, shaping the way we capture and experience moving images today.

Popularization of Photography

Photography became more accessible to the general public with the introduction of the Kodak camera by George Eastman in 1888. George Eastman was an American entrepreneur and inventor who revolutionized photography with the introduction of the Kodak camera.

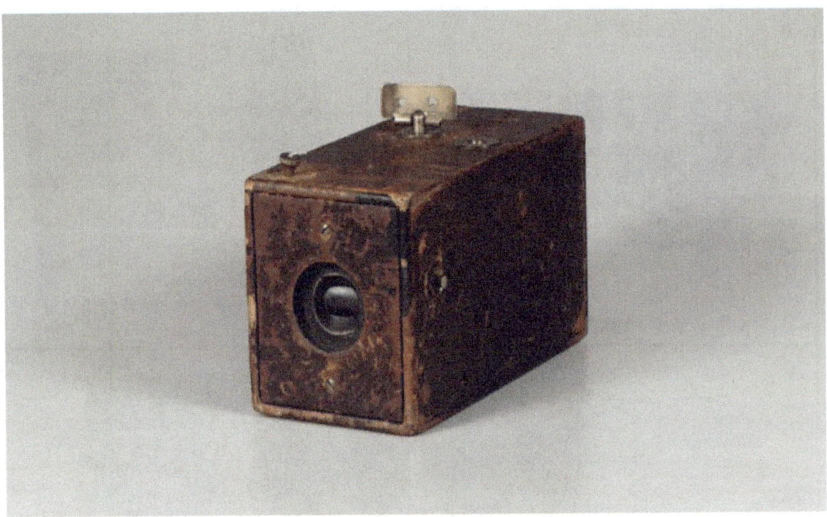

In 1888, Eastman launched the first Kodak camera, which was a compact and user-friendly device that simplified the process of taking photographs. The camera came *pre-loaded with a roll of film* capable of capturing multiple exposures, and once the roll was used up, it could be sent back to Eastman's company for processing and printing. This innovation made photography accessible to everyone, as it eliminated the need for complex equipment and darkroom processing. The introduction of the Kodak camera marked a significant milestone in the history of photography, ushering in a new era of portable and convenient image-making that would lay the foundation for modern consumer photography.

Color Photography

The Lumière brothers, Auguste and Louis Lumière, were pioneering French filmmakers and inventors who played a crucial role in the early development of cinema. In 1907, they continued their groundbreaking work by introducing the Autochrome Lumière, an innovative color photography process.

The Autochrome Lumière was the first commercially successful color photography method, based on a process of using dyed grains of potato starch to create a color filter. This filter was applied to a glass plate, which was then coated with a light-sensitive emulsion. When exposed and developed, the Autochrome Lumière produced vivid and realistic color images. Still-Life wiht Lobster Autochrome on Glass.

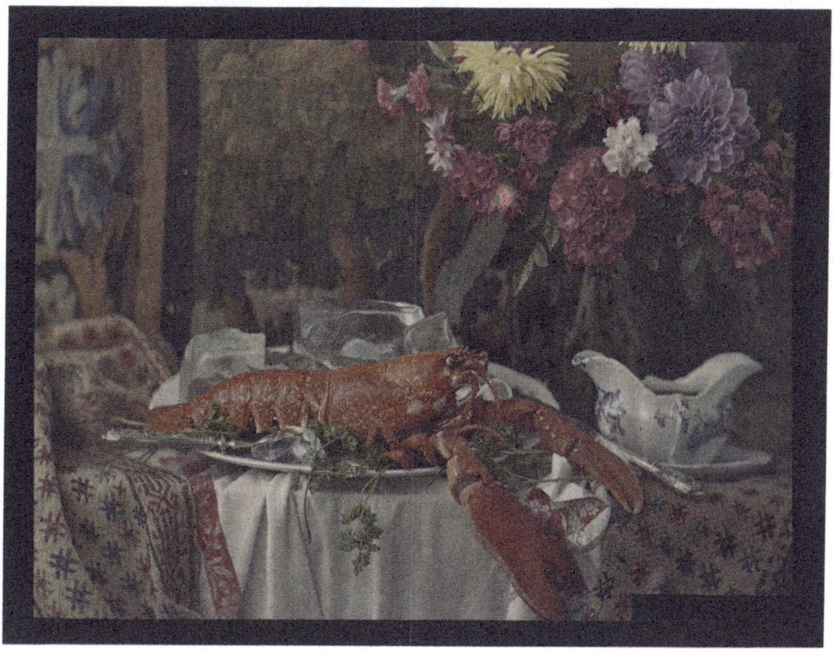

The introduction of the Autochrome Lumière was a significant advancement in the field of photography, as it allowed photographers to capture the world in color. Prior to this, color photography was a complex and often cumbersome process, and the Autochrome Lumière made it more accessible and practical.

The Lumière brothers' contributions to cinema and photography were monumental, and their innovations continue to influence the art and industry to this day. Through their inventions and films, they played a vital role in shaping the history and future of visual storytelling.

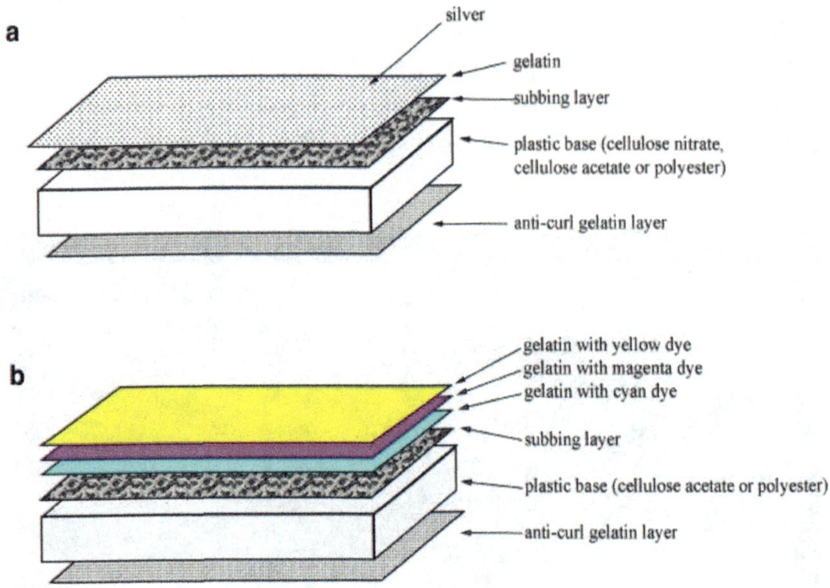

Digital Photography

In the late 20th century, digital photography emerged with the development of electronic image sensors and the transition from film to digital cameras. Digital photography revolutionized the field by allowing instant image preview, storage, manipulation, and easy sharing of photographs.

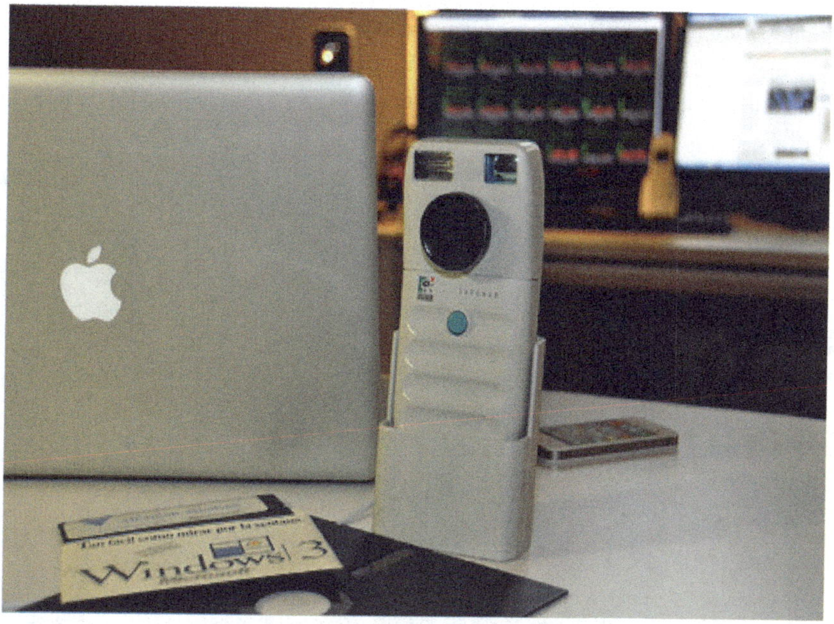

Logitech Photoman was a digital camera introduced by Logitech in the late 1990s. It was a compact and user-friendly camera designed for everyday photography needs. The Logitech Photoman featured a built-in flash, fixed focus lens, and a small LCD screen for image preview. It offered a resolution of up to 640x480 pixels, which was sufficient for capturing digital images during that time. The camera connected to computers via a serial port, allowing users to transfer their photos and view them on the computer. While the Logitech Photoman was not a high-end professional camera, it provided an affordable and accessible option for individuals looking to venture into the world of digital photography.

Rise of Smartphone Photography

The rise of smartphone photography has transformed the way people capture and share moments. With the advancements in smartphone camera technology, the quality of images has improved significantly, allowing users to capture high-resolution photos with ease. The integration of advanced camera features such as optical image stabilization, multiple lenses, and computational photography techniques has made smartphone cameras capable of producing stunning results. Additionally, smartphones offer a wide range of editing tools and filters, allowing users to enhance their photos directly on their devices.

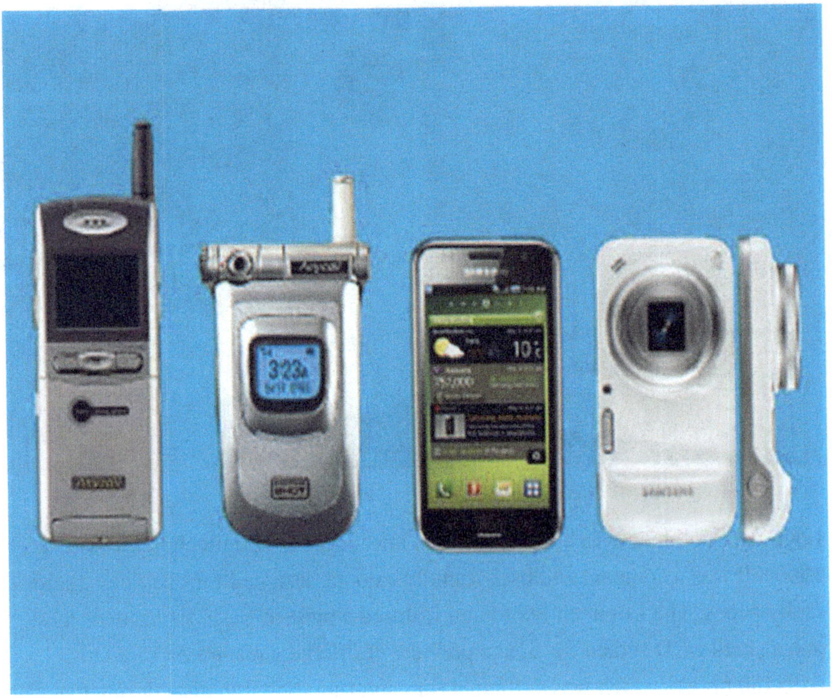

The convenience of having a capable camera in one's pocket at all times has democratized photography, enabling people from all walks of life to express their creativity and share their perspectives through images. Social media platforms and photo-sharing apps have further fueled the popularity of smartphone photography, enabling users to instantly share their photos with a global audience. The rise of smartphone photography has empowered individuals to become storytellers, capturing and documenting their experiences in a visually compelling way.

Contemporary Photography

Photography continues to evolve and adapt to new technologies and artistic trends. Various genres and styles have emerged, including documentary photography, street photography, fashion photography, and fine art photography, among others.

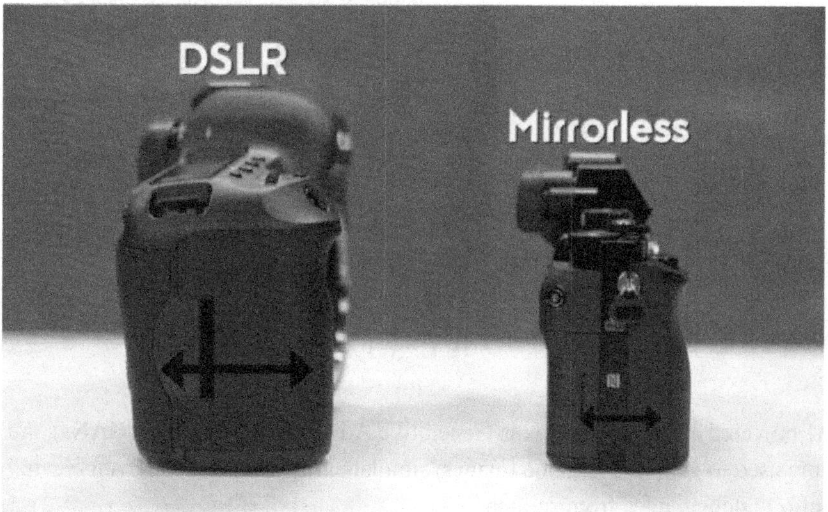

Camera technology is continually advancing, and new developments are expected to emerge regularly. At the present moment, Mirrorless Cameras appear to be at the top of the list, advancing past the standard DSLR cameras. I outline the pros and cons of each in their own Chapters in the next two Chapters.

The integration of artificial intelligence (AI) into photography has been a gradual process, but it has gained notable momentum in recent years. The exact timeline of AI's involvement in photography can vary depending on the specific applications and advancements being considered.

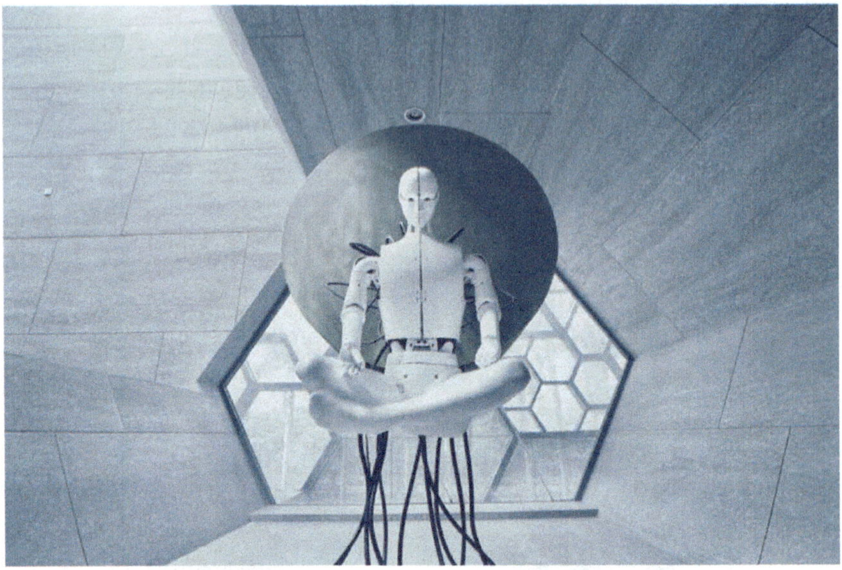

AI-powered algorithms, such as Generative Adversarial Networks (GANs), are now used to generate realistic images, simulate artistic styles, and even create entirely new images from scratch.

It's important to note that the integration of AI in photography is an ongoing process, and new developments continue to shape the field. AI is being leveraged to automate tasks, improve image quality, enhance user experience, and push the boundaries of creativity in photography.

2

DSLR CAMERAS

What is a DSLR Camera?

DSLRs, or Digital Single Lens Reflex Cameras, use a unique mirror system. They angled this mirror at 45 degrees and reflects images to the viewfinder in real-time. When the shutter button is pressed, the mirror lifts, the viewfinder goes black momentarily, and the image is captured as light reaches the sensor.

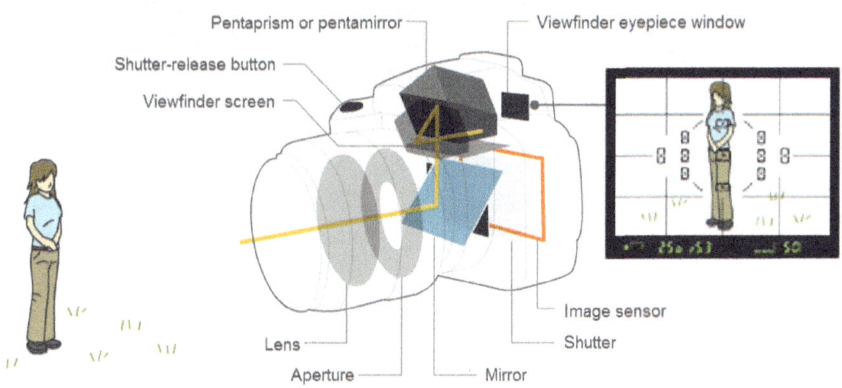

The reflected light from the lens travels through a mirror mechanism and ends up in the viewfinder's pentaprism. This clear view of your subject is possible before pressing the shutter button. The mirror's position in front of the shutter and sensor is a little trick that prevents light from reaching the sensor until it's time to take the shot. This is just one of many fascinating features of a DSLR camera that allows you to capture incredible photographs.

From wedding photographers to wildlife photographers, anyone who wants to capture stunning images knows the importance of having a good camera. What makes them stand out is their ability to combine traditional lens technology with modern image sensors. This means you get the same control over your images as you would with a traditional camera, but with better detail and sharper images.

Viewfinders Debate

When it comes to choosing a camera, one of the key decisions to make is whether to opt for an optical or electronic viewfinder. And now there is a new hybrid option. While optical viewfinders have long been the standard, electronic and hybrid viewfinders are increasingly gaining popularity.

Advantages of Optical Viewfinders

DSLRs come with optical viewfinders. Some Mirrorless cameras employ electronic viewfinders. Instead of using mirrors and prisms to reflect the scene, an electronic viewfinder uses a digital display, much like the one on the back of the camera. This can be a game-changer for those who like to experiment with different settings or shoot in challenging lighting conditions. Whether you opt for an optical or electronic viewfinder camera depends on your preference and the photography you want.

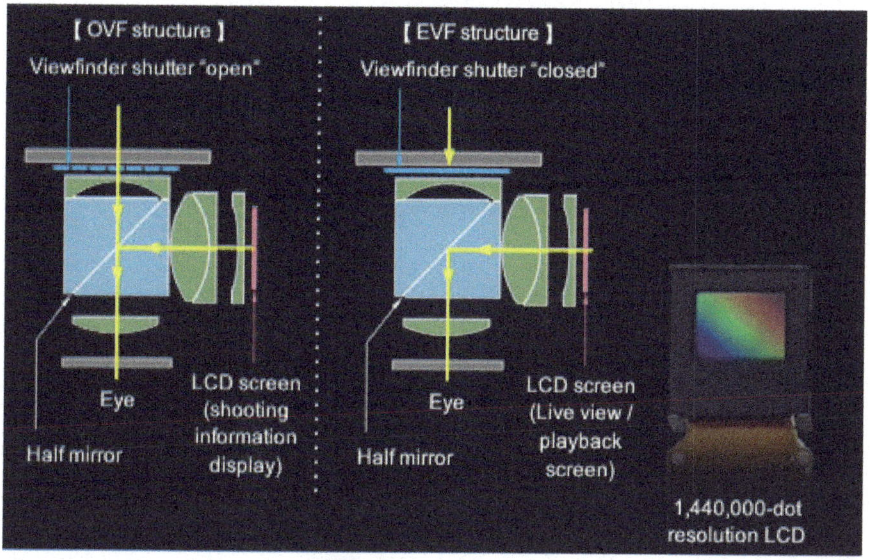

For photography enthusiasts, the quality of the image captured is of utmost importance. And while modern Mirrorless cameras offer fancy electronic viewfinders, there's something to be said about the reliability and clarity of an optical viewfinder. By using actual light passing through the camera, as opposed to a digital processing system, optical viewfinders provide a superior view of the environment. They offer a better dynamic range, allowing for the capture of scenes with extreme differences in brightness. And, unlike some electronic viewfinders, there is no delay - so you won't miss out on capturing the perfect moment.

Advantages of Electronic Viewfinder

By displaying images directly from the sensor, the electronic viewfinder mode offers the benefit of seeing accurately exposed images. With this feature, you can be confident of your shooting exposure settings. Electronic viewfinders have focus aids like focus peaking. This helps you see what's in focus before taking the shot. However, they can suffer from slight lag, making them a less desirable option for sports and action photographers. In low light, high-ISO noise can cause cloudiness.

Are you a sport or action photographer? Opt for an optical viewfinder over an electronic viewfinder - even if the electronic viewfinder has useful features like focus peaking. They suffer from lag, which can be a critical factor in capturing fast-moving subjects. In low light, electronic viewfinders can get cloudy due to high-ISO noise. Optical Viewfinders perform far better in these scenarios. Choose the right viewfinder to get the best shots every time.

Digital Sensor Technology

Digital cameras employ a fascinating process to capture images, utilizing countless minuscule light cavities known as "photosites." When the camera's shutter button is pressed and the exposure commences, these photosites gather photons and convert them into an electrical signal. Once the exposure concludes, each photosite closes, and the strength of the electrical signal is measured, revealing the number of photons that entered each cavity. These signals are subsequently converted into digital values, with the level of precision determined by the bit depth. However, the resulting precision may be diminished depending on the file format, typically ranging from 0 to 255 for an 8-bit JPEG file.

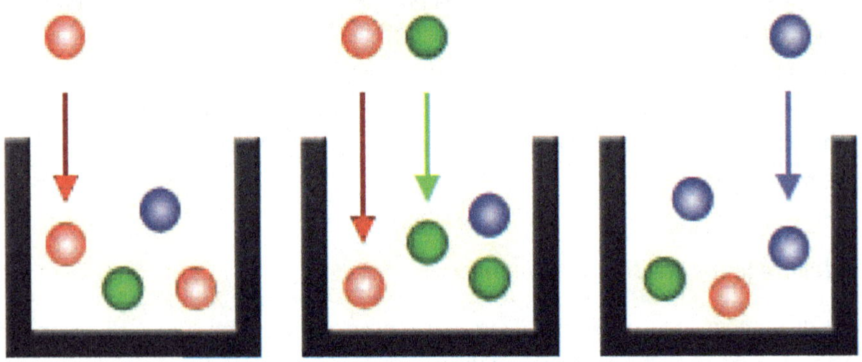

When capturing an image using these cavities, a grayscale representation is obtained. To capture color images, a filter is necessary to permit specific light colors through each cavity. Presently, digital cameras only capture one of the three primary colors, discarding two-thirds of the incoming light. The camera then approximates the other two primary colors, ultimately achieving full-color representation at every pixel. The most commonly used color filter array is known as the "Bayer array."

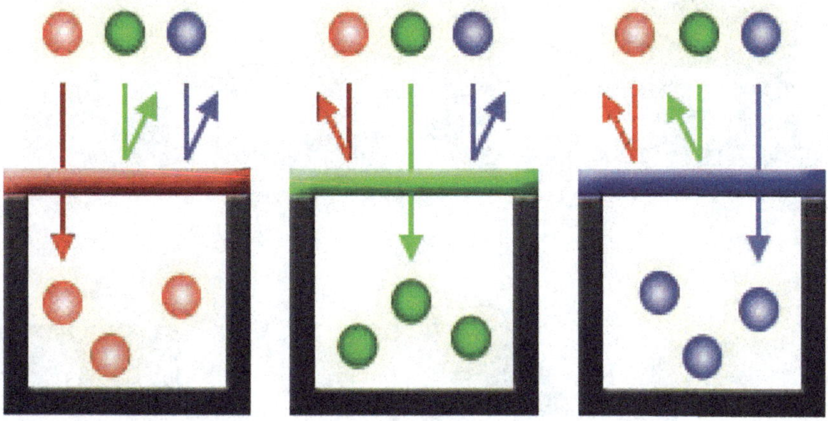

Digital Sensor Sizes

In addition to technological advancements, digital cameras have revolutionized the way photography is practiced and experienced. Here are some further points to consider:

Ease of Use: Digital cameras have made photography more accessible to everyone, from amateurs to professionals. With user-friendly interfaces and intuitive controls, capturing images has become simpler, allowing photographers to focus more on their artistic vision rather than technical settings.

Immediate Feedback: Unlike film cameras, digital cameras provide instant feedback through the LCD screen, allowing photographers to review their shots immediately. This feature enables them to make on-the-spot adjustments to composition, exposure, or other settings, leading to more accurate and desirable results.

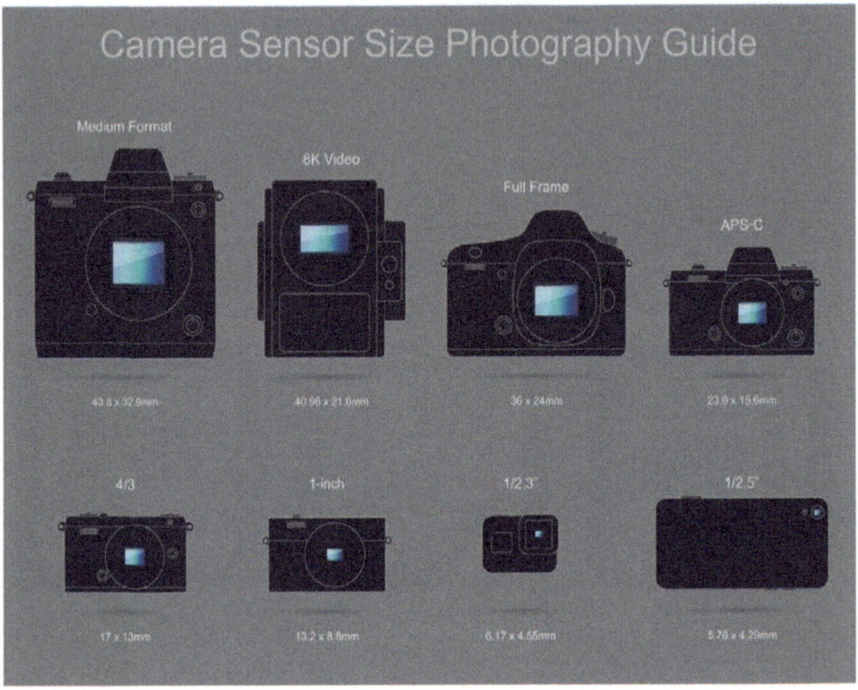

Flexibility in Post-Processing: Digital images can be easily edited and enhanced using various software applications. Photographers can adjust exposure, contrast, color balance, and apply creative filters without compromising the original image quality. This flexibility opens up a wide range of possibilities for artistic expression and experimentation.

Image Storage and Organization: Digital cameras eliminate the need for physical film rolls, reducing the cost and hassle of storage. Images can be stored on memory cards or directly transferred to computers or cloud storage, making it convenient to organize, categorize, and search through vast collections of photographs.

Increased Shooting Capacity: Digital cameras typically have larger storage capacities, allowing photographers to capture many images without having to constantly change film rolls. This feature is particularly beneficial in scenarios where continuous shooting or capturing fast-paced events is required.

Low Cost per Shot: With digital photography, photographers no longer need to worry about the cost of film and development. They can take as many shots as they want without additional expense, which encourages experimentation and the exploration of different creative angles and techniques.

Sharing and Connectivity: Digital cameras enable the seamless sharing of images across various platforms and devices. Photographers can instantly share their work with a global audience through social media, websites, or online galleries, fostering a sense of community and providing exposure for their talent and skills.

Environmental Impact: Digital photography has a significantly lower environmental footprint compared to film photography. By eliminating the need for chemicals and paper associated with film processing, digital cameras contribute to the reduction of waste and harmful pollutants.

Overall, digital cameras have propelled the field of photography into new dimensions, empowering photographers with powerful tools that enhance their creativity and capabilities. As technology continues to evolve, we can anticipate further breakthroughs that will shape the future of photography and inspire even more remarkable imagery.

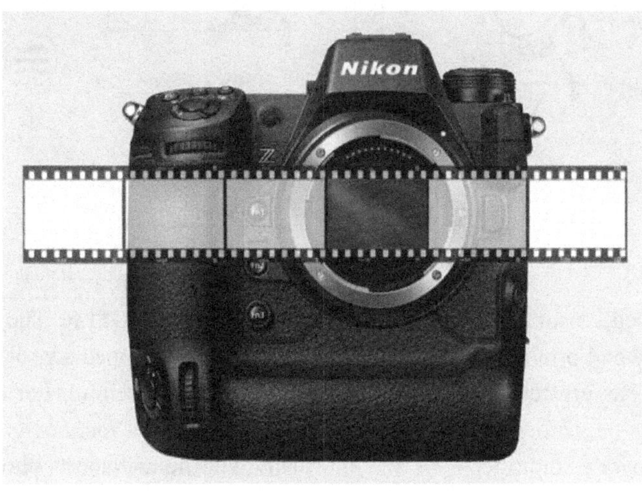

The digital image sensor may be compared to an old fashion film roll. It is the most crucial feature of your camera. They collect and store light on the light-sensitive sensor to create your image. They produce a final picture using information from the sensor. Your memory card receives an electrical signal created from an optical picture by the image sensor. There are two different sensors on a DSLR: *cropped sensor* and a *full-frame sensor*. You can get the same results with both types of sensors.

Cropped Frame Sensor

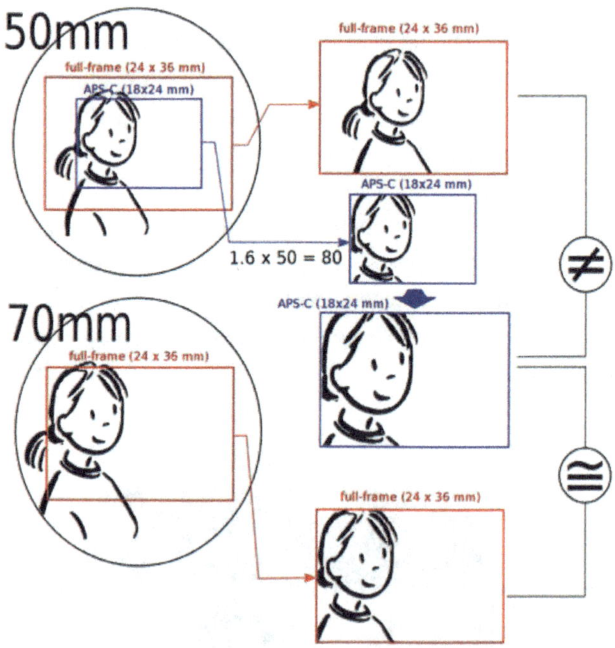

The cropped sensor camera (APS-C) is the most popular DSLR. They are often less pricey and provide excellent images. Because the cropped sensor is smaller, your lens has greater "reach" into your photo (example below). For example, a 50mm lens on a cropped sensor camera will have the *same focal length* as a full-frame camera's 80mm lens. As a result, many wildlife and sports photographers preferred cropped sensor cameras.

Full-Frame Sensor

With a full-frame camera, you can get the exact lens angle promised - for example, 50mm has an actual image angle of exactly 50mm. This type of sensor offers greater control over the depth of field than other sensors and is ideal for portrait or macro photography, where you want to make your subject stand out from the background! That's why many professionals are turning to full-frame camera systems for their portraiture projects.

The allure of evening photography is undeniable, but capturing stunning shots in low light can be challenging. Luckily, the full-frame sensor saves the day. With its ability to pick up even the faintest hints of light, these powerful sensors capture images that were once impossible to achieve. And with their larger size and higher ISO settings, full-frame sensors create portraits with breathtaking bokeh backgrounds, bringing your subject into sharp focus. Moreover, you can get closer to your subject than ever before, giving you a whole new perspective on night photography. With the full-frame sensor, the possibilities are endless.

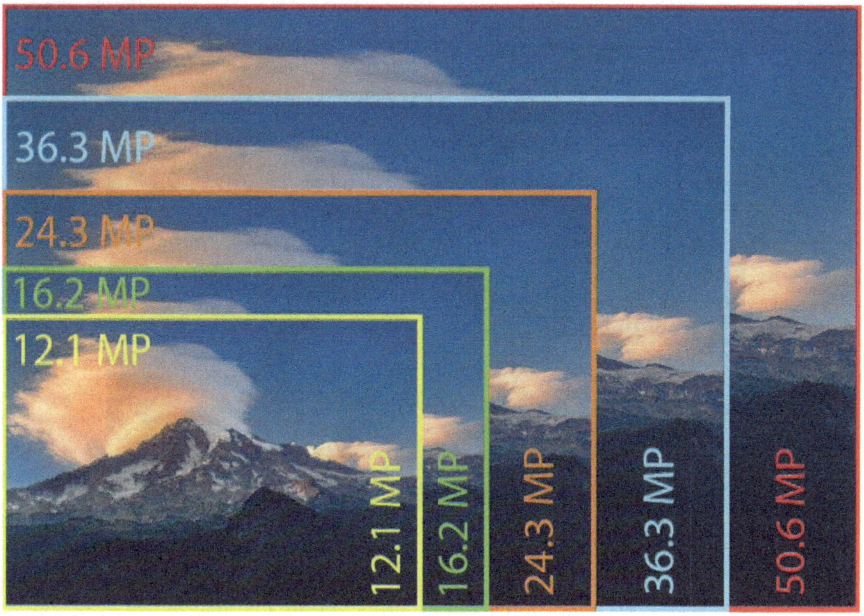

This is where more megapixels genuinely make a huge difference. With a larger sensor, the pixels can absorb more light, making clearer and sharper images. You'll be able to capture every intricate detail of your subject with ease, whether it be the delicate texture of a flower petal or the subtle nuances of a person's expression.

Auto-Focus Systems Debate

By choosing a camera, one of the other key decisions is whether to opt for one with Phase Detection Auto-Focus, Contrast Based Focus, or a Hybrid Focus. As technology advances, so are the options and features of focusing systems. This is a short review of each of them:

Phase Detection Auto-Focus

DSLRs have revolutionized photography with their dual-focusing systems - one for traditional viewfinder capture and another specialized system designed to facilitate stunning live-view images.

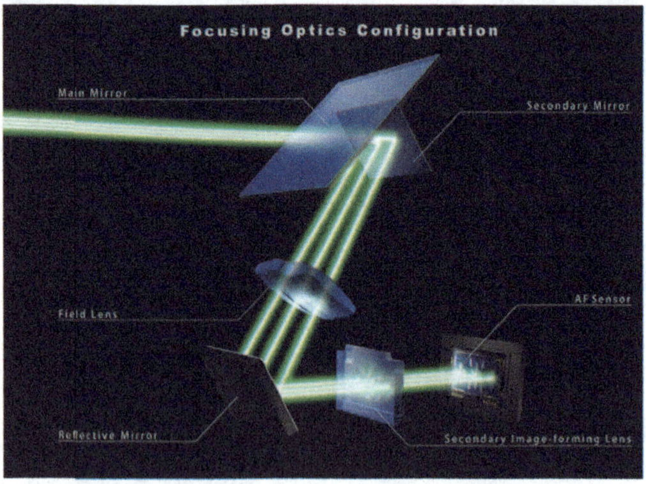

Hidden beneath the back mirror, *phase detection focusing sensors* are utilized when using the DSLR's viewfinder mode; however, this is inaccessible during live-view photo moments, which calls for a second AF system that uses direct sensor imaging. Thanks to these advancements in technology, photographers now enjoy an unprecedented level of control over every shot!

The light entering is divided into pairs of pictures and compared in phase detection systems. Two optical prisms collect light beams traveling through opposing sides of the lens in this setup. This image shows how the light path is split in a DSLR camera to direct light to a beam-splitting sensor that measures how the lens elements should be moved to focus on the subject. These beams are directed to an AF sensor below the mirror via a beam-splitting, semi-transparent mirror (or a semi-transparent portion on the primary reflex mirror).

The waveform of the two photos is then compared to see whether they are identical. As stated in the graphic below, the phase difference between the two images is used to calculate how much and in which direction the lens elements should be changed. The lens motor will then move the optical components to achieve proper focus.

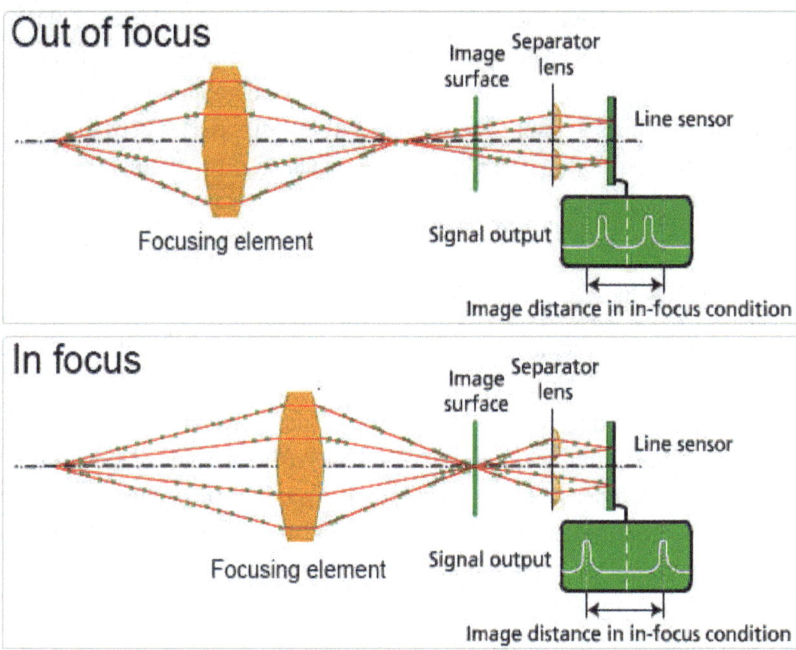

Contrast-Based Auto-Focus

Contrast-detection autofocus may sound complicated, but it is a method that relies on measuring contrast within a sensor field through the lens. Essentially, this means that the camera determines the clarity of an image by examining the difference in intensity between adjacent pixels of the sensor. It's a clever approach, but it presents some challenges, particularly with tracking moving subjects. This is because a loss of contrast doesn't show whether the subject is moving towards or away from the camera, making it challenging to maintain focus. This method is still widely used and can produce exceptional results in the right conditions.

When it comes to autofocus technology in digital cameras, contrast detection is a widely used method. This is particularly true for DSLRs that use live-view modes to focus. However, Canon digital cameras with Dual Pixel CMOS AF are an exception to this by combining both contrast and phase-detection autofocus. Meanwhile, mirrorless interchangeable lens cameras have traditionally relied on contrast measurement autofocus, but they have gradually shifted toward phase detection. The latter has enabled mirrorless cameras to offer better AF tracking performance, making them a preferred option for photographers who want fast and reliable autofocus in their shooting. Overall, the differences between contrast and phase detection autofocus highlight how digital cameras continue to push the boundaries of imaging technology.

Hybrid Auto-Focus

A hybrid autofocus system is a fascinating technology that combines multiple methods to achieve accurate and reliable focus on your subject. These methods can include active and passive techniques, phase detection, and contrast measurement. By utilizing multiple tactics simultaneously, weaknesses within each method can be compensated for to improve overall performance. This hybrid approach can cause faster autofocus speeds and more accurate shots. Whether you're capturing fast-moving action or shooting portraits with shallow depth of field, a hybrid autofocus system can be an essential tool in achieving the perfect shot every time.

Auto-Focus Line Sensors (Line vs. Cross-Type)

Line Sensors

Gone are the days of fuzzy, out-of-focus photographs. Thanks to the advancement of technology and line sensors, photographers can now capture stunning, crystal-clear images. By utilizing phase detection, these line sensors can measure the distance between a subject and the camera accurately. This unique auto-focusing technology uses horizontal and vertical-orientated sensors to track movement in different directions for more precise results. With the ability to gather data from individual points organized as lines, photographers can use phase-difference detection AF for unparalleled focusing accuracy. The result is a photograph that captures every intricate detail with stunning clarity.

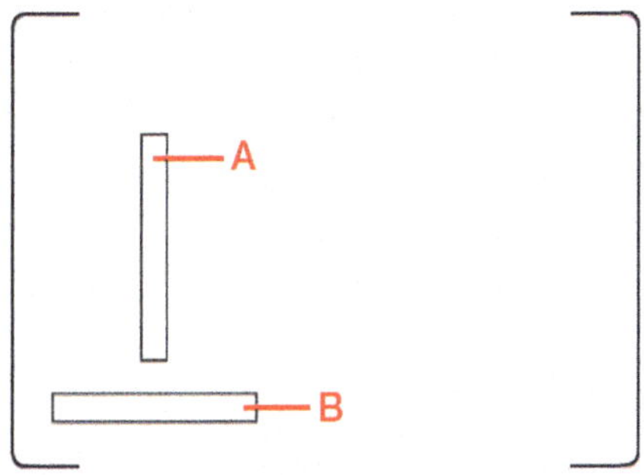

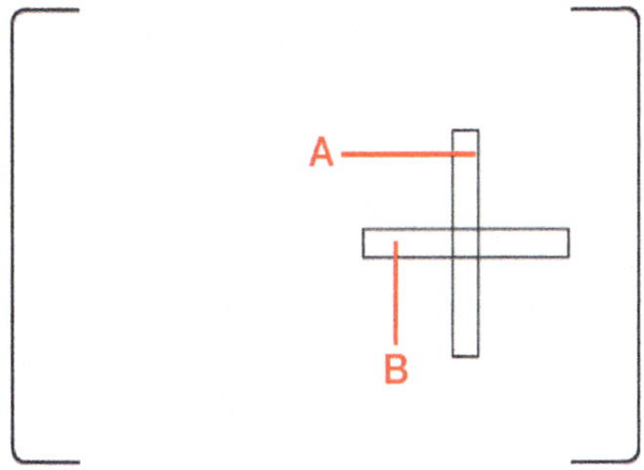

Cross-Type Sensor

Cross-type sensors provide a distinct advantage over traditional auto-focus sensors, offering unmatched focus accuracy and reliability. Thanks to their unique design of crossing-line sensors that work together in horizontal and vertical directions, even two-dimensional subjects such as trees or walls can be accurately focused on without worrying about accidental backdrop engagement. This significantly reduces errors from center out-of-focus issues - providing exceptional results every time.

Understanding AF-A, AF-S, AF-C, and MF Focus Options

As photographers, we all want our autofocus to be spot-on every time. But when it isn't, we often blame the lens calibration. However, the settings we choose to use on our cameras play a much larger role in the consistency of our autofocus. With many options in the focus menu, it's overwhelming to know where to start. But taking the time to dive into the nuances of these settings can make all the difference in achieving the sharpness and clarity we desire in our images. So, let's not overlook the power of the focus menu and experiment with different settings to see how much of an impact they can have on our autofocus.

	Single (AF-S)	Continuous (AF-C)	Auto (AF-A)
Nikon	Single servo	Continuous servo	Auto
Canon	One shot	AI Servo	Auto
Sony	Single	Continuous	Auto

When it comes to capturing that perfect shot, every photographer has their preferences on how to do so. And while the default camera setting, AF-A, can be pretty useful, some photographers would instead make the decision themselves. After all, there's nothing like taking control of the situation and feeling that excitement when the perfect shot comes into focus. Whether capturing a beautiful landscape or a fast-paced sport event, photographers know that the proper focus setting can make all the difference. This is how the icons show up on our camera settings.

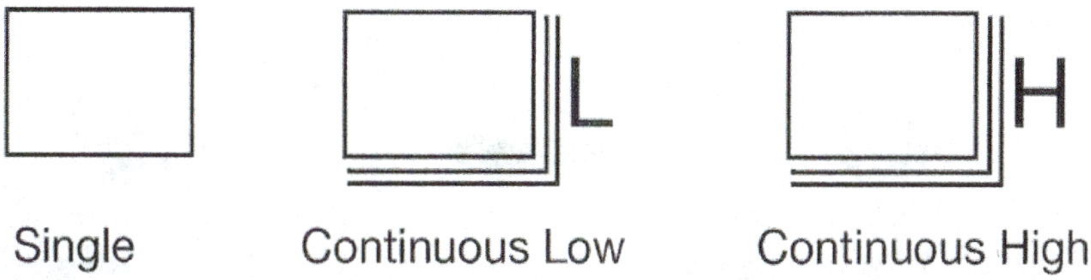

AF-Continuous

Capturing the perfect action shot can be tough, especially when your subject is constantly in motion. But with AF-C, your camera does the heavy lifting for you, ensuring that your moving subject stays in focus. This feature is especially handy when photographing animals on the move, like a playful pup or galloping horse. Simply set your camera to AF-C, point it at your subject, and hold down the shutter button. The camera will continuously adjust the focus as your subject moves, allowing you to capture crisp, clear shots that truly capture the moment's essence. It's the perfect tool for any photographer to up their action shot game.

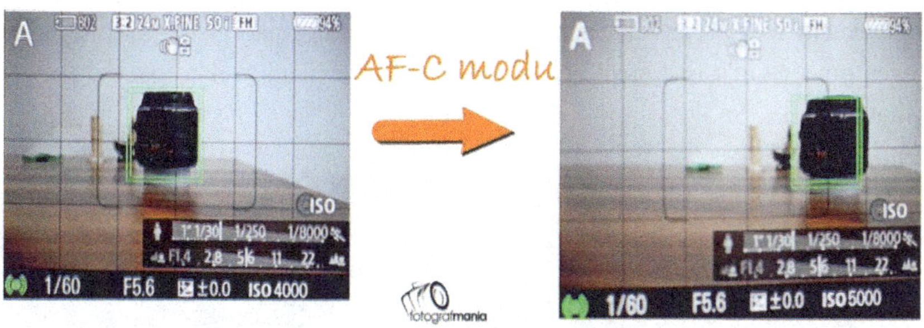

AF-Single

In photography, capturing a subject that doesn't move can be a real challenge. That's why AF single mode is such a valuable tool to have in your arsenal. Whether snapping photos of flowers or taking classic portraits, this mode lets you lock in on your subject and ensure that the focus stays in place while you compose the perfect shot. With AF single mode, you've got the freedom to move and experiment until you find the angle and setting that works best for you.

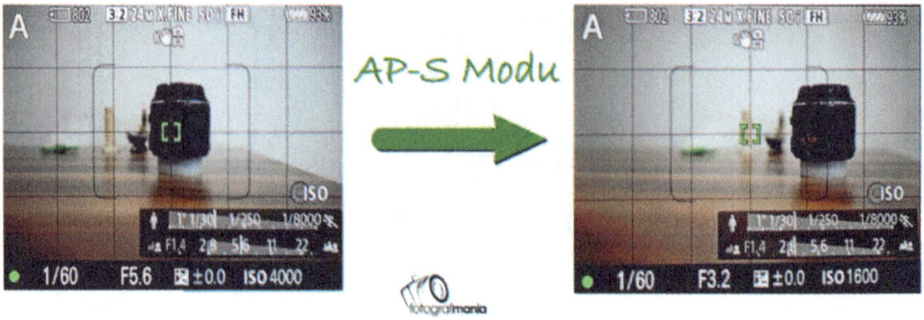

AF-Automatic

As photographers, we all strive to capture the perfect shot. However, sometimes capturing that perfect moment can be tricky, especially when the subject is constantly on the move. That's where AF-A comes into play. This nifty feature allows your camera to think for you and choose between the last two modes depending on the situation. When your subject is stationary, the camera automatically selects AF-S focus mode to ensure crisp and clear shots. But, when your subject is on the move, AF-C focus mode takes over to track and capture every movement with precision. So, whether you're photographing sports, wildlife, or even your child's first steps, AF-A makes it easier than ever to get the perfect shot.

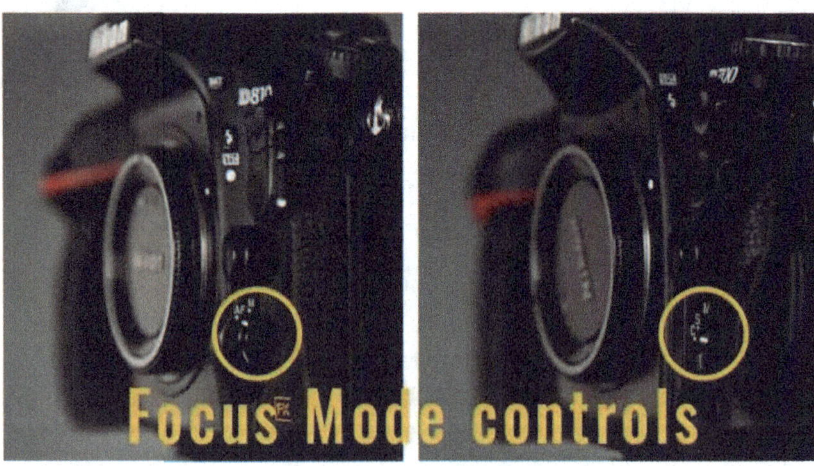

MF - Manual Focus

It's unclear why this focus mode is included because, nowadays, there is usually an option to switch between auto and manual focus on the side of the actual lens. Maybe it's in case you come across a lens that doesn't give you that option.

Auto Focus Dot Points

Have you ever wondered how your DSLR camera can capture life's moments with such precision? Well, with just the flick of a switch, your camera's auto-focus mechanism interprets different spectra points to determine which regions are proper for focusing. As if by magic, red and green boxes appear on your LCD or EVF screen, ensuring that you're all set up to capture that perfect shot.

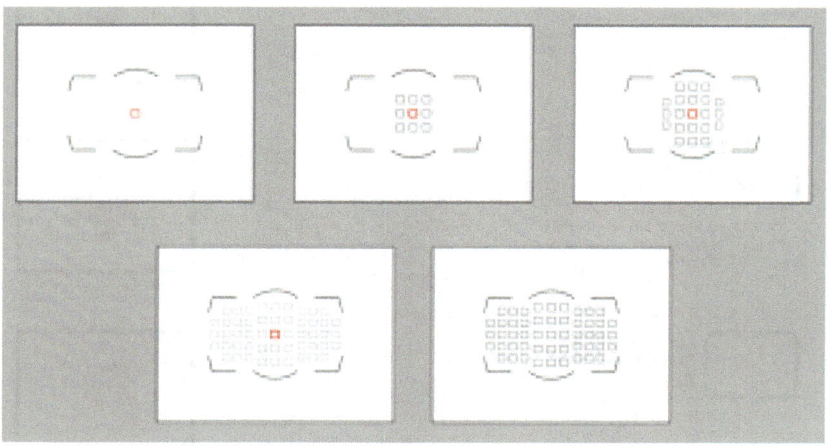

Achieving perfect focus can be a real challenge, especially when trying to capture a moment on the go. But with manual focus, you can take control of your photography and ensure that your shots are always pin sharp. While relying on your camera's sensors can be useful, it's not always easy to get the result you want. But if you're shooting from a tripod and benefit from Live View, you can dial in your focus precisely to create the perfect shot. So don't be daunted by the prospect of getting your focus right – with a bit of practice and the right tools, you can enjoy precision and creativity in your photography.

Metering Modes

If you want to ensure your photos are correctly exposed, understanding and using light metering is essential. DSLR or Mirrorless cameras come with built-in sensors that allow photographers to get an accurate reading of the ambient light in a scene to make adjustments accordingly. Dive into my chapter on Understanding Light Metering for all the tips and tricks needed to master this advanced photographic technique!

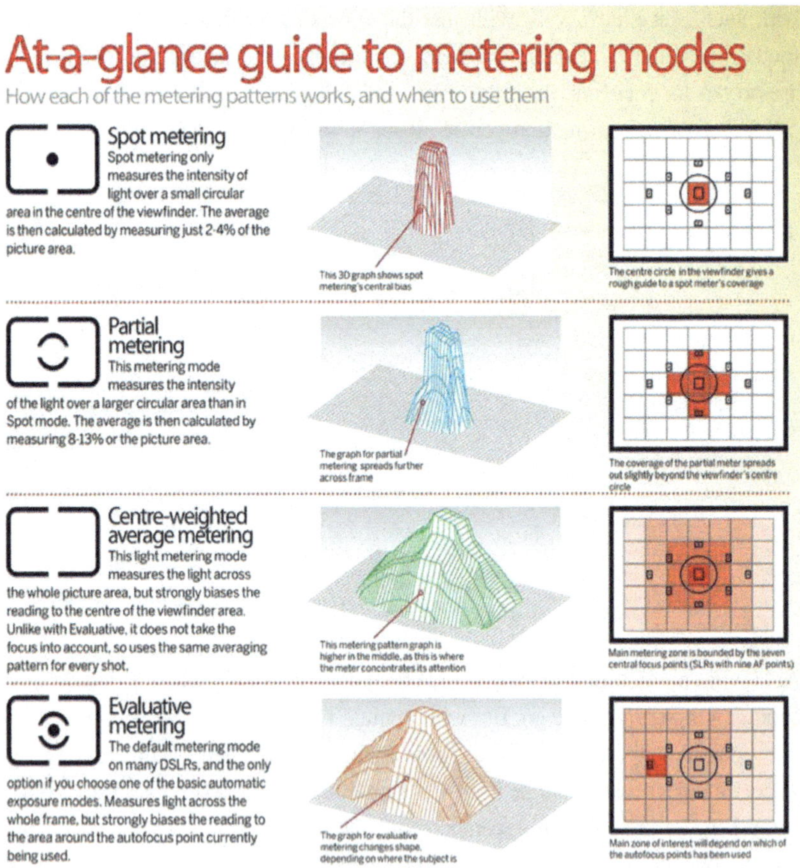

It's a jungle out there when with camera metering modes! Different manufacturers offer various options, each identified by their unique terminology and symbol. If you're still learning your way around the DSLR or Mirrorless settings on your device, don't fret - chances are that with enough practice, any mode will become second nature. So aim and snap away for stunning shots every time! Here are the varied metering modes:

Spot Metering

Capture riveting photos by unlocking the hidden potential within spot metering mode! This unique form of light measuring allows you to take control and create a masterpiece, emphasizing either white or black tones for an attention-grabbing effect. Take advantage of your camera's center points as targeted spots—your results will be beautiful and versatile just by using one set. Remember: Identify the point over a mid-tone that best brings out your subject's creative side. With this advanced technique, it's time to unleash stunning visuals!

When photographing music concerts, Spot Metering is the way to go! This method helps guarantee a quality image despite unpredictable light variations that often occur at such venues. You never know when the stage lights will shine brightly on an artist or dim down - but Spot Metering ensures your camera can still effectively measure and capture every moment in perfect clarity.

Partial Metering

Partial metering is a technique photographers used to capture exceptional images in difficult lighting conditions. Unlike center-weighted or spot measure, partial metering offers an "extended" area for exposure evaluation which benefits the photographer seeking high-quality results despite intense backlighting and illuminated backgrounds. Partial meter mode allows more precise control over subject illumination while simultaneously overexposing part of the backdrop – making it ideal for creating stunning compositions!

Center-weighted Average Metering

Capture the perfect picture - even in high-contrast settings! With center-weighted metering, your camera will prioritize the light data from where you need it most:

at the heart of your subject. Whether that's a beautiful portrait or an unexpected scene like a broken headlight after an accident, this mode gives more focus to whatever is in the middle of the viewfinder and less importance to lighting on its edges.

Matrix or Evaluative Metering

Matrix or Evaluative Metering is the go-to metering mode for most photographers because of its convenience and ease of use. It works by calculating light from all areas within your frame's composition and automatically determining which parts are most important when it comes time to expose your shot. This smart system ensures that you get consistently great results, having no prior technical expertise.

With matrix metering mode, your camera can break down a scene into distinct sections and precisely evaluate light. Not only that, but the number of points in the internal computer can influence its accuracy, so upgrading to a 6-point or 9-point matrix may be worth it! This mode is perfect for capturing landscapes, cityscapes, and even group shots with lots of white space or dark shadows - just beware if there are too many areas requiring extra exposure, as you could run into an over/under-exposed image problem.

Camera Flashes

On-Camera Flash

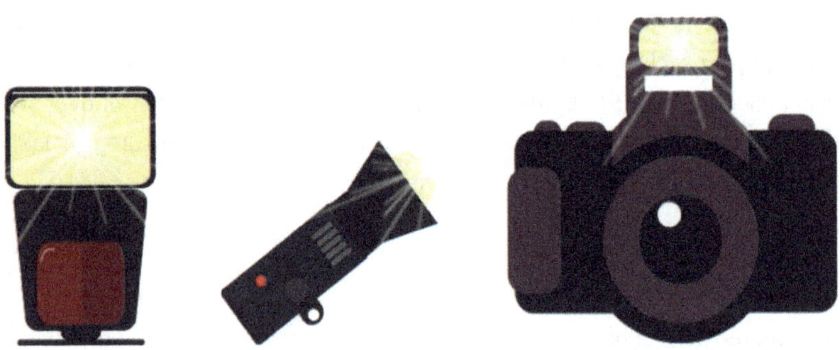

For any photographer, an on-camera flash is a must-have accessory. It can be incredibly useful when lighting conditions become too dark, allowing you to capture shots even when you can't handhold your camera comfortably easily. But an on-camera flash is helpful in low light. It can also help you achieve more balanced exposures in daylight, freeze fast-moving subjects, and even control or trigger other light sources. Also, an external flash is an excellent creative tool that can help to elevate your imagery in aesthetically exciting ways. While carrying an extra piece of equipment may seem like a drawback, the benefits of using an external on-camera flash far outweigh any inconvenience.

Have you ever taken a photo of someone in low light conditions and been disappointed by the red eyes staring back at you? This is a common problem when using built-in flashes near the camera lens. But fear not, there is a solution! By using an on-camera flash source off-camera and from a different angle, you can eliminate the red-eye effect in your photographs of people. This technique not only removes red-eye but also gives your photos a more professional look. So next time you take photos in dimly lit conditions, try moving your flash source to a different angle and see the difference it makes.

Off-Camera/External Flash(es)

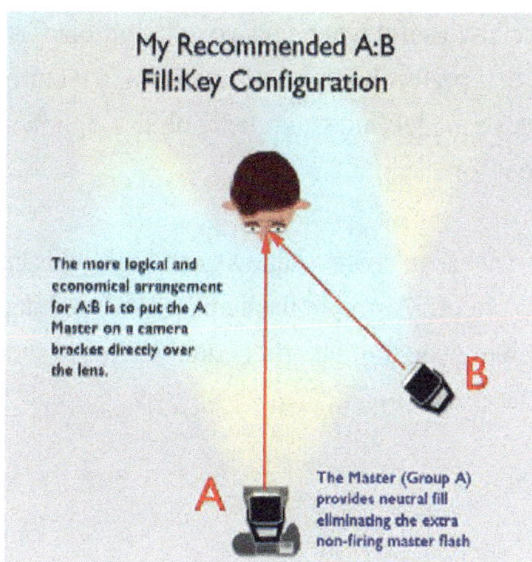

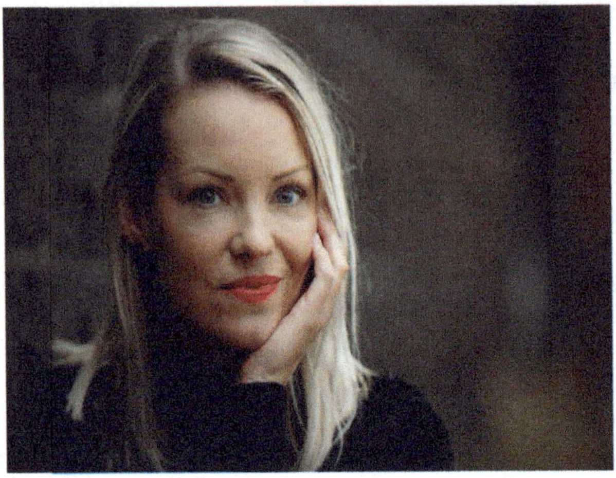

With photography, lighting is crucial. But what do you do when your setting is dark, and there isn't enough natural light to work with? This is where your flash comes in handy. Whether indoors or outdoors, using your flash can make a huge difference in the quality of your photos.

If you're looking to get creative with your camera, why not go a step further and explore the capability of controlling off-camera lighting from your DSLR? This nifty feature is especially useful when you've got multiple flash units dispersed around or if there's that perfect but hard-to-reach angle requiring adjustments. More recent, expensive models are equipped with this option in their menu system - so take it out for a spin!

Using your flash or flashes to create shadows and highlights can lead to some truly amazing photo effects. A simple flash change can add depth and dimension to your images, allowing you to highlight certain elements and obscure others.

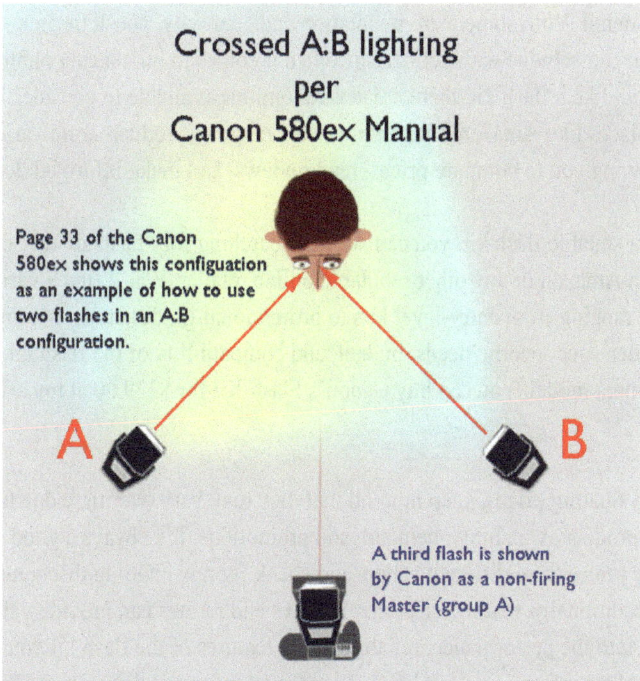

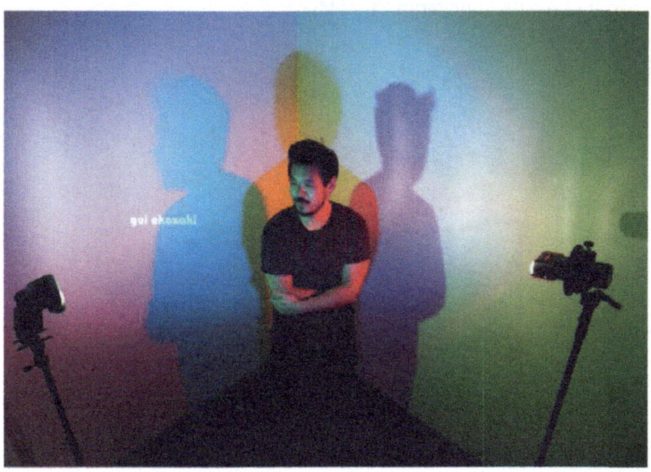

Move your flash off center from your subject to capture more flattering shadows and highlights. You might even play with the position of the flash itself, elevating it for a more dramatic effect or directing it in a particular way to emphasize a specific detail. With some experimentation and creativity, you'll be amazed at what you can achieve with your flash. When it comes to purchasing photography equipment like a flash kit, there are several options available to consider. Online marketplaces like Amazon often offer a wide range of products from various sellers, allowing you to compare prices, read reviews, and make informed decisions.

To find a suitable flash kit, you can start by searching for "flash kit" or "camera flash" on Amazon or any other reputable online retailer. You'll find a variety of options, ranging from entry-level kits to professional-grade setups. It's important to consider your specific needs, budget, and compatibility of the flash kit with your camera model. You can buy Canon's Flash Kit for $229.00 at my affiliate link.

When evaluating prices, keep in mind that they may vary over time due to factors such as product availability, demand, and promotions. It's always a good idea to compare prices from different sellers and check for any ongoing discounts or deals. Additionally, reading customer reviews and ratings can provide valuable insights into the performance, reliability, and features of the flash kit you're interested in. This information can help you make an informed decision and ensure that the product meets your requirements.

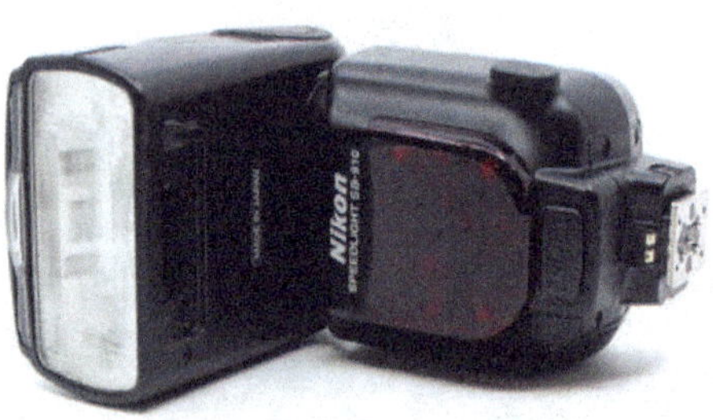

You can buy Nikon's Flash Kit for $326 and the Sony Flash Kit for $298.00 at my Amazon affiliate links.

LCD Screen

The LCD screen, found on the back of most cameras today and can range in size from small to large, has completely replaced traditional viewfinders for a much better viewing experience. Not only does it offer a larger area than the old-school method, but many professionals have moved towards utilizing Live Mode when focusing their shots - or "Back Button Focusing," as they call it - directly from behind the LCD panel.

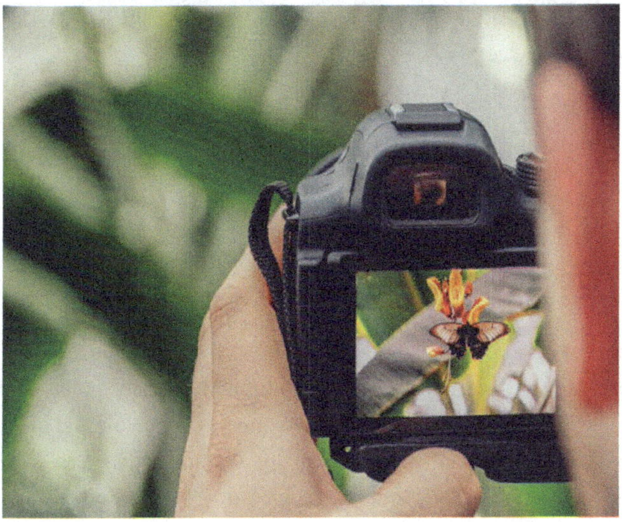

As technology progresses, so does the world of photography. The Sony DSLR-A300 and DSLR-A350 are shining examples of this advancement, taking the live view mode to the next level. With their innovative autofocus feature that engages when you press down on the shutter release, these cameras offer a new level of precision in photography. Reducing mirror flipping enhances camera performance, making the experience smoother and more efficient. It's exciting to see how far technology has come and how much it continues to improve. With these camera models leading the way, the future of photography looks bright.

Videos

Whether you're a budding video photographer or an experienced one, there are plenty of cameras to choose from - but few compare to the incredible DSLR line-up. Not only do these offer unbeatable prices and easy access to lenses suited for different shooting styles, but if you know what model's right for your projects, they'll be tremendous tools for capturing jaw-dropping movies.

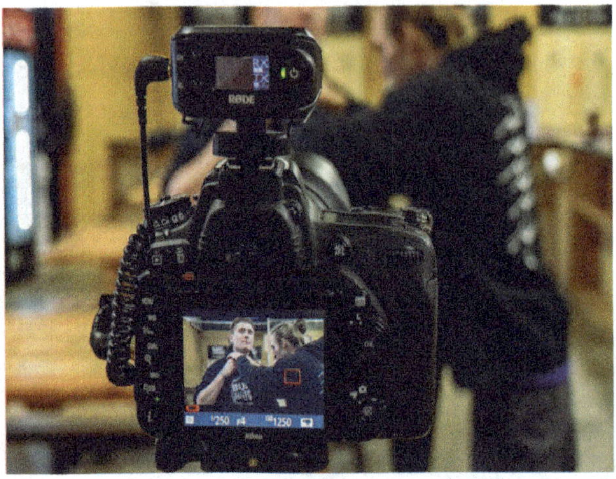

For videographers, navigating through the multitude of camera options can be an intimidating task. With newer DSLRs becoming less available and older models offered at lower prices, knowing where to put your money is no easy feat! It's important to remember the best photographic cameras might not always double up as great video gear; having specific characteristics will help ensure you make a purchase suited for filmmaking. To guide you along this journey, we've compiled a list outlining some essential features - all designed with creativity in mind.

1. **Resolution Shooting pixels:** Now that 4K is the industry standard, you'll want to be sure your DSLR can record video at this quality. Professionals and clients alike will demand it, and many of them do. When shooting in 4K, be aware that some photographers may crop the

image so severely that it is almost worthless. Full HD is more than sufficient if you take a video casually or post it on social media.

2. **LCD:** For videography, an articulated LCD screen is essential. It is critical for solitary video content producers they can assemble their footage from various points of view and even turn the screen around so they may shoot themselves.
3. **Auto-focus:** As a filmmaker, you'll likely use a manual focus system. However, having a decent video auto-focus system is a tremendous weapon in your arsenal and provides much freedom. With Live View video recording, you'll want to see how well a DSLR can auto-focus in Live View mode (using the LCD screen).
4. **Frame Rates**: Regarding the video, a camera can record, resolution and frame rate are only two parts of the puzzle that need to be considered. Using 24p or 24fps, for example, will give your video a cinematic feel since this is the frame rate used in motion picture filmmaking. There are advantages and disadvantages to both 30p and 60p. Increasing the frame rate to 120 fps or more can bring you into slow motion, which may be beneficial.

Flexibility and Versatility

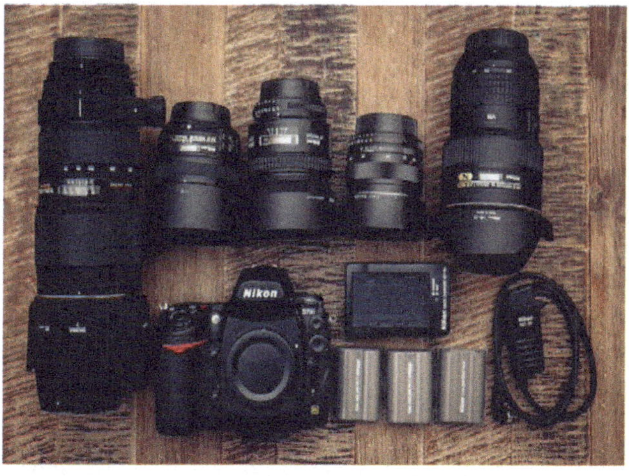

Crafting the perfect shot is an artistic endeavor, and when equipped with a DSLR camera, it becomes an experience that is both adaptable and versatile. The primary advantage of utilizing a DSLR camera lies in its ability to accommodate interchangeable lenses. This feature grants photographers the liberty to effortlessly capture a diverse range of shots, including expansive wide-angle compositions and magnified telephoto images, all without the need to switch camera bodies, a process that can be burdensome and time-consuming. By employing separate lenses and camera bodies, photographers can easily switch between different lenses offering various focal lengths and additional advantageous features, such as image stabilization or weather sealing. Opting for a DSLR camera bestows upon photographers the freedom to tailor their equipment precisely to their artistic vision, enabling them to artistically capture awe-inspiring and visually captivating images.

Speed and Performance

Furthermore, DSLR cameras offer a notable advantage in terms of their speed and performance capabilities. These cameras are equipped with advanced processors that allow for swift image processing, surpassing the capabilities of other camera types. Consequently, DSLRs boast faster shooting speeds, enabling photographers to capture a series of shots in rapid succession. This feature is particularly advantageous when photographing fast-moving subjects such as athletes in action, wildlife in motion, or any other fleeting moments that require precise timing and swift reflexes.

One contributing factor to the exceptional performance of DSLR cameras is the size of their sensors. DSLRs typically employ larger sensors compared to point-and-shoot cameras, which results in several benefits. Firstly, larger sensors have a greater light-gathering capacity, enabling them to capture more light and detail in each shot. This translates to superior image quality, with vibrant colors, rich tones, and enhanced dynamic range.

Moreover, the larger sensors of DSLR cameras contribute to reducing noise in images. When capturing photos, noise refers to the random variations in color or brightness that can occur, especially in low-light conditions. Due to their larger pixel size and superior sensor technology, DSLRs are capable of producing images with significantly less noise compared to cameras with smaller sensors. This noise reduction capability allows photographers to achieve cleaner, crisper, and more professional-looking images, even in challenging lighting situations.

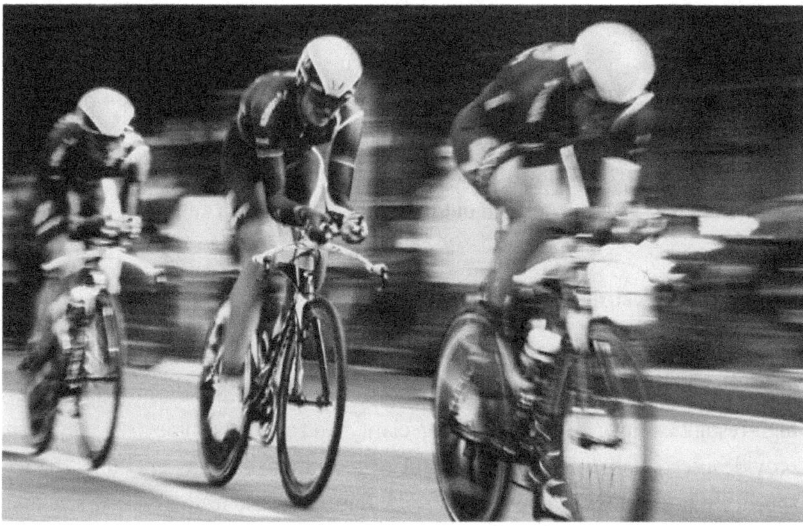

The combination of speed and performance, along with the enhanced image quality, makes DSLR cameras particularly well-suited for capturing fast-paced subjects such as sports or wildlife photography. The ability to shoot at faster frame rates ensures that photographers can freeze action and capture those split-second moments with precision and clarity, without compromising image quality or suffering from motion blur.

In conclusion, DSLR cameras excel in speed and performance, thanks to their powerful processors and larger sensors. Their faster shooting speeds enable photographers to capture a continuous burst of shots, making them ideal for capturing dynamic subjects. Additionally, the larger sensors of DSLRs allow for exceptional image quality, with reduced noise and enhanced light sensitivity. These advantages make DSLR cameras the preferred choice for professionals and enthusiasts alike who require both speed and image excellence, especially when photographing fast-moving subjects or situations where every moment counts.

Control Options

Finally, one of the main reasons DSLRs are so popular among professional photographers is their control options and manual settings capabilities. With manual settings, you have complete control over how your photos turn out–from shutter speed to aperture size–allowing you to get creative with your photos rather than relying on auto mode settings. This gives you more freedom to capture unique images that stand out from others taken with automatic settings.

Benefits of Investing in a DSLR Camera

For those who plan to use their camera regularly or professionally, investing in a high-quality DSLR is often the best choice. Not only do these cameras produce high-resolution images with stunning clarity and color accuracy — they also provide users with full manual control over settings such as aperture, shutter speed, ISO sensitivity, white balance, and more. Because of their larger size and heavier build quality compared to smaller point-and-shoot models or even some Mirrorless options — professional-grade DSLRs remain popular among those who need reliable equipment in challenging conditions such as extreme weather or rugged terrain.

The ability to change lenses is also a game-changer, as it allows for a broader range of shooting options and enhances the quality of the final image. If you're looking to improve your photography skills or take your art to the next level, investing in a digital SLR camera is a wise decision. However, Canon, Nikon, and Sony have ceased making new DSLRs in recent years, only producing Mirrorless models. Presented below is a selection of renowned brands currently dominating the market. To facilitate your shopping experience, I have conveniently embedded affiliate links throughout my book, granting you instant access to these recommended products. It is worth noting that I receive a small commission from each sale, which greatly contributes to supporting my photography endeavors and ensures my ability to provide you with valuable tutorials and instructional content in the future.

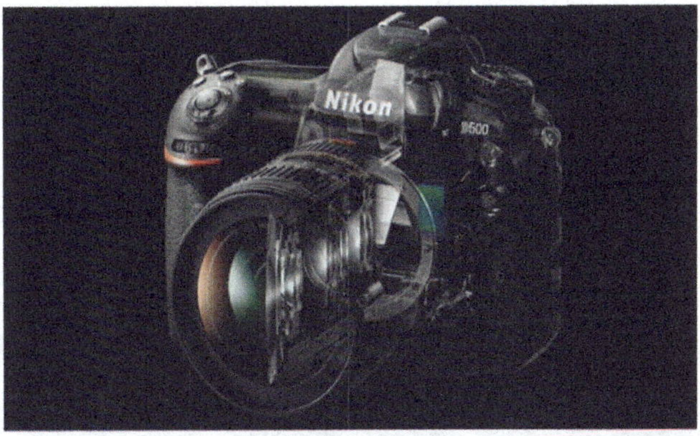

Nikon D500 DX-Forma DSLR with a 16-80mm lens is for sale on Amazon Affil-iate Link for $1,999.99.

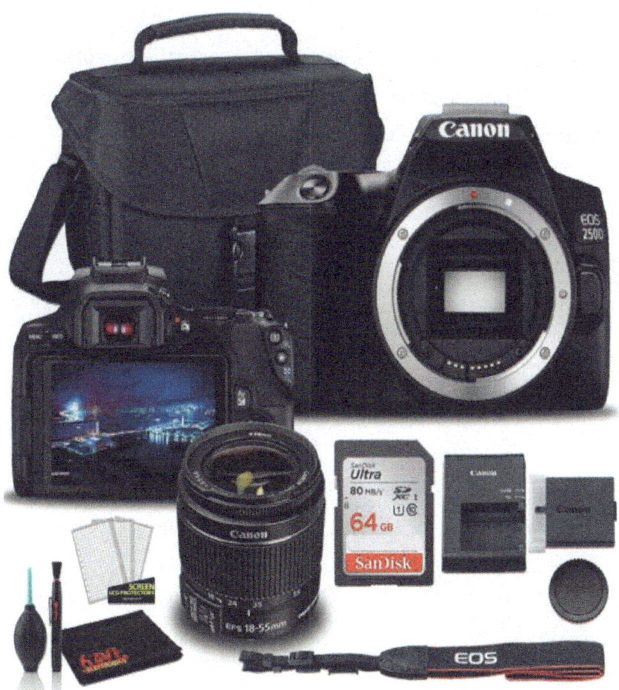

Canon EOS 250D DSLR Camera with 18-55mm Lens (Black) (3453C002), EOS Bag, Sandisk Ultra 64GB $720 on the Amazon Affiliate Link.

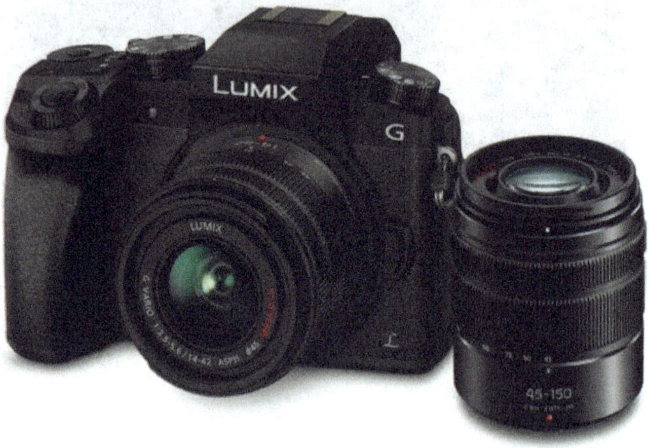

Panasonic Lumix G7 4K Digital Mirrorless Camera Bundle with Lumix G Vario 14-42mm and 45-150mm Lenses, 16MP, 3-Inch Touch LCD, DMC-G7WK (USA Black). Amazon Affiliate Link for $697.00.

3

MIRRORLESS CAMERAS

What is a Mirrorless Camera?

Curious about the disparities between Mirrorless cameras and DSLRs? It appears that the Mirrorless system offers a simpler and more straightforward approach. Unlike DSLRs, Mirrorless cameras eliminate the need for a mirror to reflect light onto the viewfinder and sensor. Instead, they directly expose the sensor to light, providing a real-time preview of your scene through the electronic viewfinder. This method not only enhances efficiency but also enhances user-friendliness, making it effortless to capture breathtaking shots. Please refer to the accompanying diagram for visual reference.

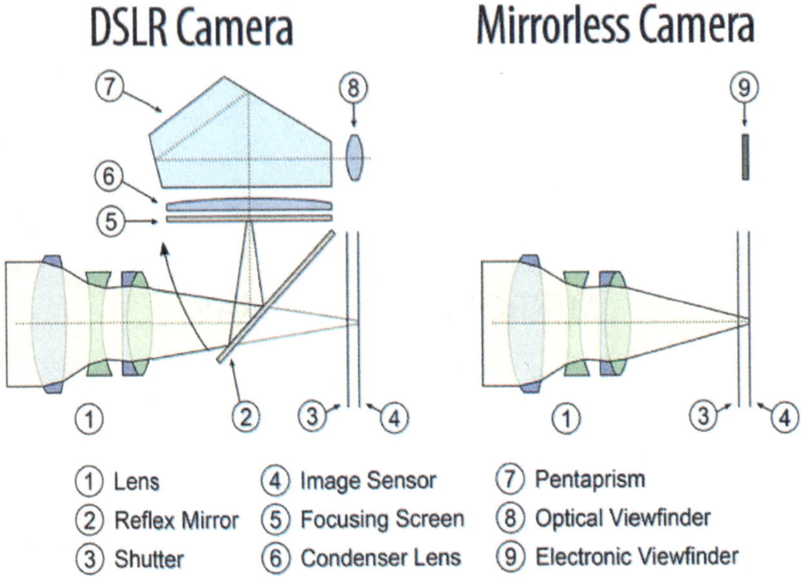

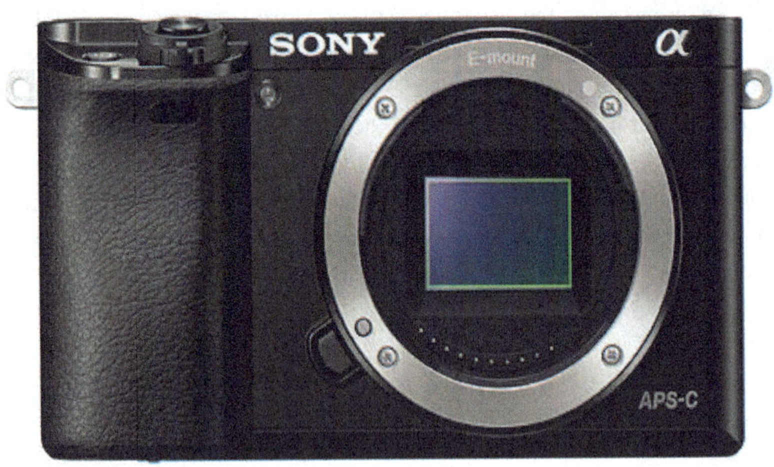

These cameras are also known as "Mirrorless interchangeable-lens cameras" (MILC), "hybrid cameras," and "compact system cameras" (CSC). The body is thinner than a standard DSLR because it does not use a mechanical mirror to switch the scene between the optical viewfinder and the image sensor. This means the Mirrorless camera is also relatively lighter and more compact than a DSLR. Mirrorless cameras were first introduced around 2008 and became very popular in 2011.

Plus, because they have fewer moving parts, they operate much more quietly than DSLRs. So, if you're looking for a top-quality digital camera that offers better portability and quieter operation than a standard DSLR, then a Mirrorless camera is worth considering.

Viewfinder - Electronic (EV) Sensor

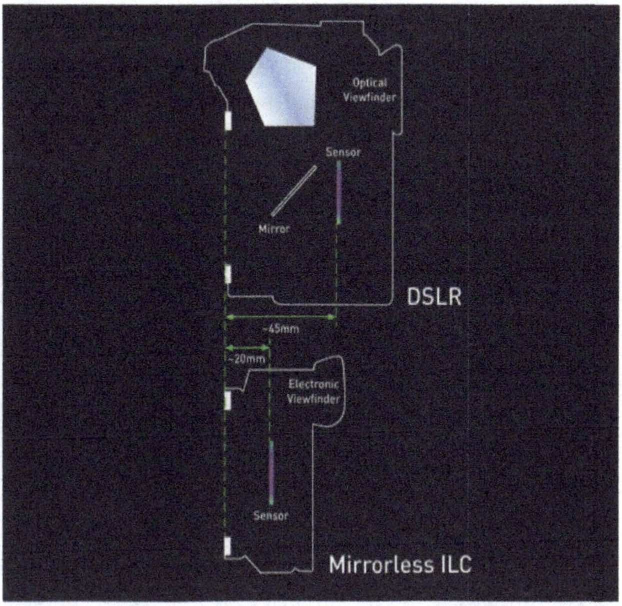

Have you ever pondered the reasons behind the increasing preference of photographers and camera manufacturers for Mirrorless cameras over DSLRs? The answer lies in the contrasting designs of these two camera types. Unlike traditional DSLRs, Mirrorless cameras are devoid of the reflex mirror and pentaprism components. This key distinction results in Mirrorless cameras being smaller, lighter, and more compact. Their design with fewer moving parts grants them the advantage of operating silently compared to DSLRs.

By displaying images directly from the sensor, the electronic viewfinder mode offers the benefit of seeing accurately exposed images. With this feature, you can be confident of your shooting exposure settings. Electronic viewfinders also have focus aids like focus peaking. This helps you see what's in focus before taking the shot. This allows you to view both in-focus and out-of-focus areas of the scene as you capture the shot.

However, they can suffer from slight lag, making them a less desirable option for fast-moving subjects like sports and action photographers. In low light, high-ISO noise can cause cloudiness. Optical Viewfinders on DSLRs perform far better in these scenarios. Photographers believe Mirrorless cameras will soon replace DSLRs. Camera makers seem to agree and are putting Mirrorless options in almost every brand. They may differ in construction and design, but not in their sensors, image quality, tech, and add-on features.

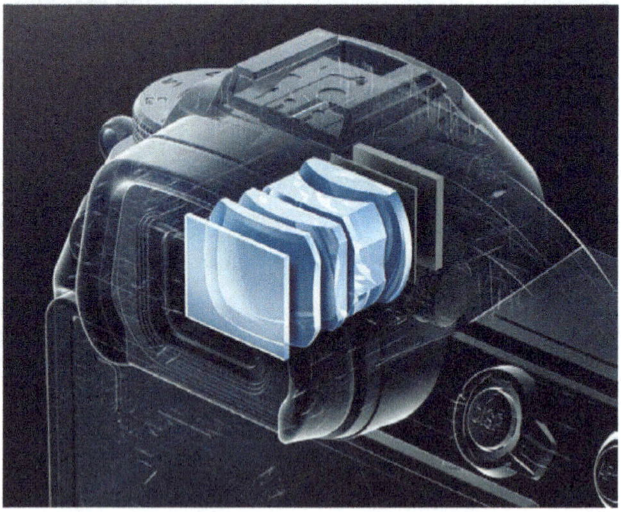

Digital Sensor Technology

Trying to choose between a Mirrorless and a DSLR camera based solely on sensor size? Here's what you need to know: Both types of cameras have the exact standard sensor sizes - Four Thirds, APS-C, 35mm full frame, and even medium format. So, if sensor size is your main concern, don't stress - you'll find various options regardless of which camera style you choose.

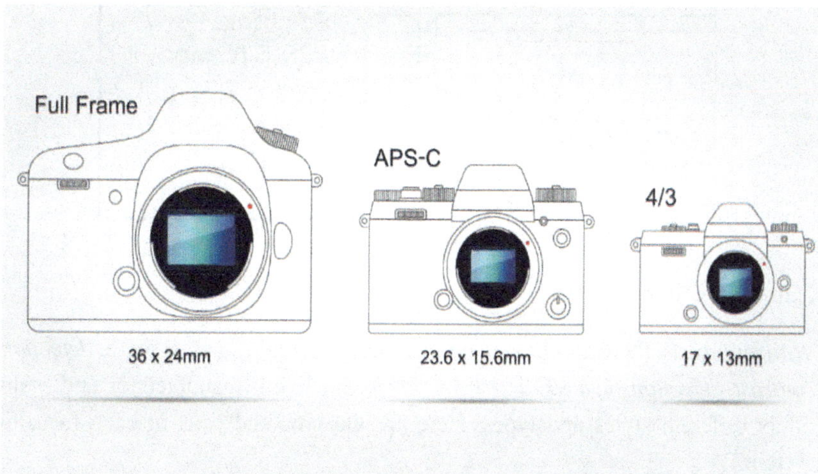

Remember, however, when taking photos, you can adjust the ISO, aperture, and shutter speed to control the amount of light that enters the camera. By balancing these settings, you'll capture stunning images no matter the size of the sensor.

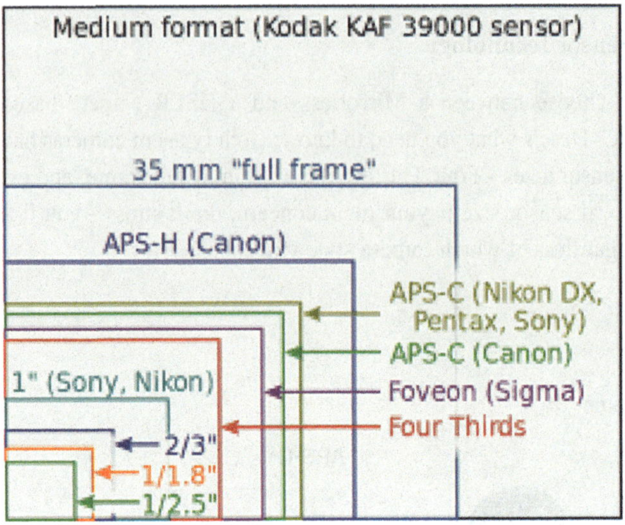

Auto-focus Systems

With autofocus, there are three main methods in digital cameras: p*hase detection, contrast detection, hybrid, and Peak Focusing*. Every manufacturer and brand offers different styles and types. Here are the pros and cons of each focusing system.

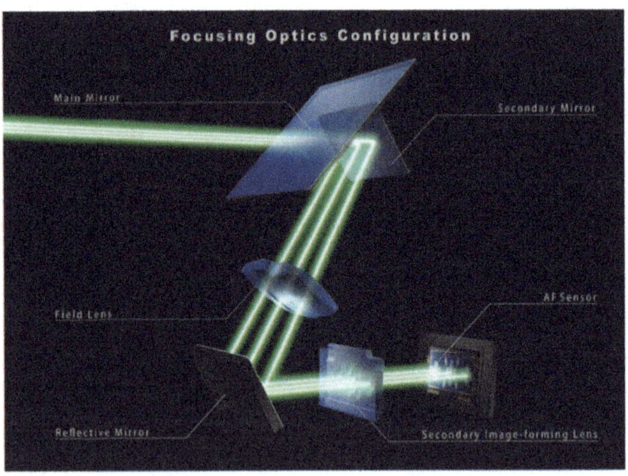

Contrast-Based Auto-Focus

When it comes to autofocus technology, contrast detection is both simple and accurate. It's not only the most straightforward method but the most cost-effective as well. This method involves the camera analyzing the contrast between edges and adjusting the focus until the image is as sharp as possible. So if you're looking for a straightforward and budget-friendly option, contrast detection may be just what you need.

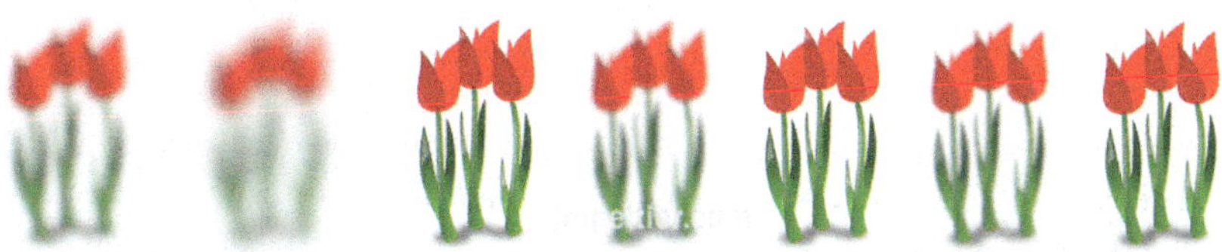

The camera may move the focus motor in the wrong direction first, and may pass through proper focus as it searches for optimal contrast.

Have you ever wondered how our brain functions when we use unaided manual focus? It's simple - we focus on edges and keep adjusting the focus ring until the edge contrast is the hardest - aka "sharp." Contrast detection autofocus is known for being the easiest, cheapest, and most accurate method of focusing. However, it also comes with a downside–it's the slowest.

Phase Detect Auto-Focus

As photography continues to evolve, so does the technology behind it. One significant advancement that has become commonplace in modern cameras is phase detection autofocus. This impressive feature operates by using a semi-transparent mirror within the camera to split incoming light, sending it to the viewfinder and a specialized autofocus unit. It is within this unit where light rays from either side of the lens come into focus on two or more micro-sensors. This intricate process produces sharp, clear, and perfectly focused images that even the most seasoned photographers can appreciate.

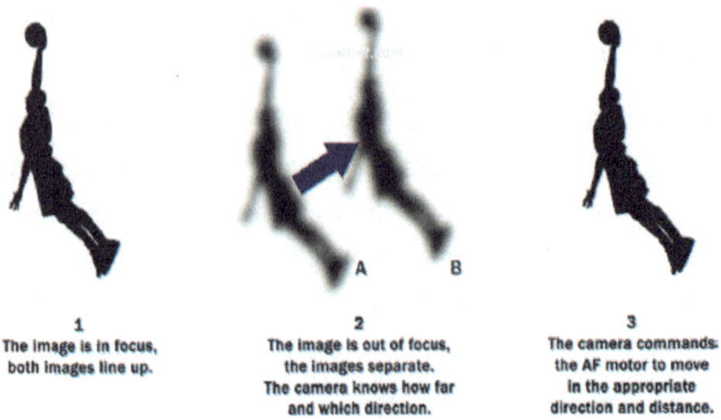

Have you ever experienced the frustration of capturing a photo that ended up slightly out of focus, despite your efforts to line up the perfect shot? Thankfully, the introduction of micro AF sensors has revolutionized the way we tackle this issue. These minuscule strips play a crucial role by measuring the patterns of light intensity and analyzing them to assist in adjusting the focus of the lens. By precisely matching the patterns detected by these micro-sensors, the resulting image can achieve a remarkable level of crystal-clear focus. It's truly remarkable to consider how such a small strip can have such a significant impact on the overall quality of a photograph. With the assistance of micro-sensors, the days of blurry photos will soon be relegated to the past.

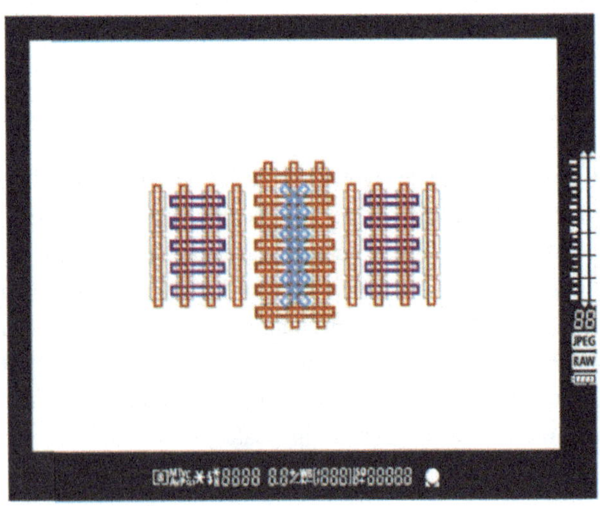

With phase detection autofocus, that frustration could soon become a thing of the past. By analyzing the way light falls on the sensors, the camera can detect whether it's front- or back-focused and make adjustments to the lens accordingly. This technology has a significant advantage over traditional autofocus methods, as it reduces the time the lens spends "hunting" for focus, resulting in sharper and more accurate images. Say goodbye to blurry photos and hello to stunning, crystal-clear shots with phase detection autofocus.

Dual Pixel Focusing

By using Dual Pixel focusing, the camera sensor can harness the potential of every pixel – a massive improvement from just 5 percent used in standard PDAF technology. This revolutionary approach unlocks unprecedented levels of focus accuracy for photographers!

As technology continues to improve, manufacturers of digital cameras are innovating new and better autofocus systems. The current challenge has been solved by placing the focus sensors directly on the image sensor. Still, a challenging side-effect is that this takes away from pixels that would generally collect light information for photos. To work around this issue, camera makers use interpolation - an educated guess based on surrounding pixel data–though it often results in issues like loss of resolution or banding appearing within images. It remains to be seen what advancements will come next when attempting to perfect autofocus capabilities!

Focus Peaking Focusing

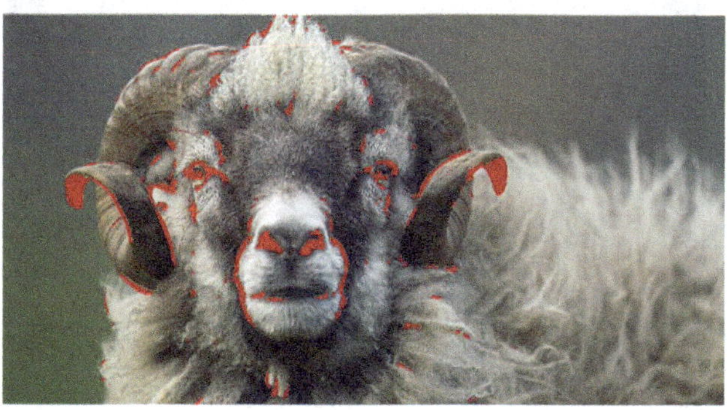

With features like eye tracking and touch-and-drag autofocus, getting sharp focus in any frame is easier than ever. If you shoot with manual lenses, the Mirrorless camera's focus peaking is especially handy. Once you turn on focus peaking, you can quickly identify the sharpest areas in your shot through the evaluative viewfinder. No more guesswork! With just the touch of a button, you can magnify your image to ensure that your subject is ideally in focus. Seeing details has never been this effortless.

Focus peaking is the ideal solution for photographers who want to focus manual lenses more quickly and accurately than with typical Live View methods. It's especially useful when it's difficult to quickly assess which areas are in focus, such as in low-light conditions. If you want to capture slow-moving objects, such as clouds in the sky, without using autofocus, try using focus peaking as a technique. It helps you identify the ideal depth of field for your shots. However, always keep a close eye on your adjustments, including your ISO.

There are cases where using focus peaking is not recommended for the best results. For instance, if your camera lenses have an incredibly shallow depth of field (e.g. f/1.2 on a full frame), it's advisable to avoid using this feature. When the scene you are trying to capture is too shallow, even the most advanced algorithms may not accurately display the sharpest areas.

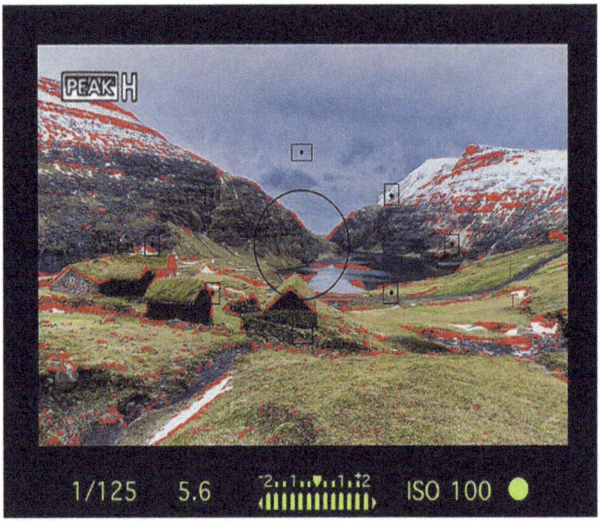

Any Mirrorless camera released in the past five years has built-in focus peaking, including older models from Sony, Fujifilm, and Panasonic. New DSLRs from Nikon, Sony, and Pentax also have focus peaking, but it can only be used in live-view. Canon DSLRs do not feature focus peaking, but Magic Lantern is third-party software that adds this feature to Canon cameras. However, Magic Lantern is not yet available for many of Canon's newest DSLRs, including the 1DX series, 5D MkIV, 7D MkII, 80D and 90D, and their newer entry-level devices.

Hybrid Autofocus

Combining the advantages of the other focusing systems, many cameras now use a dual-focusing system to ensure precision in any situation. For instance, SONY sensors integrate these two technologies, while Google Pixel employs PDAF with Laser autofocus for optimal image quality.

Drive Speed (FPS)

Contrast detection autofocus is known for being the easiest, cheapest, and most accurate method of focusing. *However, it also comes with a downside–it's the slowest.* If you've ever witnessed autofocus "hunting" back and forth, you're experiencing contrast detection at work. The process involves comparing focus distances to locate the point of maximum contrast.

The drive speed (the frame rate) differs somewhat between cameras. The Sony a7 iii can shoot 10 frames per second (fps), whereas the Canon EOS R can only do 8 fps. When photographing sports or animals, you may have heard the expression "spray and pray." It's possible to capture excellent photographs you wouldn't usually get by pressing the shutter button and taking hundreds of photos per minute. It's possible to fire and capture 80 images in three-second intervals throughout a weekend. There are 1,920 photographs captured with the Canon EOS R and 2,400 with the Sony, a difference of 480 photos! The Sony 7 iii is the sole camera you should choose if getting more images quickly is critical to your business's success.

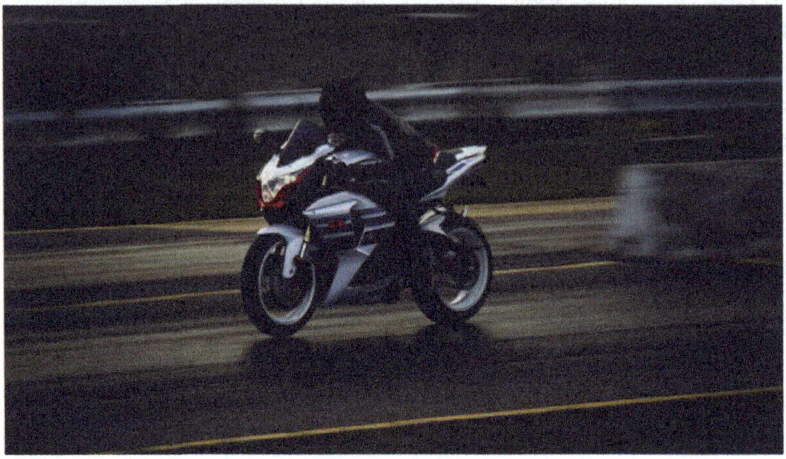

Lenses

DSLRs had a head start on their lenses' quality, options, and price. But production appears to be declining. Canon and Nikon now almost entirely use Mirrorless lenses. Other advantages of Mirrorless lenses include more oversized Mirrorless lens mounts and shorter back-focus flange distances. While creating their new full-frame Mirrorless cameras, Nikon and Canon have shown exceptional ingenuity and creativity. Besides the growing number of lenses for the Nikon Mirrorless Z 6 and Z 7, an FTZ mount converter, which allows you to use any of Nikon's current DSLR lenses with the Nikon Mirrorless Z 6 and Z 7, can be purchased to supplement the growing number of native lenses for the Nikon Mirrorless Z 6.

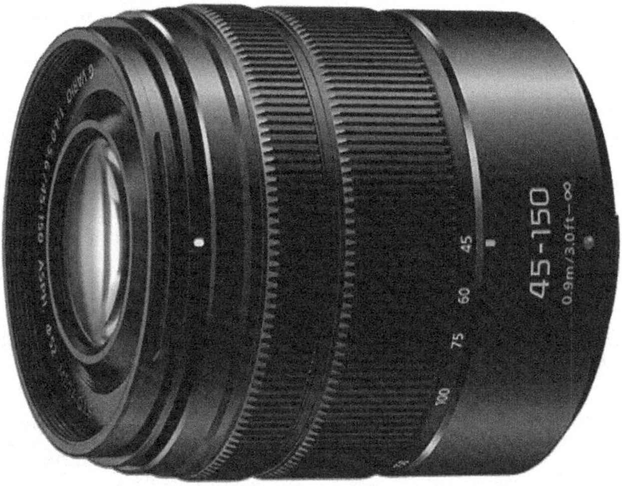

By introducing the new Canon lens adapters, users can use the complete Canon EF DSLR lens family with the EOS R full-frame Mirrorless cameras, allowing them to take advantage of the whole Canon EF DSLR lens family. The project will take some time to complete. Additionally, Nikon's newest DX Mirrorless cameras, the Nikon Z50 and Nikon Z FC are the world's most miniature DX cameras, with only three native APS-C lenses, making them the most miniature DX cameras currently available.

The outcome has been that Fujifilm and Olympus have had time to develop their native lens systems to where none of the Mirrorless camera manufacturers are presently at a competitive disadvantage regarding lens choices. The size of the sensor has a considerable influence on the length of the lens. Several Mirrorless manufacturers have developed small or retractable lenses, but these come with additional sacrifices. Manufacturers are producing larger and heavier lenses than their previous DSLR counterparts to take advantage of the more giant Mirrorless lens mounts.

Contrary to popular belief, small-body-large-lens Mirrorless camera pairings might be challenging because of their size and weight. The G Master lenses that comprise the high-end Sony A7 series are pretty big compared to other cameras in their class. Your Mirrorless camera may need a battery grip to enhance the handling of your most often-used lenses.

Your DSLR lenses will work on your Mirrorless camera with the right adapter. However, lenses designed specifically for Mirrorless cameras will not work on your DSLR cameras.

Videos

Interchangeable lenses were not available in popular video production until the introduction of DSLRs, which made high-definition cameras more accessible. The Canon EOS 5D IV and Nikon D780 are excellent options for video recording, comparable to Mirrorless cameras. However, Mirrorless cameras are advancing in high-definition recording and offer several advantages, including size, weight, manual focus, low-light focusing, and faster video speeds. Camera manufacturers are focusing on Mirrorless cameras for the future. Fujifilm and Panasonic now provide cameras like the X-T4 and Lumix GH5 series, capable of capturing 4K video at 60/50 frames per second for smooth slow-motion effects. Sony's full-frame Mirrorless A7 series, such as the A7 III, excels in high-quality "over-sampled" 4K videos. Netflix has approved the Panasonic Lumix S1H for unique content creation.

Nikon Z 30 APS-C 20.9MP 4K Video Mirrorless Digital Vlogging Camera Bundle with Content Creator's Accessory Kit for Z 30 and NIKKOR Z DX 16-50mm Lens for $796.91 at Amazon. Here's my affiliate link.

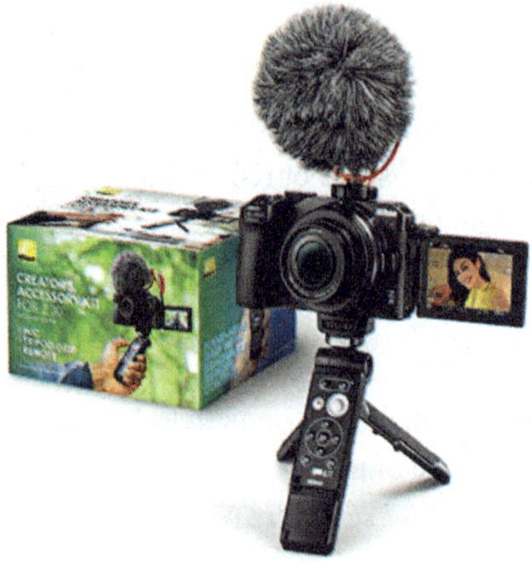

Commercial photographers working for customers that want video and still photographs may use DSLRs to capture them. The most excellent Mirrorless cameras have closed the gap between them and full-blown movie cameras and broadcast-quality camcorders in terms of features and performance. So, if you only use video cameras sometimes, Mirrorless cameras are better than DSLRs. Mirrorless lenses employ high-tech focus actuators and quiet stepping motor auto-focus technology during shooting.

Body Size Comparison

Mirrorless systems are typically touted as smaller than DSLRs—the same sensor size and picture quality as a DSLR without the heft. However, producing a Mirrorless camera body that is small frequently means sacrificing battery life, handling with bigger lenses, and additional dials and controls. Smaller Mirrorless bodies have smaller controls, which may not be convenient for bigger hands. Many pro users like the Nikon D850 DSLR's size because it makes it easier to see and change camera settings and balances well with big lenses, which we'll cover in the next section.

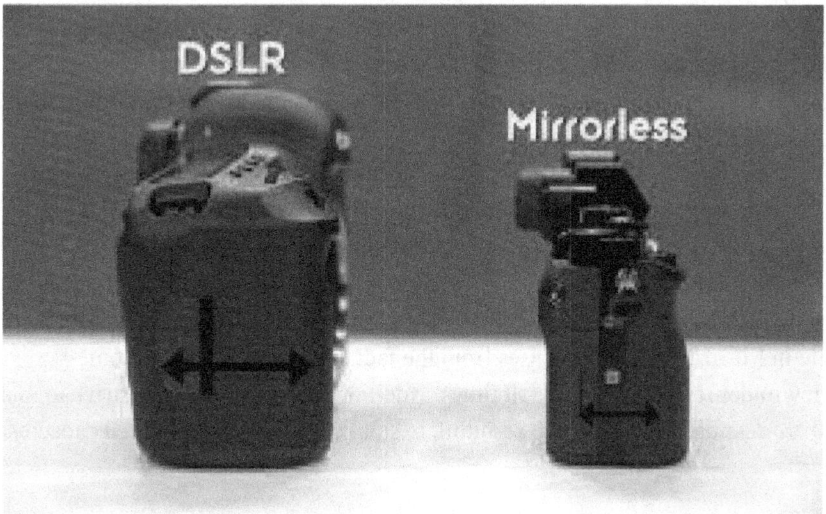

Batteries

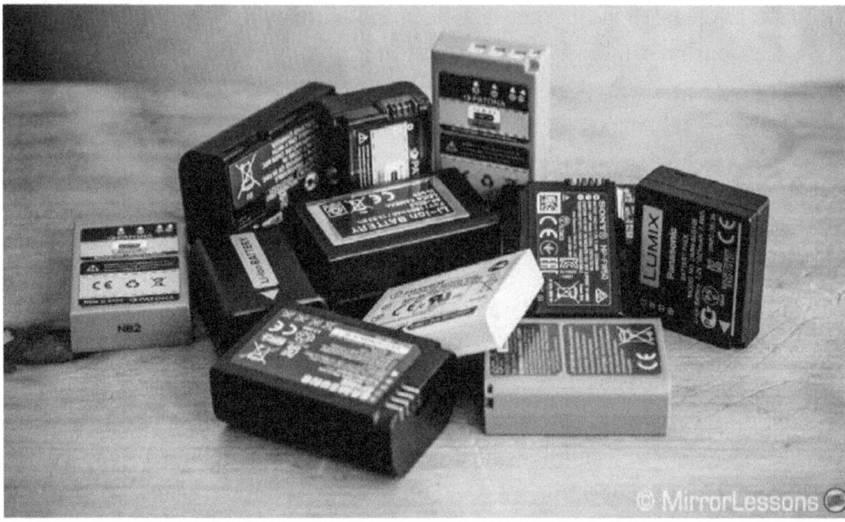

Mirrorless cameras generally have fewer frames per charge compared to their competitor, DSLRs. Entry-level DSLRs like the Nikon D3500 can capture up to 1,550 photographs on a single charge, while high-end pro DSLRs can shoot over 4,000 frames per charge using larger batteries. For instance, the Nikon D6 pro-DSLR boasts an impressive battery life of 3,580 shots and even more for high-speed continuous shooting.

On the other hand, Mirrorless cameras typically offer an average of 350-400 frames per battery, with some models providing even fewer shots. The Sony A7R III introduced a 650-shot battery life, slightly improved upon by the Sony A7R IV, while the Canon EOS RP can handle only 250 shots. The concern with battery life in Mirrorless cameras arises from the fact that the LCD or electronic viewfinder remains active at all times. Additionally, manufacturers strive to make Mirrorless cameras compact, resulting in smaller batteries and limited capacity.

Conclusion

The DSLR vs. Mirrorless camera debate may settle as Canon and Nikon have not released new DSLR models in two years. However, DSLRs remain a budget-friendly choice for dedicated photographers. While most manufacturers have shifted towards Mirrorless cameras, Pentax continues to use DSLRs. DSLRs still have a strong presence and are worth considering due to their lower price point. They are larger and heavier compared to Mirrorless cameras, as they house a mirror mechanism internally. DSLRs also offer a wider range of accessories and third-party lenses. They are well-suited for art and portrait photography.

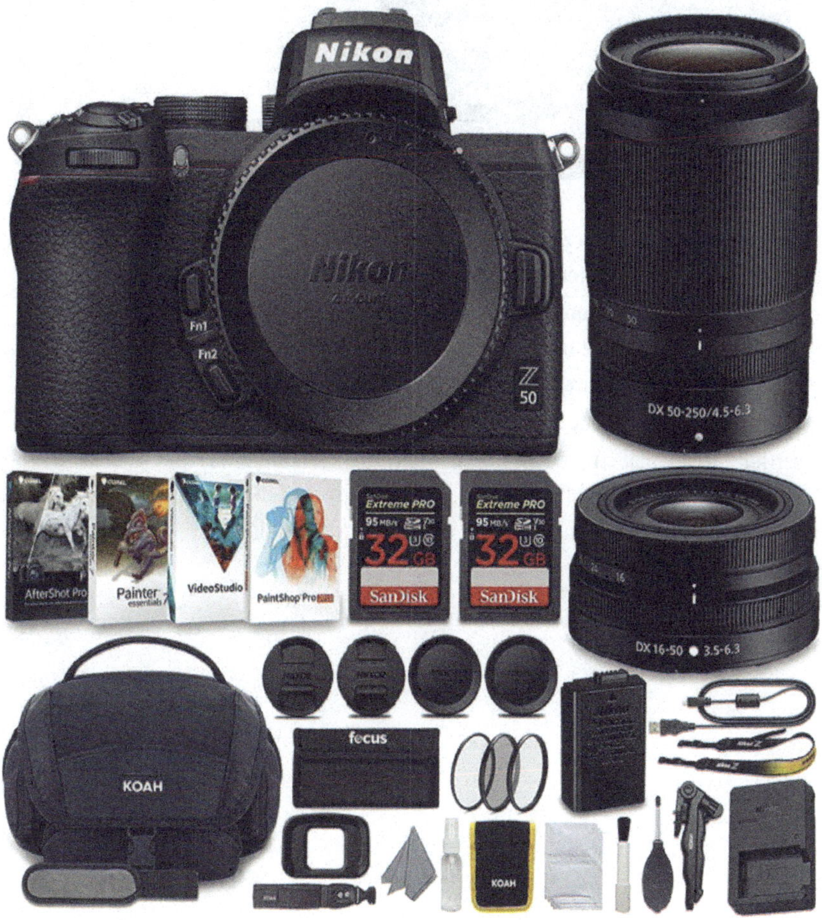

Here are some fantastic deals on mirrorless cameras you can find on Amazon. Above is a Nikon Z50 Mirrorless Camera with NIKKOR Z 16-50 and 50-250mm VR Lenses and 64GB Card Kit with Deluxe Accessory Bundle for $1,229.95.

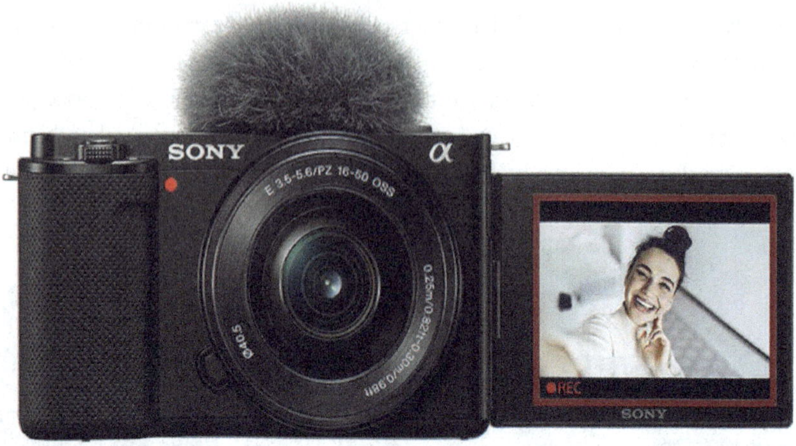

Here is the Sony Alpha ZV-E10 - APS-C Interchangeable Lens Mirrorless Vlog Camera Kit. APS-C Interchangeable Lens Mirrorless Vlog Camera Kit - Black. You can buy on Amazon affiliate link. **It's on sale for $798.** On the other hand, Mirrorless cameras are lighter and smaller, but they can drain batteries faster than DSLRs. MFT (miniature full-frame) Mirrorless cameras are the smallest within the Mirrorless family, featuring tiny sensors and compact lenses. Real-time settings are displayed on the camera. Many professional travel and landscape photographers opt for Mirrorless camera systems, and they are also popular among filmmakers because of their excellent video quality.

Canon EOS M50 Mirrorless Camera (Black) w/M-Adapter & Canon Lenses - EF-M 15-45mm f/3.5-6.3 is STM and EF 75-300mm f/4-5.6 III + 500mm Preset Telephoto Lens + Deluxe Travel Accessory Bundle for $1,129.00.

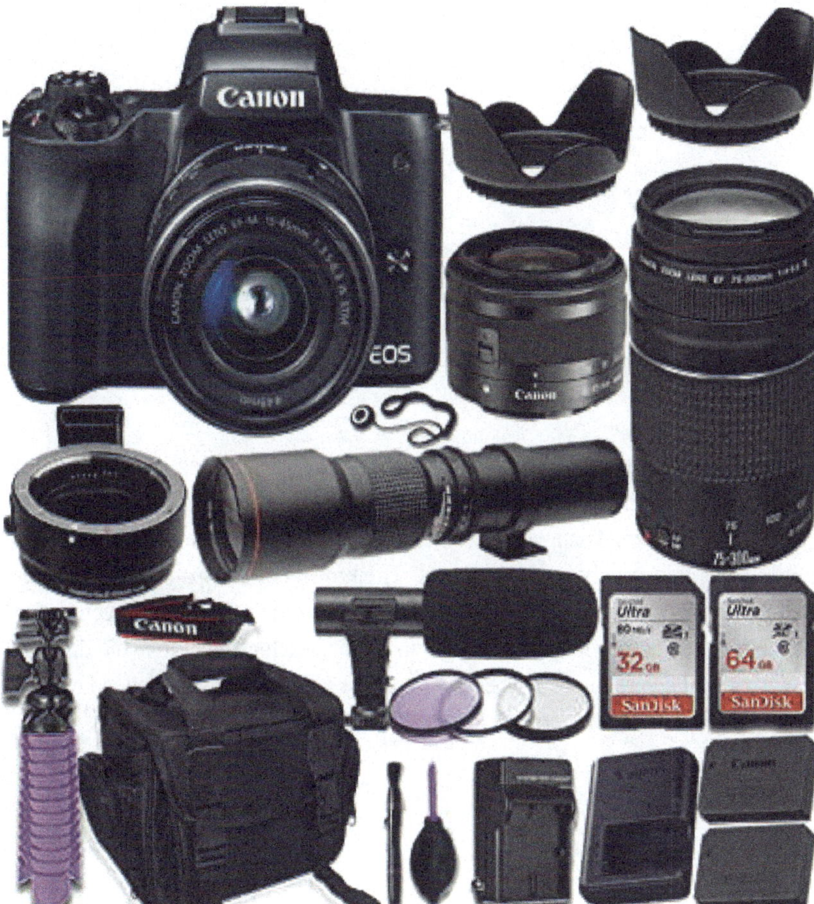

4

EXPOSURE TRIANGLE

Capturing the ideal picture entails skillfully managing of three crucial elements: Shutter Speed, ISO, and Aperture, collectively known as the Exposure Triangle. Achieving a harmonious blend among these factors guarantees impeccably exposed photos. Think of them as *three* steering wheels on a dashboard of a car—over-adjusting just one of them in either direction can lead to unfavorable outcomes. It's vital to balance each element to avoid disaster. With careful control of each wheel, your photos will turn out stunning, conveying your desired vision with precision.

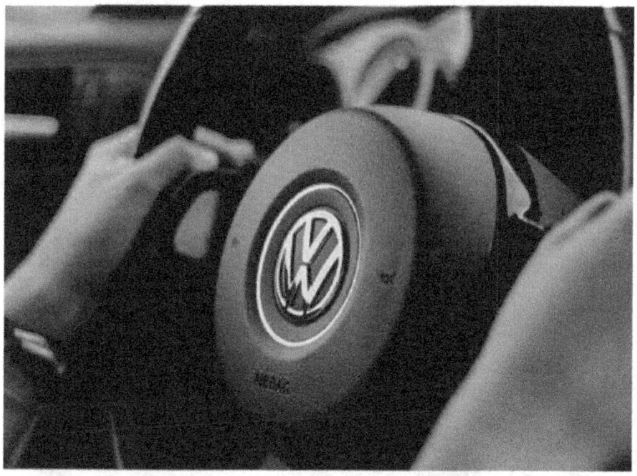

Achieving a precise equilibrium among these three elements is vital to capturing a well-exposed photograph. Excessive light can cause overexposure, causing important highlights to be washed out and fine details to be lost. Insufficient light can lead to underexposure, obscuring details in shadows and producing a lack-luster image. Thus, comprehending which element to adjust within your exposure triangle is crucial in mastering the art of photography. To aid your understanding, I have included an illustration showcasing the behavior of each element.

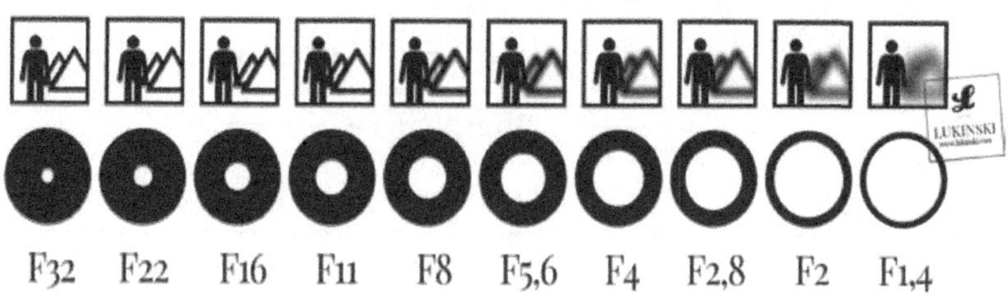

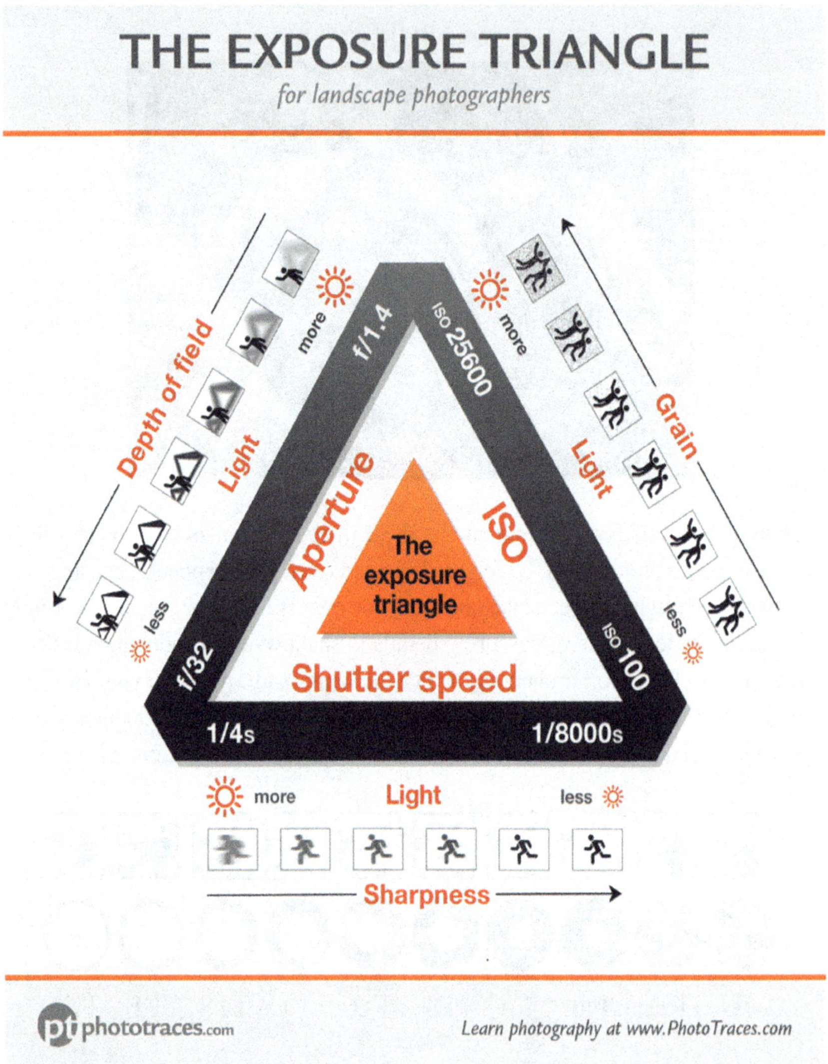

Shutter Speed (Motion Blur)

When you hear that signature "click!" of a camera, what's really happening is the shutter speed within the lens working to capture light. The longer and harder you press down on your shutter button, the slower this process becomes - allowing for more time between clicks! With an understanding of these speeds, photographers can create stunning photos with artistic clarity. Here is how slow, medium and fast shutter speed appear when you take a picture.

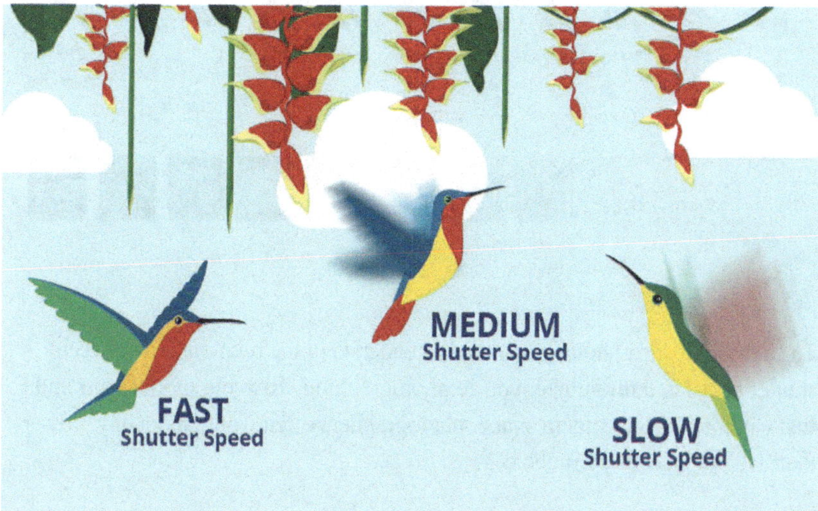

In photography, shutter speed is everything. A slower shutter can capture more light and make your images brighter - almost like a window opening up for the perfect shot! But with increased brightness also comes motion blur- so if you're looking for sharpness in your shots then increasing the shutter speed will help achieve that goal. It's all about finding a balance between capturing enough light and keeping movement at bay.

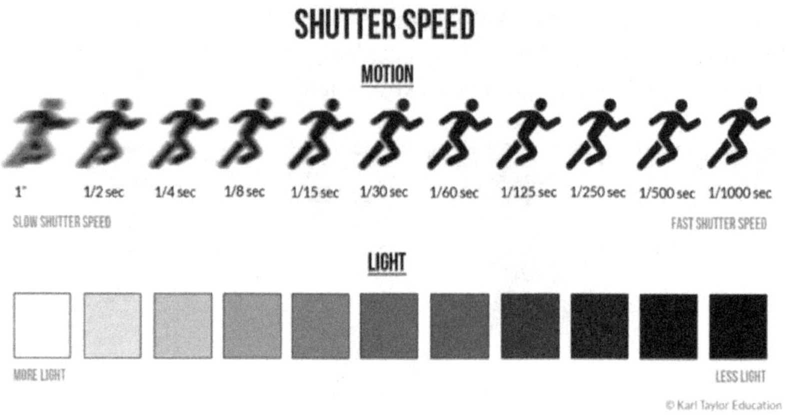

To capture the best photos, you need to understand the relationship between shutter speed and the subject you're photographing. To avoid motion blur and fuzzy pictures from camera shake, photographers often won't shoot any slower than 1/60 of a second handheld.

Raising the shutter speed is one solution, but for those interested in longer exposures, invest in a tripod. This diagram shows you why a tripod would be necessary. Anything past 1/60 and your subject blurs out.

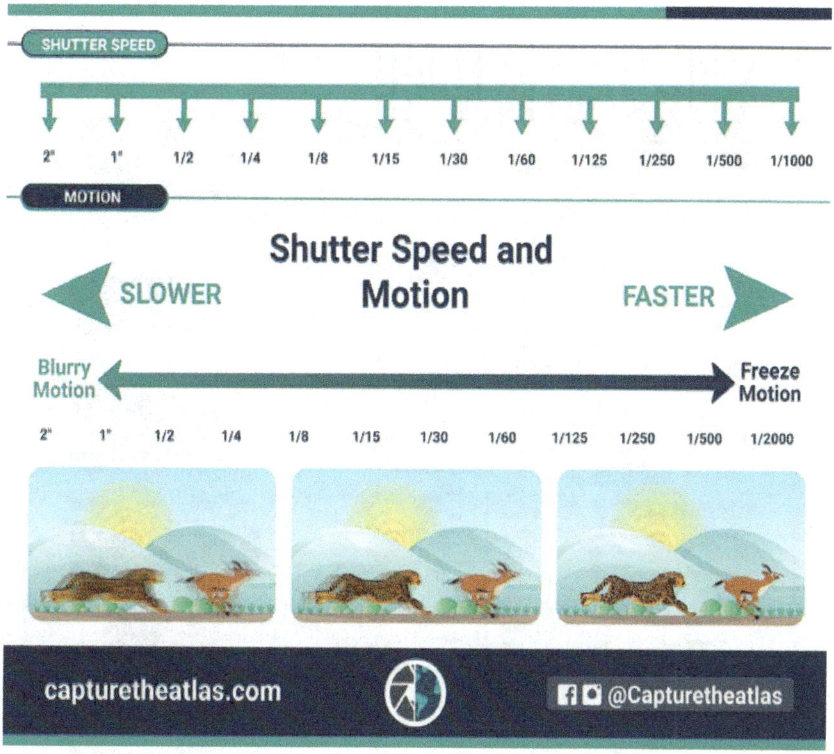

Shutter speed is the measurement of how long the camera's shutter (or eye) remains open, which is typically expressed in seconds or fractions of a second. The sequence usually follows a standardized format, progressing from slower to faster speeds:

1 second → 1/2 second → 1/4 second → 1/8 second → 1/15 second → 1/30 second → 1/60 second → 1/125 second → 1/250 second → 1/500 second → 1/1000 second → and so on.

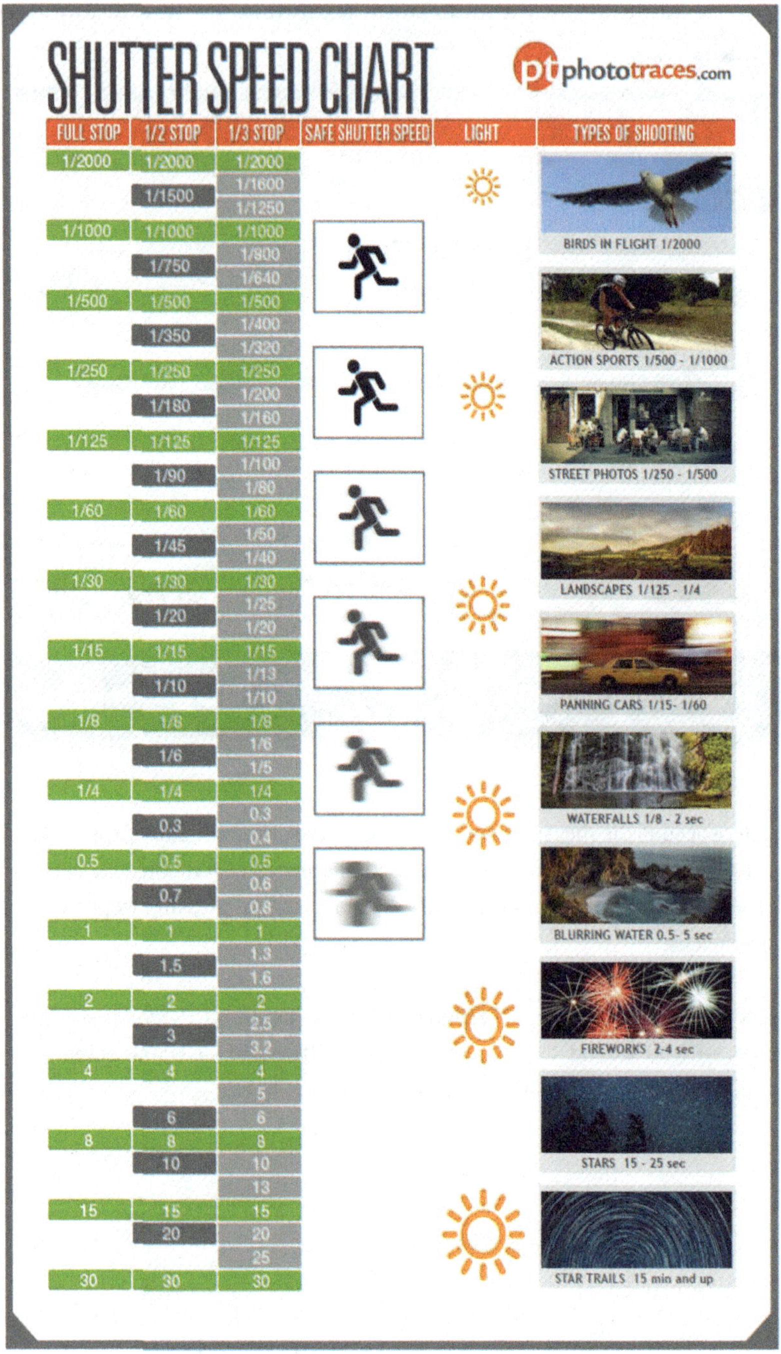
SHUTTER SPEED CHART
phototraces.com
FULL STOP
1/2 STOP
1/3 STOP
SAFE SHUTTER SPEED
LIGHT
TYPES OF SHOOTING
1/2000 1/2000 1/2000
1/1600
1/1500
1/1250
1/1000 1/1000 1/1000
1/800
1/750
1/640
1/500 1/500 1/500
1/400
1/350
1/320
1/250 1/250 1/250
1/200
1/180
1/160
1/125 1/125 1/125
1/100
1/90
1/80
1/60 1/60 1/60
1/50
1/45
1/40
1/30 1/30 1/30
1/25
1/20
1/20
1/15 1/15 1/15
1/13
1/10
1/10
1/8 1/8 1/8
1/6
1/6
1/5
1/4 1/4 1/4
0.3
0.3
0.4
0.5 0.5 0.5
0.6
0.7
0.8
1 1 1
1.3
1.5
1.6
2 2 2
2.5
3
3.2
4 4 4
5
6 6
8 8 8
10 10
13
15 15 15
20 20
25
30 30 30
BIRDS IN FLIGHT 1/2000
ACTION SPORTS 1/500 - 1/1000
STREET PHOTOS 1/250 - 1/500
LANDSCAPES 1/125 - 1/4
PANNING CARS 1/15- 1/60
WATERFALLS 1/8 - 2 sec
BLURRING WATER 0.5- 5 sec
FIREWORKS 2-4 sec
STARS 15 - 25 sec
STAR TRAILS 15 min and up

ISO Settings (Grainy/Noise)

ISO stands for International Organization for Standardization, but in the context of photography, it refers to the sensitivity of your camera's image sensor to light. It is a crucial setting that allows you to control the exposure of your photographs.

ISO is represented by a numerical value, such as 100, 200, 400, 800, and so on. A lower ISO number indicates low sensitivity to light, while a higher ISO number indicates high sensitivity to light. When you increase the ISO, your camera becomes more responsive to light, allowing you to capture properly exposed images even in low-light conditions. However, higher ISO settings can introduce noise or graininess in your photos, reducing overall image quality.

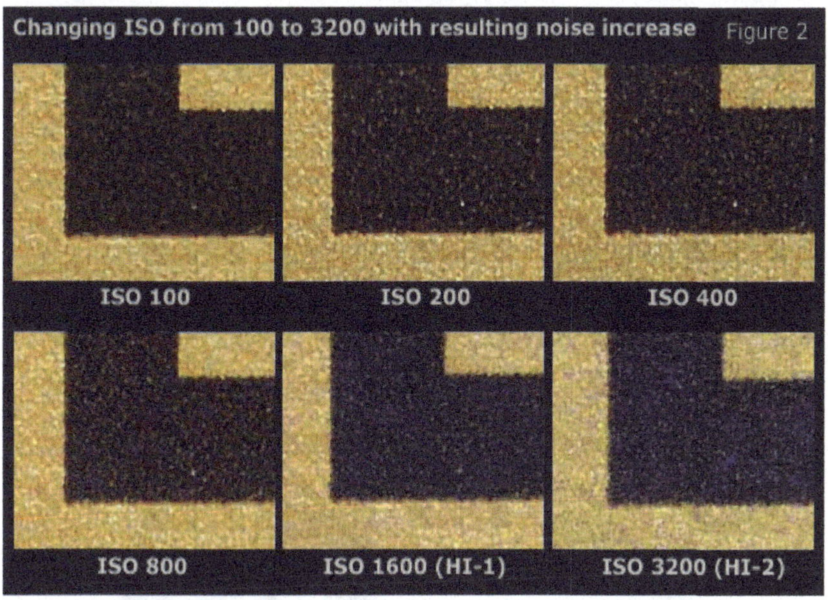

Conversely, using a lower ISO setting produces cleaner and less noisy images but requires more light to achieve proper exposure. Therefore, it's important to strike a balance between ISO, aperture, and shutter speed to achieve the desired exposure while minimizing noise.

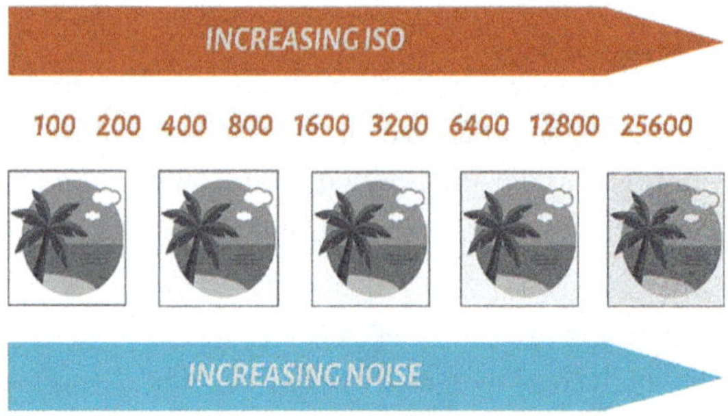

In low-light conditions, such as indoors or during twilight hours, higher ISO values, like 1600, may be necessary to avoid underexposed photos plagued by unwanted "noise" or graininess. By adjusting the ISO, you can optimize the exposure and capture stunning images in various lighting situations.

DSLRs and Mirrorless cameras offer superior low-light performance compared to cell phone cameras. This is because their larger sensors are packed with significantly more pixels, allowing for less digital noise when shooting at higher ISOs - perfect for capturing those stunning night shots! Simply put: a bigger sensor = fewer noisy photos; even the tiniest of pixel sizes make a difference.

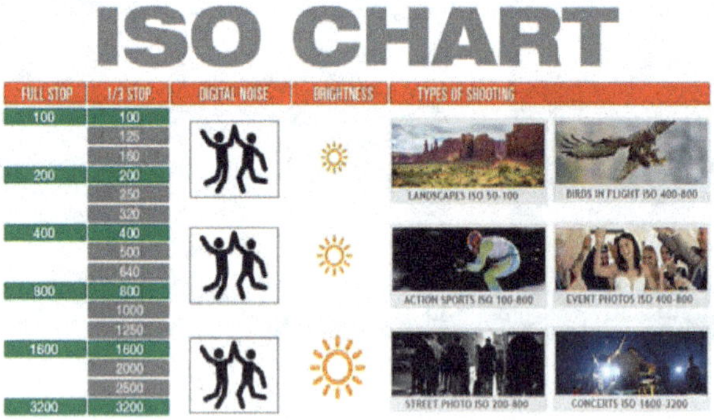

Learning how best to use auto ISO can be a great way for aspiring photographers to take their skills up a notch - it may just mean the difference between an amateur shot and one fit for a professional display.

Aperture (Depth of Field)

Photographers can create stunning images by simply mastering the art of depth of field (DOF). By adjusting the lens aperture, they can control how much clarity they achieved in each shot. Our eyes provide us with the ability to observe and appreciate life's beauty, but we don't normally think of them in terms of photography. Yet cameras rely on a part of the camera just like our own pupils - the aperture! This crucial component affects both how much light enters your lens and what you capture through its shutter action.

Aperture values may be expressed by fractions known as **f-stops,** and are essential for taking beautiful photos!

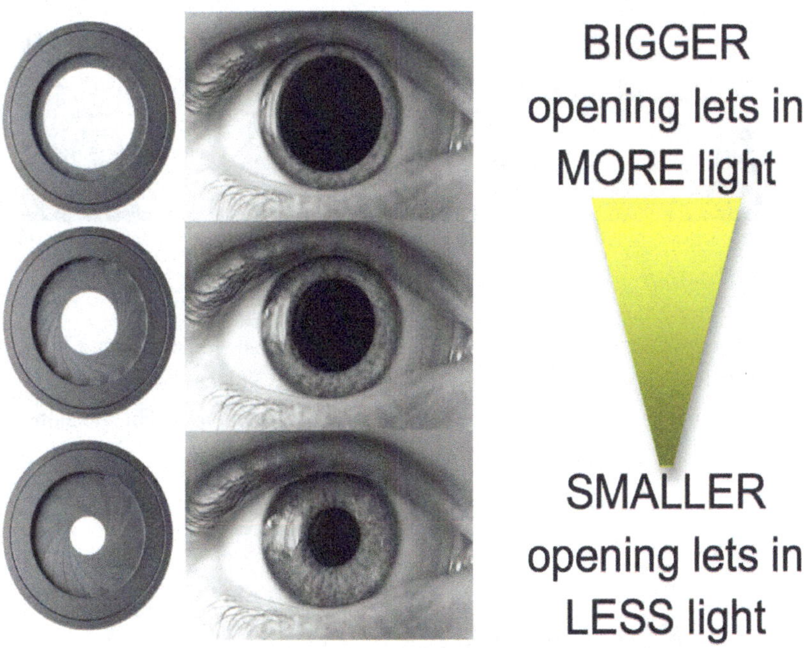

Narrow vs. Large Depth of Field

Photographers who are looking for a narrow (aka shallow) depth of field and crisp focus need to widen their shutter's aperture. The f/stop number, which corresponds with the size of the open space in your lens' pupil, is determined by how much light can enter at once. By opening and closing it like an adjustable pupil, you can control both how much light hits your sensor and where the focal point lies within the frame.

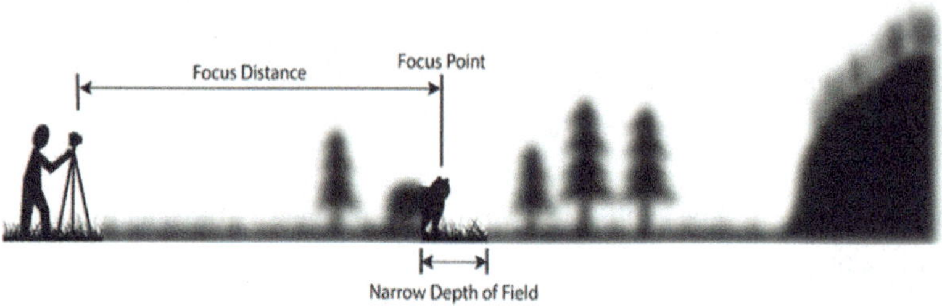

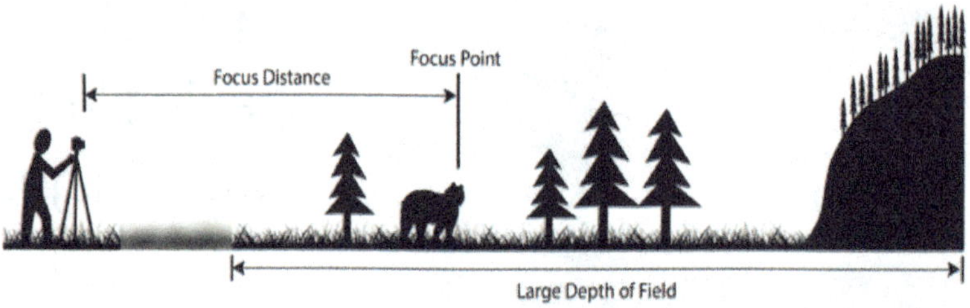

However, if you want a larger (aka deeper) depth of field with everything from front to back sharply focused, then shrink the pupil to a higher f/stop instead! Blurring out any distractions allows for creative compositions and breathtaking visuals.

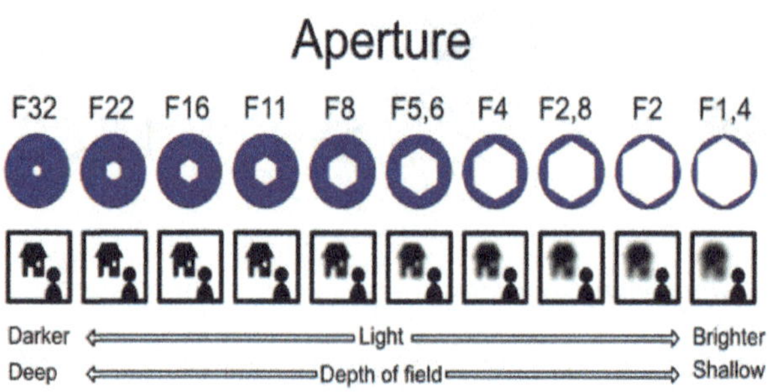

With more light entering through this wider aperture, photographers can create bolder portraits of their subjects even in low-light settings - making these lenses perfect both for professionals looking for that extra touch and enthusiasts wanting some serious fun with sports photos!

Based on the example above, if you're shooting shots such as portraits on a bright day, lower numbers like 1.4 would be recommended. If you are taking high-detail photos, relying on natural lighting - think architecture or landscapes– go higher around 22 so fewer rays will hit your sensor simultaneously, providing better clarity when zooming into details.

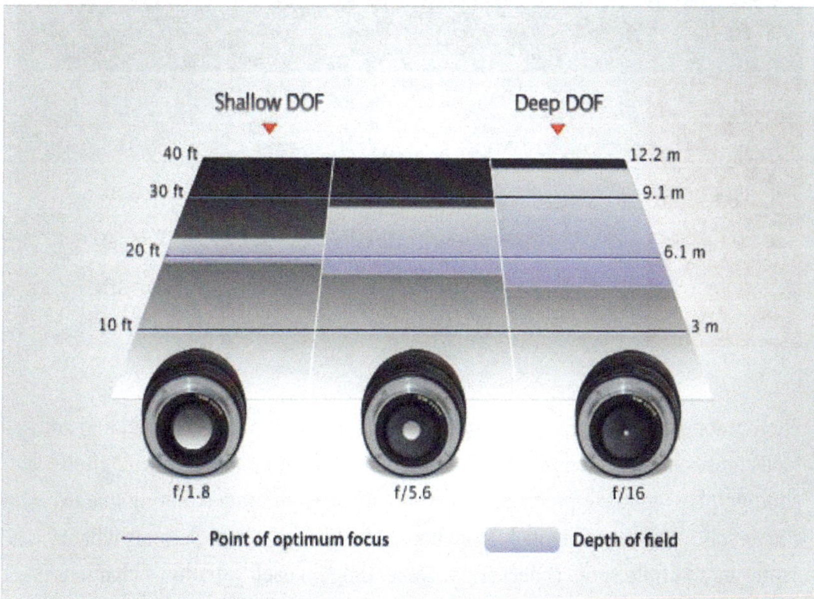

Capturing the unbridled beauty of nature through photography takes skill and precision. Using a low lens aperture enables photographers to bring detail, clarity & crispness into their pictures - all the way from close range to as far out in nature as they can see. This tool may be double-edged since it reduces light reaching the sensor, consequently resulting in darker images that require more post-editing effort; however, done right, this technique unlocks stunningly beautiful landscape photos that truly capture mother earth's magnificent scale!

Lens Focal Lengths

Achieving a dreamy depth of field and bokeh in your photographs requires careful decision-making with lenses and other details. Focusing on focal length, aperture size, picture sizing, camera type, and viewing distance will all play an essential role in getting those desired blurred backgrounds you're looking for! Taking these factors into account is key if you want consistent results every time– no matter the setting or environment.

Lens focal length (DX cameras)	Dispersal of Depth of Field		Total Depth of Field
	Closest acceptable sharpness	Furthest acceptable sharpness	
18mm	3.55 metres	infinity	infinity
25mm	5.15 metres	171.16 metres	166.01 metres
55mm	8.38 metres	12.51 metres	4.03 metres
100mm	9.45 metres	10.62 metres	1.17 metres
200mm	9.86 metres	10.15 metres	0.29 metres
300mm	9.94 metres	10.06 metres	0.13 metres

Photographers looking for the most versatile solution can have manual and auto-focus lenses. Manual lenses offer a more significant amount of control, allowing photographers to make precise adjustments while generating stunning images; conversely, auto-focus is much more convenient in fast-paced settings where capturing multiple shots is necessary. Depending on each situation's characteristics and needs, having access to both lens types opens up various creative possibilities for anyone behind the camera!

Stop of Light Defined

In photography, a "stop" is a unit of measurement that represents a doubling or halving of the amount of light reaching the camera's sensor. It is used to adjust the exposure triangle elements either by increasing or decreasing the amount of light. Here's a brief explanation.

FULL STOPS

	Aperture	Shutter Speed	ISO	Flash Power
	1.4	1"	12800	1/1
Most Light:	2.0	1/2	6400	1/2
	2.8	1/4	3200	1/4
	4.0	1/8	1600	1/8
	5.6	1/15	800	1/16
	8.0	1/30	400	1/32
	11	1/60	200	1/64
	16	1/125	100	1/128
	22	1/250	50	
	32	1/500		
		1/1000		
		1/2000		
Least Light:	**affects flash intensity**	**affects ambient light only**		

Stop of Light and Aperture

In aperture settings, each "stop" represents a specific doubling or halving of the amount of light that passes through the camera's lens and reaches the sensor. The aperture refers to the opening within the lens that controls the amount of light entering the camera.

Aperture settings are commonly referred to as f-numbers or f-stops. The sequence of f-numbers typically follows this sequence: f/1.4, f/2, f/2.8, f/4, f/5.6, f/8, f/11, f/16, f/22, and so on. Each subsequent f-stop represents a halving or doubling of the amount of light.

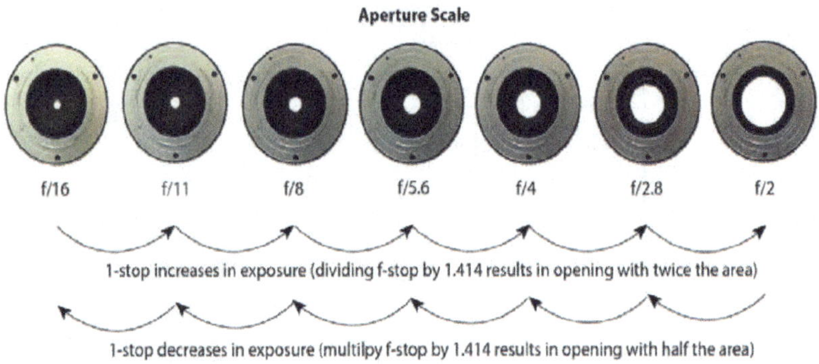

When you adjust the aperture by one stop, either by increasing or decreasing the f-number, you are changing the size of the lens opening. Going from a larger f-number to a smaller f-number (e.g., from f/4 to f/2.8) increases the size of the lens opening, allowing double the amount of light to pass through. Conversely, going from a smaller f-number to a larger f-number (e.g., from f/2.8 to f/4) decreases the size of the lens opening, reducing the amount of light by half.

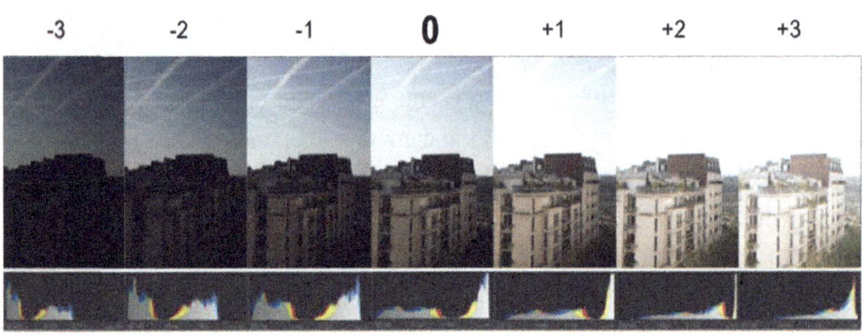

Each stop change in aperture also affects the depth of field. A larger aperture (smaller f-number) creates a shallow depth of field, where the foreground or background is blurred while the subject is in focus. A smaller aperture (larger f-number) produces a deeper depth of field, where more of the scene appears in focus from foreground to background. Understanding stops of light in aperture settings allows photographers to control the exposure and depth of field of their images, providing creative options to achieve the desired look and visual effects.

Stop of Light & Shutter Speed

In photography, the concept of a "stop" of light also applies to shutter speed. Shutter speed refers to the duration for which the camera's shutter remains open, allowing light to reach the camera's sensor.

Similar to aperture, each stop change in shutter speed represents a doubling or halving of the amount of light that reaches the sensor. Shutter speeds are typically measured in fractions of a second, such as 1/500, 1/250, 1/125, 1/60, 1/30, 1/15, and so on.

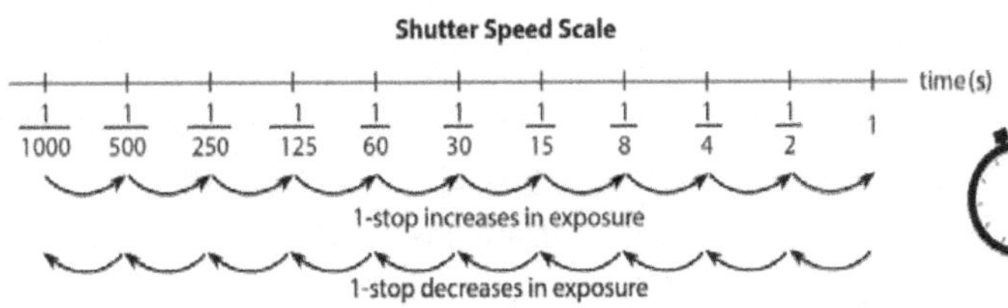

When you increase the shutter speed by one stop, such as going from 1/60 to 1/125, the amount of time the shutter remains open is halved, allowing half the amount of light to reach the sensor. Conversely, when you decrease the shutter speed by one stop, such as going from 1/125 to 1/60, the amount of time the shutter remains open is doubled, allowing twice the amount of light to reach the sensor.

Adjusting the shutter speed also has an impact on motion blur. Faster shutter speeds, such as 1/1000 or 1/2000, freeze fast-moving subjects and result in sharp, crisp images. Slower shutter speeds, such as 1/30 or 1/15, allow for longer exposure times, which can introduce motion blur if there is movement in the scene. Understanding stops of light in relation to shutter speed enables photographers to control the amount of light entering the camera and capture subjects with different levels of motion blur. It provides flexibility in adjusting the exposure and capturing moving subjects in various creative ways.

Stop of Light & ISO

In photography, the concept of a "stop" of light also applies to ISO. ISO refers to the sensitivity of the camera's image sensor to light. It determines how effectively the sensor captures and records the incoming light.

Each stop change in ISO represents a doubling or halving of the sensor's sensitivity to light. ISO values are typically represented as numerical values, such as ISO 100, ISO 200, ISO 400, ISO 800, and so on.

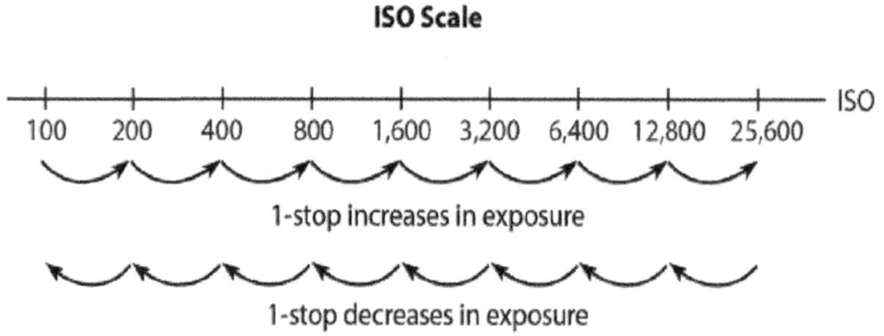

When you increase the ISO by one stop, such as going from ISO 200 to ISO 400, the sensor becomes twice as sensitive to light, allowing it to capture more light in a given exposure. This results in brighter images but may introduce additional digital noise or graininess to the image. On the other hand, when you decrease the ISO by one stop, such as going from ISO 800 to ISO 400, the sensor becomes half as sensitive to light, resulting in darker images but with potentially less noise.

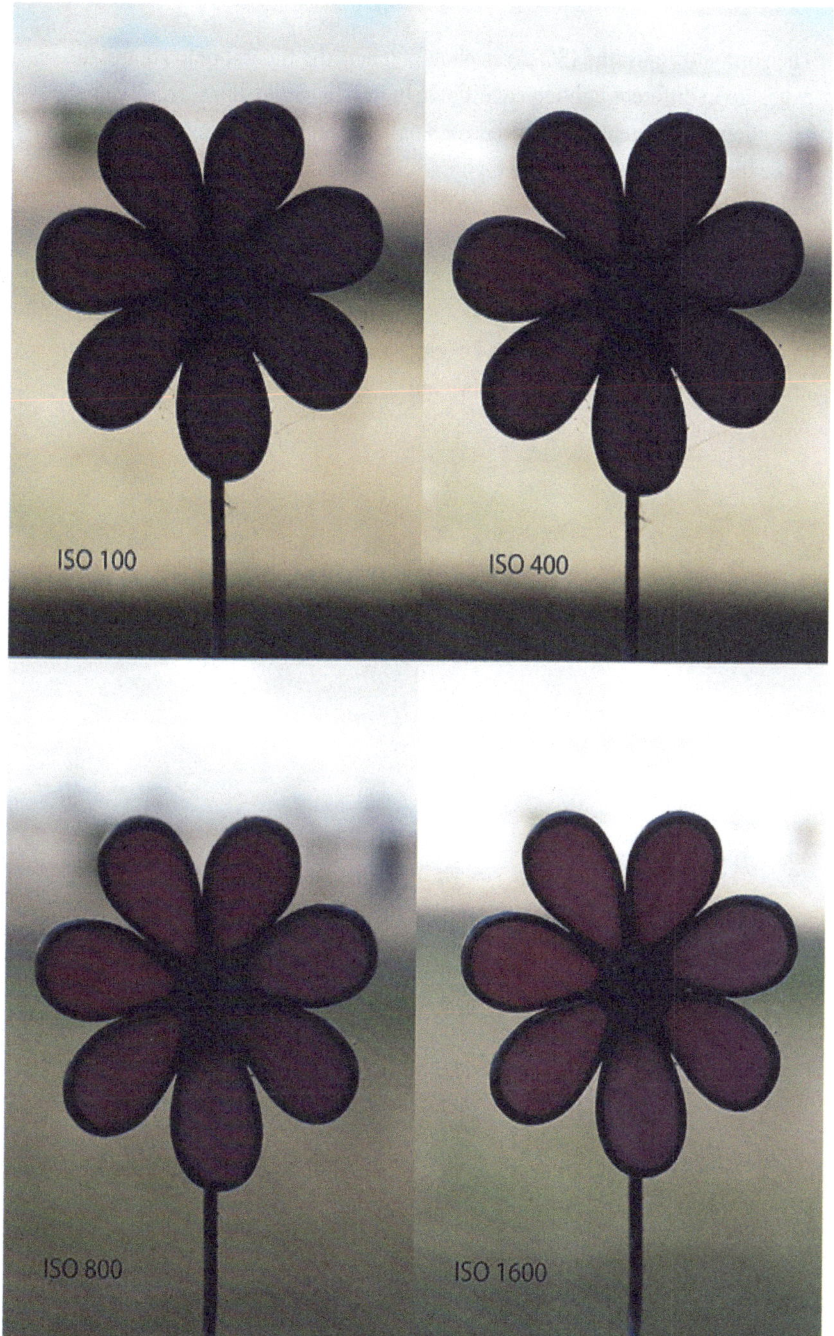
ISO 100
ISO 400
ISO 800
ISO 1600

The ability to adjust the ISO gives photographers the flexibility to control the exposure in different lighting conditions. In low-light situations, increasing the ISO allows for faster shutter speeds or smaller apertures, helping to capture properly exposed images. However, higher ISO settings may introduce more noise, so finding the optimal ISO value is important to balance image brightness and noise levels.

Understanding stops of light in relation to ISO empowers photographers to adapt to different lighting conditions and achieve the desired exposure while considering the trade-off between image brightness and noise.

5

LANDSCAPES

The principles of mastering light are important for taking better photographs. The size of the light source (like a flashlight) will create different shadows in the photograph. Our sun is bright, but because it is far away, it acts like a large light source. To make the scene look its best, you need to find the right intensity for illumination and then add or subtract elements to balance the exposure.

Lighting plays an essential role in determining the quality of images. Experienced photographers learn to master both natural and artificial light sources for optimal results. With proper setup positioning, exposure settings, and supplemental lighting tools such as reflectors or flashes, they can make any subject look stunning regardless of its environment.

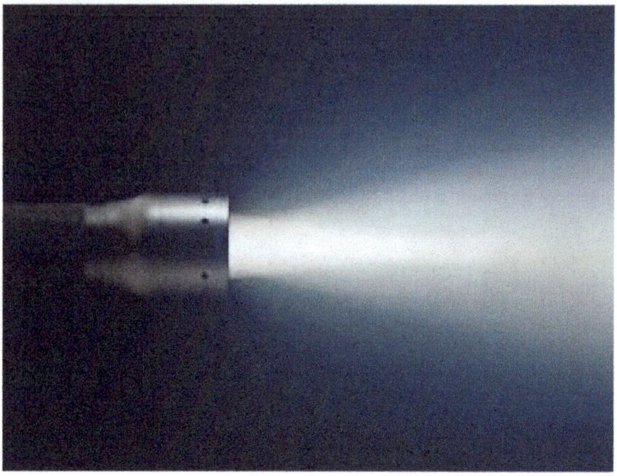

With a bit of skill, you can become a pro landscape photographer. You only need the right attitude, equipment, and patience to succeed. For over four decades, my experience as a professional photographer in the US and worldwide has taught me insider tips on taking amazing pictures - even if it's your first time picking up a camera. I have had several landscape photographs "favorited" by the editors of National Geographic, and even had a landscape image as a runner-up for the cover of National Geographic (below).

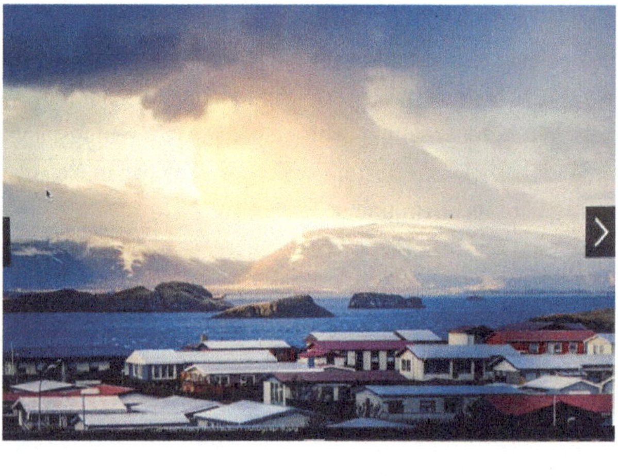

Lighting Quality and Direction

Lighting quality and direction are critical factors that can make or break your photographs. In this book, we'll explore the differences between hard and soft lighting, as well as the importance of lighting direction.

Lighting Direction

Lighting direction refers to the angle at which the light falls on your subject. The direction of light can add depth and dimension to your photos. For instance, noontime sunlight hits the subject from above, while evening sunlight hits it from the side.

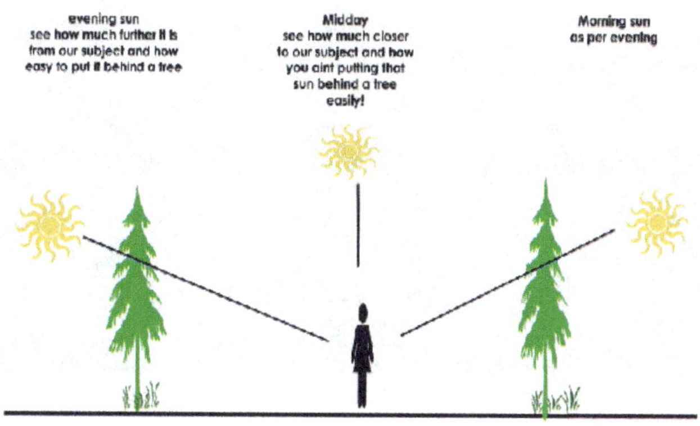

Whether a professional photographer or a beginner, understanding lighting direction is the first key to taking breathtaking photos. It's incredible how simple changes in lighting can transform an image, and that's why experimenting with lighting is so important. Photography is all about painting with light and mastering different lighting techniques. But where do you start? There are several types of lighting you should understand, including natural, artificial, diffused, and direct lighting. Once you start playing around with these different lighting options, you'll be amazed at the stunning results you can achieve. So go ahead, grab your camera, and start experimenting with lighting to take your photography to new heights!

Lighting Quality

The hardness or softness of the light plays a significant role in photography. Soft light produces saturated colors and limited shadows, while hard light adds contrast and heavy shadows. Harsh lighting usually happens in the middle of the day. Understanding lighting quality is essential because it can distinguish between mediocre and great photos. I always try to find cloudy days to photograph. It acts like a filter, defusing the intensity of the sunlight. If you don't have a cloudy day, consider shooting at sunrise or sunset when the light is less intense.

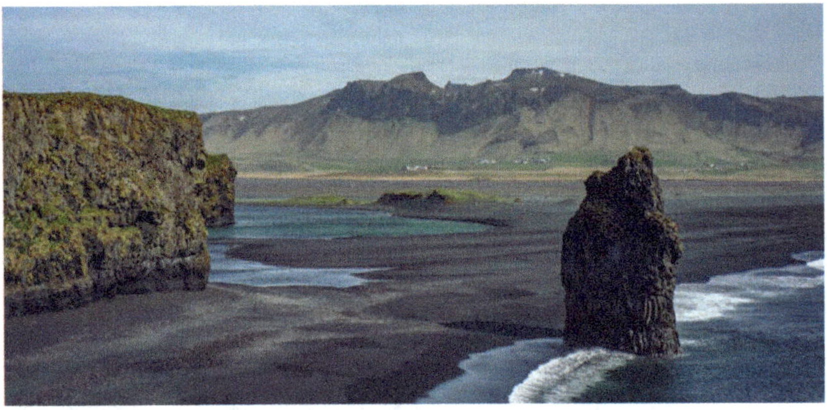

You can buy this Iceland image on my website. https://tracy-mccrackin-photography

This image taken of Iceland's famous black beaches shows nice, even lighting. Overhead, clouds were blocking the harsh sun rays from washing the colors out of this beautiful scene. You can see soft shadows being cast by the sun under the black rock formation. This is the type of lighting you want to capture. My camera had no filter on it. I barely touched it up in Photoshop just to bring back the black rock details. This is exactly how it looked in person in all its natural colors. This is the day you should scout for when you are shooting landscapes.

Types of Different Lighting Setups

Reflected Light

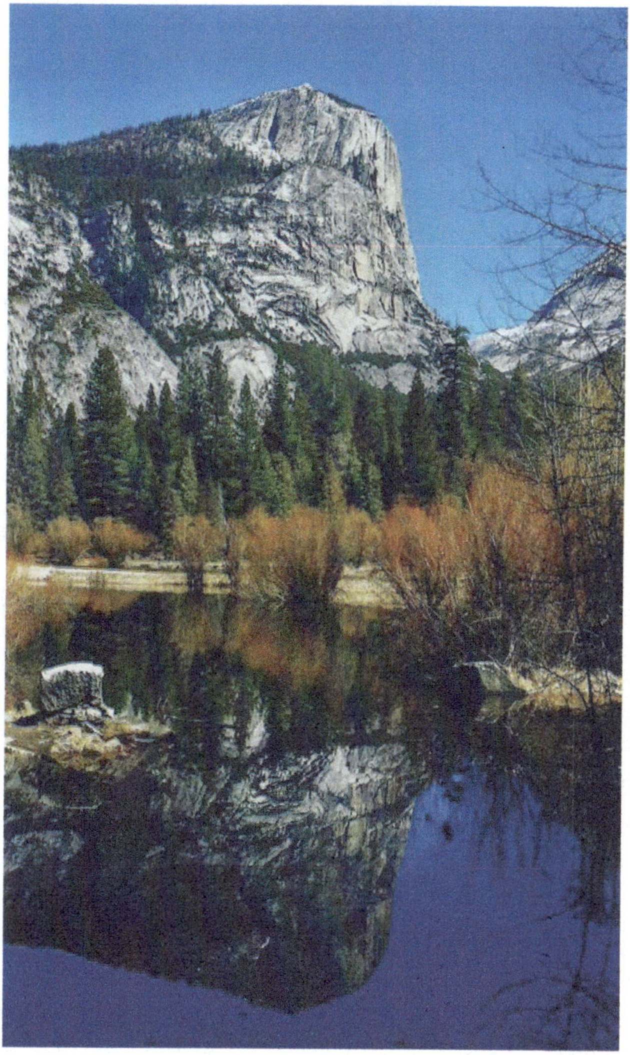

You can buy this Yosemite Image from my website at www.tracymccrackin.com

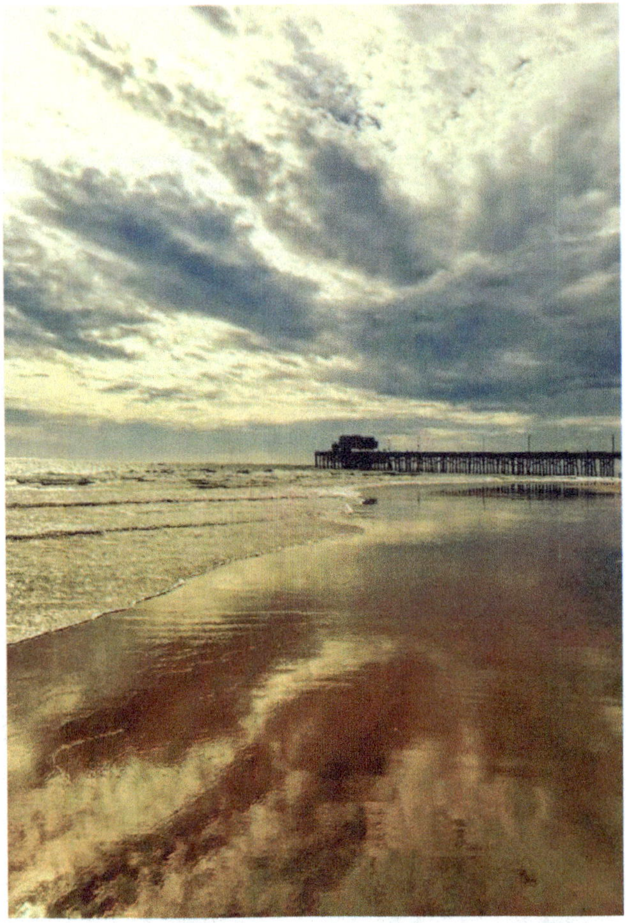

*You can buy this Newport Beach Image from my website at www.
tracymccrackin.com*

Reflected light, or diffused or bounced light, adds a soft and gorgeous effect to your pictures. This occurs when sunlight bounces off a nearby surface, creating a stunning and even glow. Capture mesmerizing photographs with the magic of reflected light. Experience stunning reflections with these tips. Water is a great place to find these reflective scenes. It can create wonderful mirror effects in the water. I used a filter on the Yosemite image because it was the middle of the day. When the light is even, the colors are always preserved.

In the Newport Beach image, I could get this image without a filter because the clouds acted as a filter for me. Achieving a beautiful reflection effect is easier than you think. To work with reflected light, find a bright surface like pale rock walls or a white beach. Steer clear of dark surfaces as they won't reflect light well. Follow these tips and get ready to capture breathtaking reflections!

Overcast Light

Colorful landscapes, such as flower meadows, seem especially nice on cloudy days. The gentle illumination is perfect for capturing delicate, rich colors. This is my favorite kind of light. Light is dim, moody, and blue during cloudy, foggy days. There are hardly any shadows, and the effects of light directionality are minimal. The lack of contrast and the softness of hazy light makes it ideal for landscape photography, but you still need to be cautious; a cloudy sky may make for a dull shot, so try to obscure it with trees, mountains, or anything else in the scene. Both images were taken on overcast days. I didn't have a filter, and I didn't have to Photoshop them to get their colors to pop. This is a simple and easy method to use when shooting your scene.

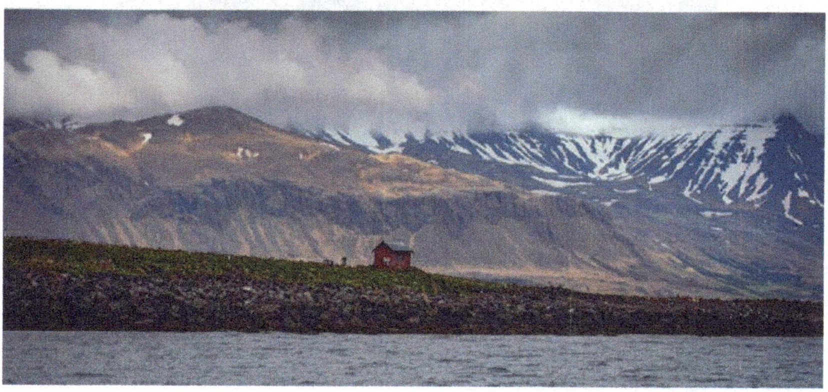

You can buy this Iceland Image from my website at www.tracymccrackin.com

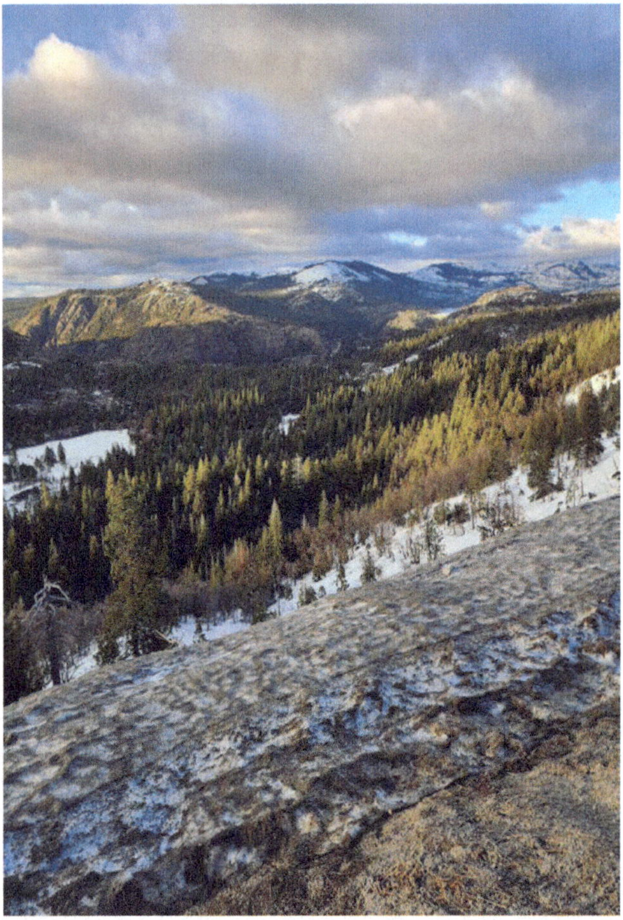

You can buy this Colorado Image from my website at www.tracymccrackin.com

Foregrounds and Backgrounds

Have you ever taken a photo that looked flat and uninteresting, despite your best efforts? You might be missing the crucial element of layering. Each photo comprises three distinct layers - foreground, middle ground, and background - that combine to create depth and interest. The foreground is the closest layer to the viewer, with the middle ground further back and the background furthest away. By using these layers to your advantage, you can create a visually compelling photo that draws the eye. So next time you're setting up a shot, don't forget to consider the different layers in play and how to use them to compose a better photo.

To truly captivate those looking at it, add depth with a texture that surpasses traditional two-dimensional photos for an unforgettable result! This image is from Haiti. I found harsh light that day, so I tucked behind this old building and discovered the most amazing scene. The rocks block the harsh sunlight and keep the colors of the ocean scene from being washed out. It also gives great depth by having a foreground of rocks, a middle ground of the ocean, and a background of the clouded sky.

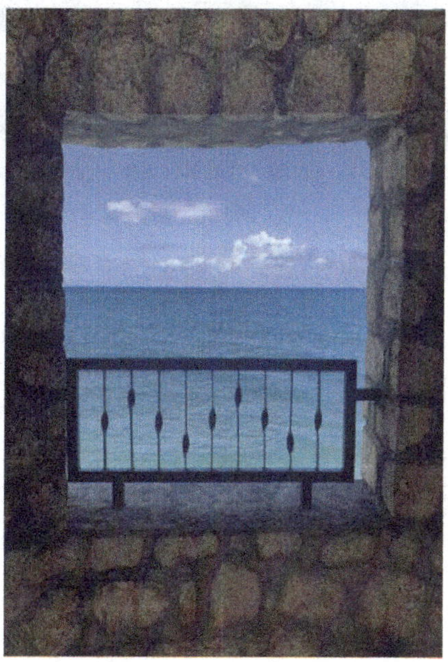

You can purchase this Haiti Image from my website at www.tracymccrackin.com

Also, consider creating a three-dimensional landscape view by positioning your camera close to an object in the foreground, like the azaleas, and aiming off into the horizon. This classic composition technique will impress! This gives your image the beach image dimension and interest.

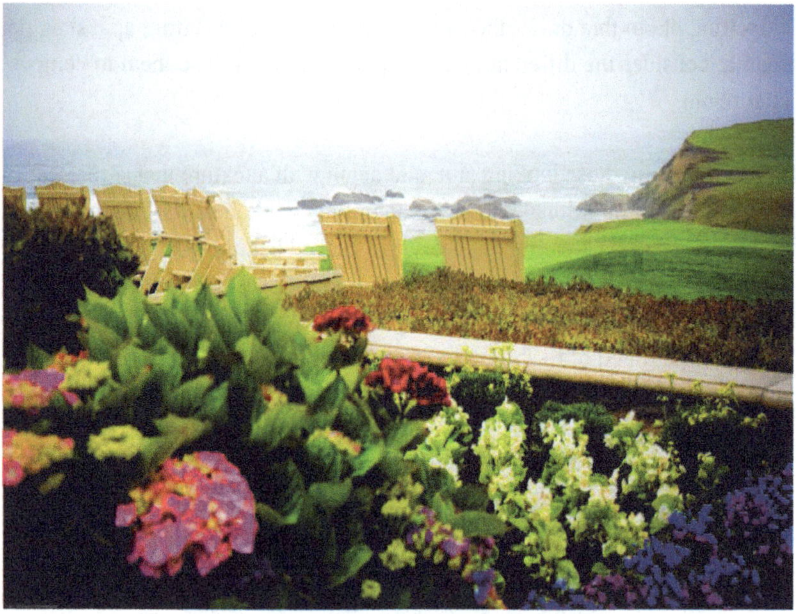

You can buy this Carmel, CA Image from my website at www.tracymccrackin.com

I recently snapped this image with my cell phone, for example. Nothing fancy about it, but it shows the type of dimension you want to look for when setting up an interesting scene. You have your foreground of the sailor statute, the flowers along the rail as the middle ground, and the island as the background. Your eye is drawn out and back. You don't know what to look at first, which makes it interesting. If I had just taken the image from the flowers, out toward the island, it would have felt boring and flat.

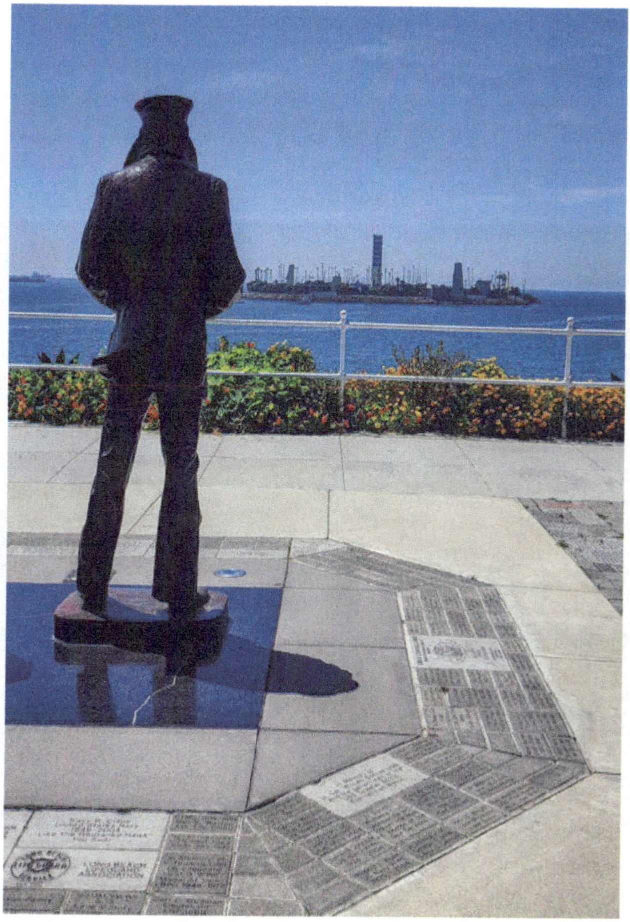

Reduce Glare or Use It As Backlighting

While photography is equal parts art and science, one of the most annoying issues when it comes to composition is glare. Unsightly, unwanted glare can appear at highly inopportune moments and ruin your shot. I see this often in scenes like glass reflecting from a model's eye, across a body of water, or the camera's lens. Glare can be extremely troublesome to tackle, but it also allows creative problem-solving. Or embrace the glare and make it your personal artsy statement to the image. Or use the glare as a creative option. It is important to note that partial backlighting occurs when the sun shines from about behind the subject, and complete backlighting occurs when the sun shines exactly behind the subject. Backlighting is a favored technique in landscape photography, particularly when the sun is barely over the horizon. Why? Backlighting is dramatic, whether paired with HDR effects (as in the picture above) or used to capture magnificent silhouettes.

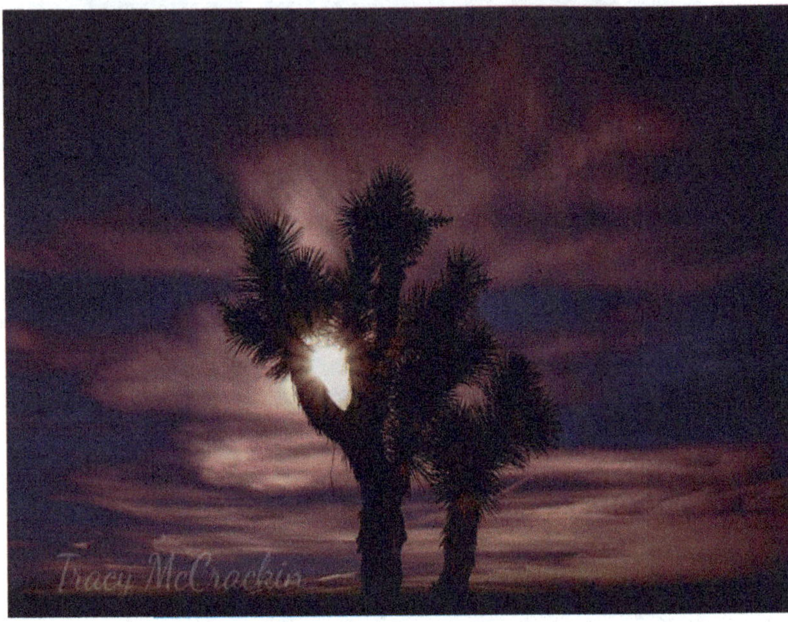

You can buy this Joshua Tree Image from my website at www.tracymccrackin.com

Pay close attention to the location of the sun in your frame. You want to partly block the light with a solid edge so that you may catch a lovely Sunburst. To avoid blown-out skies, keep the sun out of the frame or put it behind a substantial object, such as a tree or a rock. This Joshua Tree image took place just as the sun was rising right after a huge storm. Storms create excellent moody colors of blues and purples.

Direct Light

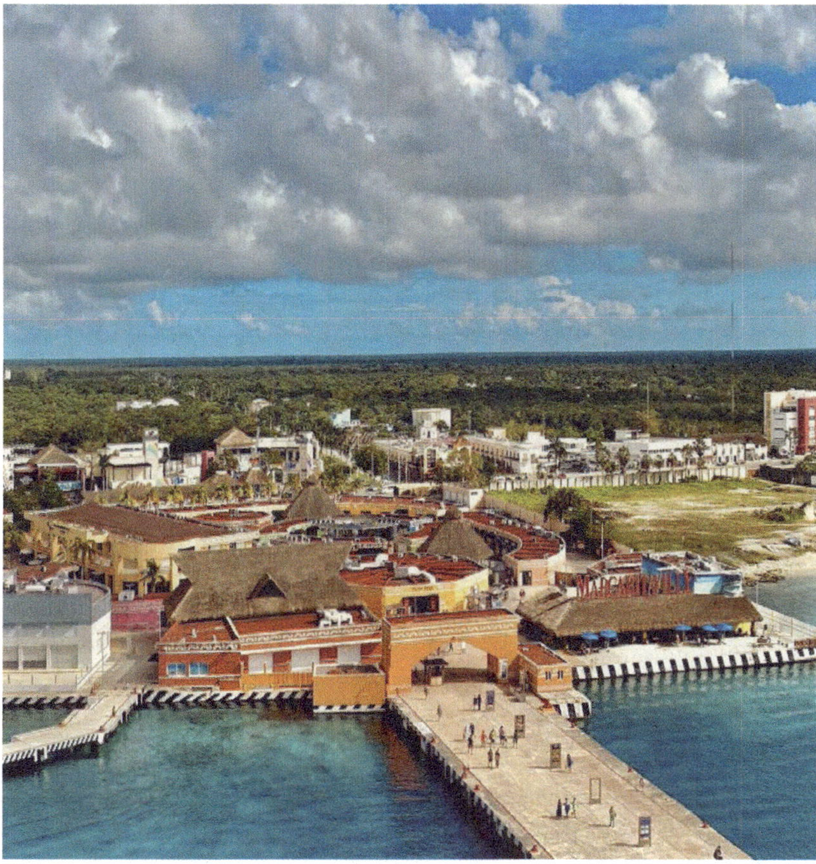

You can buy this The Caribbean Image from my website at www. tracymccrackin.com

Direct sunlight is notorious for being strong, harsh, and unforgiving. It is typically present a few hours after sunrise and before sunset, but as the sun rises higher in the sky, the light becomes even less flattering. For this reason, some landscape photographers steer clear of direct light altogether. While I don't go that far, I suggest using a filter or converting your image into black and white. So, if your photos appear dull and uninspiring when shooting in direct light, seek subjects that offer substantial tonal range. These subjects should span from deep black shades to bright white hues, as seen in the photo above.

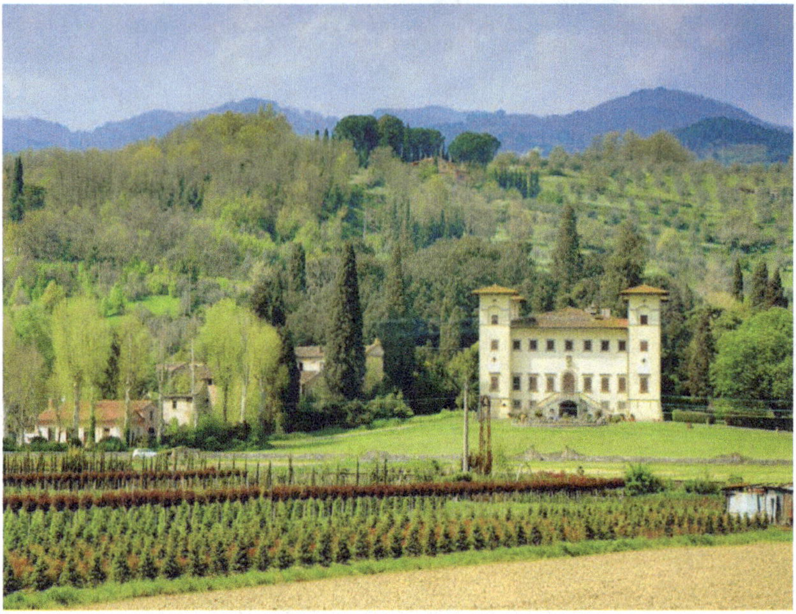

Change Positions

Spice up your artwork with a change of perspective! Try shooting from an unexpected angle, like rising above the scene in a bird's-eye view or getting down low for that dramatic worm-eye shot. Use images of everyday subjects in novel ways to make them stand out and show people something they haven't seen before.

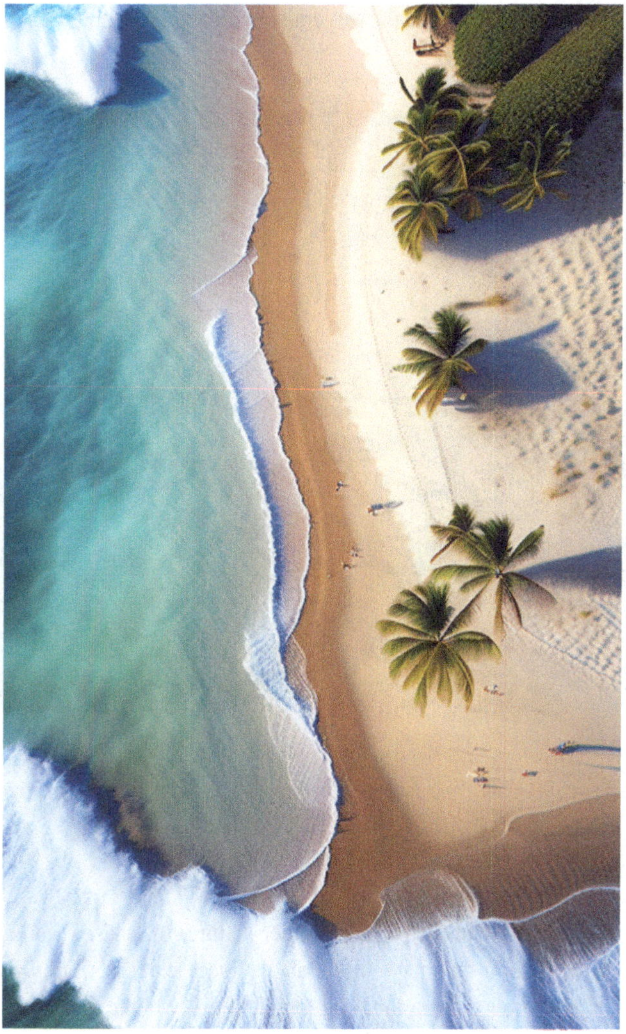

This aerial image is available on my website: www.tracymccrackin.com

- **Eye-Level Shot**: Place the camera at the same height as the subject.
- **Low-Angle Shot**: Place the camera below the subject.
- **High-Angle Shot**: Place the camera above the subject.
- **Worm's-Eye Shot**: Place the camera low to the ground and close to the subject.

- **Bird's-eye Shot**: Place the camera up high and photograph downward (like a bird's view).

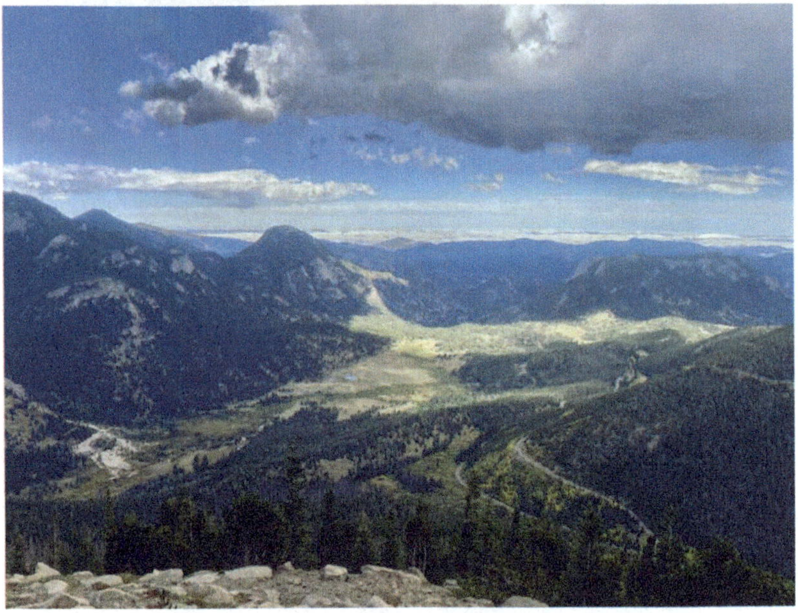

You can buy this Colorado Image from my website at www.tracymccrackin.com

Choose the Golden Hour - Morning/Evening

Get the perfect shot with help from Mother Nature. Instead of working around harsh sunlight (like in the image of me above), seek clouds or tall wooded areas (like the image below), for optimal lighting that diffuses the light and eliminates glare. Or, wait until later in the day, called "the golden hour," when it's not so bright; this could give you just enough softness on your subjects while still providing a great contrast between shadows and highlights. This image was taken in Lake Tahoe just as the sun started setting behind a grove of trees.

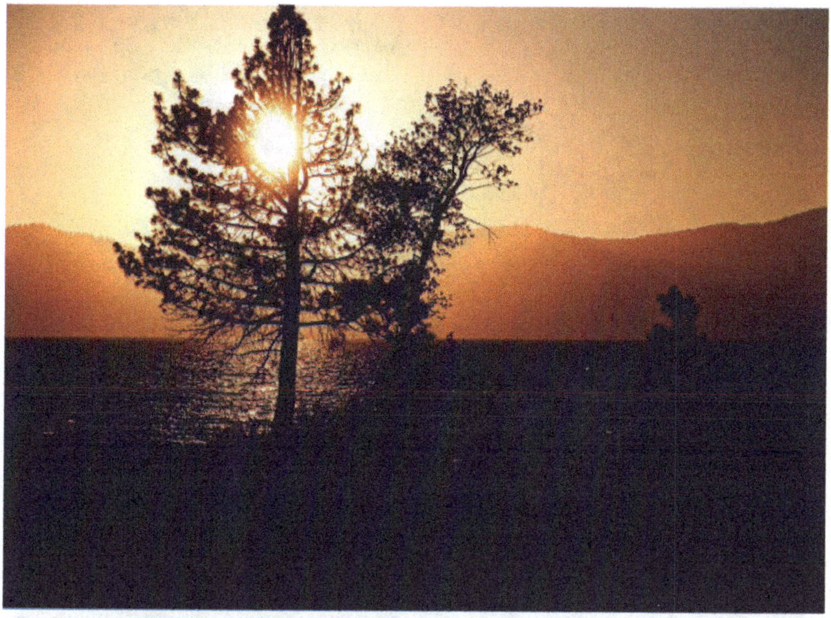

This Lake Tahoe image is for sale on my website at www.tracymccrackin.com

A beautiful sunrise or sunset can be what it takes to bring out the full potential of any location's beauty. This was undoubtedly true for capturing China's Victoria Harbour - in all its kaleidoscope of colors, set against dark hills in the foreground. It felt otherworldly, with the illuminated city in the background. I was lucky to see this scene while we were touring the hilltop. It had just rained, and the city lights were illuminating the clouds. This is one of my favorite images from my trip to China. I have learned over the years to wait until there are clouds in the sky before going out to photograph landscapes. Without them, images can look flat and uninteresting.

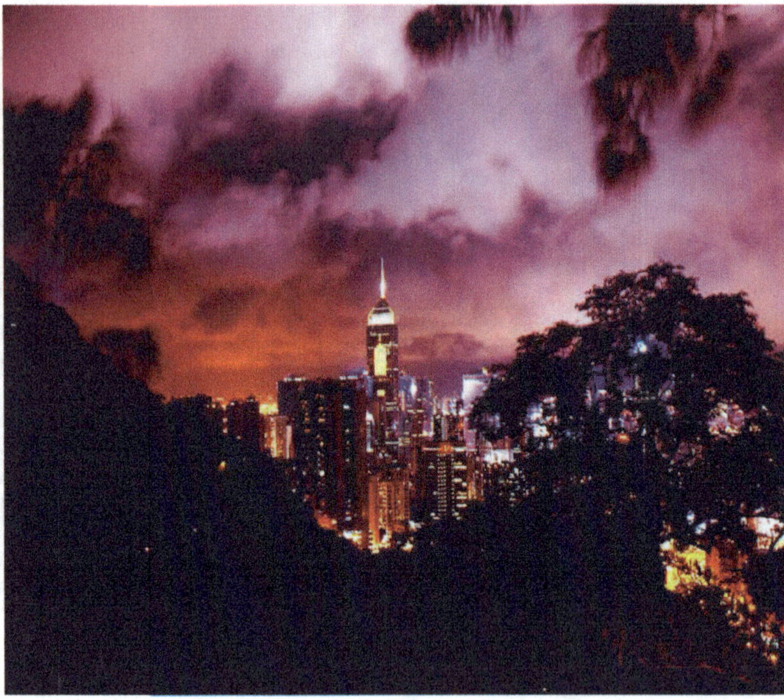

YOU CAN BUY THIS IMAGE HERE

Use Scale to Wow

Magazines often use wide-angle shots to captivate viewers and emphasize the vast expanse before them. By positioning a person or people far away from the lens, they create an intimate connection between the audience and the scene - prompting everyone who views it to imagine themselves standing in that same place. Such was my intent with this photo taken at the majestic Grand Canyon: an image so full of wonder you feel you are right there in its grandeur! On my website, I have other incredible panoramas for sale.

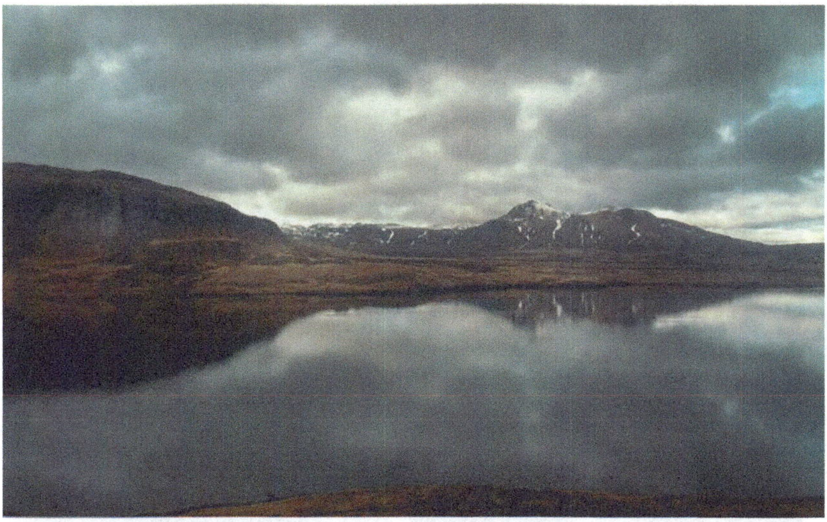

This Iceland image is for sale on my website at www.tracymccrackin.com

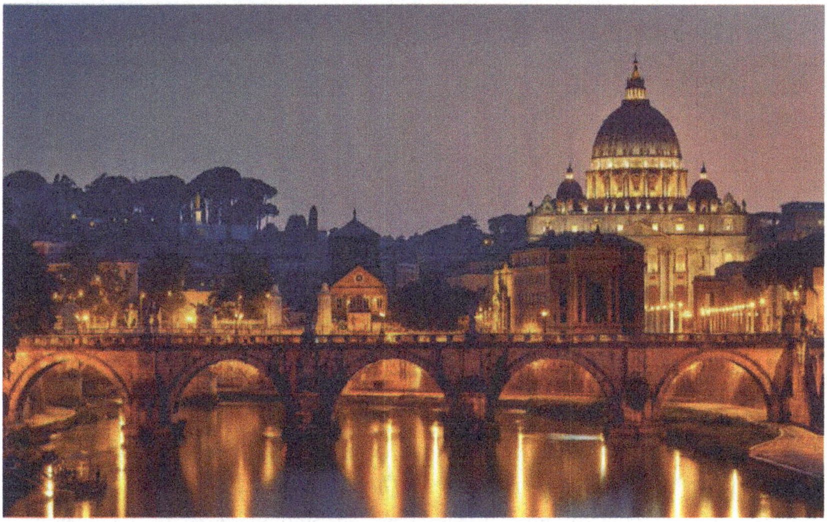

You can buy this Italy Image from my website at www.tracymccrackin.com

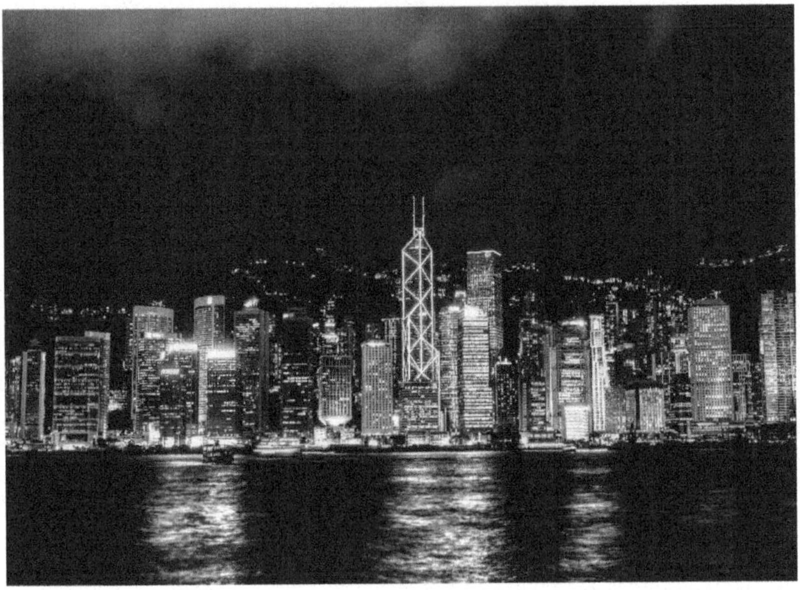

You can buy this Hong Kong Harbor B&W Image at www.tracymccrackin.com

Tools and Tips

Bring Various Lenses

If I were to give you any simple, sage advice on lenses, after years of trial and error, I would recommend to the person just getting into the industry you spend more money on your lenses and less on your camera body. Shocker right? Others might disagree, but this is how I see the camera. *Think of the camera's sensor as a canvas and the lenses as individual paintbrushes. The textured canvas is nice, but the paintbrushes give you all the visual effects. Just like paintbrushes, each lens gives you a different look and feel. The sensor just absorbs the quality and amount of light.* Now, if you're already a pro photographer already, then that may not apply to you.

So why would anyone spend thousands of dollars on a **high-end** Pro Camera and leave themselves with just one lens? It would be like working with one cheap paintbrush. Your creativity would be severely limited, and the range of projects you could take on would be limited. I suggest you start with a good **entry-level** camera from one of the top brands and put most of your money into getting multiple lenses (Wide, Telephone, and Normal).

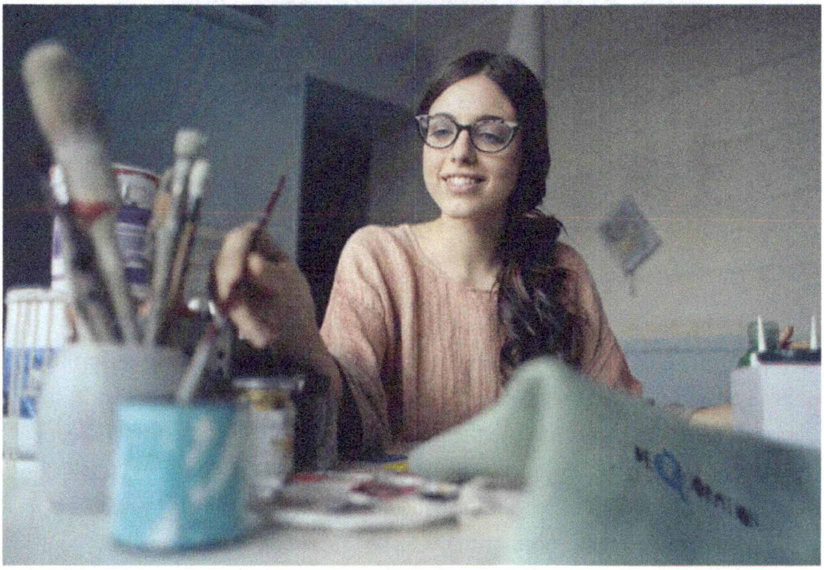

It's easy to get caught up in the hype of the high-tech camera world. I did the same when I first started. These brands advertise spending in the millions, preaching that you need Pro Cameras to make great pictures. It's a marketing lie. You can take great pictures with your cell phone. You can take great pictures with an old film camera. Half of the time, there are so many features in these Pro Cameras you have to take a class just to learn how to use them. After 8 years of having a great Nikon Pro Camera, I still hadn't used half its features! Remember, when buying your lenses and camera body, stick to the same brand of camera manufacturers, or your lenses won't work fit. Otherwise, you have to buy a universal ring to get them to fit, which may make you lose sharpness in your lens.

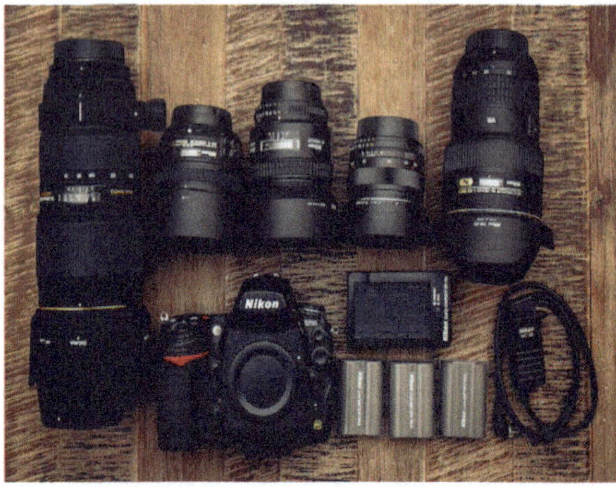

Wide-Angle Lens (3/4): If you're a landscape photographer, you probably already know that anything about 24mm or wider is considered a wide-angle lens. While these lenses may be the most popular choice for capturing sweeping landscapes, it's important to remember that there are other ways to create stunning photos. While it's true that a wide-angle lens can help to exaggerate the foreground and capture more of the scene in one shot, it's not the only tool in your arsenal. So, don't be afraid to experiment with other lenses and compositions to create unique and captivating landscapes.

Normal Lens: Looking for the perfect lens for landscape photography? A "normal lens" with a full-frame equivalent of 28mm to 70mm may just be what you need. While they may not provide the same exaggerated foregrounds of a wide-angle or subject isolation of a telephoto lens, they have a natural and unforced feel that can't be beaten. In fact, as a seasoned landscape photographer, I find myself gravitating more toward this focal length range. Don't let the maligned reputation of these lenses fool you–they can produce stunning landscape photography results.

Telephoto Lenses: Telephoto lenses have always been popular for wildlife and sports photography, but did you know they're also great for capturing distant landscapes? In fact, more and more photographers are using them to take stunning landscape shots.

Remote Shutter Release

A remote shutter release may seem like a fancy accessory, but it can make a big difference in achieving sharp and clear photos. One of the most common tools in landscape photography. Used for long exposures since it allows you to go beyond the typical 30-second limit. But did you know that a remote shutter release can also help avoid camera shakes caused by pressing the shutter button? It's also wonderful for portrait photography when you want to take selfies.

This Pixel Shutter Release is Wireless and Nikon and Canon cameras. Right now it's only $39.00 on Amazon. Affiliate Link for Nikon: https://amzn.to/44nyMbX and Canon: https://amzn.to/3nzzWAx

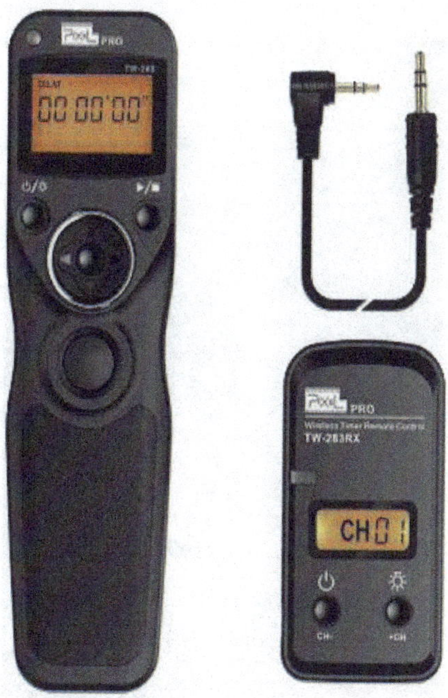

While some cameras today offer longer exposure times and self-timer modes, a remote shutter release remains an affordable and practical option. Don't settle for blurry or shaky shots – make the most of your camera and upgrade to a remote shutter release. As a photographer, I used to rely on remote shutter releases.

However, in the past few years, I've reached for them less and less. While some landscape photographers might consider them essential, I can manage just fine without them. What's your take? Are remote shutter releases a crucial component of your photography kit? Let's discuss this.

Buy Waterproof Gear

Picture this: it's a rainy day, you've got your camera in hand, and you're ready to capture some stunning shots. But wait, the raindrops pelt your camera, leaving you frantically trying to shield it while also getting the perfect shot. This is where rain gear and large covers come in. I enjoy sticking my bare head into crazy places like this waterfall. It's exciting and part of the fun! But it will seriously **ruin** your camera gear in a flash if not protected from the elements!!

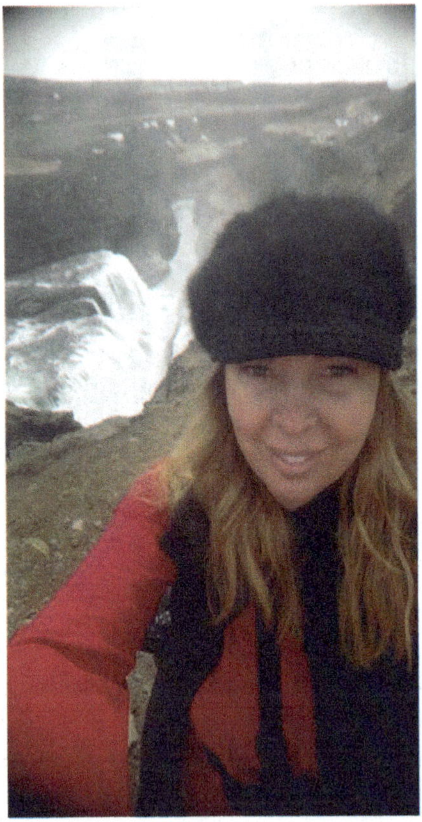

If you're out there chasing waterfalls like I was in this Iceland image (which was taken with my waterproof cellphone) or waves on the beach, waterproofing is necessary! Be smart about your choices. If you take care of your camera, it will take care of you (and give you long years of adventuring enjoyment). My own Nikon almost met its demise several times in Iceland from the extreme weather, despite all my precautions. I'm wearing a waterproof backpack in this image.

Waterproof Backpack: As an avid photographer and outdoor enthusiast, investing in high-quality weatherproof gear is essential before any hiking or photography trip. While I appreciate feminine colors in my everyday life, when trekking through nature, practicality outweighs style.

My camera equipment is too valuable to risk damage from dirt or wear and tear, so I choose durable black backpacks and cases. A sturdy backpack with ample padding is necessary to transport camera gear over rugged trails safely, and it doubles as a chair in a pinch. Though less glamorous than pink or purple, weatherproof black gear is a pro photographer's best friend on any outdoor adventure.

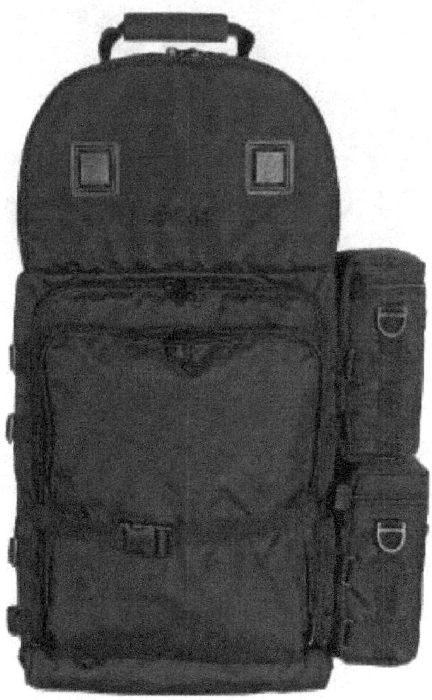

This is a very large Pro Backpack that is Waterproof. This one is affordable and got 4.5 stars on Amazon. They can be expensive. This one is only $159. Here is the affiliate link: https://amzn.to/44lRhOd

Looking for a camera that can handle all your adventures and won't break the bank? Look no further than the Tarion waterproof camera! This little gem has generated buzz among photographers for its impressive features and affordable price tag. With a tripod holder conveniently on the bottom, you can capture stunning shots without worrying about stability. Plus, the $49 price point is hard to beat, especially considering its impressive 4.7-star rating on Amazon. Whether you're a seasoned pro or just getting started, the Tarion camera is definitely worth checking out.

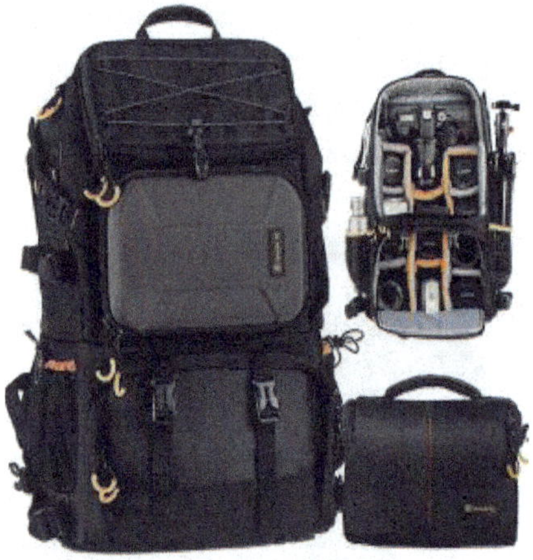

To buy it, you can go to this Amazon Affiliate link: https://amzn.to/420kbBD

Rain Cover For Your Camera: I vividly remember my trip to Iceland and the many epic waterfalls I encountered. But there was one waterfall that gave me a rude awakening about protecting my camera equipment. After that experience, I knew I needed to invest in a reliable camera rain cover. That's when I stumbled upon this gem - the one I used in Iceland. It's comfortable to wear, velcro shut for easy access to your camera, and can easily be rolled up and stowed away in your backpack. And the best part? It covers both you and your camera, ensuring that your equipment stays dry even in the harshest of conditions.

Spending a mere $29 on this rain cover is a smart investment that could save you thousands of dollars in damaged equipment. Here's the affiliate link on Amazon: Movo CRC27 Storm Raincover Protector

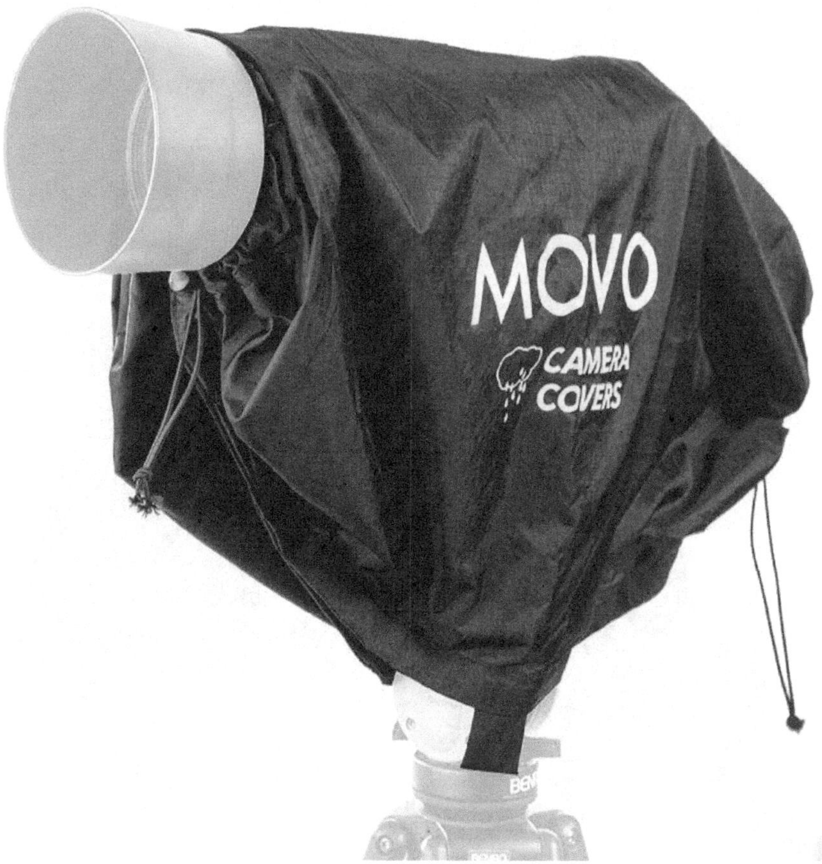

Raincover for Your Tripods: Don't let the unpredictable weather ruin your camera tripod! This amazing product has got your tripod legs covered - literally! No need to worry about rusting parts because this protective gear saves the day by securing the bottom and keeping wind and rain away. Plus, it comes in two stylish colors - black and white - making it not only functional but also a fashionable accessory. And at an affordable $24, you don't have to break the bank to keep your photography equipment in tip-top shape. Here is the affiliate link on Amazon: https://amzn.to/3Luonmc.

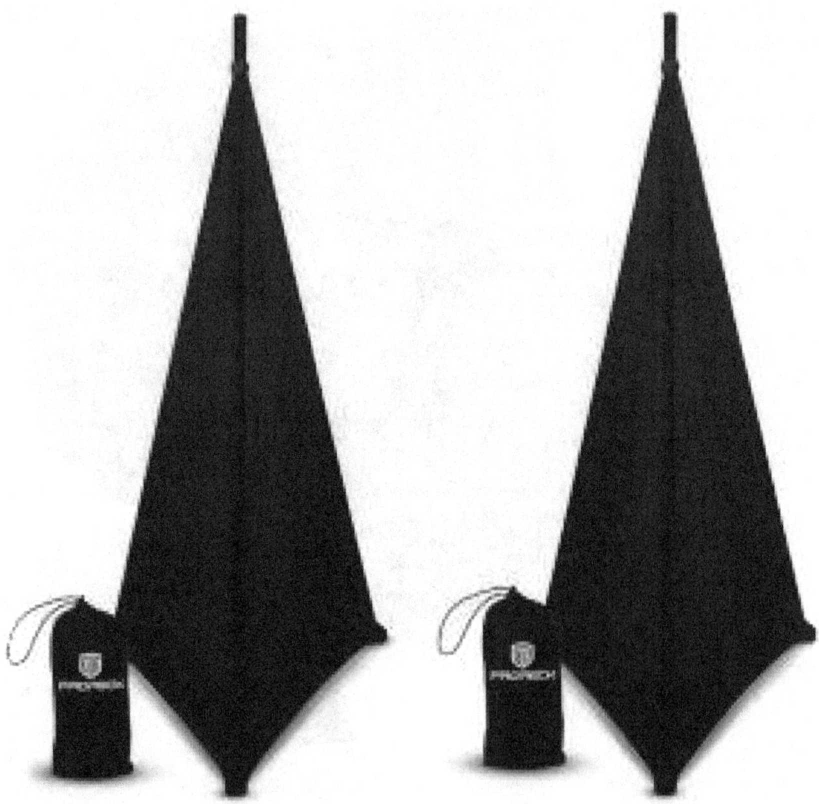

Raincover for Yourself: I can't help it, I'm totally addicted to this brand! I just wore this set to Iceland, and it was a lifesaver. The best part is they have different colors, so you can really choose which one fits your style. I will say the material is pretty thin and not padded like a winter coat, but that's actually a plus. If you need padding, just buy a size up and wear it over your regular coat. Plus, when you're taking photos on the beach or running around trying to get the perfect shot, thin layers make it so much easier to move around in without feeling weighed down. And let's not forget the snaps. They make it easy to pull on and off when you're done taking photos.

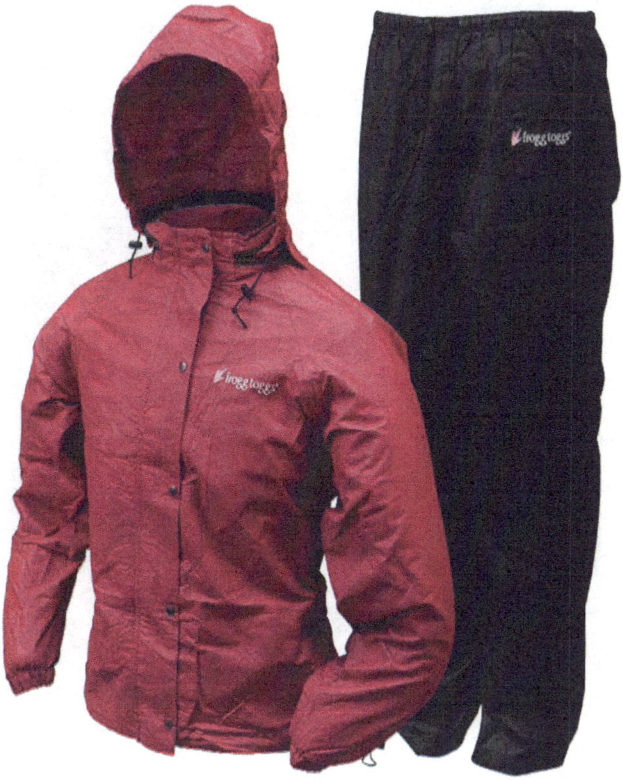

Seriously, if you're in the market for a new set, give this brand a shot. For $39 you won't regret it. Frogg Toggs Waterproof Rain Suit Amazon Affiliate Link: https://amzn.to/413tRtO

Use a Polarizing Filter vs. an ND Filter:

Polarizing filters and ND Filters are two tools savvy photographers used to achieve the perfect shot, especially during bright days. Neutral Density (ND) filters darken scenes without altering color - great if you wish to capture movement or detail when too much outside light is available.

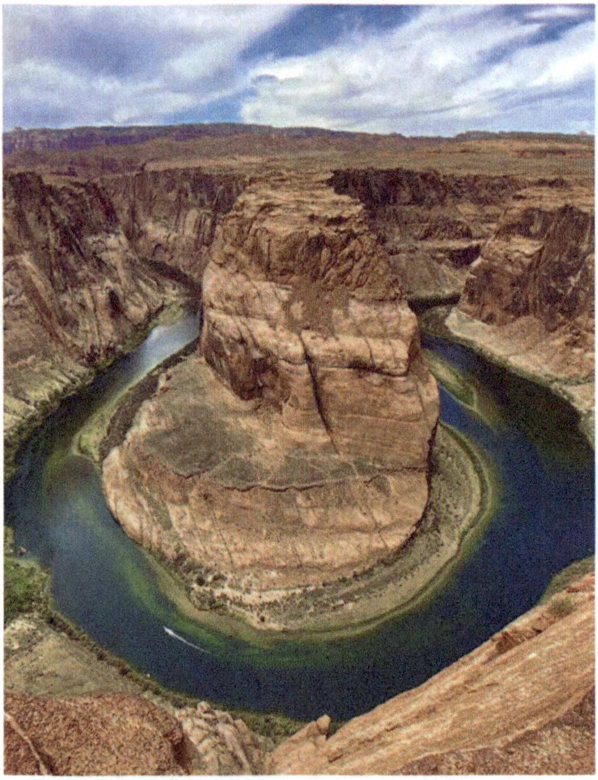

You can buy this Utah from my website at www.tracymccrackin.com

Polarizers block light reflected off surfaces, allowing for brighter colors with deeper saturation in your photos. They can range in price from a high-end kit from $100-$200 to a cheaper version between $50-$100. They also come in different sizes to fit the size of your lenses.

A popular and affordable one on Amazon is the K&F Concept 43mm UV/CPL/ND Lens Filter Kit (3 Pieces)-18 Multi-Layer Coatings, UV Filter + Polarizer Filter + Neutral Density Filter (ND4) + Cleaning Cloth+ Filter Pouch for Camera Lens (K-Series). It is approximately $40 for the kit and it includes *a Polarizer and the ND filter!*

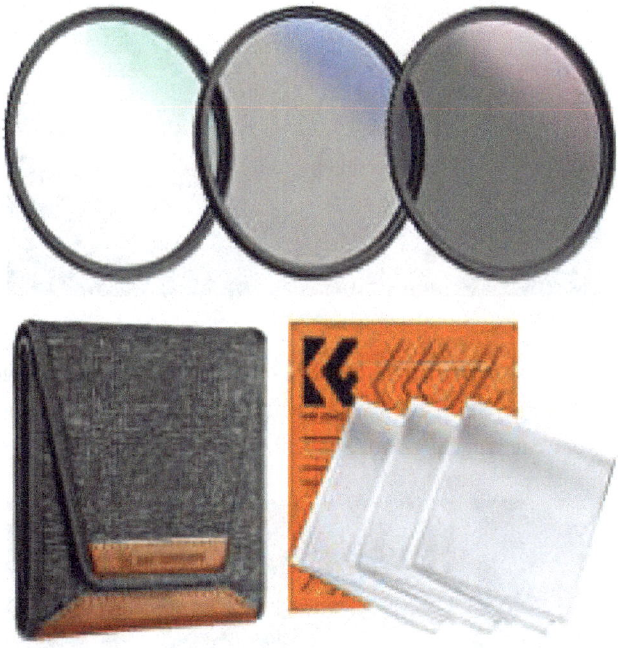

BUY NOW ON AMAZON Affiliate link

Add a Hood to Your Camera

Lens hoods are a great way to reduce those pesky sunspots which often spoil the perfect shot. They block out any disruptive light while still allowing your lens to get plenty of natural lighting, ensuring that you capture quality photos each time! If sunspots seem unavoidable no matter what angle or focal length you try, then perhaps it's worth investing in a more specialized piece of equipment and equipping yourself with an unbeatable tool for tackling glare.

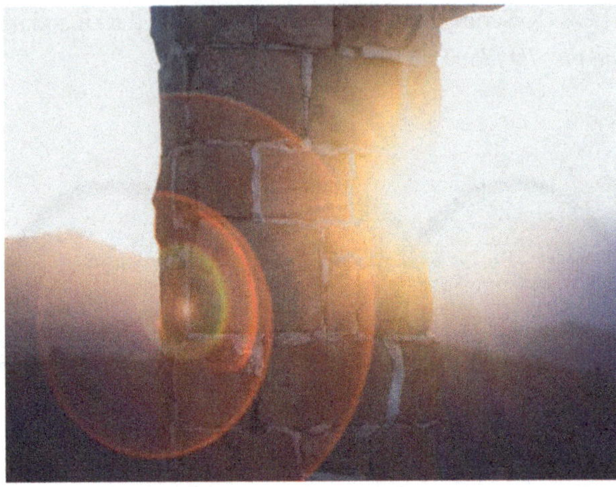

Every manufacturer makes a hood for their cameras. You can also buy generic brands from several retailers. Make sure you get a hood that matches the size of your lens. They can range in price from $30-$100.

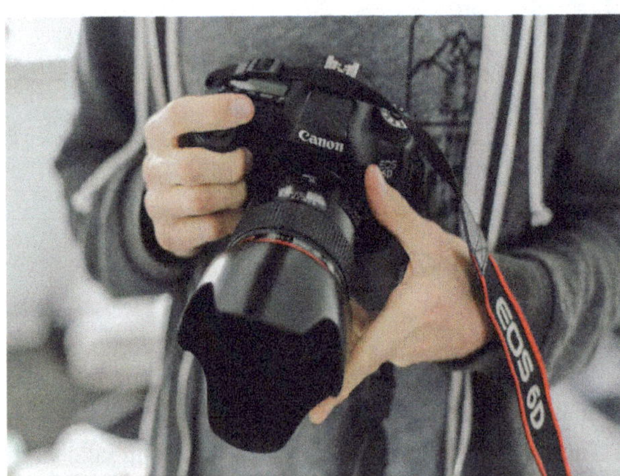

BUY NOW ON AMAZON Affiliate Link

Use Editing Software

Capturing a vivid image free of any harsh glare or over-saturation can be tricky. Luckily, there's an easy fix — editing software. Editing software should be a part of any photographer's workflow and tool chest. But it should never be overdone unless that's the artistic impression you're trying to make with your image. I did an entire Chapter in this book titled "Photo Manipulation" to explain editing software in greater detail. This image was taken of Florida's coastline and turned into a tiny world look and feel using editing software. This image was picked as an editor's favorite on the **NatGeo YourShot's website.**

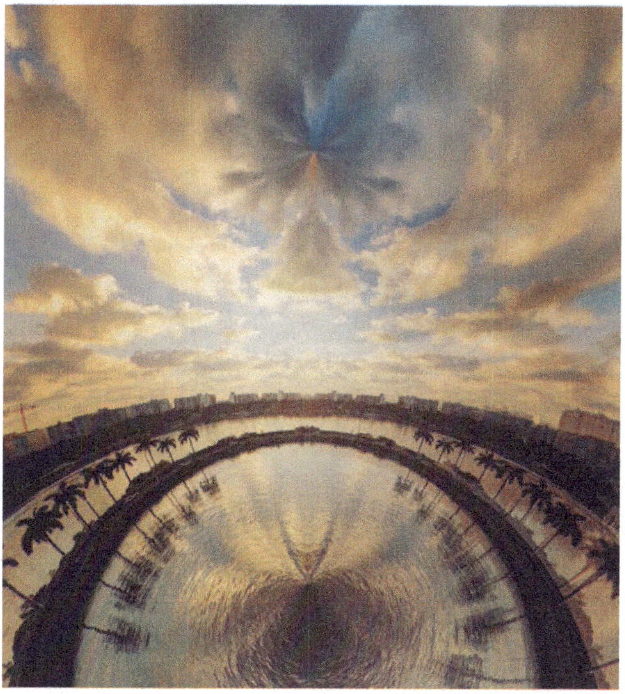

You can buy this Florida image from my website at www.tracymccrackin.com

Memory Card & Extra Batteries

We've all been there, ready to capture those breathtaking moments, and then bam! Our camera dies or our memory card is full. It's the worst. But fear not! With a little of planning, you can avoid this headache altogether. Always remember to pack a couple of extra camera batteries and a memory card with more capacity than you think you'll need.

If you want to be a pro, bring a spare memory card and keep it in your car. I know it can be tempting to skimp on gear and go for the smallest memory card possible, but trust me, it's not worth it. Not only do you risk running out of space, but if you lose your only card, you lose your whole trip. So, until you can afford that beefy 1TB card, go for two 512GB cards, etc. And don't forget to make sure your memory card is compatible with your camera - Sandisk is a great brand that works with many of the major ones, but not all of them. Happy shooting!

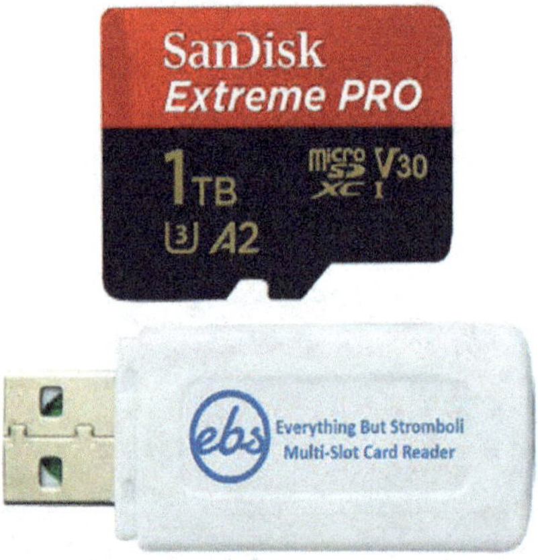

If you'd like to buy it, here's the affiliate link: https://amzn.to/4232qBU

Lastly, who wants to lug around heavy equipment all day? That's why I'm excited to tell you about this killer deal on waterproof memory cards right now. ,You can get two (2) 512GB cards and a memory stick for only $111.00! That's a steal for high-capacity, reliable cards that won't weigh you down. Don't miss out on this hot deal.

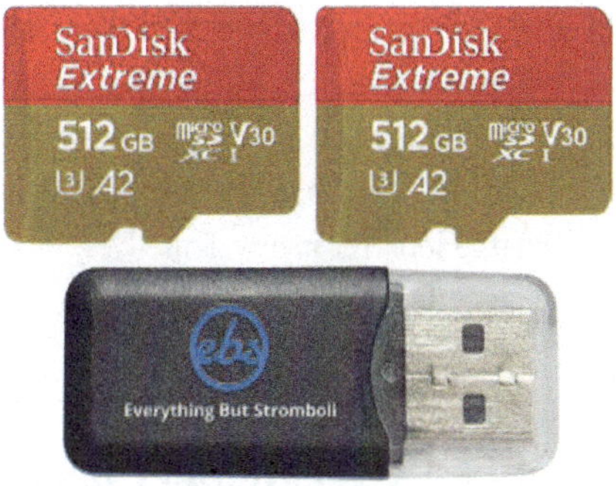

Here's the Affiliate Link to Amazon's Sale: https://amzn.to/42dCKSK

Take a Tripod

Are you tired of blurry or poorly focused photos? Look no further than a trusty tripod to take your photography to the next level! With a stable base, you'll be amazed at the sharpness and depth of focus your images can achieve. Sure, you could go for a cheaply made tripod, but be prepared for frustration and disappointment. I made that mistake and ended up with collapsed equipment and subpar shots. Believe me, investing in a quality tripod from the get-go is worth every penny. So take the leap and see what amazing shots you can capture with this essential piece of equipment. Your photography game will never be the same!

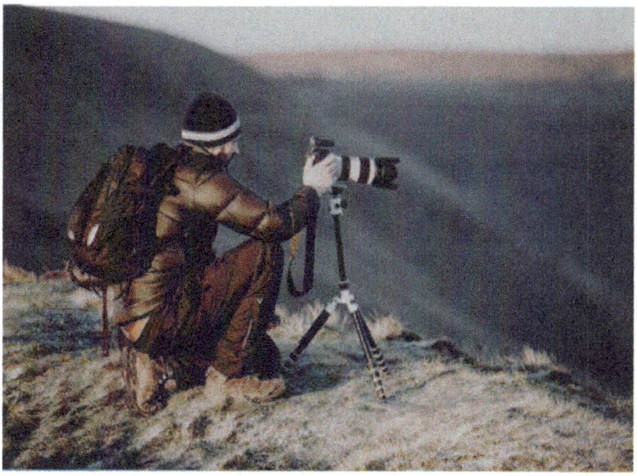

If you're anything like me, you're always on the hunt for the perfect tripod to take with you on your outdoor adventures. And having a reliable, lightweight tripod is crucial when you're hiking and climbing in the great outdoors. But if you're looking for a tripod to use for *portrait work*, this might not be the best option for you. Here's what to look for in any Tripod:

360 Swivel Ball Head.

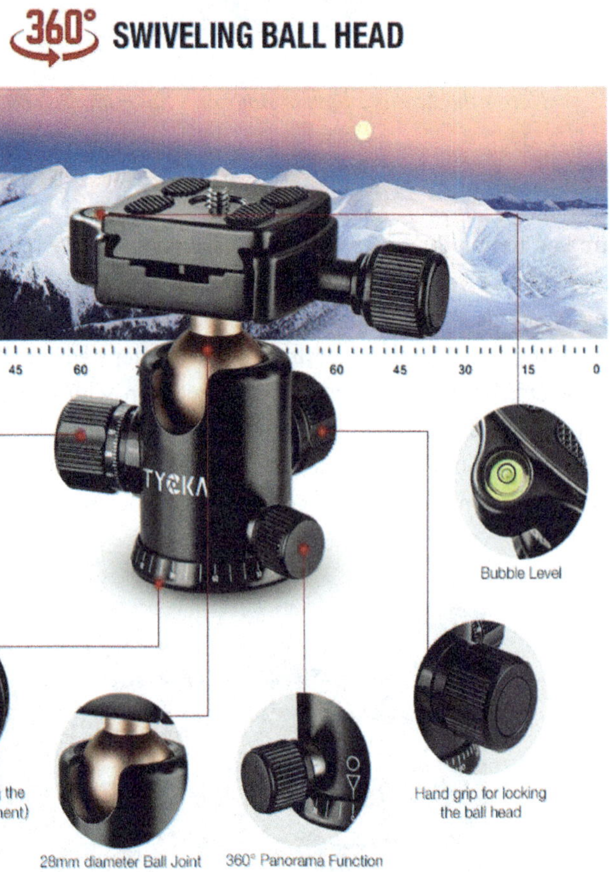

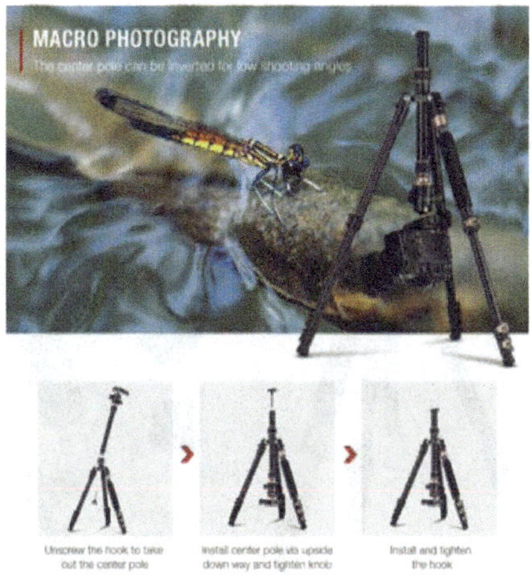

Can flip upside down for Macro work.

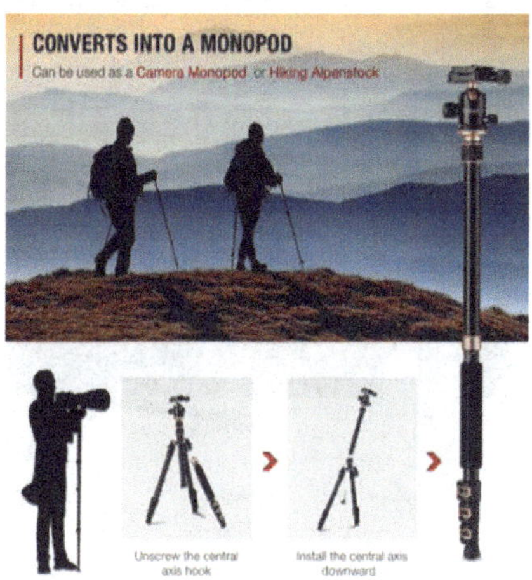

Converts to a Monopod.

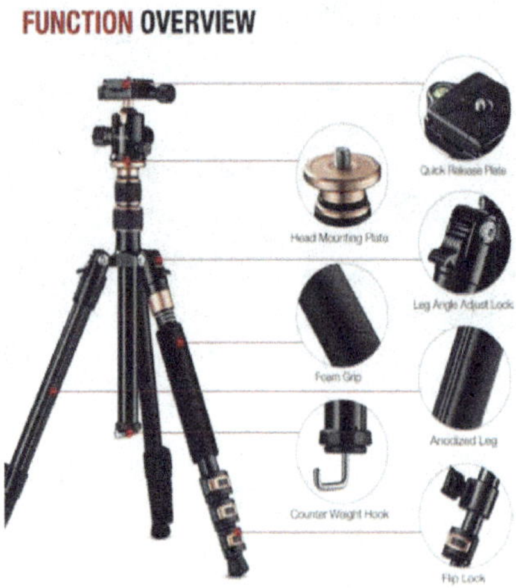

A quick-release plate so you can take your camera on and off the tripod quickly.

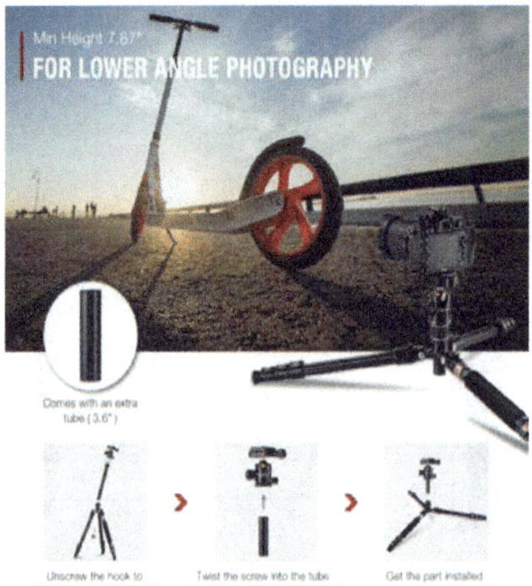

Can change height quickly.

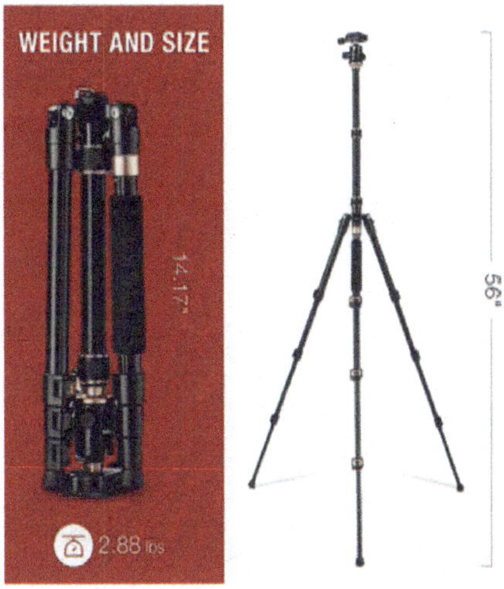

Lastly, is the proper weight and size for your project. With outdoor photography you need small and lightweight. With indoor photography you need sturdy and tall.

I've listed the top 5 choices from Digital Camera World 2023, which does a wonderful job testing out gear and providing a stellar review. If you'd like to read their reviews or see pictures of the tripods, click this link to go right to their review: https://www.digitalcameraworld.com/buying-guides/best-tripod

1. 3-Legged Thing Winston 2.0 - Price $449

Affiliate Link to Buy: Amazon
Portable and Tall
Material: Carbon fibre
Leg sections: 3Max load (legs/head): 40/30kg
Max height (with head): 194cm
Folded height: 61.2cm
Weight (with head): 2.05kg

2. Vanguard Veo 3+ 263AB - Price $301

Affiliate Link to Buy: Amazon

A versatile tripod
Material: Aluminium
Extended height: 172.5cm
Folded height: 76cm
Weight: 2.45kg
Feet: Pads & spikes
Leg sections: 3
Max load: 15kg

3. Peak Design Travel Tripod - $379

Affiliate Link to Buy: Amazon

A very cleverly designed compact tripod
Material: Carbon fiber or aluminum alloy
Extended height: 153cm
Folded height: 39cm
Weight: 1.27kg/1.56kg
Feet: Pads (spikes optional extra)
Leg sections: 5
Max load: 9kg

4. Benro Rhino Tripod - $325

Affiliate link to Buy: Amazon
Travel tripods is great all round
Material: Carbon fibre
Extended height: 174.5cm
Folded height: 49.4cm
Weight: 2.06kg
Feet: Pads
Leg sections: 4
Max load (legs, head): 20kg

5. ProMediaGear TR344L Pro-Sti - $1,249

Affiliate link to Buy: Amazon

A high-end lightweight tripod perfect for heavier kit
Material: Carbon fibre
Extended height: 180cm/70.7"
Folded height: 60cm/23.8"
Weight: 1.95kg/4.3lbs
Feet: Pads
Leg sections: 4
Max load (legs, head): 27kg/60lbs

Panorama Slide

A slide is a must-have tripod accessory for panoramas. It lets you conveniently slide your camera back and forth on the tripod head, effectively centering the "nodal point" of your camera system. By doing so, you can successfully avoid any parallax issues that can occur when taking panoramic photos - those pesky changes in object position as you take each shot. Don't let parallax ruin your perfect panorama - invest in a nodal slide today!

GVM Motorized Camera Slider,31" Wireless Carbon Fiber Dolly Rail Camera Slider with APP Control, Motorized Time Lapse and Video Shot Follow Focus Shot. **It's on sale for only $320.** You can buy this using my Amazon Affiliate Link: https://amzn.to/3LQGh42

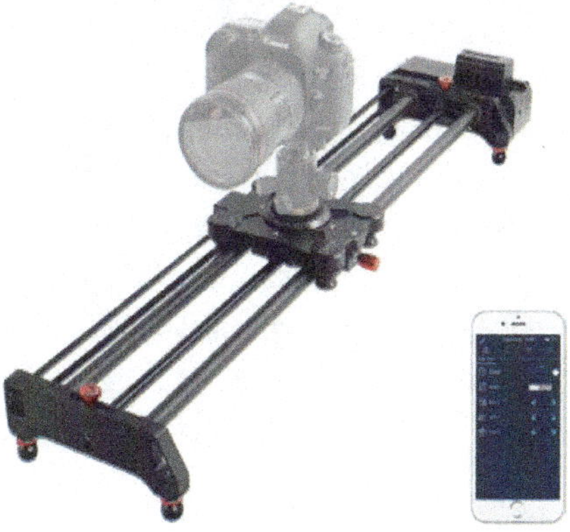

Neewer Scaled Camera Table Dolly Slider with 22 pounds/10 kilograms Load

Capacity Skater Design Aluminum Rods Rotatable Rubber Wheels 1/4-inch 3/8-inch Screw Threads for DSLRs Video Camcorders (Black). It's only $39.99. You buy this using my Amazon Affiliate Link: https://amzn.to/3LBGExT

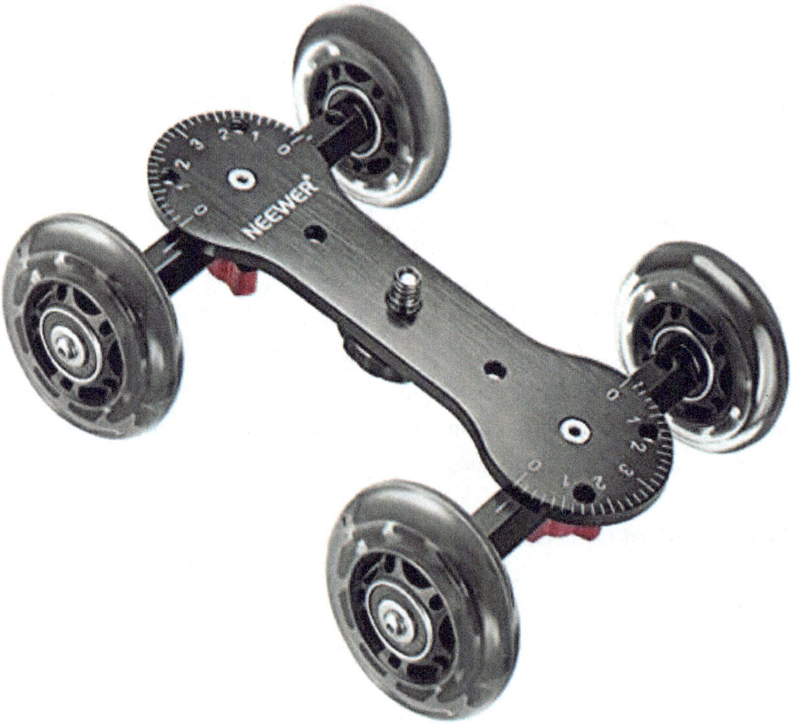

I know that sounds really obscure, but dedicated panorama photographers will find these invaluable. You'll simply have a much easier time aligning your panoramic photos in post-production if you used a nodal slide to center your camera system ahead of time. But it's also a bit of a special case that doesn't apply if you don't shoot a lot of wide-angle panoramas, so I'm not rating it any higher than "can be useful."

6

OUTDOOR PORTRAITS

Photography can be a tricky art to master, especially when it comes to lighting. Have you ever had a photographer babbling on about the different types of light they use and felt confused? You're not alone. Terms like natural, artificial, ambient, and existing light can seem like a foreign language if you're not familiar with them. But fear not because understanding the differences between these types of light is easy to learn. So, let's break it down and get to know these categories a little better.

Ambient Light Defined

Have you ever noticed how the lighting in certain places you go sets a particular mood of feeling? That's because lighting is crucial in how we perceive our surrounding space. *While some lighting sources are intentionally installed (like street lights), others simply exist in the environment already (like the moon). This is called ambient lighting.*

Some other examples of ambient light are direct sunlight, moonlight, light fixtures in a room, flashlights, streetlights, lamps, etc. Sometimes that pesky light can be exactly what you need to make a photograph pop, while other times it can ruin your shot completely. In the example above, the streetlights act as ambient light. In the image of the tattoo artist, the ambient light is coming down from his ceiling (out of view) and radiating down from his lamp.

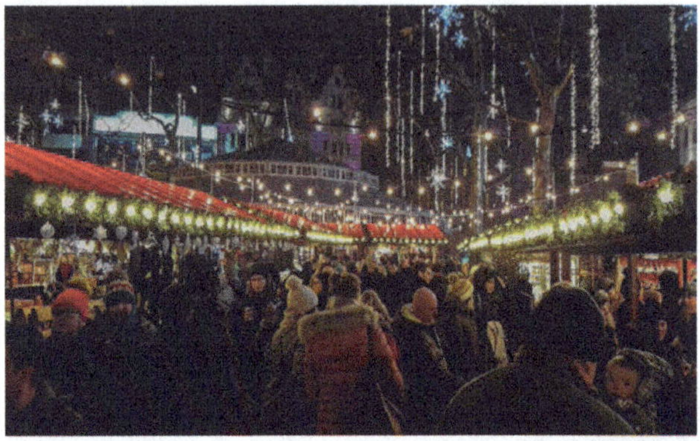

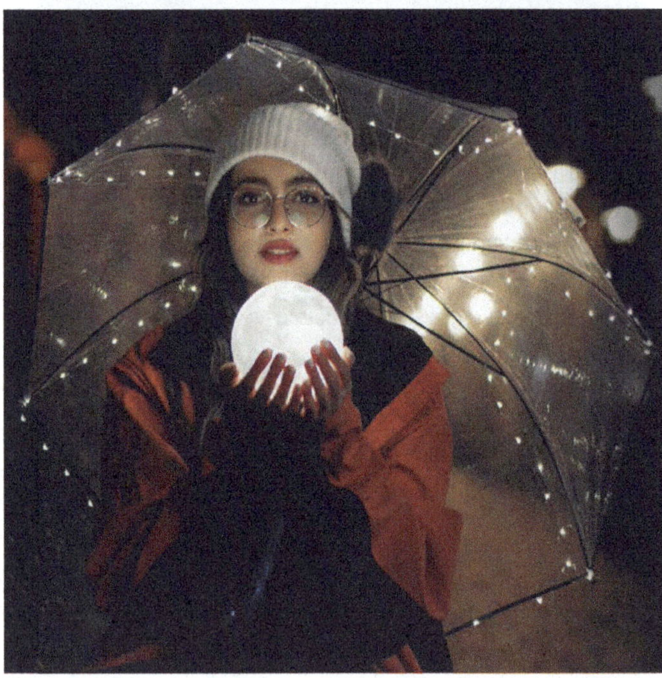

In the image of the woman using the umbrella, the ambient light is the glowing moon lamp, the streetlights behind her, and the twinkling lights in her umbrella.

Sometimes all you need is well-placed ambient light to light an entire scene properly.

Natural Light Defined

Nature provides natural light. A photographer does not bring it to a scene. It's not street lights. It's not coming from a camera's flash. It's the most basic form of light photographers use because it's cheap, all around us, easy to manipulate and bend, and comes in different colors. Examples of natural light are the sun, the moon, or some bioluminescent in water. In this image, the sunset brings warm, soft natural light to the scene. Because it's close to sunset, it brings warmth to the scene.

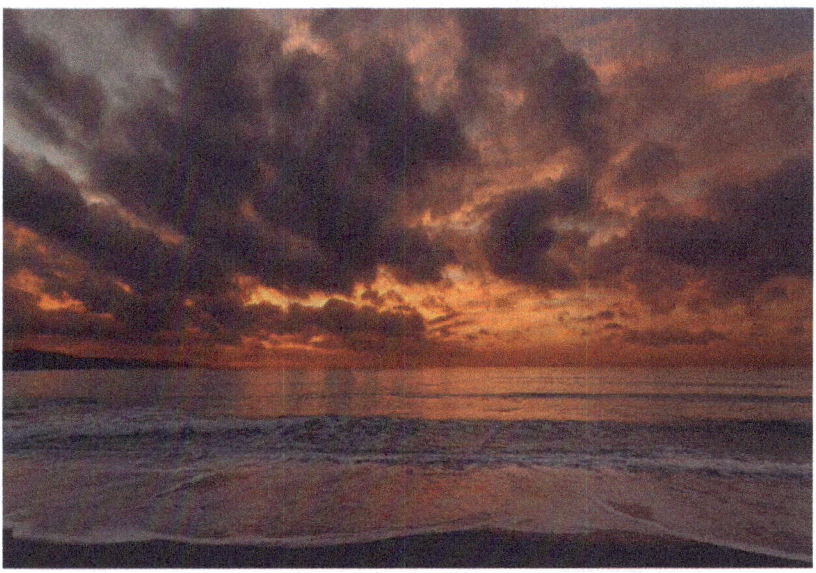

In this image of the bride and groom, the natural light comes from the indirect sun. The trees create a cooler blue color tone shade to the scene. Whether it's the warm, golden hour light, you get just before sunset or the soft, diffused cooler light on an overcast day, natural light can create a variety of moods and tones in your photos, making it a must-have in any photographer's toolkit.

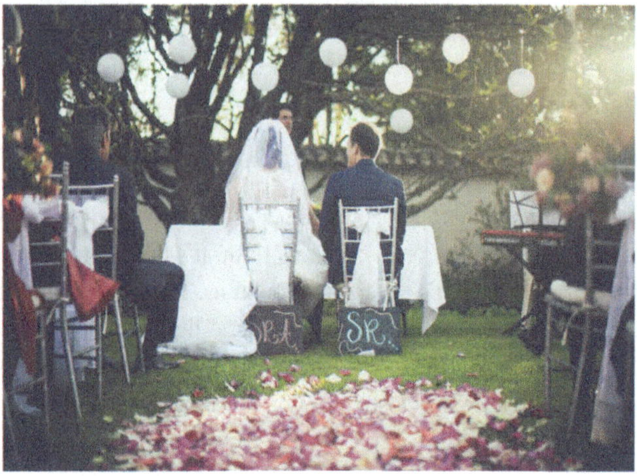

Ambient vs. Natural Light

There are some rule breakers in these two groups. For example, the sun and the moon surround us but come from nature. So they can be *both* ambient and natural light. Understanding the differences between these types of light can help you better appreciate their unique qualities and determine how best to use them.

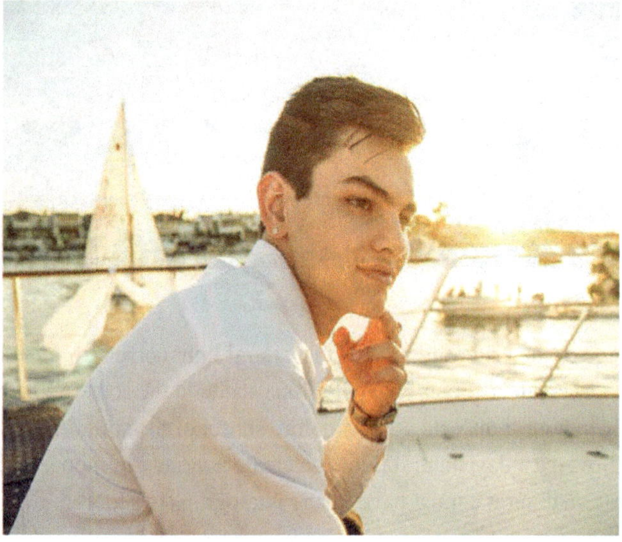

Ambient light refers to any light in the surrounding space, whether from overhead fixtures, lamps, moonlight, etc.

Natural light refers to the light that comes from nature only, like sunlight and moonlight.

Rule of Thumb: *not all ambient light is natural light, but all natural light is ambient light!*

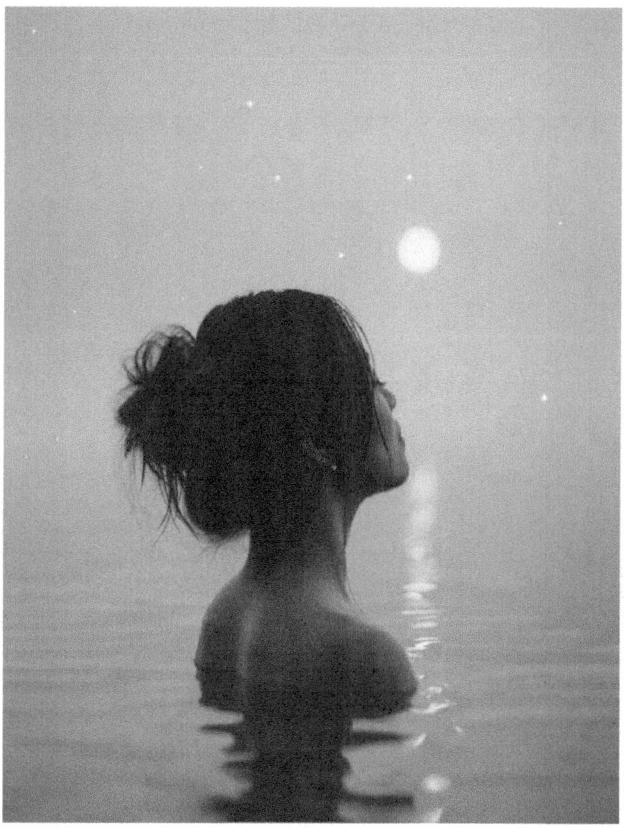

Colors of Natural Light

The same natural daylight can appear in different colors depending *on what time of day* you take your photos. Photographers refer to this as color temperatures.

At sunrise, cool light blue tones predominate, while at midday, the light is more balanced and whiter. Late afternoon is known as the 'Golden Hour,' when the light turns warmer and more orange/red because red waves of light are longer in the spectrum of visible light. Shortly after sunset, you might experience the 'Blue Hour,' or Twilight, when light reflecting off the moon produces a hint of light in the still-blue sky.

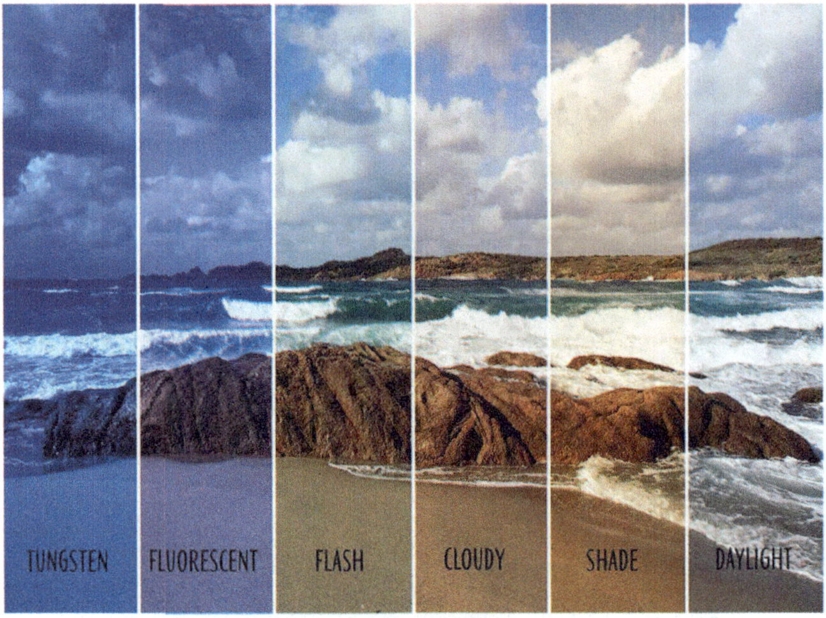

The Intensity of the Natural Light

The quality *and* color of natural light impact its intensity. If you're an avid photographer, you know that getting the perfect shot often means understanding the path of the sun and the color of the scene. But keeping track of the sun's movements can be tricky, especially if you're not an expert in astronomy. That's where apps right on your phone or computer that follow the sun and moon's patterns are a must-have for scheduling a shoot or out for a photography hike.

Sun Seeker is one of my favorite apps. This nifty app handles everything, from basic sunrise and sunset data to full-on augmented reality pathing. With the app, you can track the Sun's arc hour-by-hour, day-by-day, making it easier to get accurate intel on the amount of light your subject will receive. And at just $9.99, it's a small price for a tool that will save you countless hours of sitting in your backyard with a stopwatch.

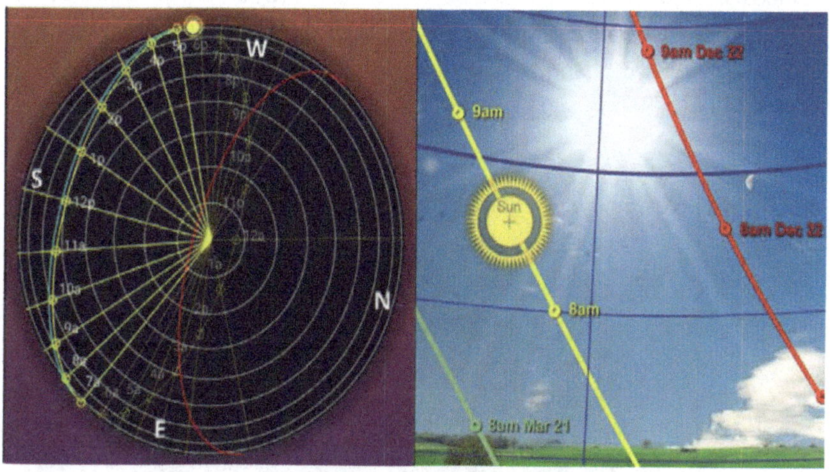

Quality of the Natural Light

Have you ever tried taking pictures outside and found the lighting was not cooperating? Natural light can be deceivingly difficult to work with. On a clear, sunny day, the bright and harsh light can cast deep shadows that ruin your photo. However, on a cloudy day, the same light can be soft and gentle, creating nuanced highlights and shadows in your picture. It all depends on the time of day and the sun's positioning. The lower the sun is in the sky, the longer the shadows it casts, and on a high-sun day, the shadows are much shorter. Understanding the different natural lights and when to shoot under each condition can make all the difference in your photography.

Soft Light

Soft light and hard light are two contrasting types of lighting in photography. While hard light produces sharp, defined shadows, soft light diffuses shadows and creates a more gradual transition from light to dark. To showcase the effects of soft light, a cloudy day is ideal. Clouds diffuse sunlight, making it less intense and more spread out. This results in a longer transition from light to dark, allowing for more shape and dimension to be captured in a subject. Soft light is also more flattering for portraits, as it is gentle on the skin and creates a smoother, more even complexion. So, if you want to capture stunning portraits or showcase the intricate details of an object, soft light is the way to go. I shot this in the wide open, at a farm, at sunset.

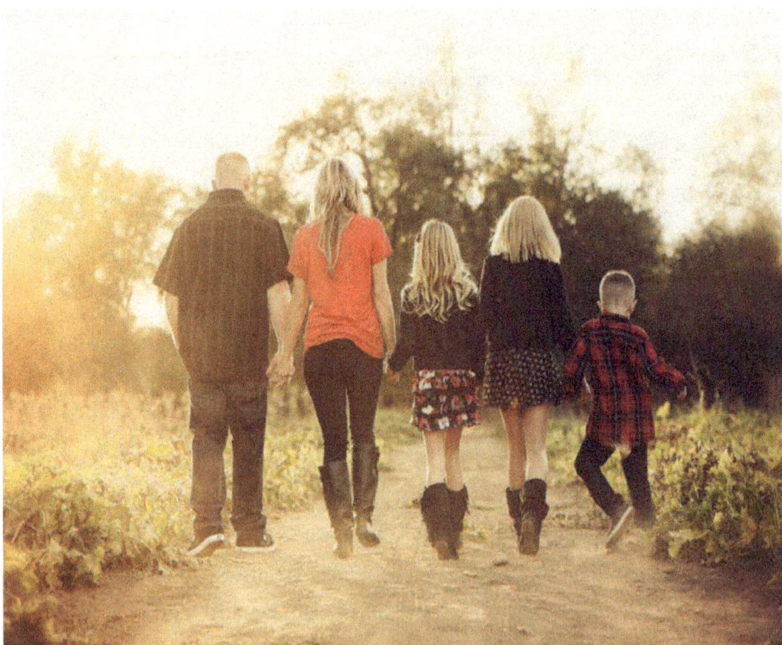

Hard Light

Strong sunlight can make all the difference in your photos. Hard light is the term used to describe the bright and intense illumination that occurs on a sunny day with no clouds in the sky. This lighting creates strong shadows that can enhance or flatten a scene, depending on how you use it. In the right conditions, hard light can make colors pop and add crispness to your images. However, it's important to remember that this type of lighting can also make your photos look flat if not used appropriately. If you want to use hard light in your photography, look for areas with quick transitions between light and shadow. With practice, you can learn to use hard light to your advantage and create stunning images that capture the beauty of a bright, sunny day.

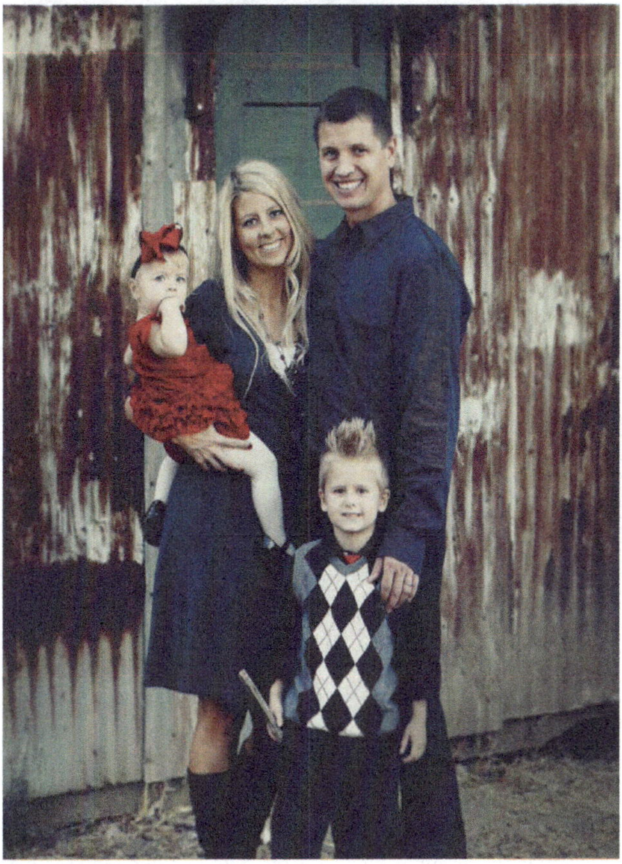

This was shot in the afternoon behind a barn, with a reflector and my on-camera flash.

Reflective Light

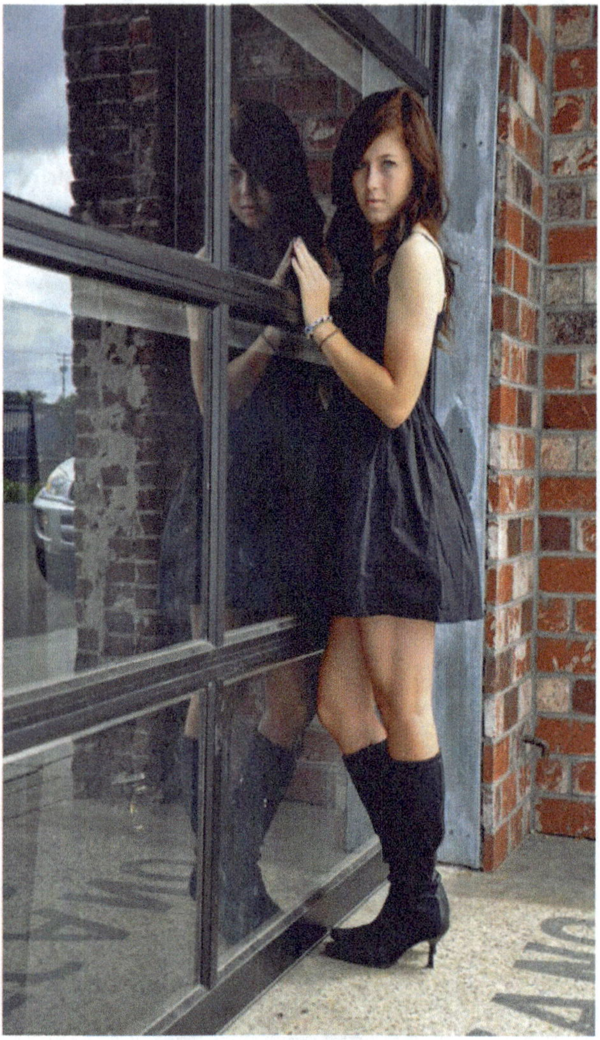

When light bounces off surfaces, we call it reflected light. It can come from walls, the ground, or any other objects. This type of light can create a soft glow in an area as it reduces the intensity of light and spreads it out. However, it's important to note that if the reflected light comes from a colored surface, it can tint the subject with that color. I shot this in the middle of the city, next to a building. It was a slightly cloudy day so that the sunlight wouldn't overexpose the image. Because it was on a cloudy day, it has a nice urbanist cool tone to the image.

Dappled Light

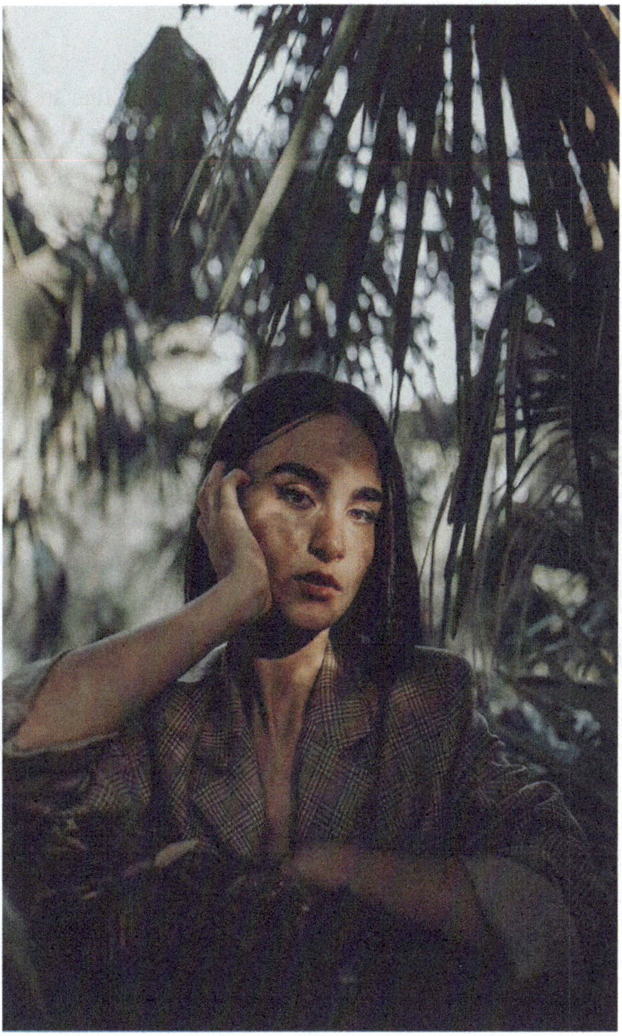

Another type of natural light is dappled light. This light appears when it passes through objects like tree branches, creating a patchy look. While it can be aesthetically pleasing when used correctly, it can also cause unwanted bright and dark spots on the subject's face. In this image, her eyes have no catchlight in her eyes, making them appear dead and lifeless.

Properties of Natural Light

Have you ever stopped to think about how photographs and film are created? It's quite fascinating! The key is exposure, which involves using light to capture an image. In the old days of film, exposure was achieved through a chemical process between light and celluloid. I discuss this more in the History of Photography Chapter of this book.

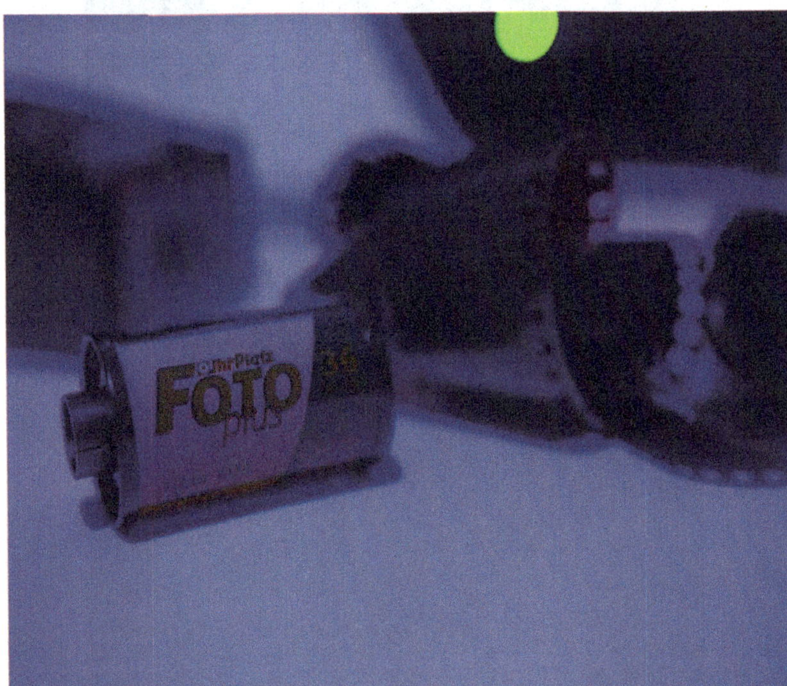

But nowadays, in the digital age, it's all about the camera sensor converting light into digital information. This incredible process allows us to capture life's precious moments and memories, and it's amazing to think how far we've come in photography.

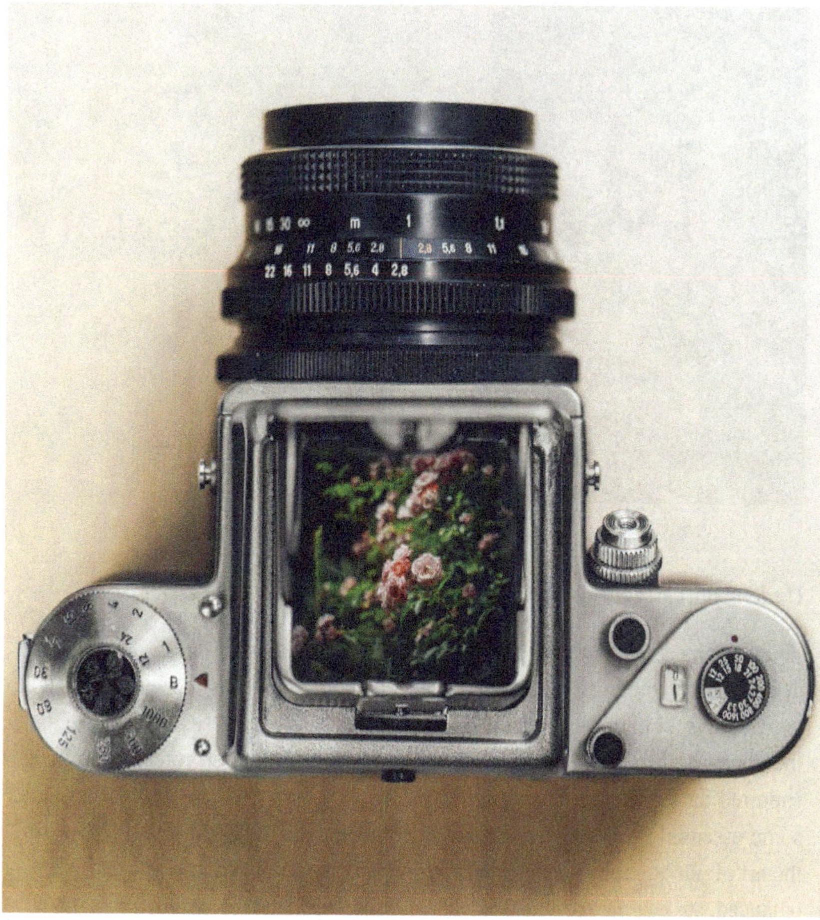

The level of brightness of an image distinguishes between the details and shadows. When underexposed, all the details are hidden in too much shadow. When overexposed, all the details get washed out into white light. Look at this example. Often, you can tell with the naked eye when an image is exposed correctly. Your eye naturally wants to find the perfect balance between color tone and details.

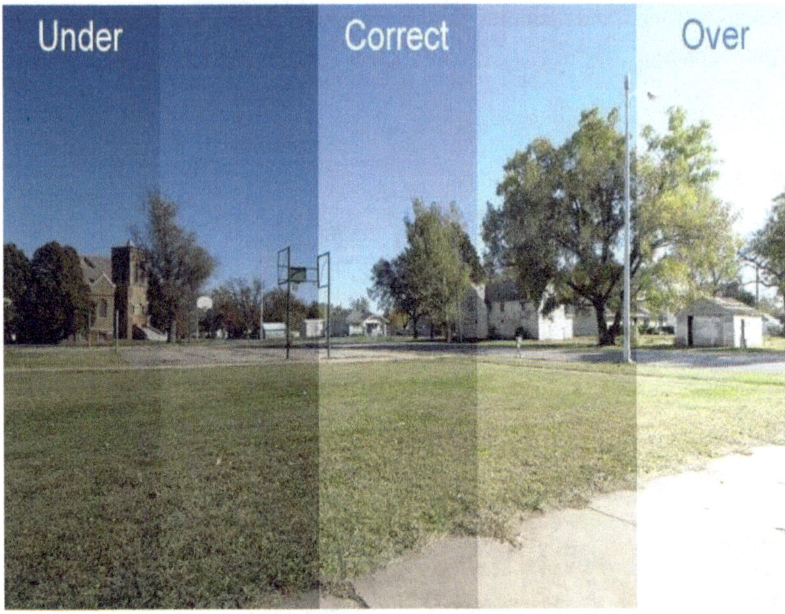

Underexposed Light Defined

Photography is an intricate art that requires patience, skill, and a keen eye for detail. One of the most important aspects of photography is working with light, which plays a vital role in capturing a stunning image. It's essential to understand the concept of properly exposed photography. Underexposed refers to an image captured darker than the balanced level. An underexposed photograph may lose some essential details in the shadows, creating an incomplete image. Mastering the art of photography requires persistence and attention to detail to create a well-balanced, striking image.

In the image of a drumming musician below. It is underexposed, and we can barely see his face and drumsticks. The ambient light of the neon signs wasn't bright enough to capture all the interesting details of the subject.

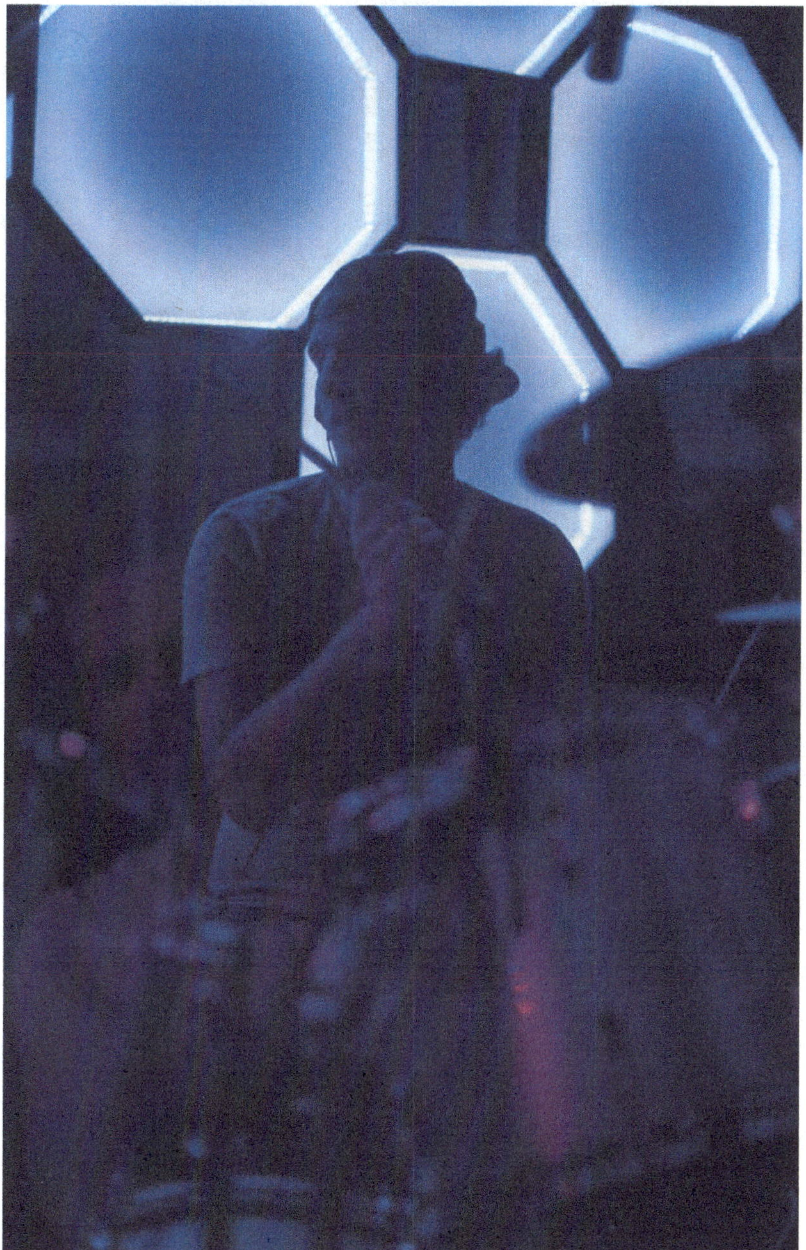

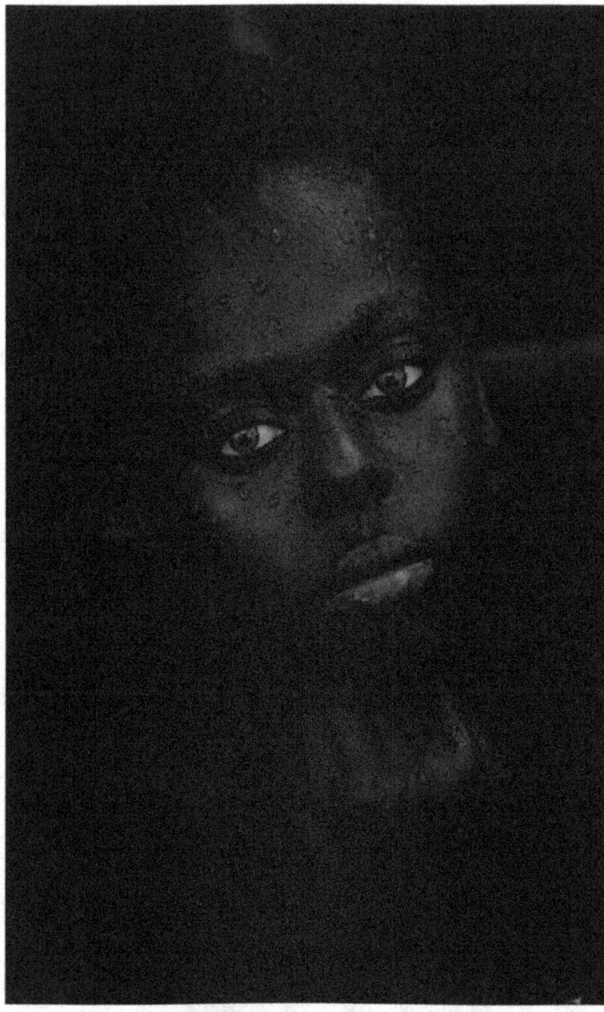

Don't worry; underexposing your image can actually work to your advantage if you set it up right. Despite being underexposed, this picture of a young boy has captured all the important facial details, leaving the rest to fade into darkness. By bringing the subject close to the camera, there was just enough light in the sky to illuminate him. It's really quite breathtaking! It just goes to show that sometimes less is more! Next time you're out taking photos, pay close attention to your subject's distance from the camera, ambient or natural light near you, to ensure your images come out just as you envisioned them.

Overexposed Light Defined

Overexposure, then and now, means something that happens to the best of us - when the camera sensor is bombarded with too much light, your image can end up looking much brighter than it should. The unfortunate thing about overexposure is that it limits the photo's detail and can rob the image of recognizable highlights or shadows. So, while some people might like the bright and almost ethereal look of an overexposed photo, for most photographers, it's a big no-no. Knowing how to avoid overexposure is key to achieving a balanced and well-exposed image.

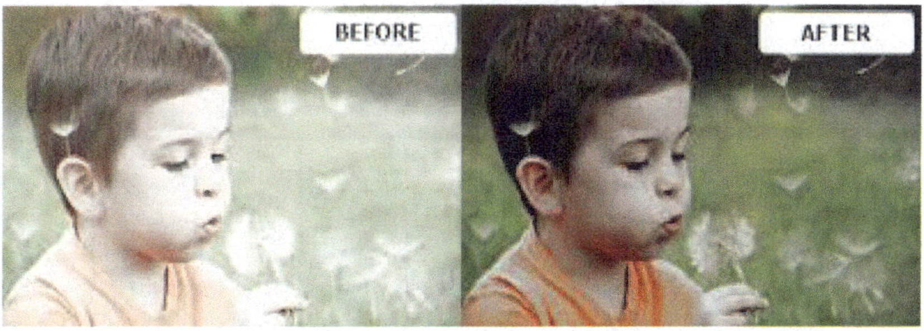

You control the amount of light that comes in by adjusting two important settings: *aperture and shutter speed.* These two settings work together to collect and bring light into the camera, giving you more control over your exposure. ISO is another powerful tool that can help regulate brightness in your photos, but it doesn't work by letting more light in like the aperture and shutter speed do. Instead, it adjusts the sensitivity of your camera's sensor to light. Think of it like turning up the volume on a microphone - it makes your camera more receptive to light. While ISO doesn't directly regulate exposure, it plays a crucial role in your overall exposure settings. So next time you shoot in low light, try adjusting your ISO and see how it affects your photos!

Sunny Day Rule

Look no further than the Sunny F/16 Rule! With a simple formula of shutter speed 1/ISO at *f*/16, you can easily dial in the correct exposure. For example, on a sunny day with ISO 100, use a shutter speed of 1/100 sec. at *f*/16 for stunning results. This rule of thumb is a great starting point for manual exposure and is incredibly accurate. Say goodbye to over or underexposed photos with the Sunny F/16 Rule.

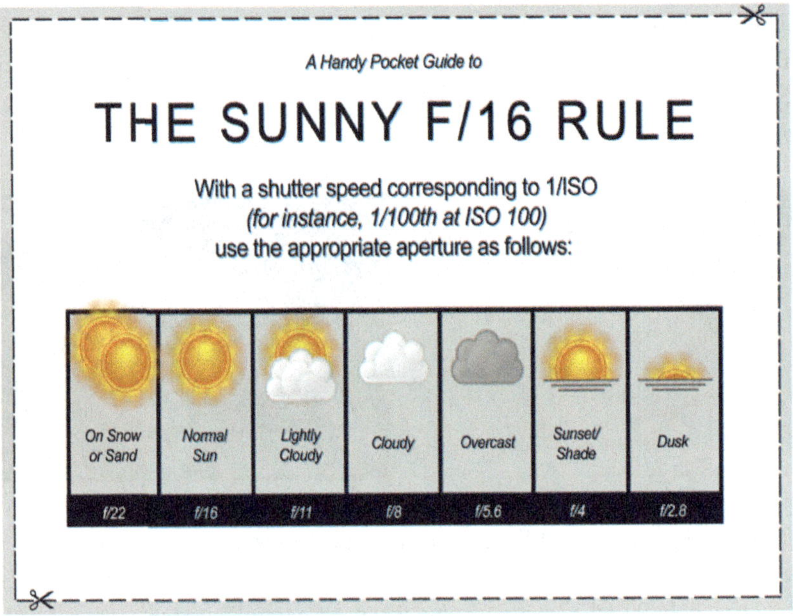

Discover an easy-to-use formula that helps you adjust your camera settings for any outdoor lighting situation. The Sunny F/16 Rule is your go-to guide, providing the perfect aperture setting for every condition, from bright sunshine to dimly lit evenings. And the bonus? No matter what, your shutter speed stays consistent at 1/ISO. Say goodbye to blurry or overexposed shots and hello to stunning outdoor photography.

Take your photography skills to the next level by gaining control over your camera and its settings. This guide will help you master manual exposure in any outdoor lighting scenario, giving you the confidence of a pro photographer. Get started on your journey to becoming the master of your camera. Slow down, think, and take better pictures. By switching your camera to manual exposure, you'll be forced to consider more than just the technical aspects of your shot. With this technique, you'll find yourself thinking about composition and creative elements as well, resulting in more captivating images. Don't underestimate the power of taking a moment to pause and think before snapping away.

Lighting Setup - Using Reflectors or Diffusers Outdoors

When working with natural sunlight, you can easily create a simple photography shoot with affordable reflectors or diffusers to bend or bounce light. With some patience and practice, you can take your photography skills to the next level. If you're struggling with harsh shadows and uneven lighting, don't worry, reflectors and diffusers are here to help!

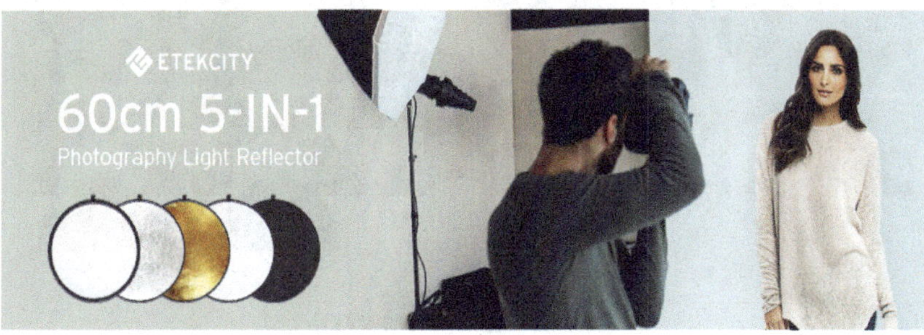

By mastering bending and bouncing light techniques, you can transform ordinary scenes into breathtaking works of art.

Silver is a good color to use when you're first, starting with reflectors. It won't change the color of your photo. A silver reflector is very reflective, so its effect will be very noticeable. You should avoid using it if there is a lot of light because it might make the highlights too bright.

White reflectors are softer and work better in brightly lit scenarios. You can use them to fill in shadows without blowing out highlights. But you must be fairly close to your subject for it to work.

Gold is a shiny color, but too much of it will change how your photo looks. It can make the photo look warmer, which can be good for shadows. But it can also look fake if you use too much.

A translucent diffuser isn't a reflector. It doesn't reflect the light. Instead, it diffuses the light to make it softer. To make the diffuser work, you must put it between your subject and the light source. It's also useful for softening the effects of a flashgun. See the sample image above.

The black side of a reflector is not actually a reflector. It is used for the opposite purpose! Black will create a shadow, perfect for use if one side of your subject's face is too brightly lit. This will also create extra depth and interest in an evenly lit subject.

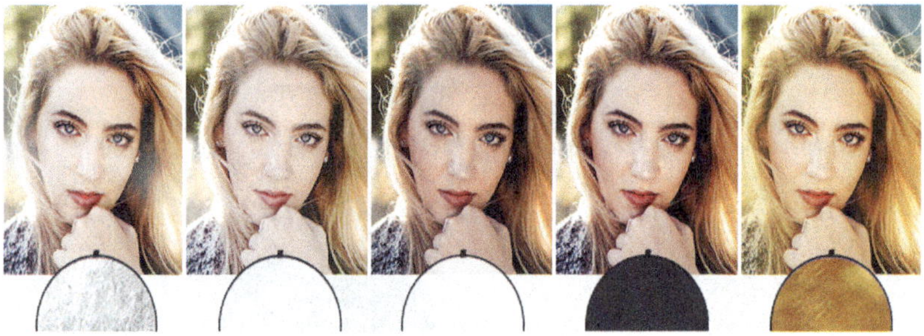

How to Correct Top Lighting

With photography, the sun is your best friend – but only if you use it correctly. By positioning the sun directly above your subject, you'll get a well-lit image that will turn out sharp and clear. However, if you're not careful, that same direct light can make your subject appear washed out.

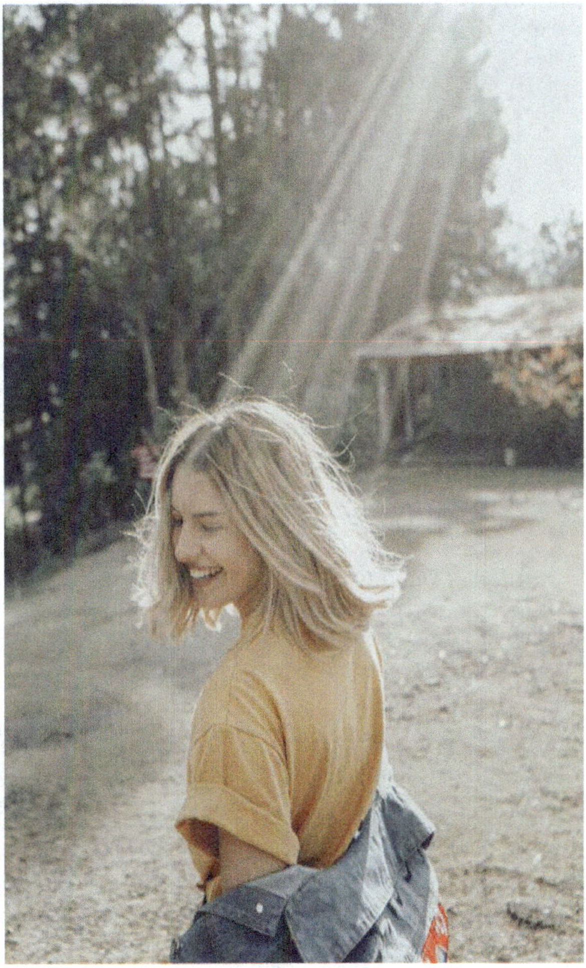

That's where using a diffuser over the subject's head and a reflector in front of the subject will even out the subject's hair and face for perfect exposure. This is the difference between an amateur snapshot and a pro portrait. And it takes only a few minutes of planning and an inexpensive photography shoot setup.

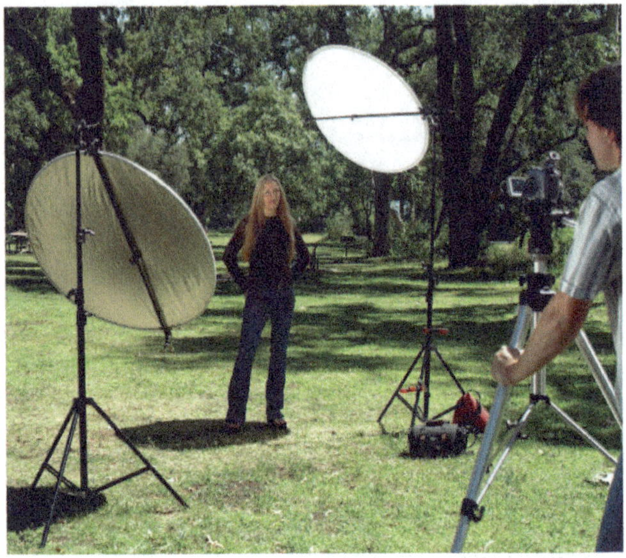

How to Correct Cloudy Day Lighting

Overcast skies might not be pretty, but they give you even soft light. However, the light can be cool in tones and heavy in shadows.

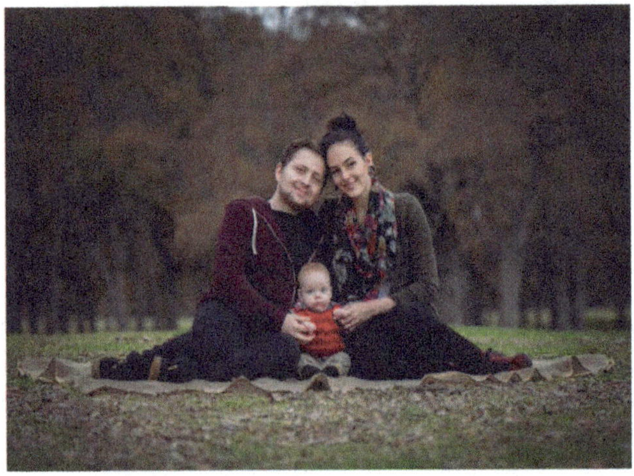

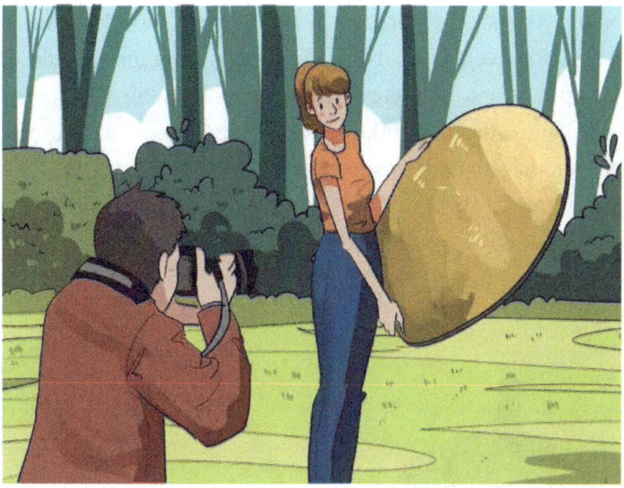

To brighten up on an overcast day, get your subject to hold a gold reflector directly underneath their face and angle upwards. If you have more than one subject, you can place additional reflectors on either side of the subjects (out of camera view) to create a warming effect, as I did in their family portrait.

How to Correct Front Lighting

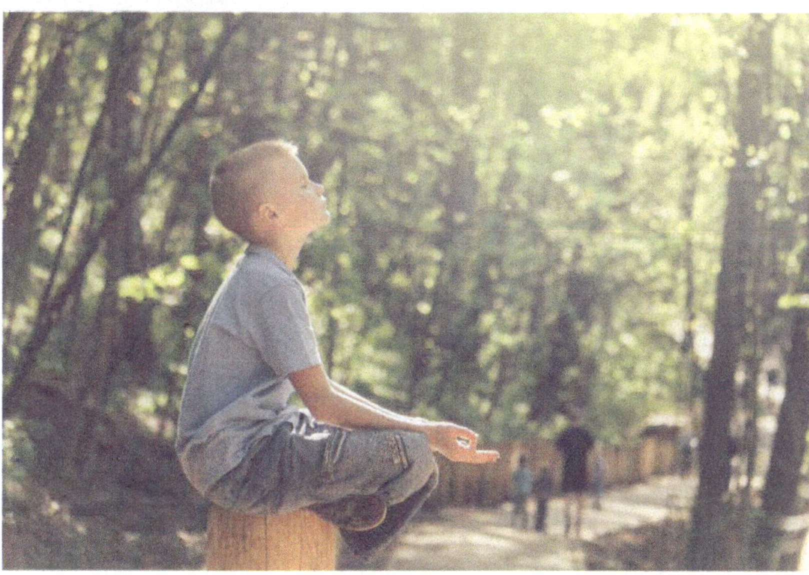

By positioning your subject directly in the path of sunlight, you can create a front-lit image. However, without angled shadows from the side, the subject may appear overexposed and uninteresting. It's also hard for the subject to spend much time looking at the sun while shooting. Simply place a diffuser in the background, between the sun and the subject. It will cut down half the light and make a well-exposed image. These diffusers usually come double-sided. You'll want to use the white side that lets light through, not the silver side that blocks it completely.

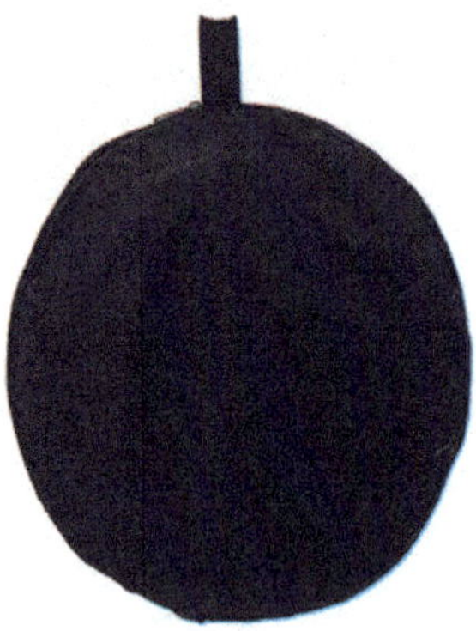

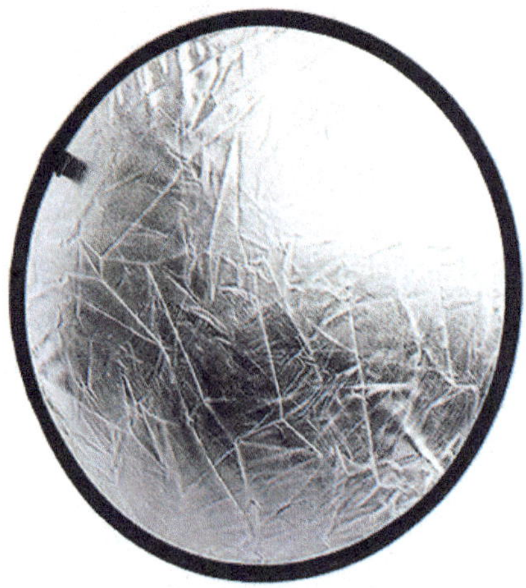

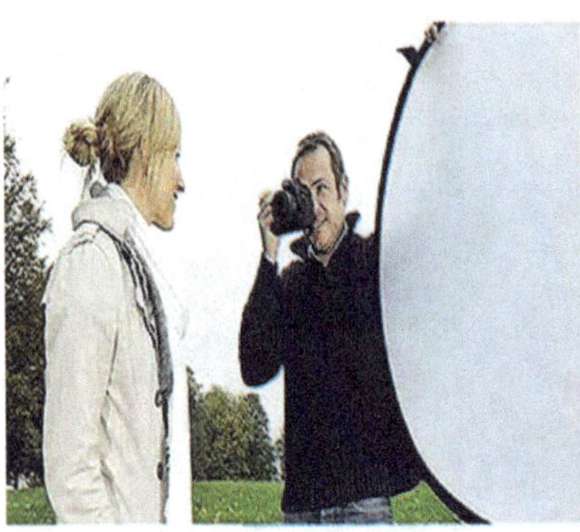

How to Correct Side Lighting

Using natural side light in portrait photography can add depth and shape to your subject. By positioning your subject at a 45-90-degree angle to the path of natural light, you can create a more 3D appearance of the person, But what if you're in a park with minimal side lighting? In this image, the light was only illuminating the left side. The right side was in complete shadows.

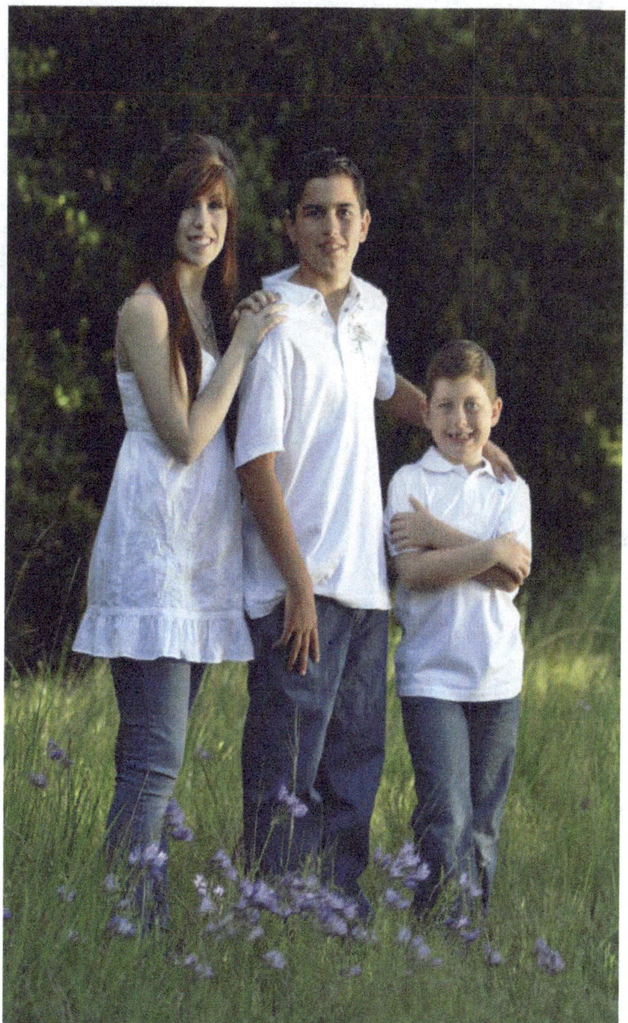

To fix this, out of sight, I placed a huge silver reflector to collect the light coming from the opposite side and then bounced it back onto the subject's right side, which was in shadow. Now they had even lighting on both sides of their bodies, creating a wonderful 3D effect. Don't miss out on the chance to enhance your photography skills with this simple and effective technique!

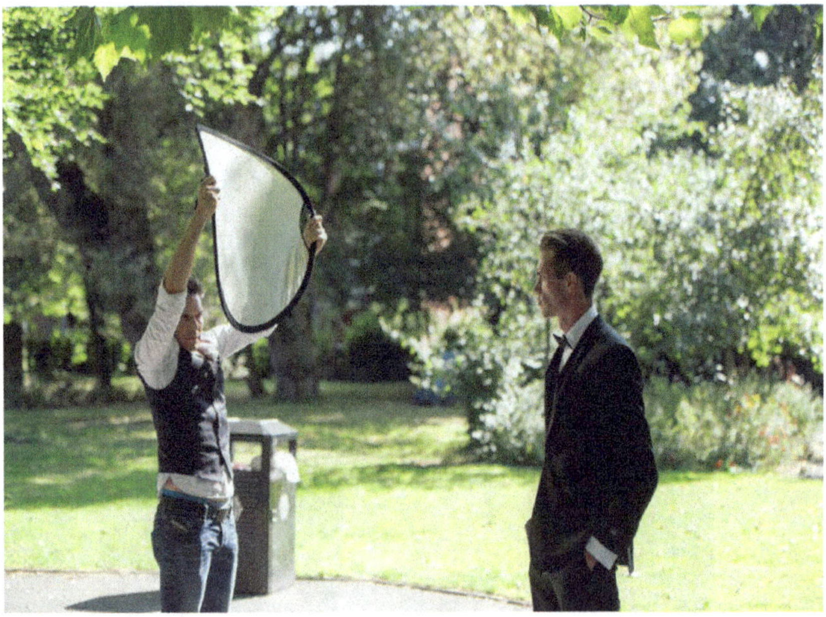

How to Correct Back Lighting

If you place your subject in front of daylight, they will appear as a dark silhouette with only their outline visible to the camera. This is because light only travels in one direction, causing the nearside (visible to the camera) darker. Backlighting is where you take a photograph with the bright sunlight streaming behind your subject. This gives an attractive rim light to the subject's hair but can overexpose the hair and shoulders.

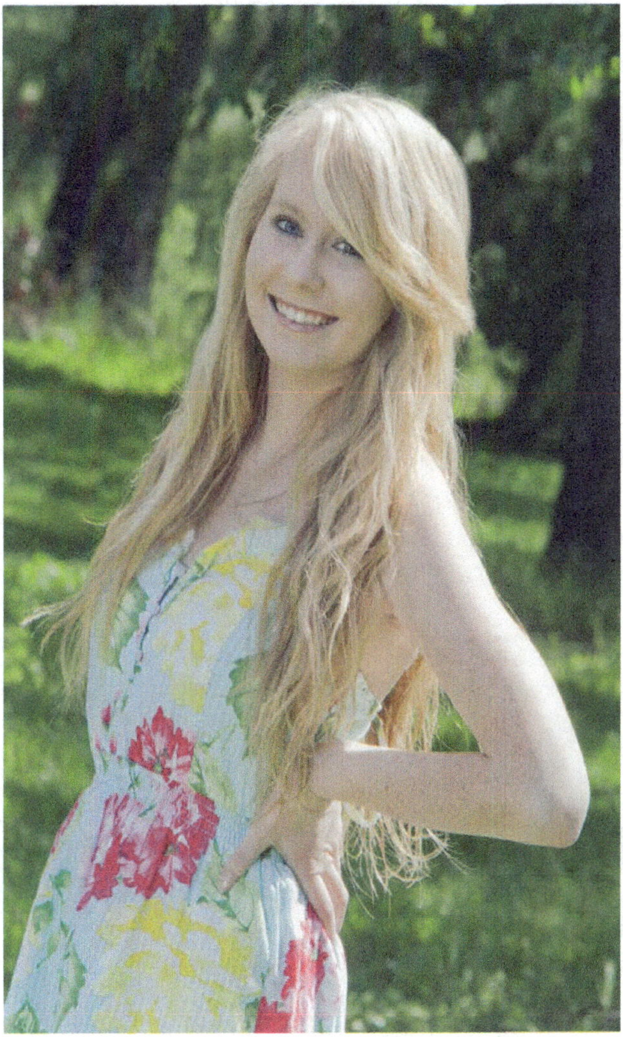

To fix this, you can use a reflector in front of the subject (to bounce light back toward their face) and a white diffuser behind their head to cut back on the light reaching her body. This will create all the necessary catchlights too!

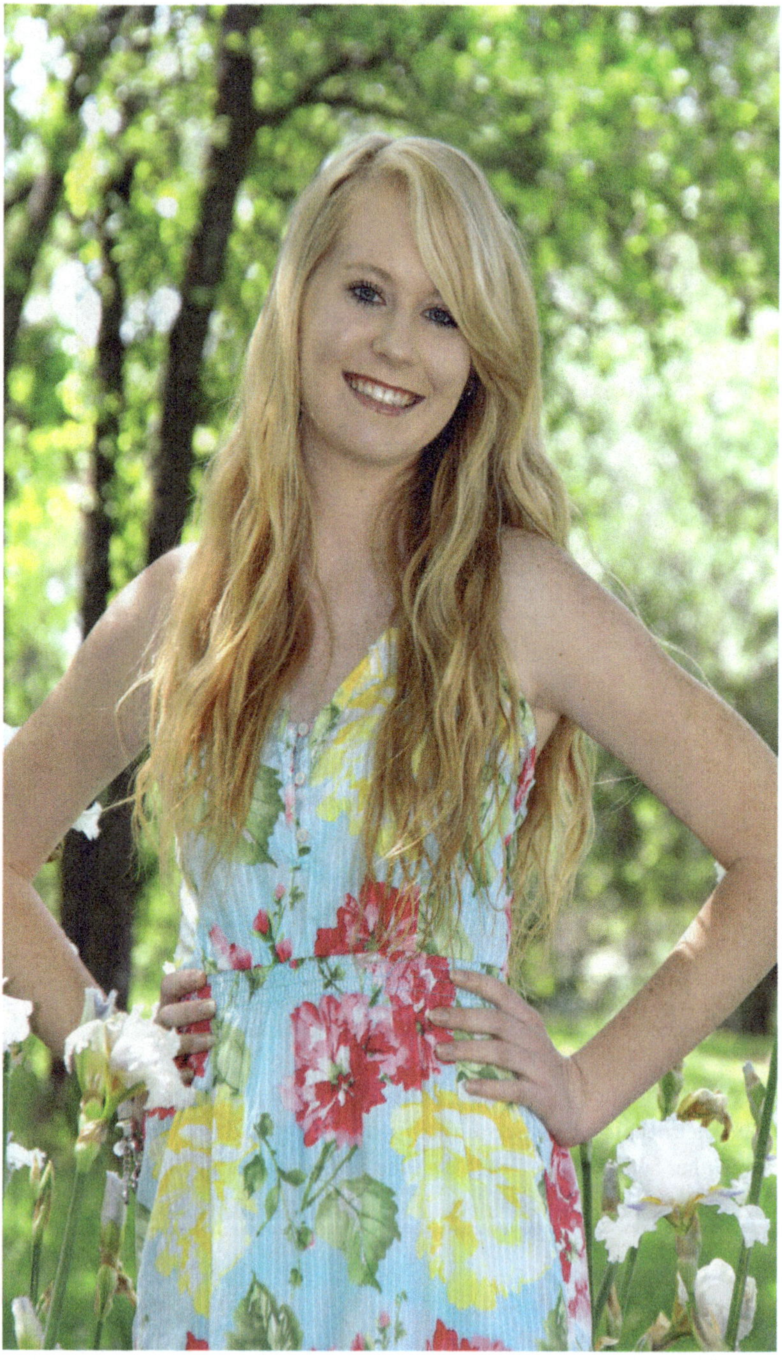

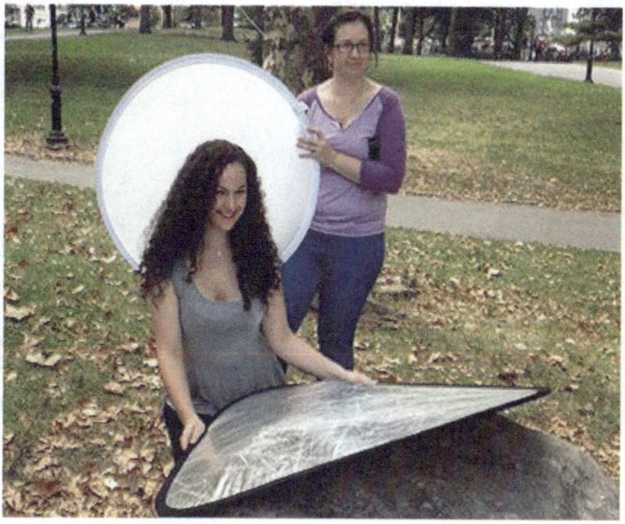

Here is the client with a white filter above her head (out of view), which cuts back on the loss of hair and skin detail.

How to Correct Missing Catchlights

Have you ever looked at a portrait and felt something was missing? Chances are - it's the catchlights. Catchlights are reflections in the eyes that add a pop of life and depth to every portrait. This is a VITAL step, and it's easy to accomplish. Use a reflector to take the light from the sun's rays near you and bounce it back into the subject's eyes. If you don't have a reflector, have your subject look up at the sky so the light reflects into them and creates this great effect. It is a sign of a pro photographer!

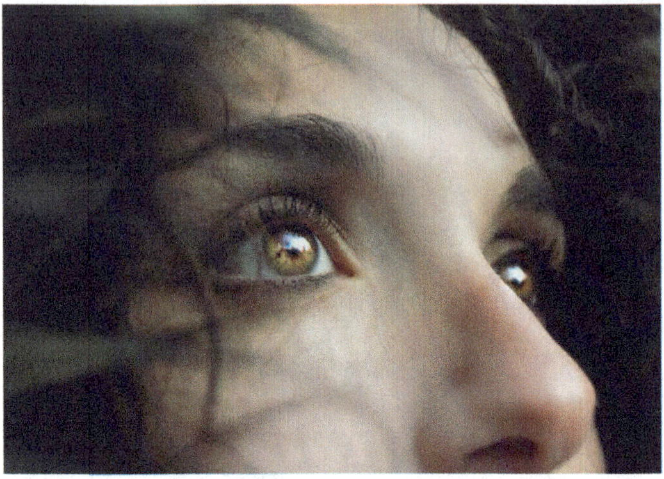

Here's a prime example of a photograph where the subject has no catchlights in his eyes. His image appears dark and lifeless. After all, the eyes are said to be the windows to the soul, so make them shine!

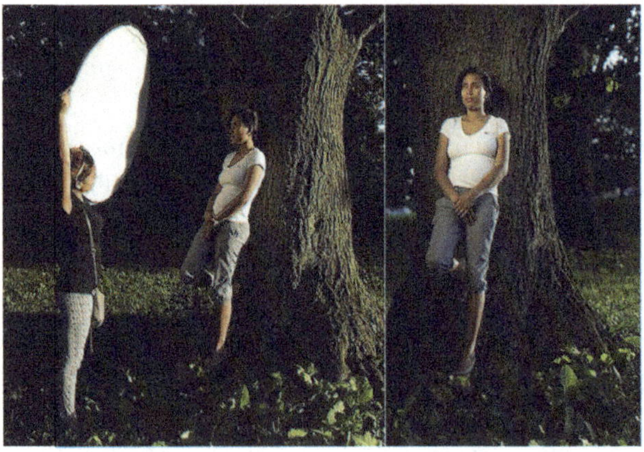

This image is of my son, my muse. It was a hot day, and we were sitting in the shade of a tall building to photograph. You can see how without the catchlights in his eyes, his image appears dark and almost sinister. Since I didn't have a flash or reflector, I directed him to turn his head, looking outward at the natural dayligh. That saved the image and gave more life to his face.

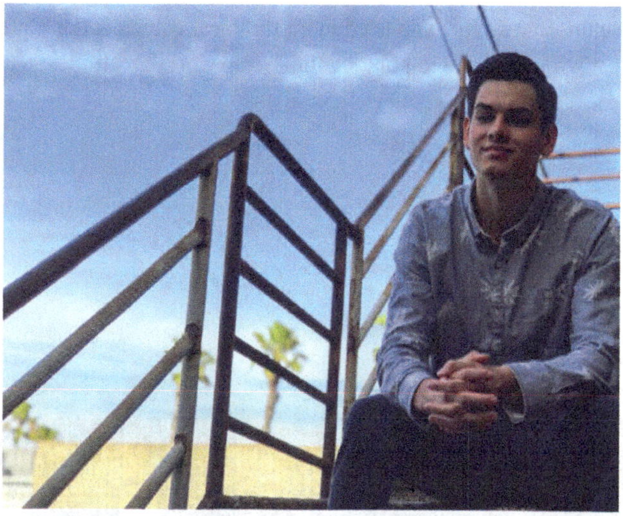

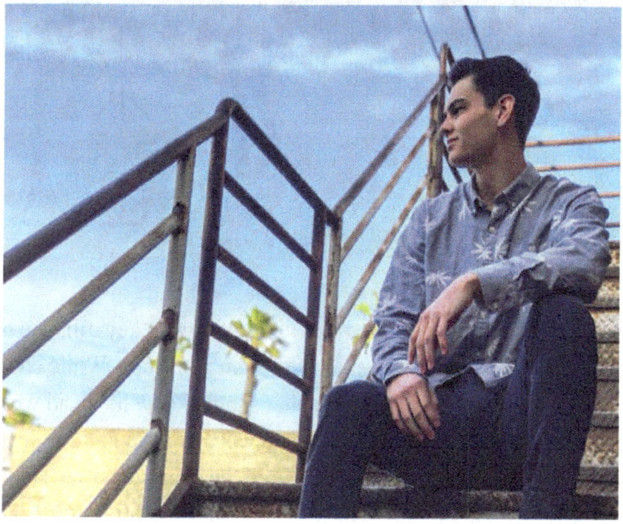

Lighting Set Up - Three-Key Lighting Outdoors

Lighting is a critical aspect of any scene, as it can create a mood, draw attention to key subjects, and set the overall atmosphere. I discussed previously in this Chapter, there are huge benefits of using reflectors and diffusers as a simple lighting setup. But what if you need more technical equipment or a professional setup? That's where the three-point lighting setup works great!

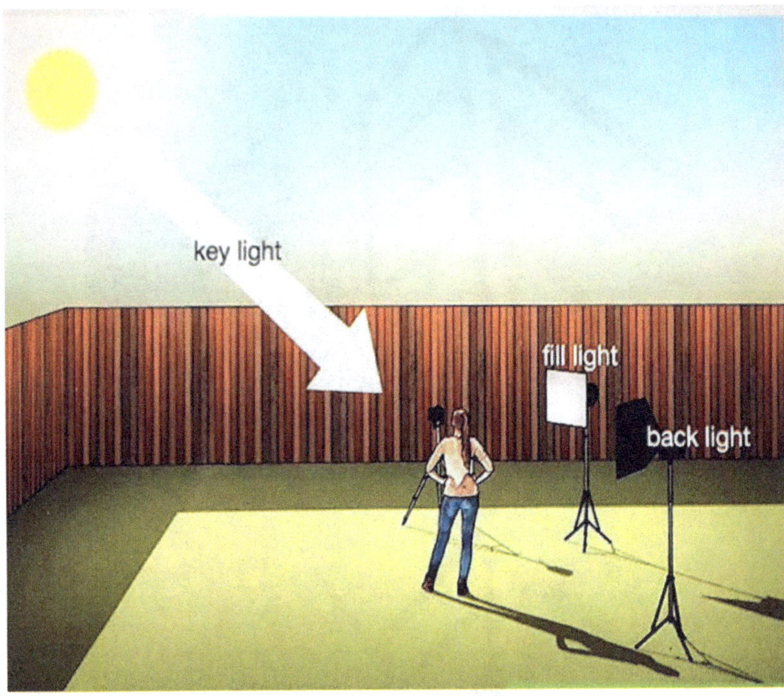

This professional technique utilizes three types of lights - key, fill, and backlight - strategically placed in distinct positions for optimal results. While commonly used for indoor portraits, every photographer should know how and when to implement this game-changing lighting setup when doing a more technical lighting situation. In this family portrait, I used the sun as a strong backlight, a gold reflector placed on the side of them (out of sight) as fill light so their backs weren't lost in shadow, and my camera's speedlight flash as the key light.

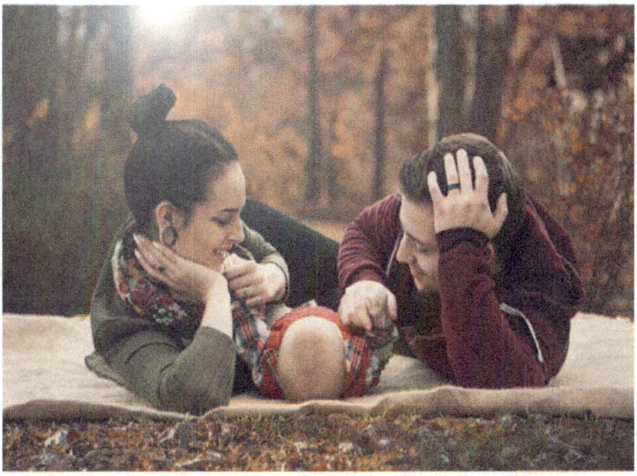

Key Light

The key light is usually positioned to the left or right side and slightly higher than the eye level of the subject being lit; it provides illumination that creates deep shape and depth on faces or objects by creating side shadows and dimension. It can be the sunlight coming into the scene lighting the subject or it can be properly placed camera lighting.

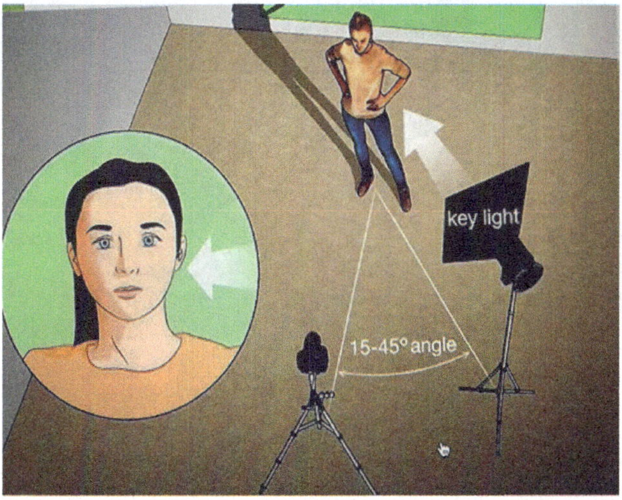

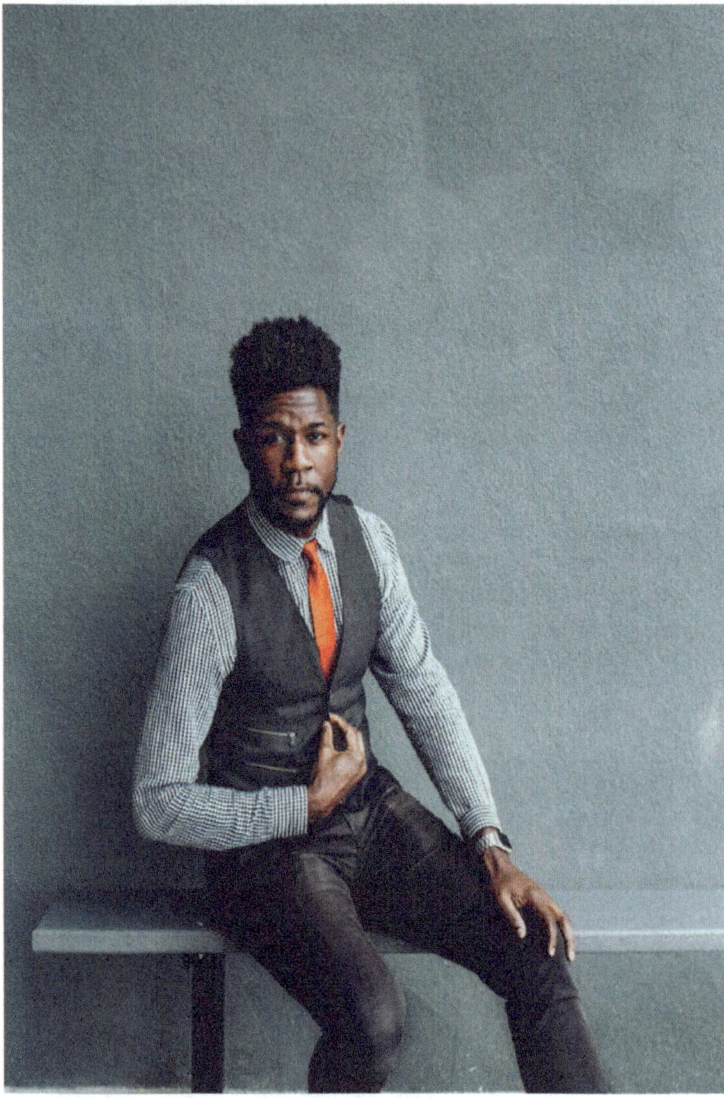

When lighting a scene, the key light is truly the star. This powerful and pronounced illumination source is the brightest light in the three-point lighting setup, casting an all-encompassing glow over the subject. But the key light is more than just bright and bold - it's also an essential tool for creating depth and mood. See the face of the subject in this example above.

Fill Light

Fill lights are placed opposite from the key light—on its other side—and provide more even coverage across face features like eyes, nose, cheeks, etc., while also reducing shadows created by the main source of illumination (key). See the example of the subject's face in the following example.

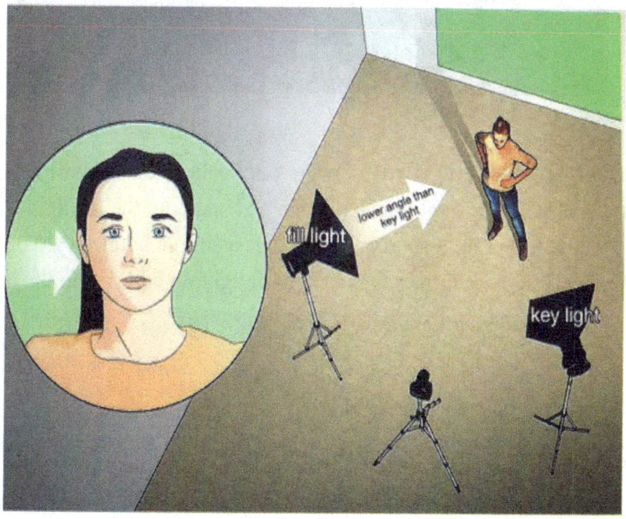

This secondary light is strategically placed on the opposite side of the camera and helps to illuminate any shadows that the key light creates on a subject. While it is typically less bright than the key light, the fill light can greatly impact the overall well-lit face. In this family portrait of the siblings, I used a similar 3-light setup. I used the fill light to the side, to create nice even lighting across all of their faces and a small amount of shadowing on their left side for depth.

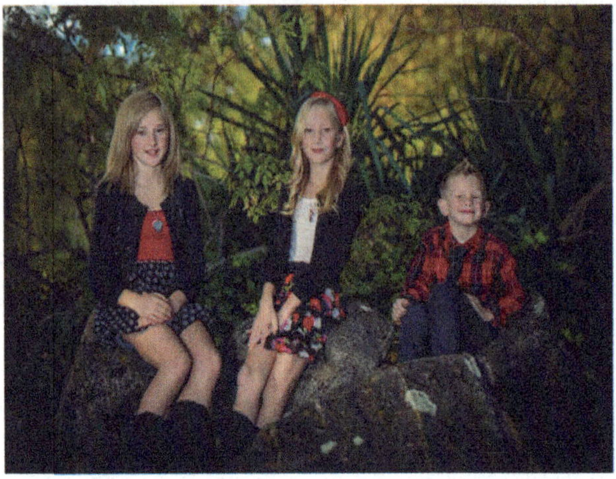

Alternatively, a brighter light with a lower, more balanced ratio will provide a more even, natural look to the subject. What's great about the fill light is that it's not always a dedicated light source - it could be a simple bounce card or even a wall that reflects light onto the subject. The fill light, in addition to the key light, is crucial in determining the mood and tone of a scene.

Backlight

Last but not least, backlights are set behind the subject, and they add detail as well as give off subtle separation between background and foreground elements in scenes with multiple characters/objects present; this ensures that none get lost in darkness! Backlight will put a highlight on the hair and separate it from the background.

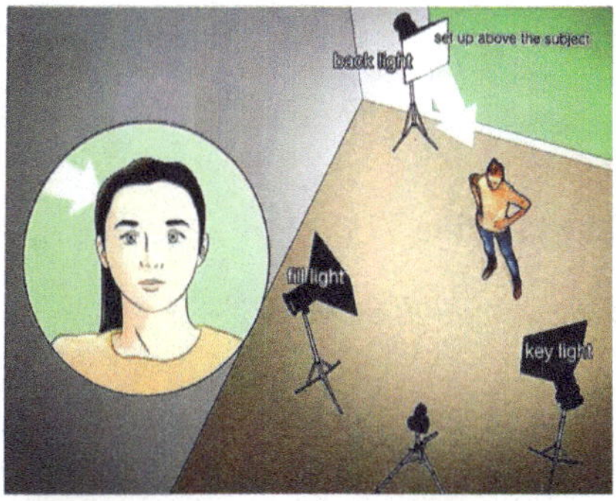

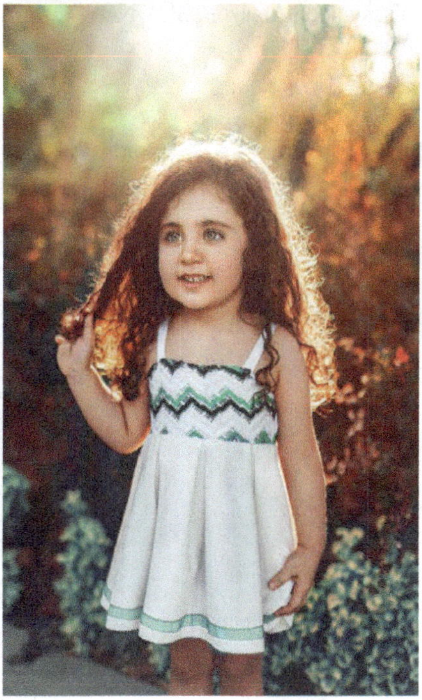

In this image, the child's red hair would have disappeared against the red bushes without backlighting. The highlights separate the subject from her background. Nowadays, photographers use various forms of lighting techniques to achieve desired effects. However, three-point lighting remains one of those most commonly used methods due to its versatility. Whether you're shooting indoors or outdoors – take advantage of this classic technique so your subjects come alive on camera!

Equipment for 3-Key Lighting

Speedlights for Key, Back and Fill Light

Portrait photography can be enhanced with a simple lighting fix - angling your flash on your camera body or adding softboxes to create the perfect setup! This costs about $50 per flashgun on Amazon. BUY NOW ON AMAZON Affiliate Link

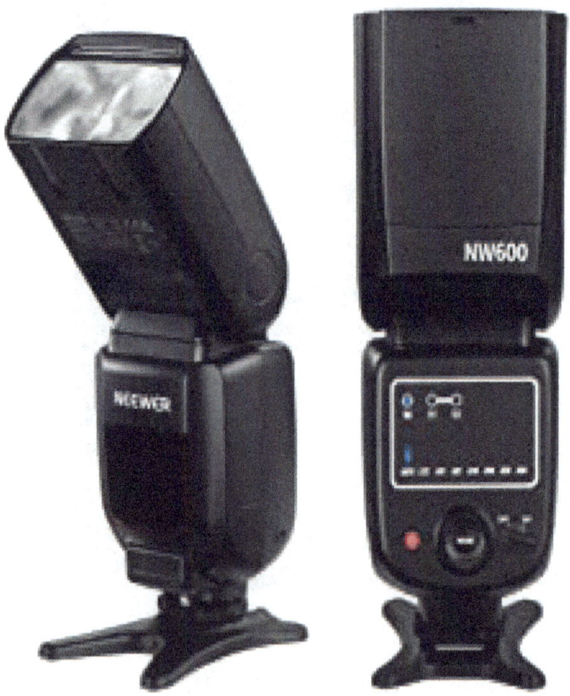

The hot-shoe connection on the camera may attach these lights, which are compact and lightweight. Here's an example of shadow and highlight placement when using the flashgun as the key, fill, and even back lighting.

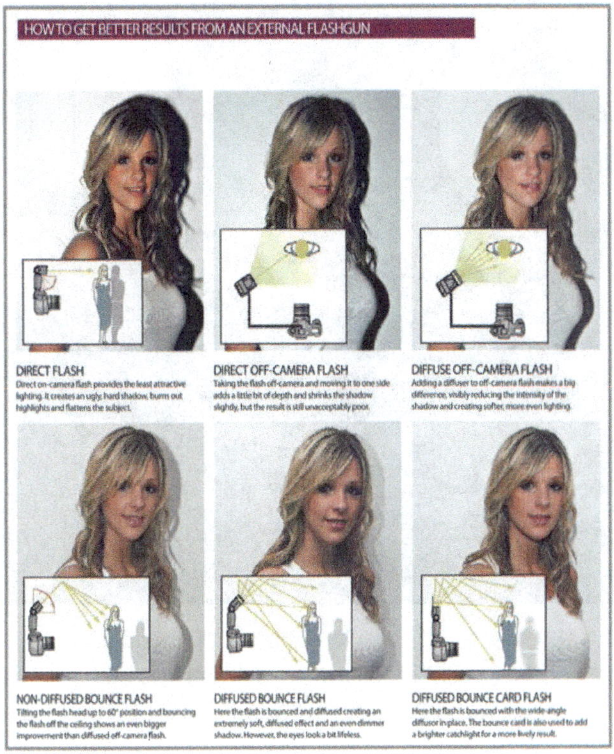

Umbrellas for Flashguns

Capturing three-dimensional subjects through photography requires a strategic approach to present them as such on a two-dimensional medium. One effective way to achieve this is by playing with light and shadows, which can be achieved by moving the light source away from the camera lens axis. To achieve this, you'll need to detach your flash from the camera and position it on a light stand or tripod, ideally using an umbrella adapter to tilt it as needed and attach light modifiers for added versatility.

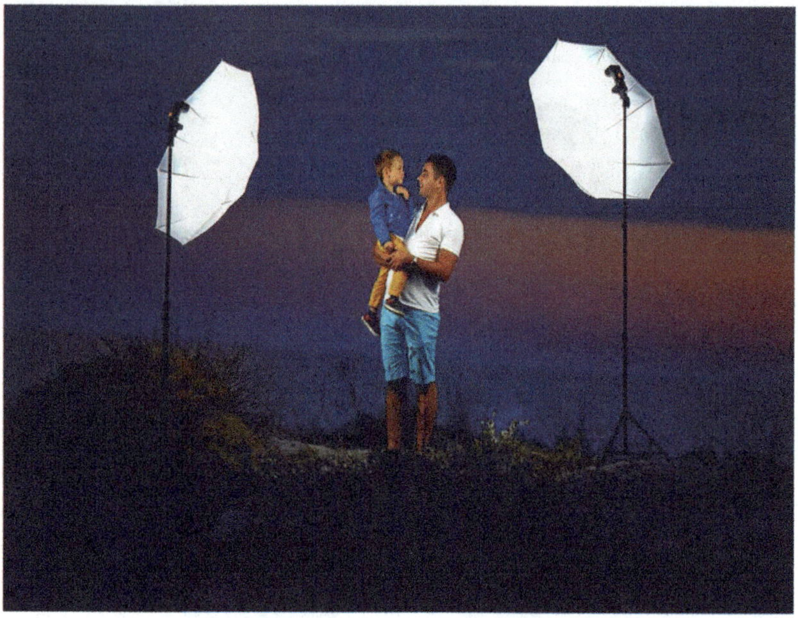

Emart Photo Studio Double Off Camera Speedlight Flash Umbrella Kit, Shoe-mount E-Type Brackets for Photography Kit with black and white umbrellas and carrying case. $67 on Amazon Affiliate Link.

Wireless Flash Triggers

For your flash trigger to connect with your camera to your umbrellas, you need this flash trigger. The more, the merrier because it gives you more options for use. Wirelessly trigger your camera flash with the Godox CT-16 3-in-1 Flash Kit. This versatile and convenient kit is compatible with Canon, Nikon, and Pentax DSLR cameras and includes a 3-in-1 transmitter and receiver for studio use. Time to elevate your photography game! It only costs $38 on Amazon through the affiliate link.

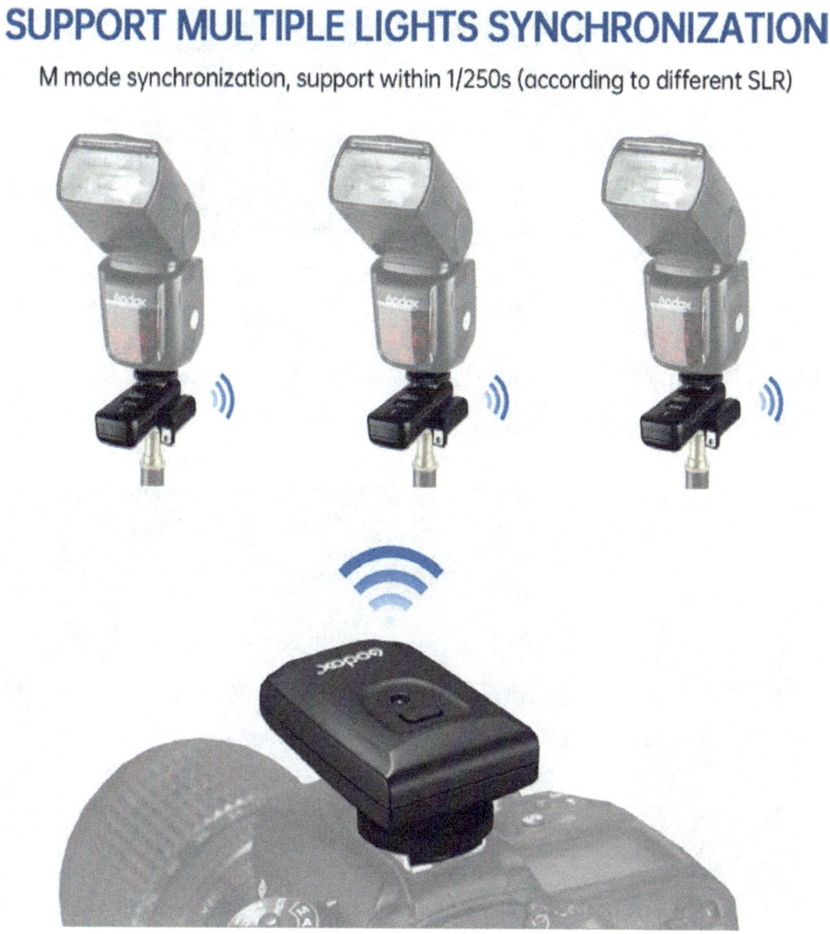

Battery Powered Light for Key, Fill, and Back Light

If you are doing photography outside, you need to be able to carry your lighting equipment with you to your shoot. With the latest technological improvements, you won't need an outlet or electricity to keep them running. And, by stocking up with rechargeable batteries, you can achieve hours of uninterrupted performance. Say goodbye to cables and hello to freedom!.

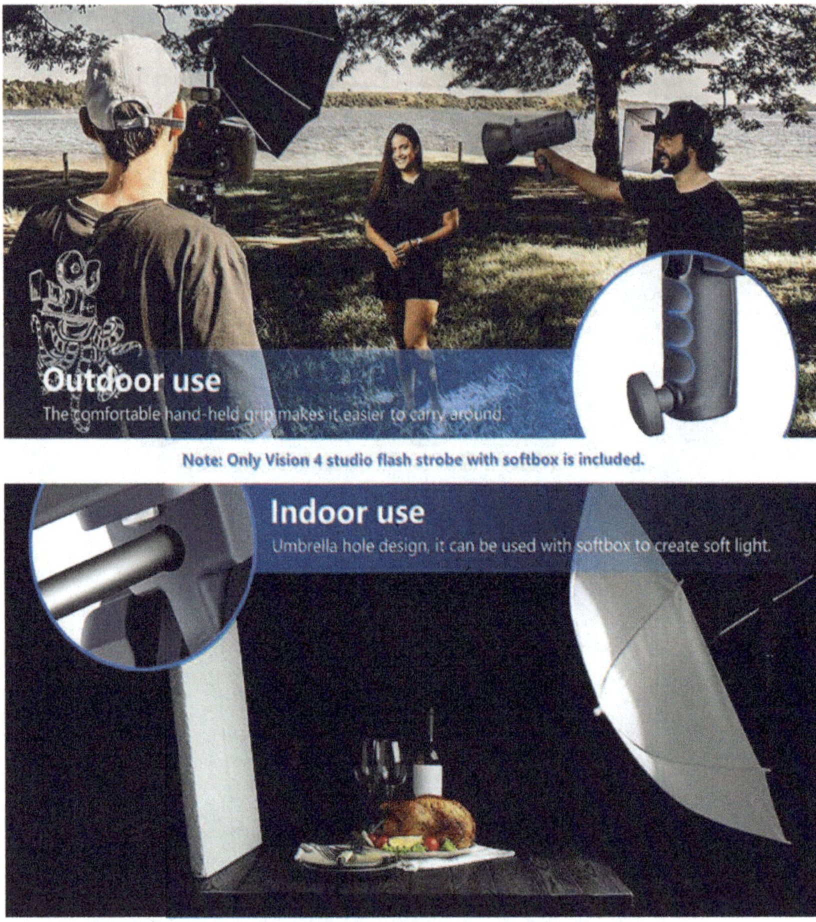

Neewer Li-on Battery Powered Strobe with Softbox Kit: This battery-powered video light offers the freedom to set up ideal lighting anywhere without worrying about pesky wires getting in the way. Say goodbye to restrictions and hello to hassle-free, high-quality footage. $290 Amazon Affiliate Link.

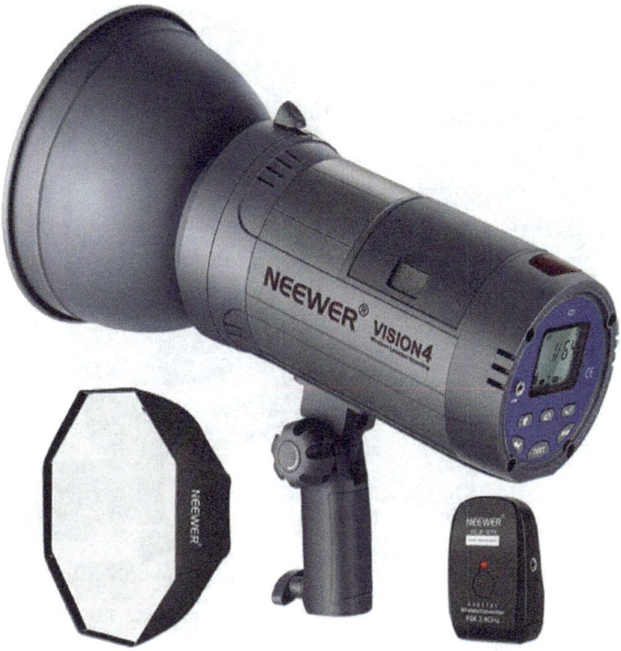

Alternatively, I like the ProFoto Lighting To Go Kit. This lighting kit can create all your necessary 3-point lighting. Looking for a powerful and portable alternative to traditional speed lights and studio flash heads? Look no further than the Profoto B2. The Profoto 2x B1X 500 AirTTL Flash Head bundle is the ultimate photography accessory. It includes 2 lithium-ion batteries, a 2.8A battery charged with power cable, a 1.8A car charger, and a backpack for easy transport. With a cordless and wireless design, you can shoot in AirTTL or manual mode without any restraints. Plus, you can connect wirelessly with other AirTTL flashes. It boasts 10 times more power than an average speedlight, with 500Ws adjustable in 1/10 f-stop increments over a 9 f-stop power range. And don't forget the bonus item - a Profoto TTL-S Air Remote for Canon cameras! You won't want to miss out on this bundle. It's the top of the line in lighting setups. $5,400 on Amazon Affiliate Link.

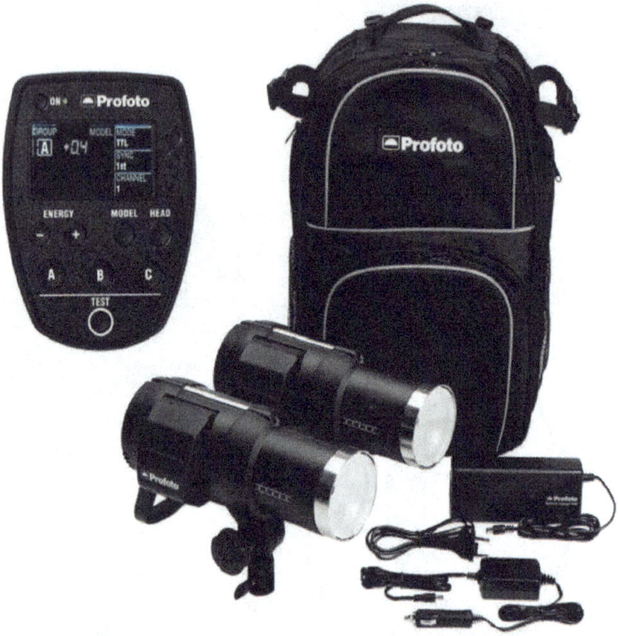

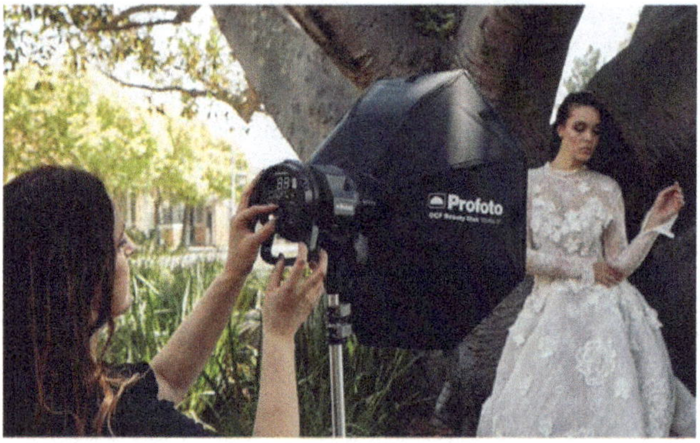

Ring Lights for Key Lighting

As a portrait photographer, nothing is more important than capturing the perfect shot of your subject. That's where ring lights come in - they're a professional favorite for a reason. By providing soft, diffused lighting on your subject, these lights help reduce shadows and are the perfect choice for close-up portraiture.

Plus, unlike other lighting options that can make your subject look washed out or change the contours of their face, ring lights allow your subject to "pop" without sacrificing any of their unique features. One sign that a model is facing a ring light? The appearance of circular catchlights in their eyes, instantly adds an extra layer of attraction and engagement to your portrait. Whether you're a seasoned pro or an amateur selfie enthusiast, these lights are the perfect selection for your next photo shoot.

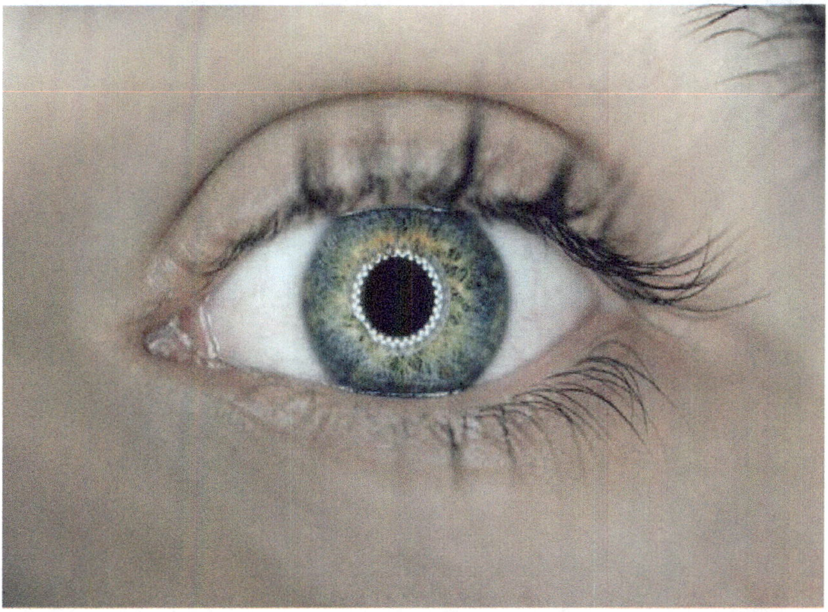

Getting the perfect shot for macro photography can be a challenge. Shadows always seem to sneak up and steal the details you're trying to capture. Fortunately, ring lights provide front-focused lighting that allows you to distribute light around your subject, hiding shadows and emphasizing crucial details. These kits work well for floral and insect photography, where every detail counts. With a variety of color temperature options, ring lights blend seamlessly with natural light, making it easy to manipulate your environment to get the perfect shot. Don't let shadows ruin your macro shots; use a ring light to bring your subject to life.

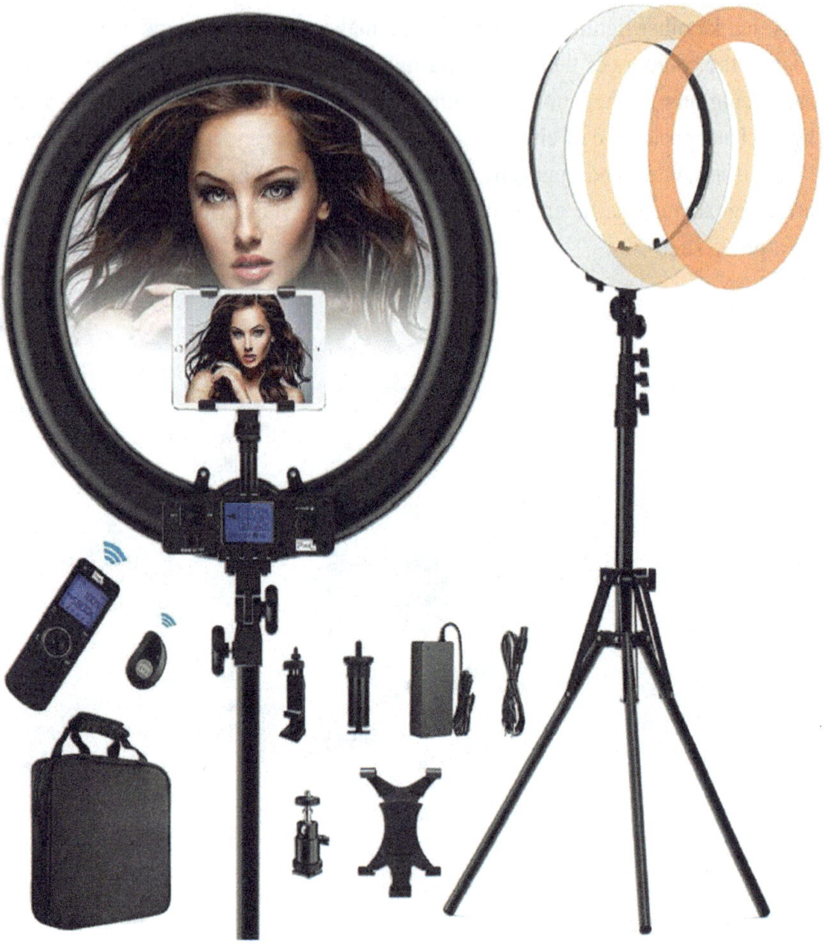

Ring Light with Wireless Remote and iPad Holder, 19 Inch Bi-Color LCD Display Ring Light with Stand and Selfie Remote, 55W 3000-5800K CRI≥97. It is only $127 on Amazon. Here is the Affiliate Link.

Reflector Stands

Selens Photography Reflector Holder Stand Kit, 32in / 80cm 5-in-1 Collapsible Light Reflectors with Swivel Boom Arm Stand and Sandbag for Photo Video Studio. $61 on Amazon Affiliate Link.

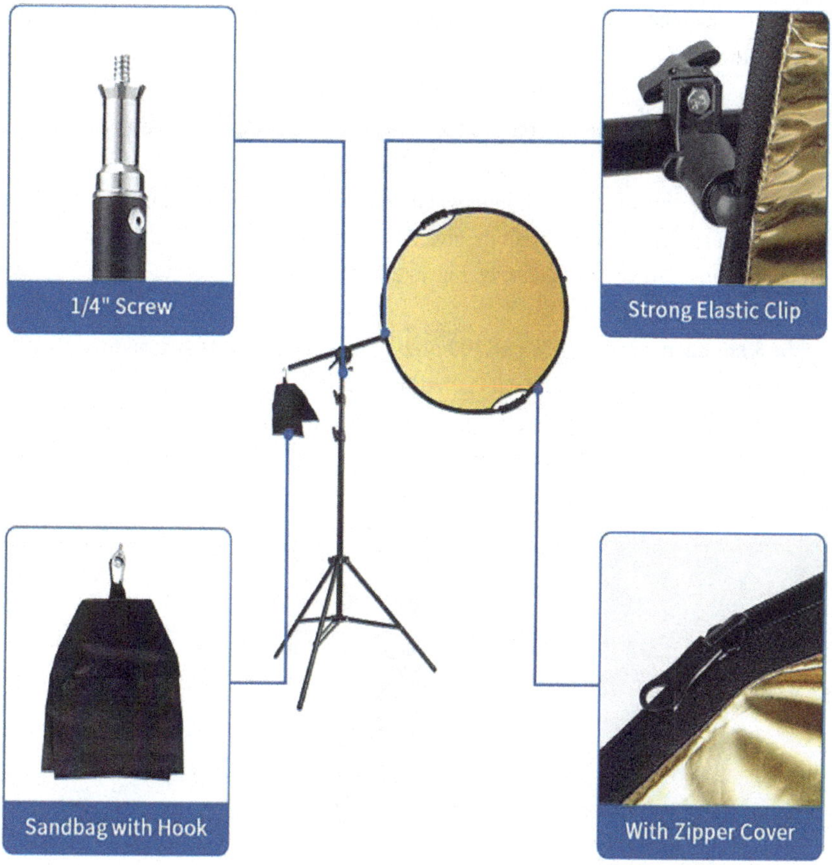

Use a Lightweight Tripod

For any photographer, capturing sharp and crisp images is the goal. However, achieving this can be challenging, especially in low-light, outdoor conditions. In such instances, it's essential to keep your camera as steady as possible to eliminate any camera shake or blurring. And the perfect tool for the job? A lightweight, sturdy tripod! A tripod is an essential accessory that can be employed in any shooting scenario, but it's particularly necessary when there's not enough light. By using a tripod, you can keep your camera level and steady when your shutter speed slows down, enabling you to capture stunning, noise-free images. Moreover, your tripod helps you maintain proper alignment for your shot, making it easier to frame the scene and eliminate unwanted distortions.

When purchasing a tripod, you want to make sure it has a quick plate release so you can quickly take the camera on and off the tripod. You also want it to have the ability to convert to a monopod when you are walking around outside. It's also great to have it do different heights. I went over this in detail in the Chapter Landscapes. Here are my favorites for outdoor portraits.

The Vanguard Alta Pro#263AB100 offers the best balance of size and stability of all the tripods we tested. It gets taller than any of our other picks (68.2 inches at maximum height), its legs can splay outward at four angles, and it's angling. Cost: $230. Amazon Affiliate Link.

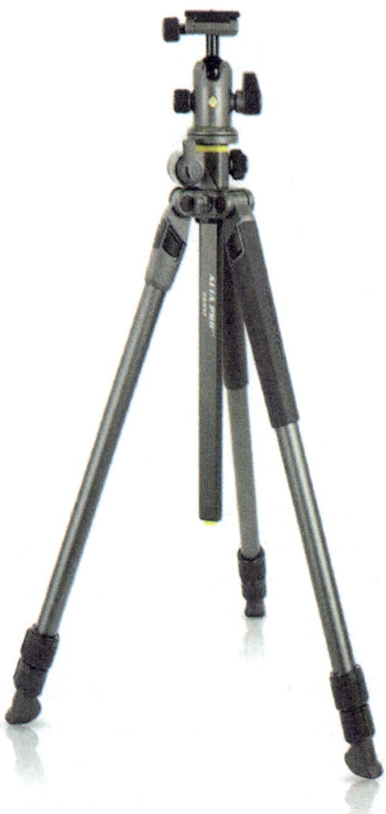

Vanguard VEO 3. A tripod that can handle two cameras. Smaller and lighter than our top pick, this tripod can also support two devices at once. But it's a little less stable and slightly more expensive. Cost: $250. Affiliate Link Amazon.

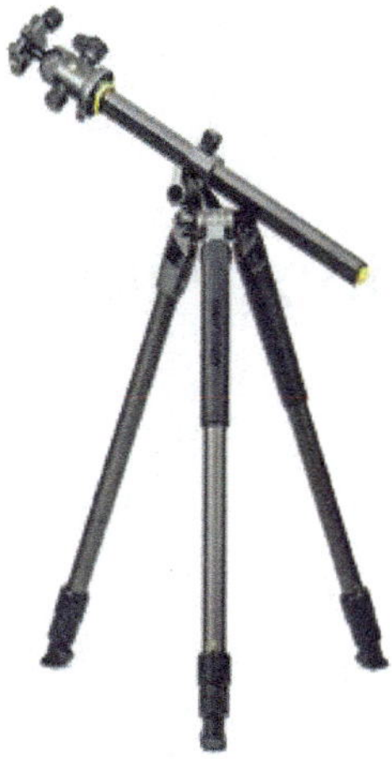

Sirui W-1004K10 Tripod Kit River Runner. A solid waterproof tripod. This tripod doesn't have an angled center column, but it's quite sturdy, designed with a greater load capacity than any of our other picks, and (most important) waterproof. Cost: $221 on Amazon. Amazon Affiliate Link.

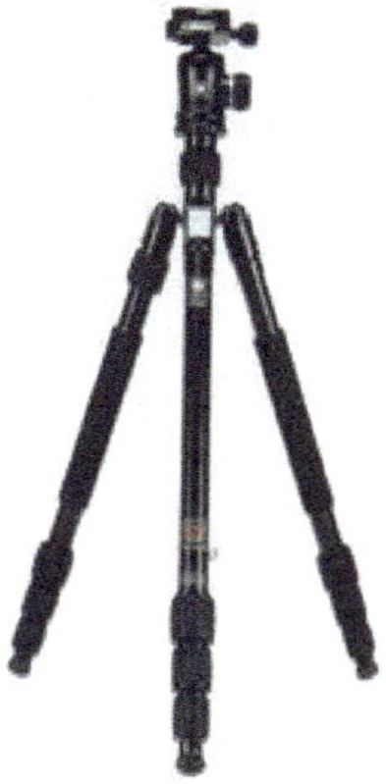

7

INDOOR PORTRAITS

Regarding photography sessions, indoor locations can be both a blessing and a curse. The controlled environment can make it easier to set up the perfect shot, but it also brings up challenges such as lighting and limited space. As a photographer, it's essential to be equipped to handle these situations quickly. With the right gear, lighting techniques, and creative vision, you can capture stunning indoor portraits. In this Chapter, we'll explore some of the best tips to help you master the art of indoor portrait photography. I will also cover basic inside lighting setups and tips and tricks to improve your understanding and skills.

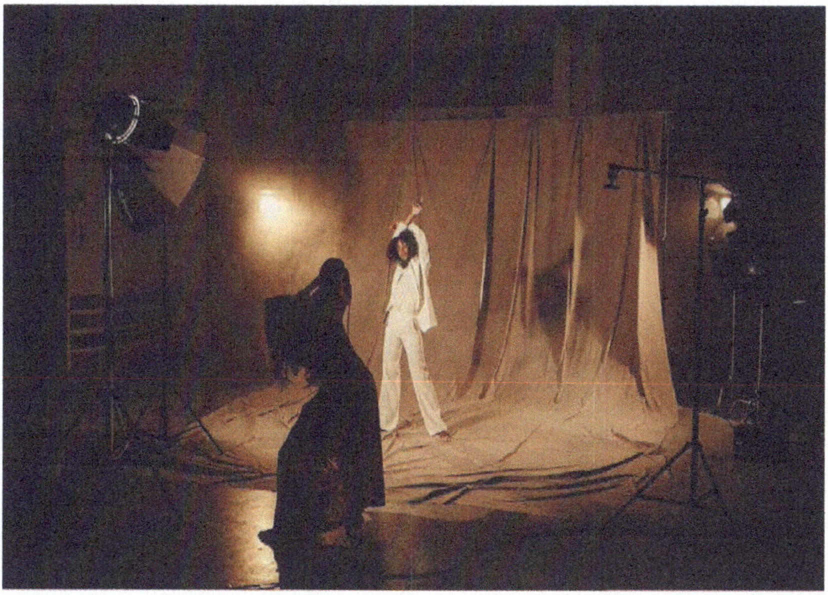

Properties of Indoor Lighting

Lighting is crucial for photographers to convey a story, evoke emotions, and engage viewers. Mastering this skill requires practice, and perfecting the desired lighting effects may take some experimentation. When photographing, you're creating a 3D illusion in a 2D space. By playing with light and shadow, you can give objects dimension and weight. And altering the lighting of the same thing can entirely change its shape and interpretation. By using a key light, fill light, and backlight in specific positions, the subject is given depth and a sense of realism. It also enhances the overall visual storytelling.

Learning to capture the light indoors (and outdoors) can be a game-changer, whether using the natural glow of windows, or getting creative with artificial lighting, and/or camera flashes; mastering this skill will elevate your photos to new heights!

Three-Point Lighting Set Up Indoors

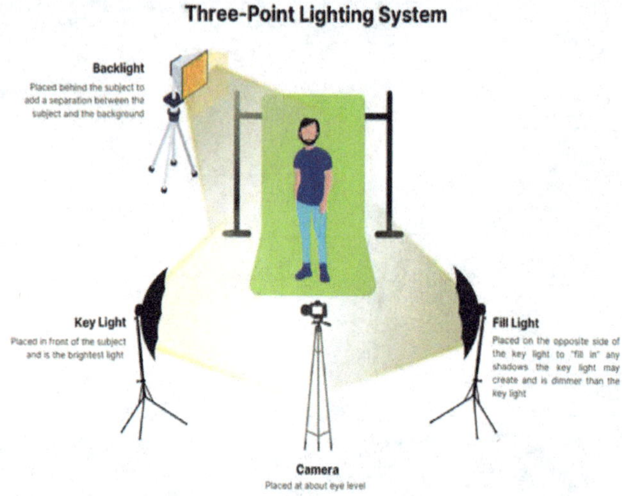

Lighting is an essential element in any scene. It can create atmosphere, bring attention to a specific subject or highlight the mood of a moment. That brings us to the popular three-point lighting setup. This is a traditional method for illuminating subjects with light sources from distinct positions: *key light, fill light, and backlight.*

Key Light

The key light is usually positioned at 30 degrees to the left or right side and slightly higher than the eye level. It provides illumination that creates shape and depth when cast on faces or objects by creating shadows and dimension.

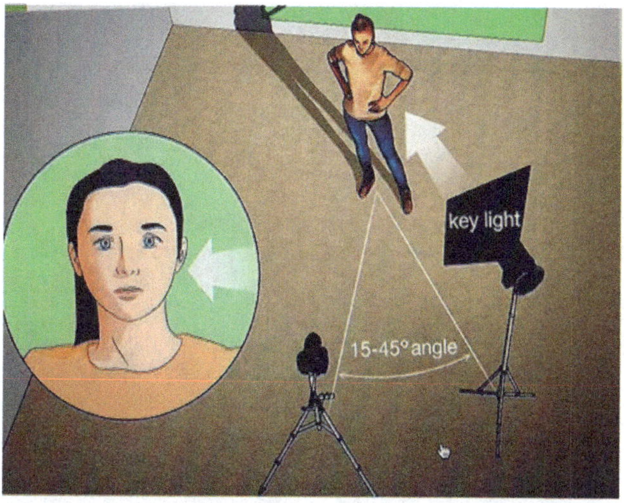

When lighting a scene, the key light is the star. It's essential for creating depth, tone, and mood. And these shadows can be softened or intensified depending on the overall lighting design, creating a *high-key or low-key image* that sets the mood and adds flair to the scene. In photography, the key light is truly the key to success. Low-key lighting creates a dramatic contrast between the lightest and darkest elements of an image, while high-key often produces smooth shadows with minimal darkness for a softer effect.

Low-Key Lighting:

If a photographer uses a higher fill ratio, such as an **8:1 ratio,** the key light will create distinct and contrasting shadows. This type of lighting is known as "low-key lighting." it can produce a range of emotional responses in the viewer. Typically seen in darker genres like fine art nudes and horror films in movies. This style of photography can create a mysterious tone that draws the viewer in. If you're looking to add an extra layer of drama and depth to your photography, experimenting with low-key lighting may be just what you need. This image is for sale on my website at www.tracymccrackin.com.

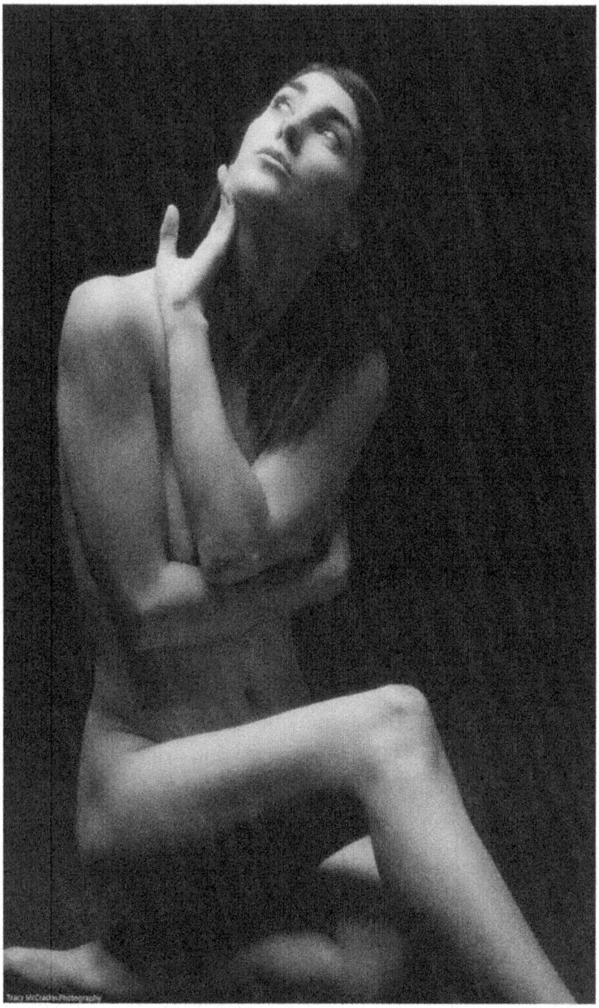

For a low-key aesthetic, please limit the natural light in your scene and be exacting about what you allow to shine through. Darker backgrounds like black or dark blue will reflect less of it, while black fabric placed strategically can help to absorb excess ambient lighting. Natural light still works for this look but requires acute attention when arranging the set or environment. It is one of my favorite lighting setups. There is very little equipment needed, and it creates such a dramatic look!

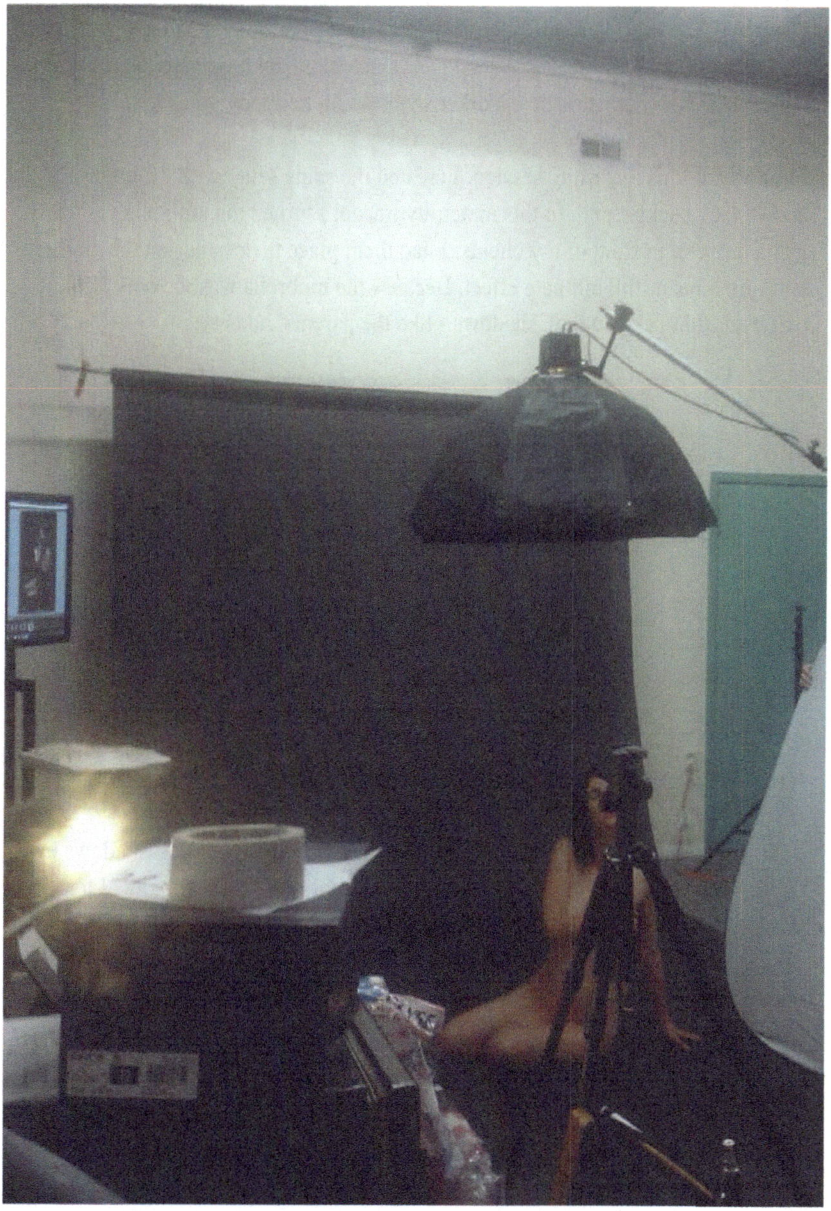

In this image above, I placed the umbrella *horizontally*, just a few feet above my client. My black background completely surrounds her body. I had her gaze up at the soft light to create beautiful shadows. The entire backdrop is jet black, which collects the light, creating even darker shadows on her body.

Similarly, in this maternity session, I created the same setup with the umbrella and a black background. In this maternity image, I turned the umbrella vertically, just a few feet in front of my clients. I had them place their hands on the mother's belly for a beautiful, intimate effect. Because the umbrella was the only light, it cast everything else in dark shadows - like the parents' bodies.

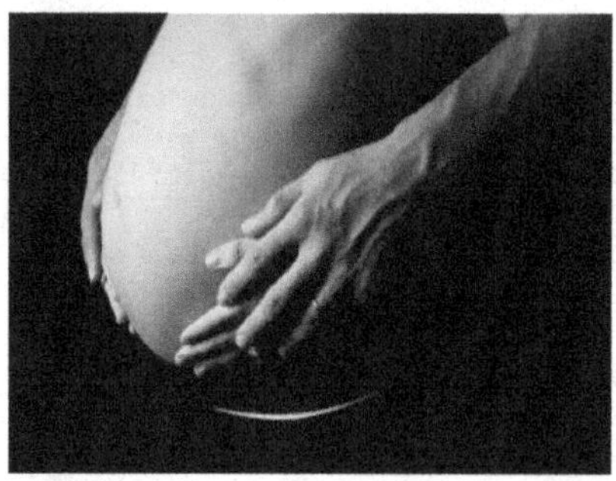

High Key Lighting

To achieve a high-key effect in your photos, you need to create soft shadows by using more extensive light sources. Diffusers or large softboxes are ideal for creating bright scenes without harsh contrast between the highlights and shadows. The bigger the source of illumination - the smoother its castes shadow." To increase brightness even more – use white background or sheet that reflects natural lighting!

By utilizing a soft key light positioned slightly off-center and employing a **2:1 fill ratio**, skilled photographers can create a flattering look that minimizes skin imperfections and highlights your subjects' best features. To capture a striking shot, place your subject in the focal point while ensuring they stay within the limits of the paper. Create a clear source of light by setting up a key light aimed towards the subject, ensuring the lighting is as even as possible. This image is for sale on my website at www.tracymccrackin.com.

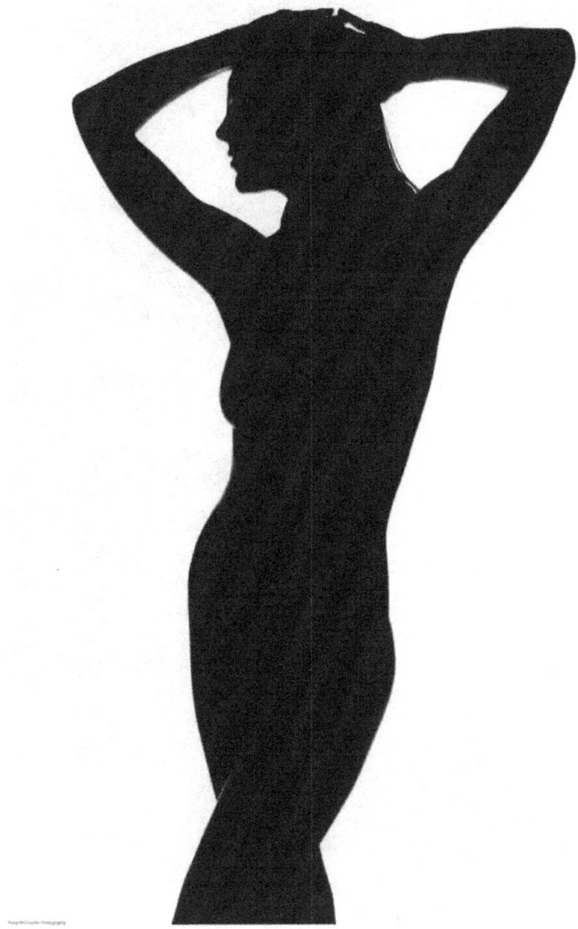

Avoid harsh shadows by setting up a secondary, less bright light on the opposite side of the subject. However, this can create a dim background. To achieve a bright white background, set up and angle a few additional lights toward the background. Be aware of the possibility of light bouncing off the scenery and creating unwanted coronas around your subject. Ensure your background disappears to achieve the desired solid white effect. So basically, you don't want to see the background at all! Otherwise, remove it in post-production.

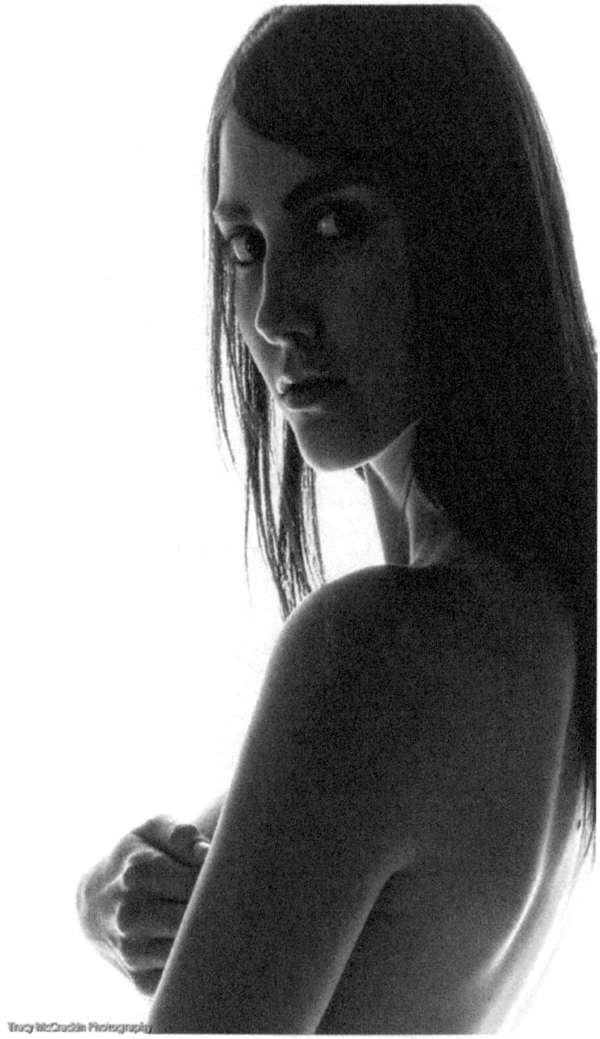

You can see how I set up a sheet in the background and asked my client to step directly in front of it and pose. In the first image, the single key light in front of her creates a stark black-and-white shadow effect. In the second image, I had her turn her face toward the camera. I had my assistant place a silver reflector in front, as the fill light on her face. A straightforward setup, and she didn't have to move around to get the needed effects. I later added catchlights to her eyes post-production.

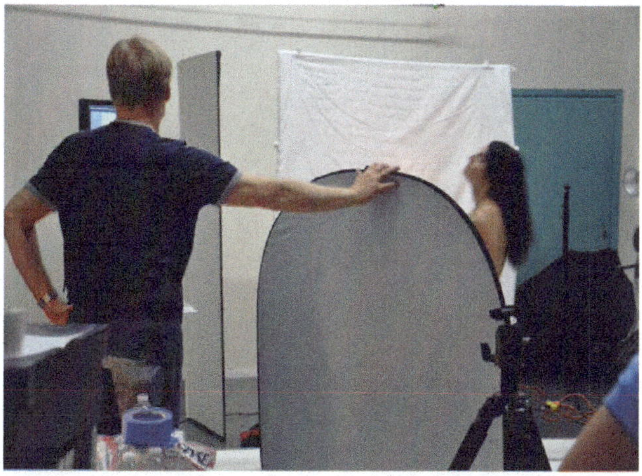

Fill Light

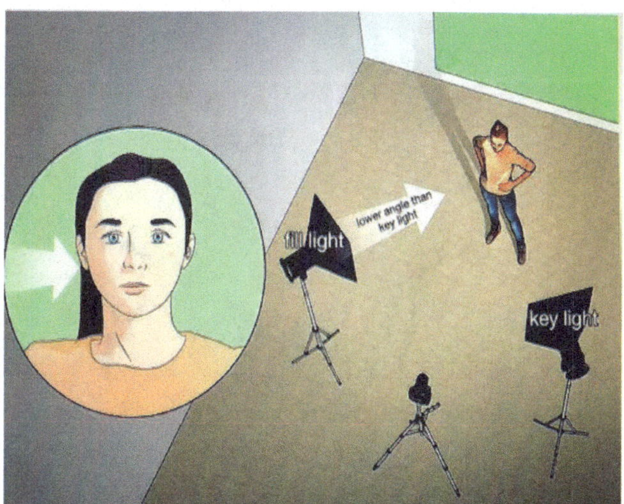

Fill lights are placed opposite from the key light—on its other side—and provide more even coverage across face features like eyes, nose, cheeks, etc., while also reducing shadows created by the primary source of illumination (key).

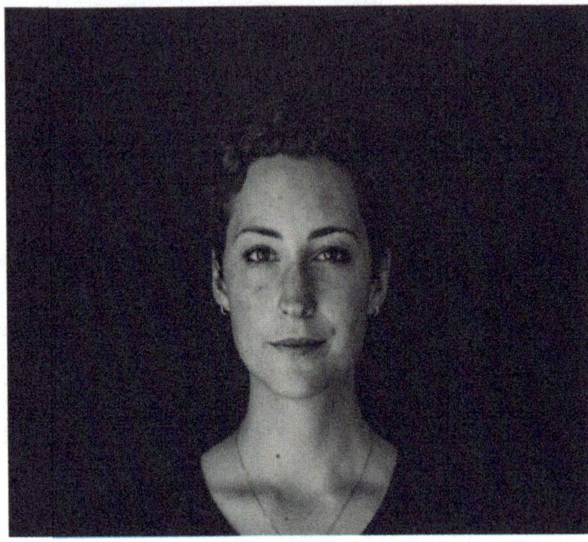

Backlight

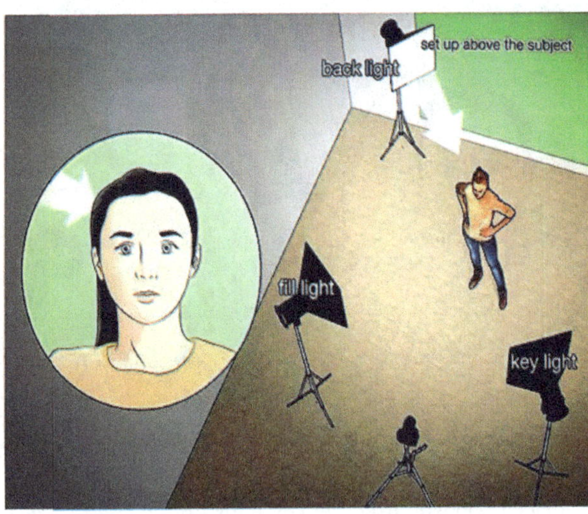

Last but not least, backlights are set behind the subject, and they add detail and give off subtle separation between background and foreground elements in scenes with multiple characters/objects present; this ensures that none get lost in darkness!

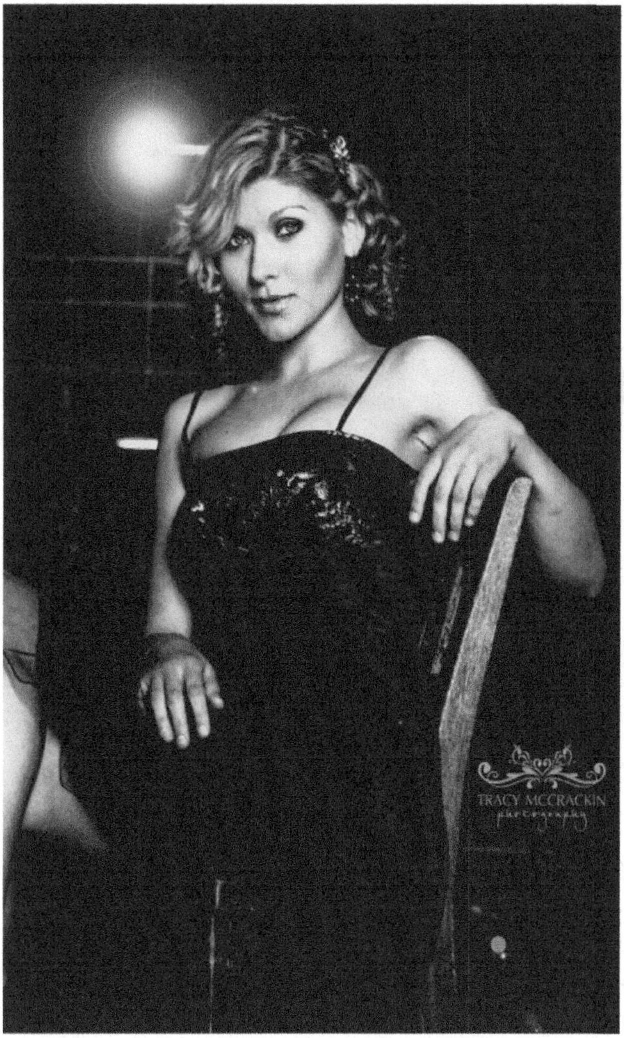

By positioning a light behind the subject, photographers can separate their subject from the background and give a sense of depth to the scene. This technique is essential in creating a well-lit and visually stunning scene. The key to effective backlighting.

Four Key Lighting

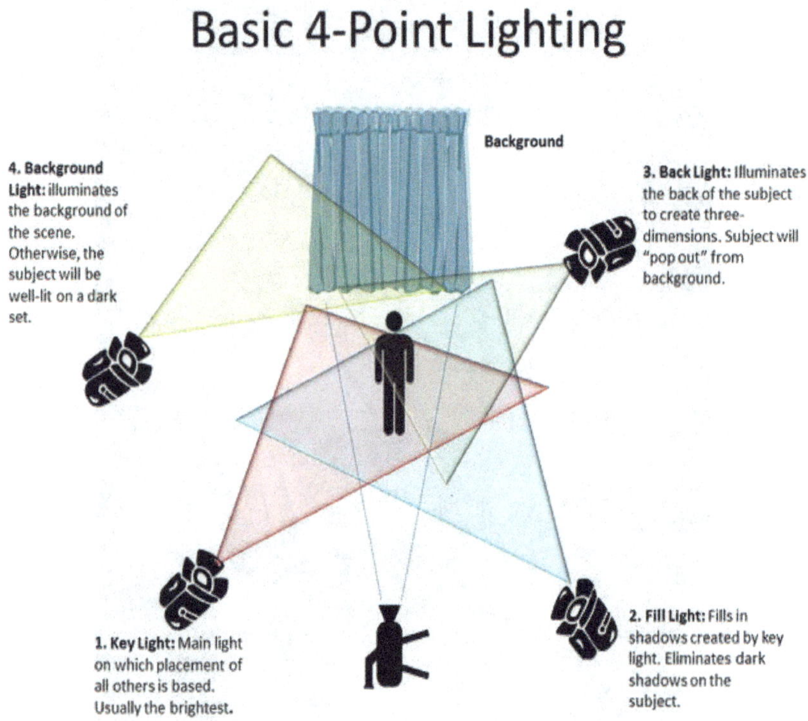

This simple technique involves using a 4th light called "background light." It is used to illuminate the background behind your subject. It's used more often in indoor portraits. Unlike a "backlight," the "background light" highlights the background, *not* the subject, It not only can you draw attention to the back-ground, but you can also create depth and focus for your subject.

It also works great at eliminating detail on a white background or sheet. This works great if you want the background to appear seamlessly behind the subject. Photographers often position the light(s) either low to the ground or high on a tripod pointing downward. The light must be directly behind the subject to avoid any unwanted glare back into the camera. This also works great for product shoots. Next time you're doing a shoot, keep an eye out for the magic of the backlight.

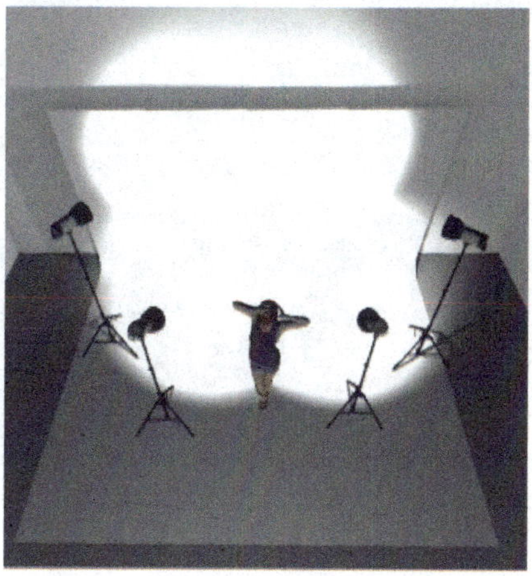

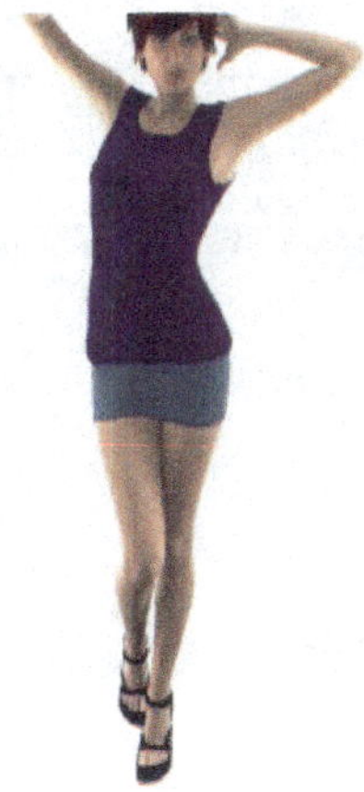

Common Key Light Face Patterns

In photography, different lighting techniques yield different effects. Flat lighting is flattering, making it ideal for headshots and glamour shots. Butterfly lighting is used in beauty shots with a reflector to soften shadows. Loop lighting creates a dramatic look by casting a shadow off the nose and showcases a subject's good side. Rembrandt lighting is even more dramatic than loop lighting, perfect for portraits of athletes. Finally, split lighting accentuates wrinkles and muscle definition, making it a go-to for athletic portraits. By mastering the 3 and 4-point lighting techniques, you can take your portrait photography to new heights!

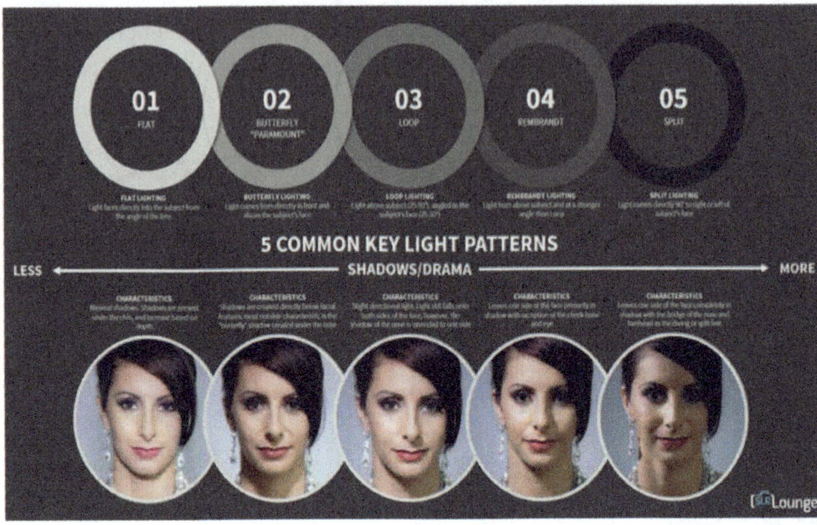

Flat Lighting Defined

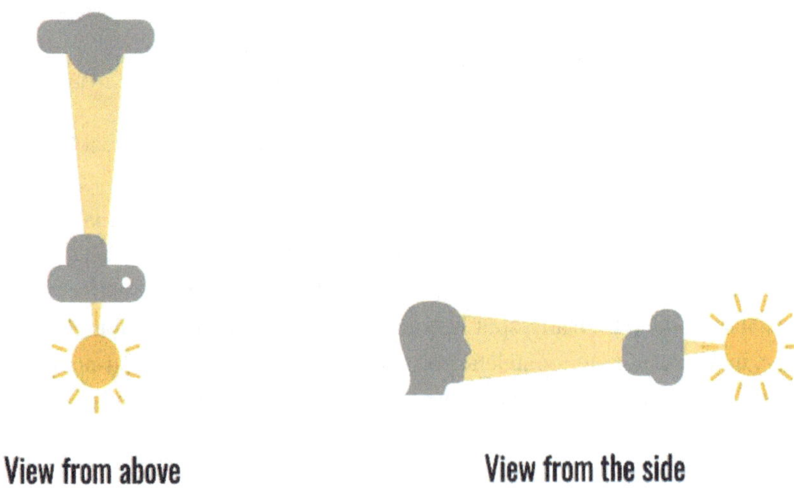

Flat lighting is the perfect choice for creating stunning headshots and glamour editorial shots. it also works great with newborn photos because it gives the skin smooth by removing all the details. It boasts a positive quality that enhances natural features and makes a more attractive appearance on camera. Flat lighting is most effective when the light direction is from the front of the subject. This allows the light to flow evenly over their face, smoothing any bumps and lines. You can see in the catchlights I'm simply using a straight key light shot with flash.

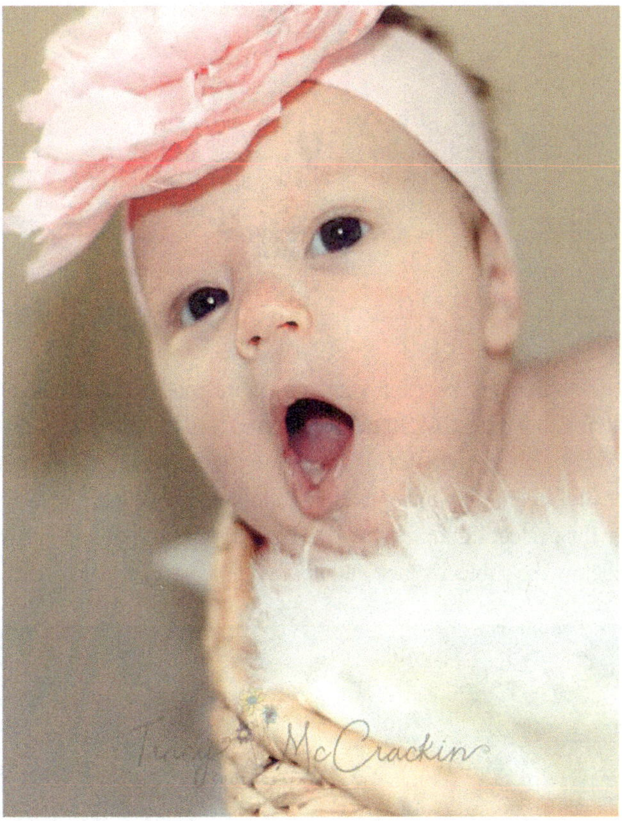

Butterfly Lighting Defined

Looking for stunning beauty shots? Look no further than butterfly lighting! With the addition of a reflector underneath, this lighting pattern softens shadows and creates the perfect look for capturing your subject's natural beauty. This lighting technique is a game-changer.

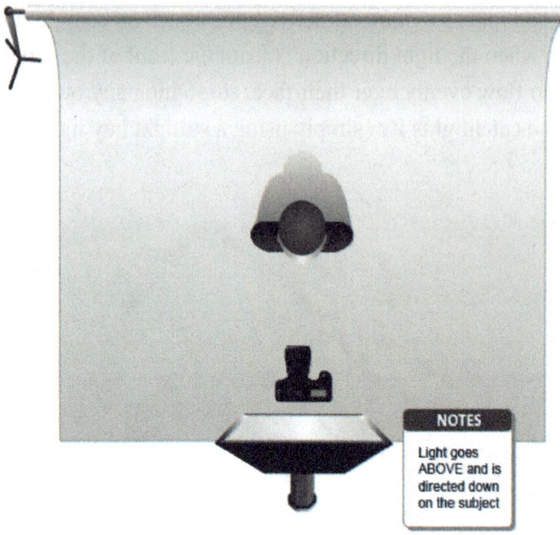

To capture the best shots, position your subject in front of the camera and add a slight angle for added interest. Remember not to turn them so much that their nose shadows the cheekbone. Ensure that your lighting source is aligned with the subject, ideally several feet in front and a foot or so above their head. This way, you'll have the perfect lighting setup. Do not forget to position the reflector a foot or so below the subject's face and angle it in a manner that softens shadows.

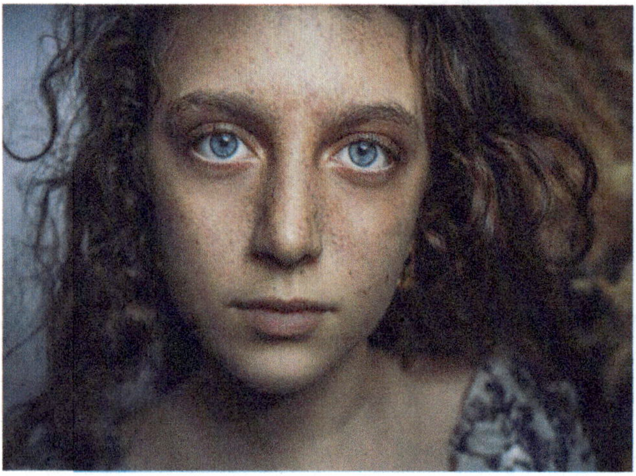

Avoid the glass being too close to the beginning, but ensure it fills in shadows slightly without being too bright. Remember to preserve the butterfly-shaded shade under the subject's nose, as it's a signature of this lighting setup. Explore harsh butterfly lighting to add drama and intense contrasts to your photos. Give your images an edgy and captivating look with this technique. In this image, you can see the nice wrap-around lighting around her face. There is just a very slight shadow under her nose.

Loop Lighting Defined

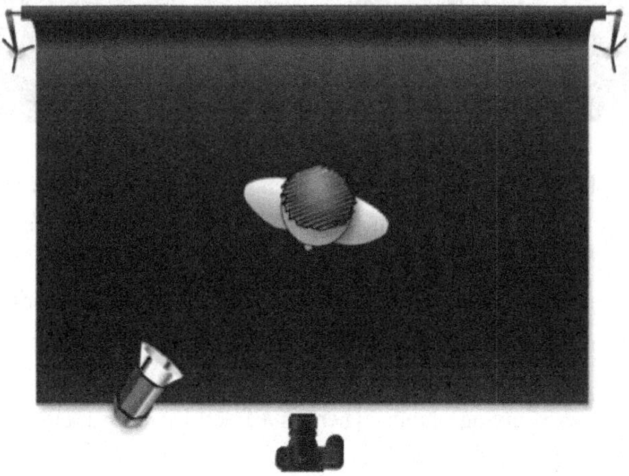

Once you've learned the basics, like loop lighting, you can use your newfound knowledge to achieve the perfect portrait look. Loop lighting is a simple yet effective lighting pattern that only requires one light and a bit of understanding of placement. In this tutorial, we'll explore loop lighting from every angle - what it is, when to use it, and how to set it up. Loop lighting is a simple yet impactful lighting pattern used in portrait photography named after the "loop" shaped shadow it produces on the subject's face. When executed correctly, this lighting creates a circular shadow under and on the opposite side of the light source. The size and intensity of the loop can vary, but it never touches the shadow on the cheek (aka Rembrandt lighting). You may have unknowingly used loop lighting by placing your flashes at 45 degrees to your subject as main and fill. Master this technique and take your photography skills to the next level!

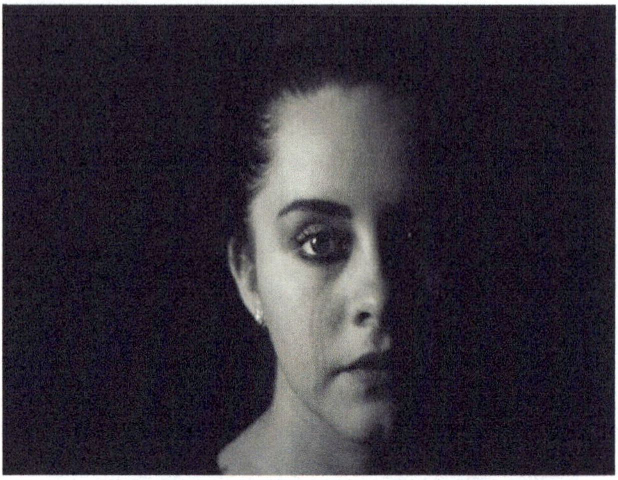

Lighting plays a crucial role in determining the outcome of photographs. By understanding the angle of light, you can create a shadow that falls off the nose, pointing down to one side. This not only adds a dramatic effect to the picture but it also illuminates the subject's face unevenly. Taking advantage of this technique requires you to know which side of the face the subject prefers to be lit up to showcase their best angle. Remember, the proper lighting can make all the difference in delivering stunning photos. There is a Loop Lighting Example Showing Nose Shadow, Cheek, and Neck Shadows.

Rembrandt Lighting Defined

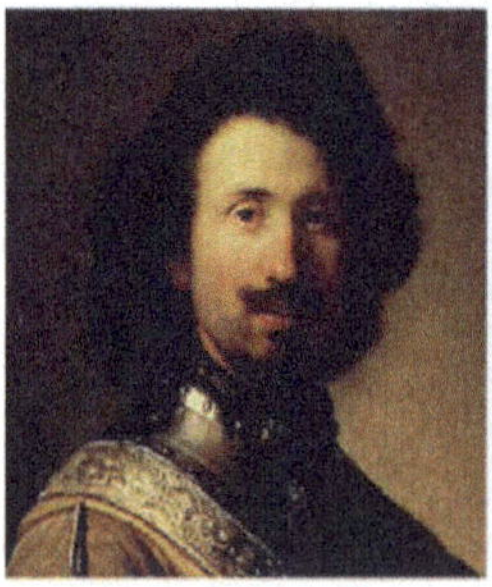

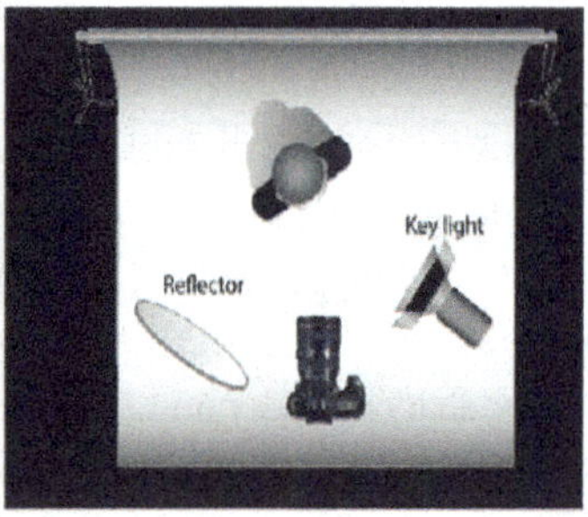

Looking to create dramatic portraits? Consider using Rembrandt lighting instead of loop lighting. By adding shadows to your subject and adjusting the angle of your light source, you can achieve stunning results that will make your photos stand out. This type of lighting is popular in portrait photography, including sports photography. Check out the video above to see it in action!

Discover the lighting technique used by Rembrandt to enhance his iconic paintings. Dubbed "Rembrandt lighting", this method involves illuminating only half of the subject's face while the other half remains shrouded in shadow. Notably, a distinctive triangle shape emerges just below the eye, adding depth and dimension to the subject's features. With Rembrandt lighting, all you need is a single light source and a reflector to produce stunning results.

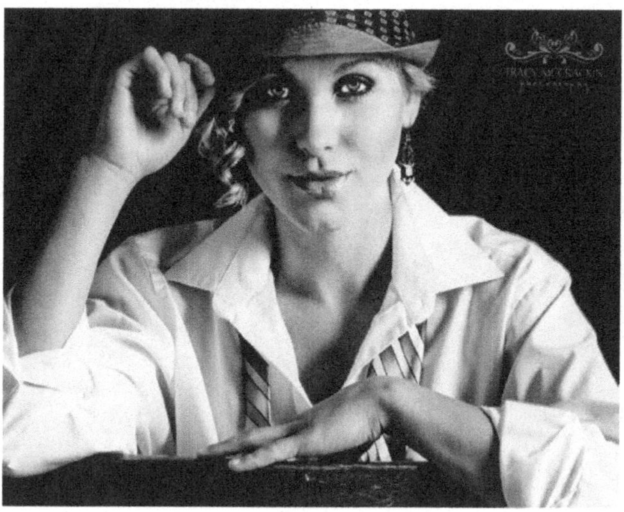

By positioning the key light source at a 45° angle on one side of the face and adding a reflector on the opposite side, you can create a beautiful triangular highlight under the eye. This lighting technique, called 'chiaroscuro,' adds depth and dimension to your photos and creates an eye-catching geometric shape. To ensure exceptional results, make sure that the triangular shape is no wider than the eye and no longer than the nose. And for softer shadows, a fill light can be added to the setup. With Rembrandt lighting, you can capture stunning images with minimal effort and maximum impact. Try it now and elevate your photography skills in no time!

Split Lighting Defined

Discover a lighting technique that brings out the best in your subject's muscular definition and body features. The split lighting pattern, commonly used in athletic portraits, creates a unique look and feel by emphasizing imperfections, such as wrinkles or fine lines. Remember that while flat and loop lighting may fill in these imperfections, split lighting accentuates them for a dramatic effect. Add depth and dimension to your portraits with this powerful lighting technique.

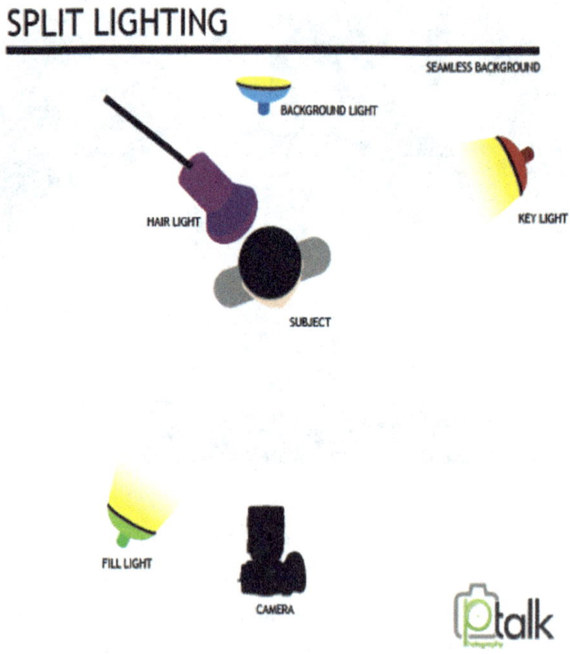

The split lighting pattern, commonly used in athletic portraits, creates a unique look and feel by emphasizing imperfections, such as wrinkles or fine lines. Remember that while flat and loop lighting may fill these imperfections, split lighting accentuates them for a dramatic effect. Add depth and dimension to your portraits with this powerful lighting technique.

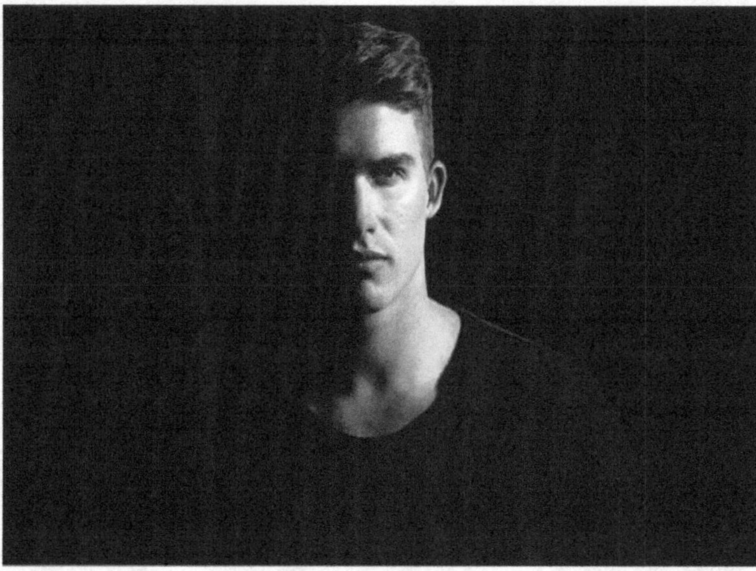

Catch your audience's attention and enhance their photography knowledge with this! Split lighting is an amazing technique in photography that adds a dramatic and breathtaking effect. By illuminating half the subject's face with light, the other half remains in shadows, creating that ideal "splitting" effect. This style is achieved by lighting the subject from one specific side, resulting in eye-catching and mesmerizing images.

Window Light for Indoor Light

When it comes to capturing the perfect image, lighting, and composition play essential roles. A straightforward technique to achieve this is to move your subject closer to a window. Windows provide direct light through the glass with just the right amount of diffusion, resulting in soft and delicate rays of light that add depth and character to your subject. Whether taking portraits or trying to capture still life, this easy trick is a surefire way to elevate your photography skills and create truly stunning photographs. So the next time you shoot, try positioning your subject closer to a window and see how it transforms your images!

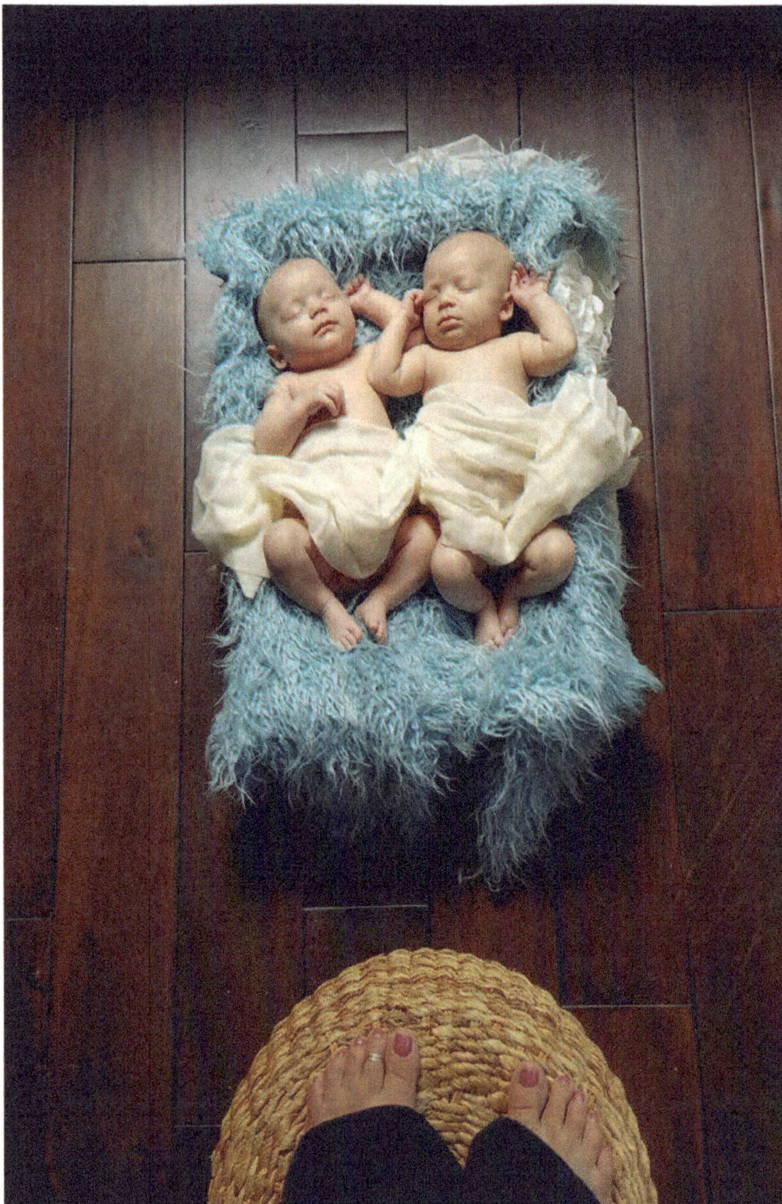

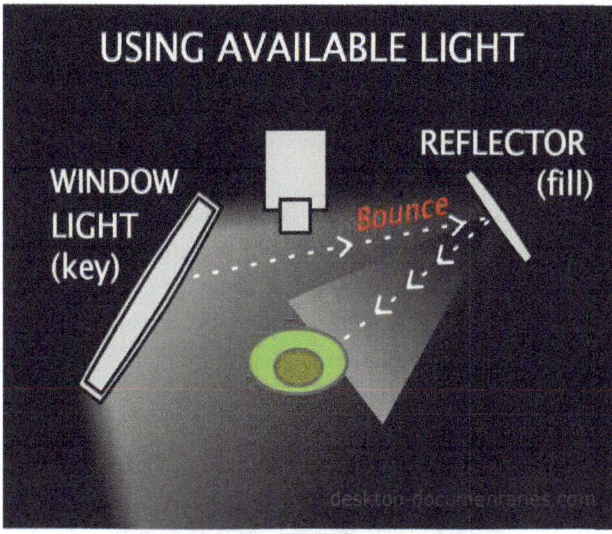

This image is of my twin granddaughters. Of course, I had to memorialize their coming into our lives by taking newborn portraits. As you can tell, I wrapped them in cream and blue gauze. I wanted to have a beach theme of them on my walls at home. As you can tell, after capturing their angelic sleeping faces, I photoshopped the rest of the background behind them. This is an excellent option if you don't like your initial surrounding. I found this one on Etsy.

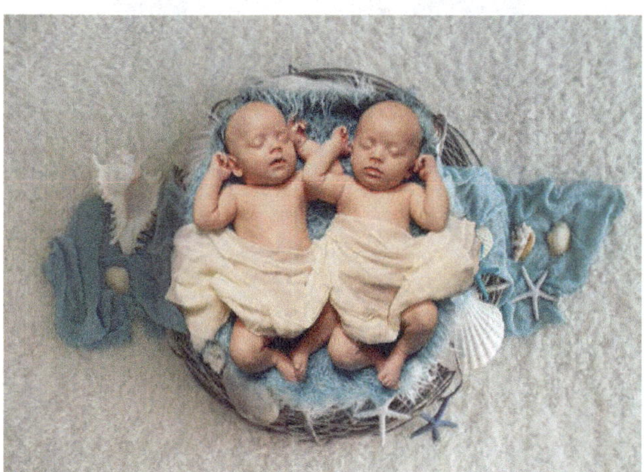

Natural lighting, as you've now learned in this book, can be a powerful, inexpensive tool for capturing stunning photographs. However, it takes careful consideration and skill to make the most of it, especially when using a window as the source.

One of the key aspects to keep in mind is the distance between the subject and the window. Bringing them too close can result in overexposure, washing out their features and leaving them dimly visible. Keeping too far away can result in a lack of illumination, making the subject appear dull. It's all about finding that perfect balance, placing the subject nearby but not too close so that their face is beautifully highlighted while retaining its natural features.

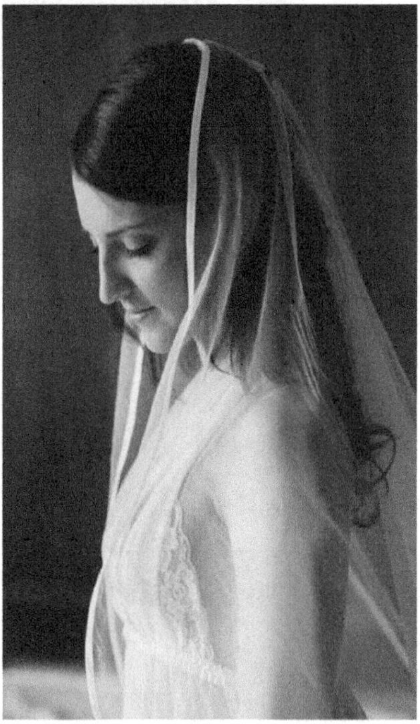

Be Creative in How You Frame Your Subject

Indoor portrait sessions can be a beautiful way to capture a moment and showcase a person's true essence. While some portrait sessions may be more centered around the subject themselves, sometimes utilizing the background to frame the person can honestly tell a story and create a mesmerizing effect.

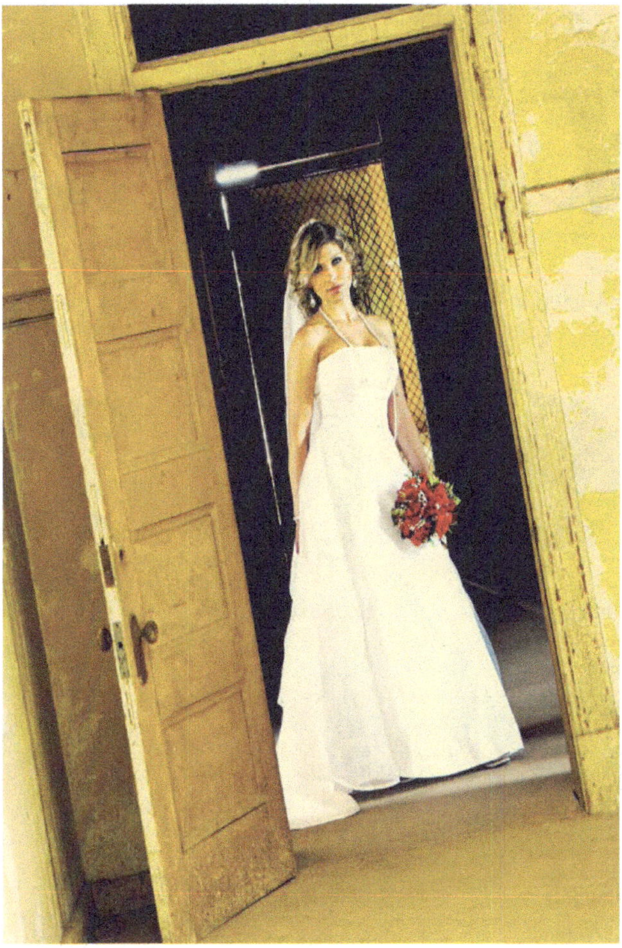

Whether you're looking to feature the issue in a particular environment or showcase their hobbies or interests, the background can be a powerful tool in conveying the message you want to share. When planning the perfect indoor portrait session, take some time to consider the backdrop and how it can help bring your vision to life. I discuss more of this in the Chapter Composition Techniques in this book. But here are a few examples.

Indoor Portrait Making Gear Terms & Uses

Understanding Studio Lighting and Light Shaping

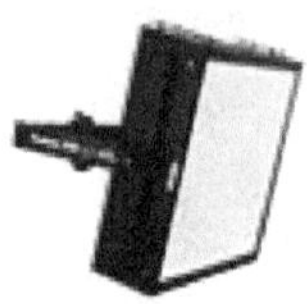

Box Lights ▸

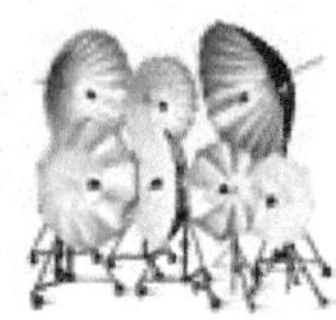

Giant Reflectors ▸

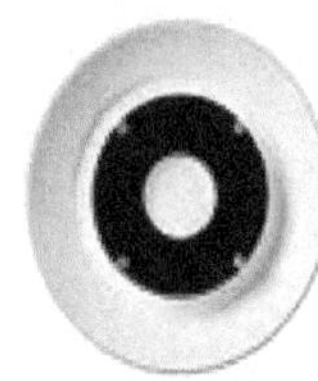

Ring Flash Reflectors and Diffusers ▸

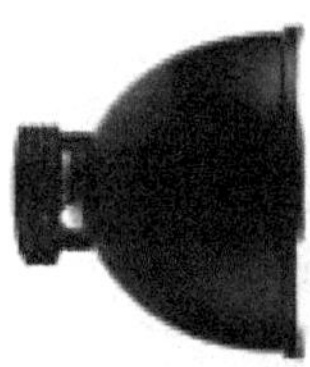

Reflectors ▸

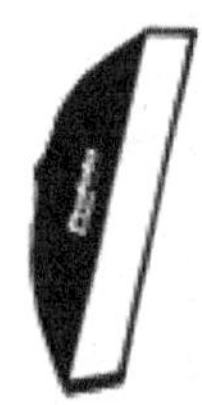

Softboxes ▸

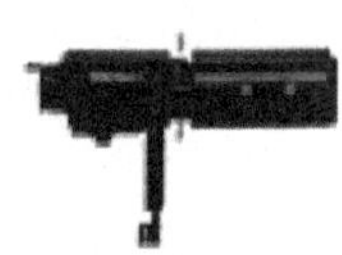

Spotlights ▸

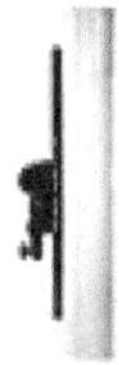

StripLights ▸

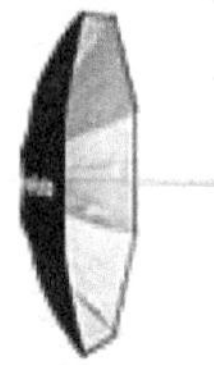

Umbrellas ▸

This is just a small list of the most commonly used lights used in studios. Each of these comes in varied sizes as well. Photographers from all over the world have come to rely on their wide range of light modifiers for all types of shoots. From studio lighting to outdoor lighting, they have it all! This means these lights allow photographers to manipulate and shape light in any way they need. The quality of this light is what makes them so popular among professionals.

Best Places to Rent a Camera or Lens:

Because of the cost of these products, it is common for photographers now to rent them. They understand that not everyone can afford to own every piece of gear they need, which is why they offer an extensive selection of rental options around the world. These rentals are perfect for traveling shooters or those who just want to augment the specific Profoto tools needed for a shoot without having to buy them outright.

1. BorrowLenses
2. Lensrentals
3. Rentglass
4. Pro Photo Rental
5. Aperturent
6. Adorama Rentals
7. LensProToGo
8. SharerGrid
9. Kitsplit

(I am not affiliated with these)

Studio Continuous Lighting

Continuous Lighting - Tungsten Lights

My journey into photography began with a humble set of continuous lights. I was on a tight budget, so these were the only option for me. Despite this, they provided an incredible amount of flexibility and quality in my amateur images. The continuous lights allowed me to gradually build up my lighting skills as I continued to experiment with different angles and exposure times. With each new shot, I grew more confident in what I could do with them - slowly but surely creating beautiful photographs. The ability to immediately see what the light is in real time made all the difference - no guesswork needed!

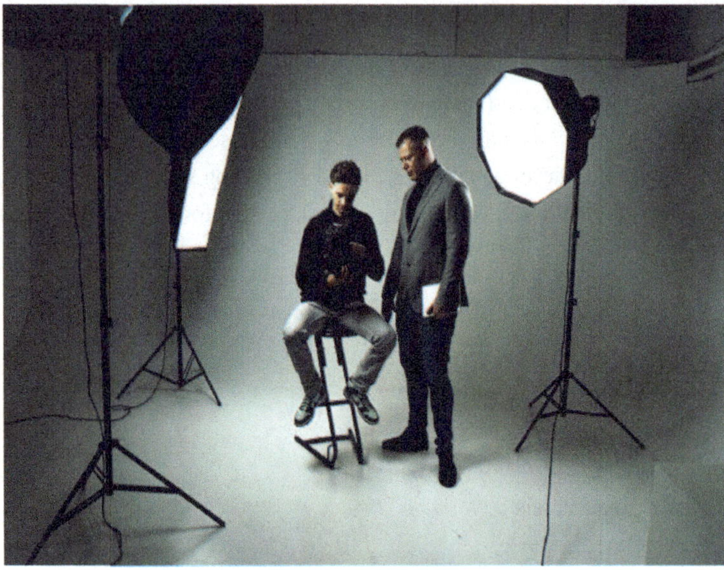

They were called "hot lights" for a reason. The tungsten or quartz-halogen lights make them very hot. These strong lights need special heat-resistant adapters for studio or residential use. During a product photography session, three 1000-watt tungsten hot lights may cause things to wilt or melt. A complex setting, for example, might frustrate you when it all comes apart. Fluorescent lights are now available, which do *not* emit as much heat. The issue is that to match a tungsten bulb's brightness, you'll need many more fluorescent bulbs. When looking for a lighting set, you always know a continuous set by the plug-in cables attached to the stands.

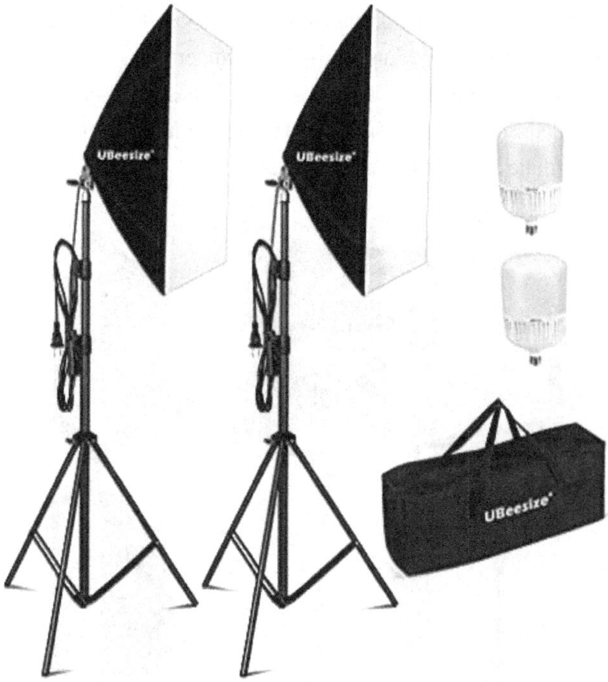

A second difficulty with hot lights is that they *cannot be dimmed.* Few continuous illumination sources provide more than one brightness setting or a basic half-power/full-power switch. Unless you shoot with f2.8-5.6, most lighting isn't strong enough to freeze action at low ISO settings. As painters, studio photographers must have total control over their "controlled environment." Many photographers and videographers use these lights because they are budget-friendly. This setup comes with two lights and a much-needed carrying case. It costs about **$79 on Amazon**. BUY NOW ON AMAZON Affiliate Link. https://amzn.to/3ZkwYxh.

Continuous Lighting - LED Softbox Panels

Over time, the technology for continuous lights has improved greatly, and so has the cost. This is another option to consider when looking at this type of lighting setup. LED lighting has gained massive popularity as a continuous light option.

This is because, unlike other lighting sources, it doesn't tend to emit too much heat. Taking advantage of adjustable color temperature settings, LED lights effectively replicate the feeling of natural light. This set is a dimmable, bi-color, remote-controlled Softbox LED light kit. **It's $283 on Amazon.** BUY NOW ON AMAZON Affiliate Link: https://amzn.to/3IrA4cu

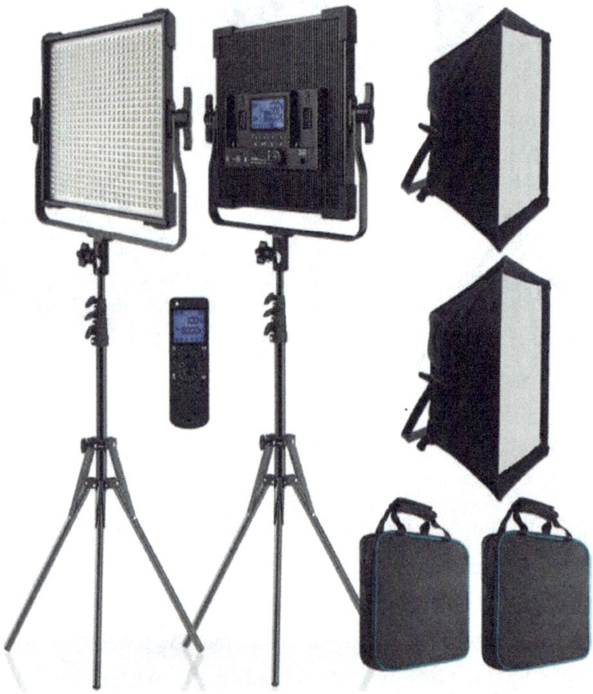

To shape and customize your lighting, modifiers such as softboxes and parabolic reflectors can be used. If you want to record video, LEDs are the way to go. They allow for adjustment of color temperature and have a flicker-free quality, making them suitable for slow motion as well. Many photographers are now expected to produce both video and stills, making LEDs a valuable addition to any studio. This is definitely the next step in studio lighting. But like with all continuous lights, you can't really take it outside the studio, like to a park, unless the tree has a plug-in.

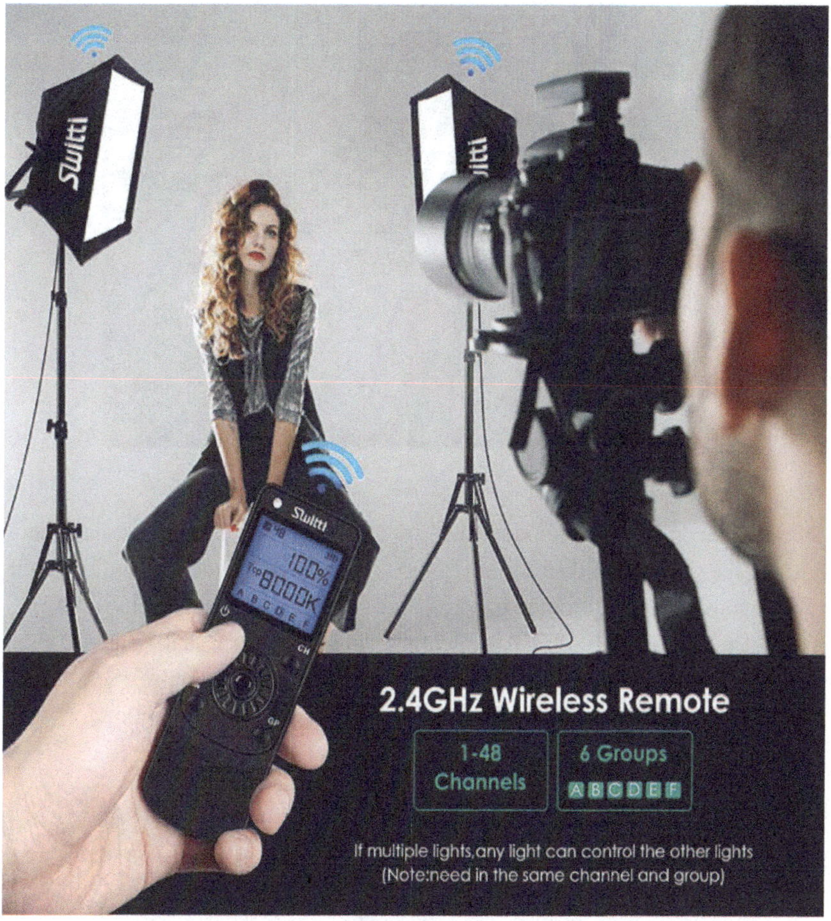

Continuous Lighting - LED Ring Light

As a portrait photographer, nothing is more important than capturing the perfect shot of your subject. That's where ring lights come in - they're a professional favorite for a reason. By providing soft, diffused lighting on your subject, these lights help reduce shadows and are the perfect choice for close-up portraiture.

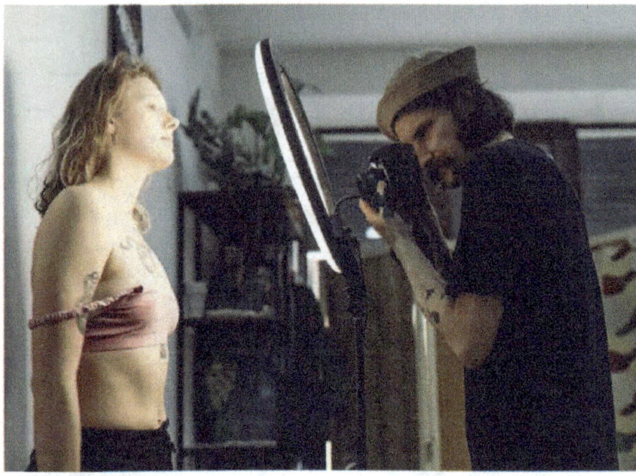

Plus, unlike other lighting options that can make your subject look washed out or change the contours of their face, ring lights allow your subject to "pop" without sacrificing any of their unique features. One sign that a model is facing a ring light? The appearance of circular catchlights in their eyes, instantly adds an extra layer of attraction and engagement to your portrait. Whether you're a seasoned pro or an amateur selfie enthusiast, these lights are the perfect selection for your next photo shoot.

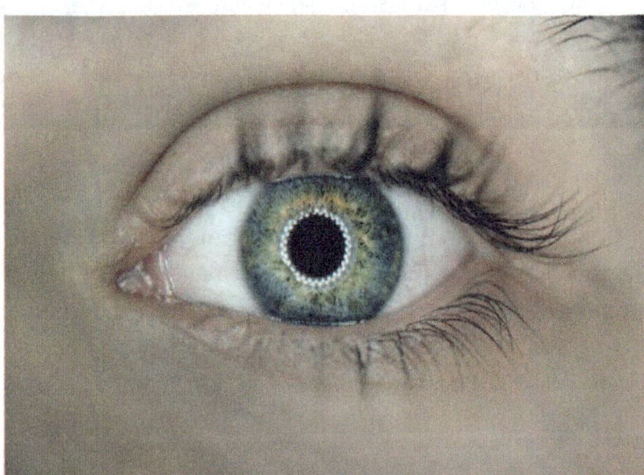

Getting the perfect shot for macro photography can be a challenge. Shadows always seem to sneak up and steal the details you're trying to capture. Fortunately, ring lights provide front-focused lighting that allows you to distribute light around your subject, hiding shadows and emphasizing crucial details.

With a variety of color temperature options, ring lights blend seamlessly with natural light, making it easy to manipulate your environment to get the perfect shot. Don't let shadows ruin your macro shots; use a ring light to bring your subject to life.

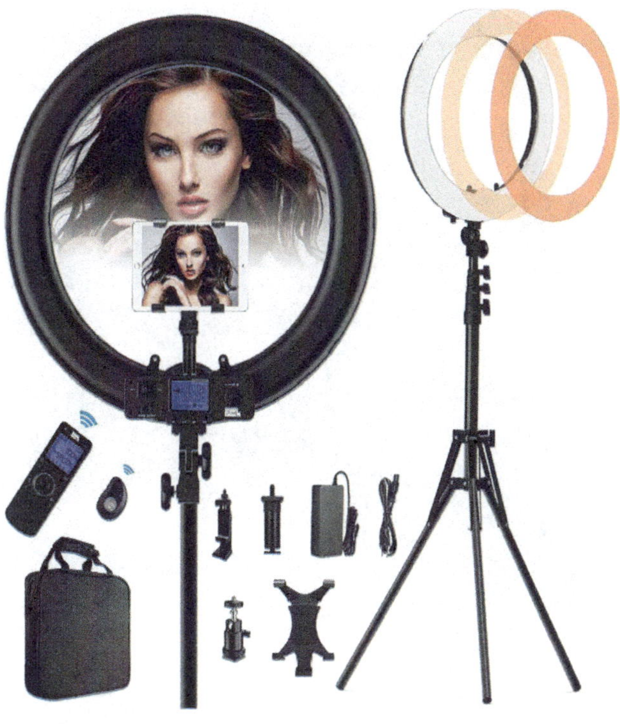

Ring Light with Wireless Remote and iPad Holder, 19 Inch Bi-Color LCD Display Ring Light with Stand and Selfie Remote, 55W 3000-5800K CRI≥97. It is only $127 on Amazon. Here is the Affiliate Link.

Continuous lighting has certain drawbacks that one needs to consider before using it for photography. One of the main disadvantages is its comparatively *low power output when compared to studio flash.* This limits the aperture and shutter speed settings that one can use, which can be a problem if the subjects are moving. Additionally, the brightness of LED lights can be off-putting to models or portrait subjects. Lastly, to use continuous lighting effectively, one needs to have the ability to completely darken the studio or shooting area, as any ambient light can interfere with the scene.

Flash Strobes

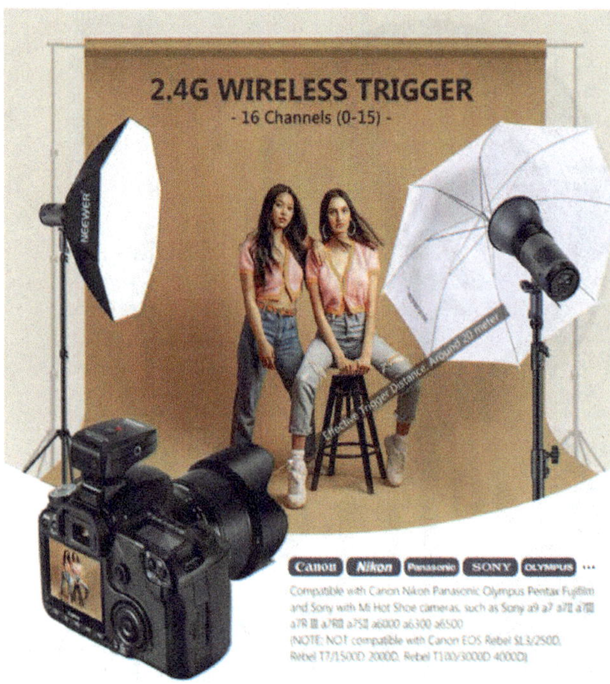

Eventually, though, the day came when it was time to upgrade from my continuous light setup to something more professional: strobe lights! While expensive at first glance, they proved their worth many times over once I got used to how they worked - allowing me to capture stunning images that otherwise would have been impossible for me before then. My journey has come full circle since those days long ago when all I had were some basic continuous lights; now having both options available gives me even greater freedom and creativity than ever before!

Studio lights offer a distinct advantage for professionals due to their power output and precise control. In comparison to LED or continuous lighting, studio flashlights offer greater flexibility with camera settings, such as depth of field. With a quick burst of flash, it's possible to freeze movement, including fast-moving subjects like smashing glasses or splashing water. Additionally, the light can be further modified using various options, which are widely available due to the longevity of studio flash lighting.

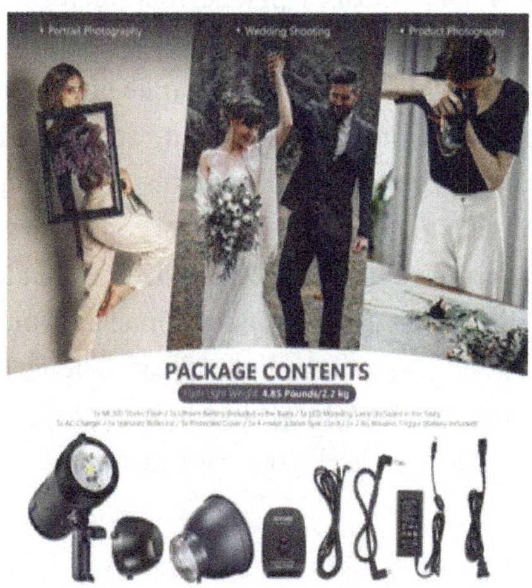

Strobes offer a distinct set of advantages and disadvantages when compared to continuous lights. With a simple activation of your camera's built-in commander mode or an optical trigger, you can synchronize off-camera flashes with your camera's flash. Unlike typical lights, strobes come with both a flash tube and a modeling lamp. The flash tube delivers a burst of light triggered by the remote shutter, while the modeling lamp provides a constant light source for the photographer to work with. In this Neewer strobe you can see the round flash tube in its face. This Neewer ML300 300W Outdoor Studio Flash Strobe Li-ion Battery Powered Monolight with 2.4G Wireless Trigger, 1000 Full Power Flashes, Recycle in 0.4-2.5 Sec. It's $248 on Amazon Affiliate Link.

Discover the difference *between strobes, such as flashes, speedlights, and flash-guns.* Although naming conventions are not standardized, we will provide general categories to help make sense of it all.

On-Camera Flash: This is the flash already built into your camera. Have you ever wished you had more creative control over your on-camera flash? While the smallest strobes built into your camera may be convenient, they offer limited creative opportunities and output. But fear not, because you can use your camera's built-in flash to trigger off-camera flashes!

Speedlight/Flashgun/HotShoeFlash: Upgrade your photography game with speedlights, the next step up from built-in flash. This type of light sits on top of your camera. By separating the flash into a separate unit, you'll get more control over direction, more power from an independent battery source, and customizable features like zoom and light patterns. A speedlight is therefore like a strobe in that it emits a burst of light which you control. Use manual flash power and lighting mods to get the perfect shot. Don't want the hassle of manual settings? Many speedlights have a TTL option for an auto mode. Adjust the zoom to control the distance and width of the light spread. Tilt the head for softer light by bouncing it off a surface. Don't forget to adjust your shutter speed to get the best results - usually 1/250 but check your camera specs.

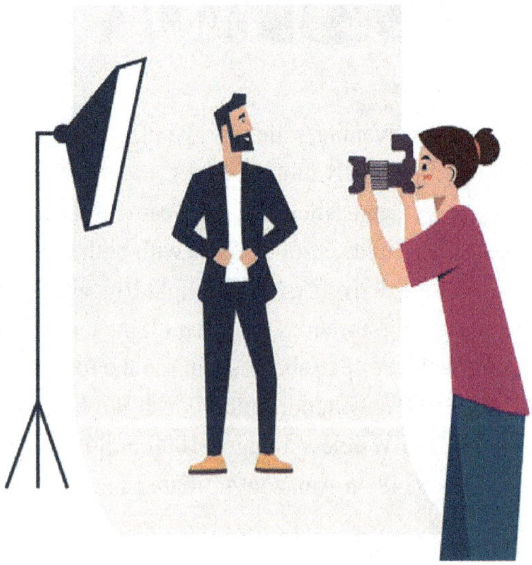

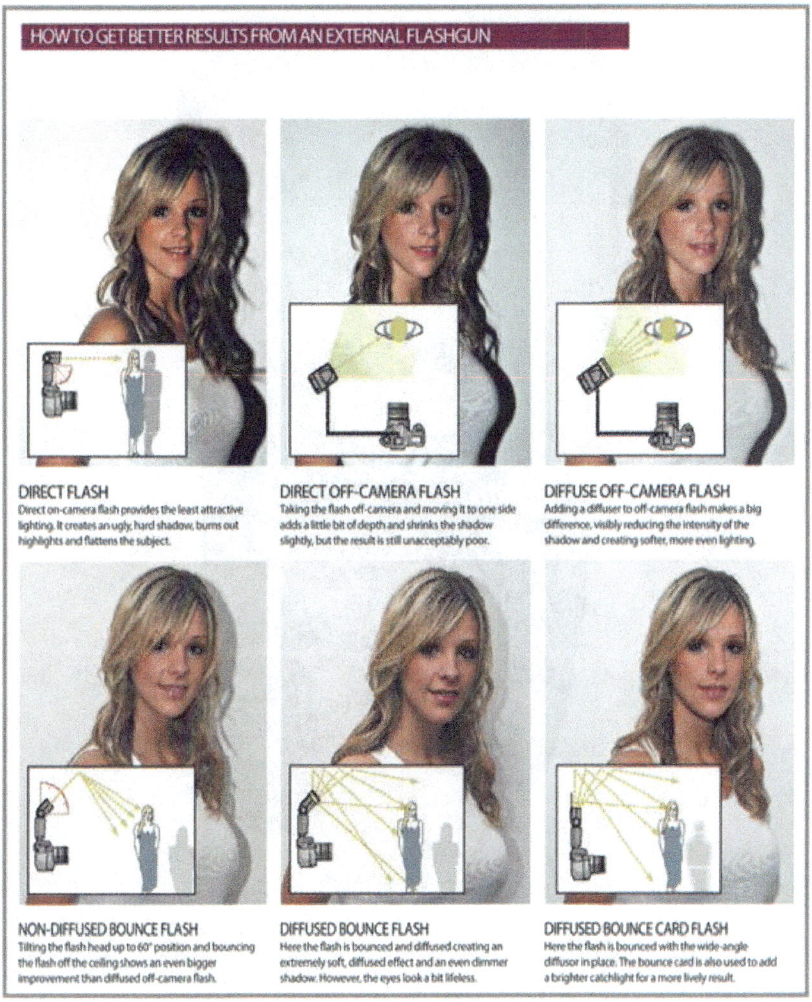

No matter the lighting conditions, you have creative control with this powerful light source. If an area is too bright or not quite right, head into a darker spot and adjust accordingly to create natural-looking shots whenever your heart desires! Go further by achieving high-key backgrounds that look unbelievably neat. - it's so easy to produce ultra-white visuals for a modern vibe.

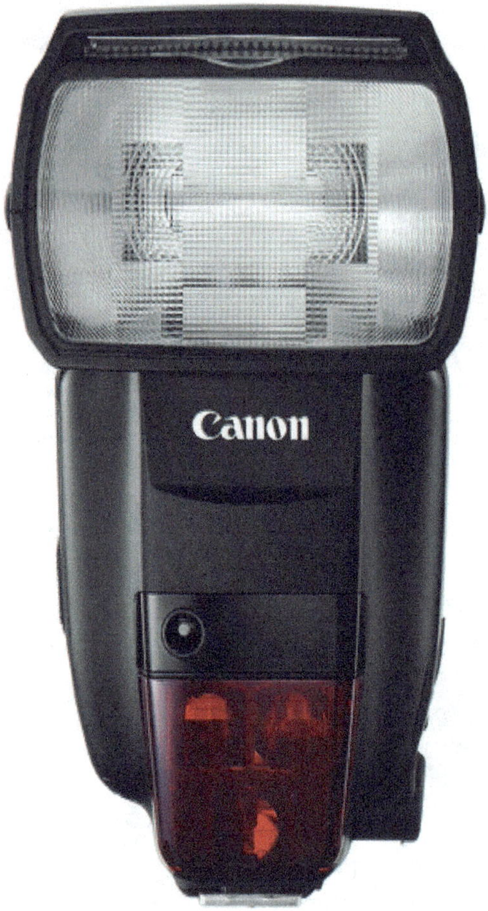

The hot-shoe connection on the camera may attach these lights, which are compact and lightweight. Here's an example of shadow and highlight placement when using the flashgun as the key, fill, and backlighting. Looking for an alternative to the aperture route for flash photography? Nikon offers another solution in their flash photography basics guide - the guide number method. By using the guide number, you can calculate the ideal distance between the subject and the flash for a specific aperture, providing accurate exposure. For instance, a GN of 12 with an aperture of f8 and ISO 100 would result in an ideal distance of 1.5 meters. If your subject is further away, adjusting your ISO or using a flash with a higher GN may be necessary. With a higher GN, your flash can reach greater distances and produce stronger illumination. Check out the illustration from Nikon for a visual guide.

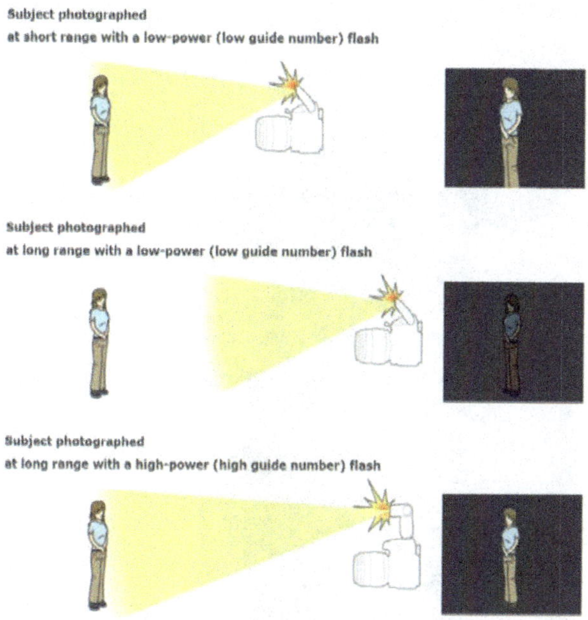

Compare Flashgun Power with Guide Numbers: Though modern flash systems have automated exposure and duration controls, you can still use Guide Numbers to determine their strength. Especially helpful for event and wedding photography, as well as capturing environmental portraits from further away. Allow your photographs to include more of the background with the ease of determining your flashgun's output. With various sizes and diffusion strengths available, there's sure to be an option that suits your needs. They require minimal space and cost while simultaneously providing maximum results: what could be better? Unlocking nature's radiance has never been easier, thanks to light diffusers.

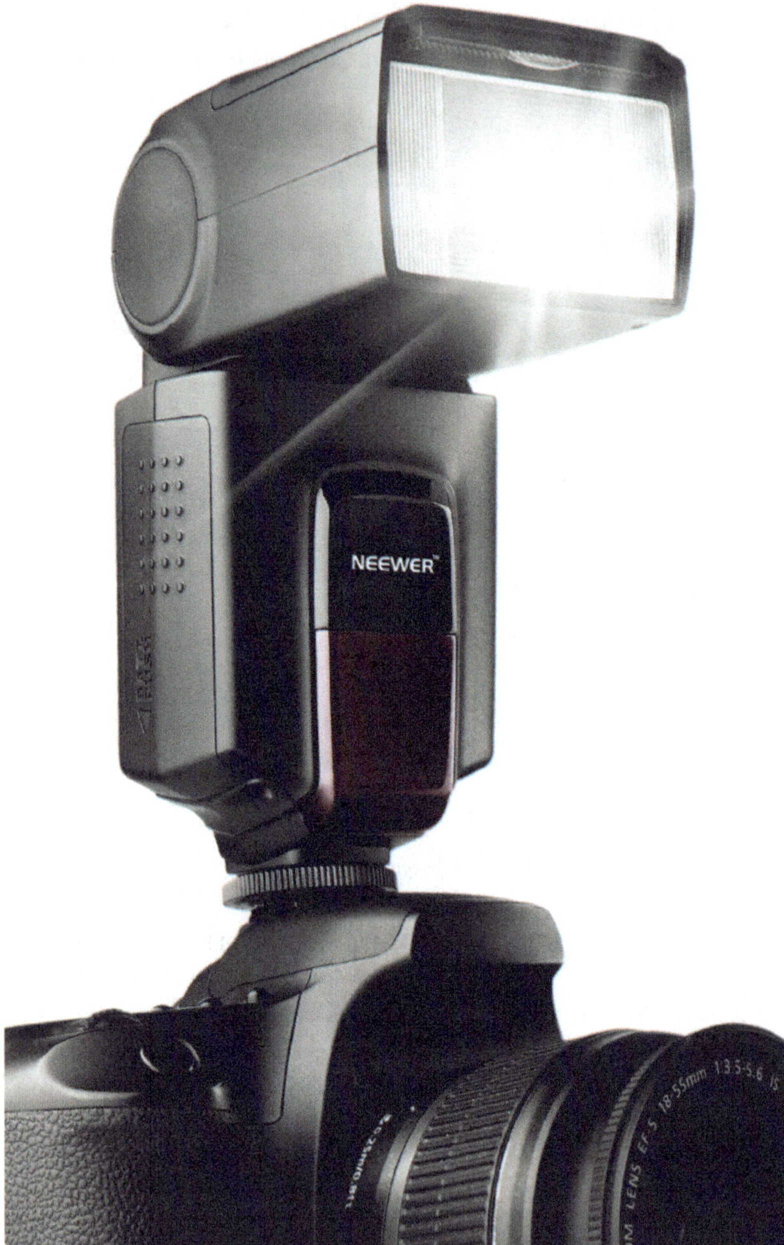
NEEWER
18-55mm 1:3.5-5.6 IS

They vary per camera manufacturer. Or you can buy his *universal brand Neewe*r. Neewer TT560 Flash Speedlite for Canon Nikon Panasonic Olympus Pentax and Other DSLR Cameras. Digital Cameras with Standard Hot Shoe. It's only $69 on Amazon Affiliate Link.

Flash Strobe Monolights:

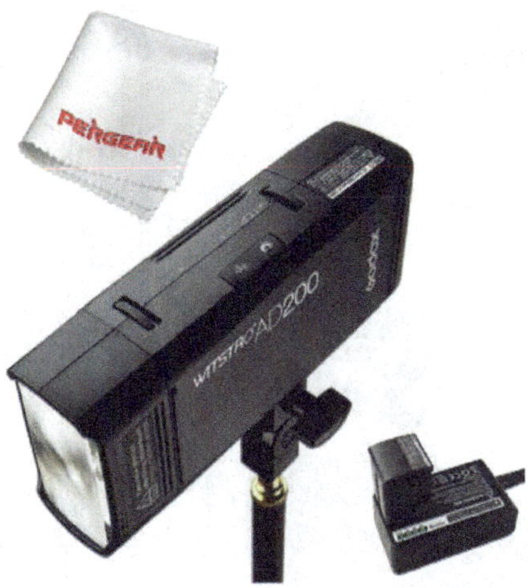

Looking for more power from your photography strobe? Consider monolights or strobe heads. These big guns pack a punch that basic speedlights can't match. Monolights have everything you need integrated into one easy-to-use unit, while strobe heads require a separate power pack. The larger size means you won't have to change batteries as frequently, and they're designed for more frequent flash use. Some monolights are smaller than you might expect, like the Godox AD200 with its hybrid design. Say goodbye to limitations and hello to stunning photography with improved strobe lighting. It's $299 on Amazon Affiliate Link.

Umbrellas

Umbrella modifiers are inexpensive and can be obtained in most photography studios. Sizes range from small to extra-large, with various colors and patterns, including white, silver, and even gold zebra prints on the inside (known as "shoot-thru"). When a light source is focused toward the umbrella's center, the light is dispersed or diffused as rays return to the source.

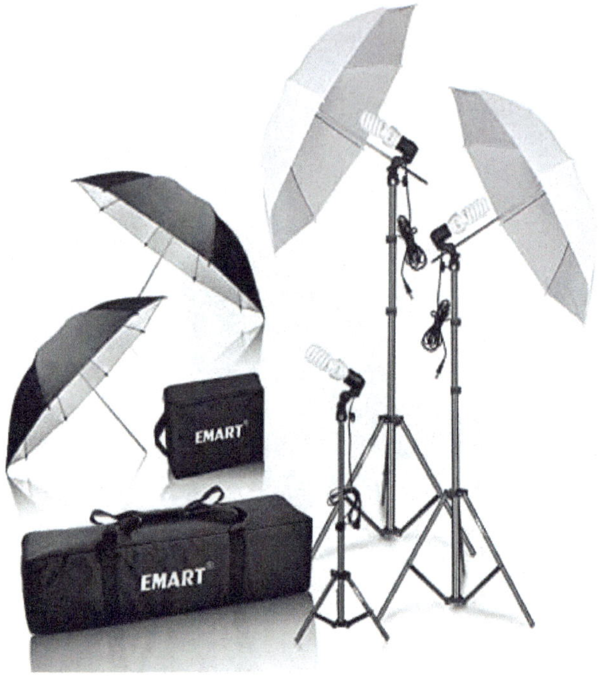

Umbrellas are the ultimate in mobility and set up fast. When two are used, they're ideal for covering a large group of people. Product photography studios aren't the most incredible place to use an umbrella. Having no control over the light is at the root of this issue. Employing "flags" or black cards may be necessary to block light from particular sections of your picture, since diffused light spreads across a large surface. **They are about $80 on Amazon.** BUY NOW ON AMAZON Affiliate Link.

Softboxes

There are many types of softboxes. When using one, the further distance the light source looks to the subject, the softer and more diffused the light. Umbrellas and softboxes diffuse and soften the light, but softboxes do it differently. They are usually rectangular boxes constructed of opaque black material on the exterior, lined with diffusion material on the inside (white or silver). They commonly contain an extra white diffusion panel called a baffle, which sits several inches from the light. There is an additional layer of white diffusing material on top of the softbox open front. The design creates a gentle light source that can be directed and dimmed.

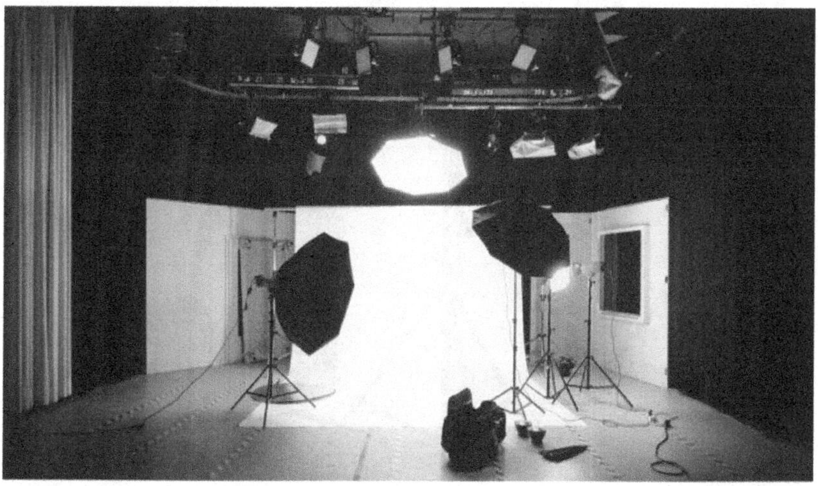

A Velcro-attached front grid is standard on most high-quality brands if a photographer needs extra security. A rectangle catchlight is produced on the subject using softboxes. There are certain drawbacks to softboxes, mainly the size. To film on location, you'll need to disassemble the boxes unless you have a large car or truck to transport them fully assembled. Although some brands are quicker to assemble, the work may not be worth it if you're on a tight schedule. As far as the price goes, they're more expensive than regular umbrellas, making them unaffordable for those just starting. Small softboxes may be attached to camera flash guns, while larger ones can light automobiles and trucks. And these softboxes can range in size from 24 inches by 36 inches to 30 inches by 60 inches.

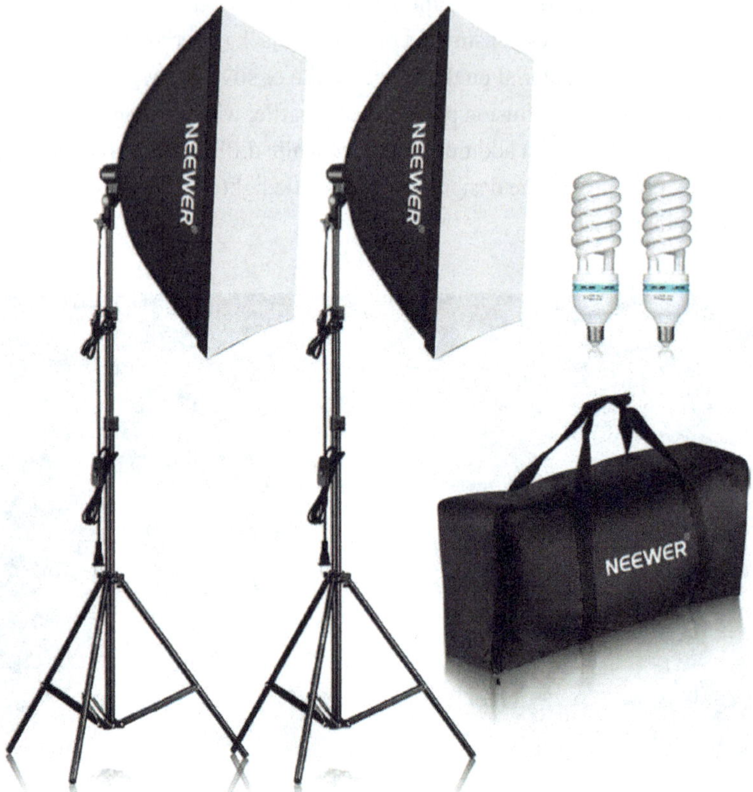

NEEWER 700W Equivalent Softbox Lighting Kit, 2Pack 5500K CFL Lighting Bulbs, 24x24 inches Softboxes with E27 Socket, Photography Continuous Lighting Kit. This is a great brand with a great price of $111.99 on Amazon. Here is the Affiliate Link.

Grids

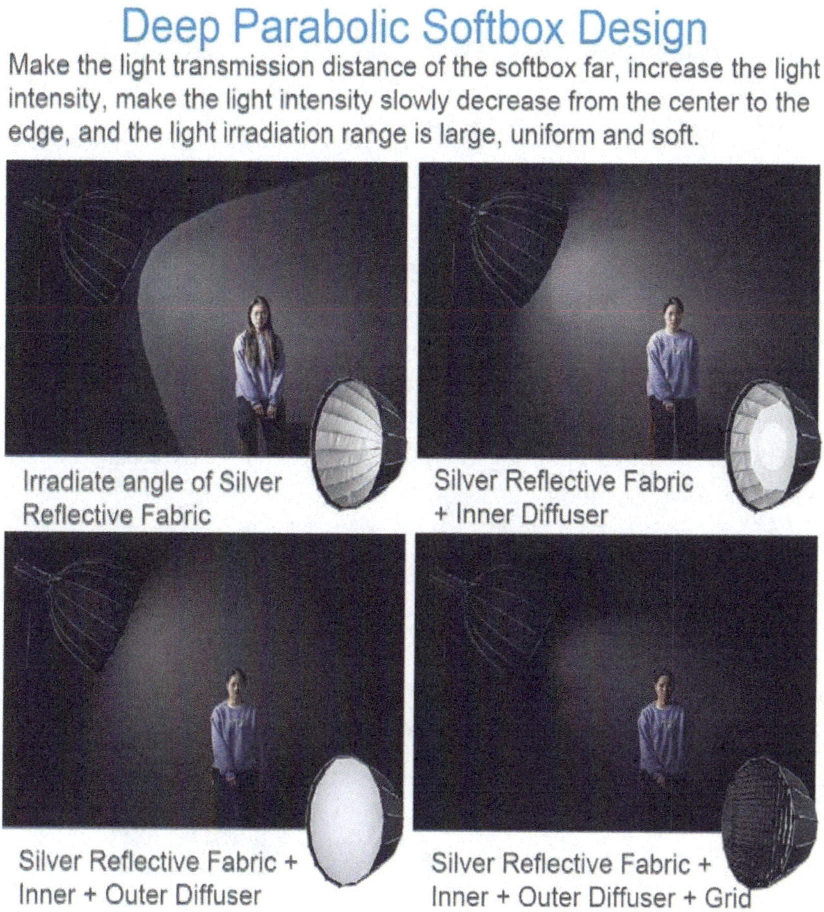

Modifiers known as grids connect to the front of the tiny conical reflector of a studio light. They narrow the light beams and alter the shadows' edge, feathering by directing the light. The most common hole designs are 10, 20, 30, and 40 degrees. The narrow beam of light produced by a 10° grid has harsh shadows, but the larger beam produced by a 40° grid has softer edges. Much of our work involves grids, and we use them all the time. When placed on a backdrop light, they may cast a circle of light over a background or emphasize a specific region of the subject brightly. In fashion and portrait photography, they frequently highlight a model's hair.

This Parabolic Softbox 35.4 inch/90cm Quick Setup Deep Soft Box II with Honeycomb Grid and Bowens Mount for Studio Monolight LED Light Photography, is just $115 at the Amazon Affiliate Link.

Gobo

Using a gobo, you can alter the way light shines. They may be found in various materials and sizes with many options. They are often employed on background lighting to produce fascinating backgrounds, like light streaming through a window or a mottled look. A Gobo example is the laser spotlight. Moving Head Lights LED Stage Lights Spot 8 Color RGBW Gobos with Magical Circle 50W DMX for DJ Disco Party Lights by U`King (White). Costs about $115 on Amazon. Amazon Affiliate Link.

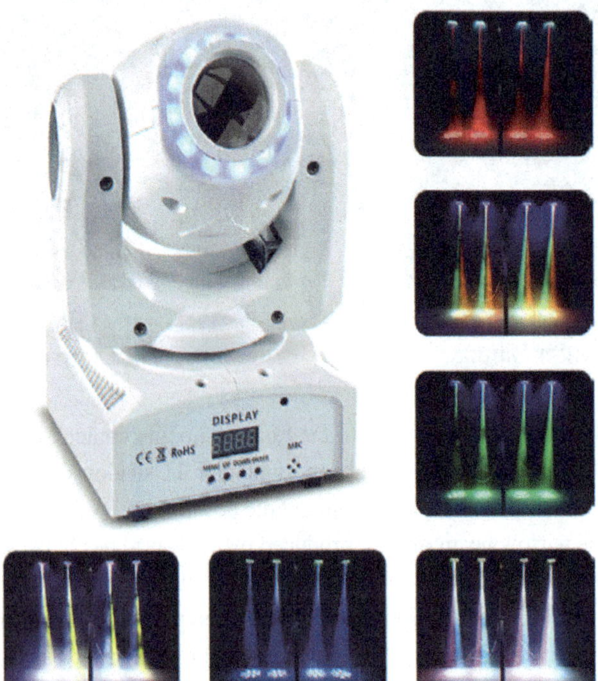

Snoot

As well as being attached to the top of your light fixture, this cone-shaped attachment is permanently attached to the housing. It provides firm shadow edges and circular forms when placed on backdrops. An object's spotlight or a particular portion of your photograph might occasionally be highlighted with a snoot, and they've only been used a few times in our studio. **They are just under $30 on Amazon**. BUY NOW ON AMAZON Affiliate Link

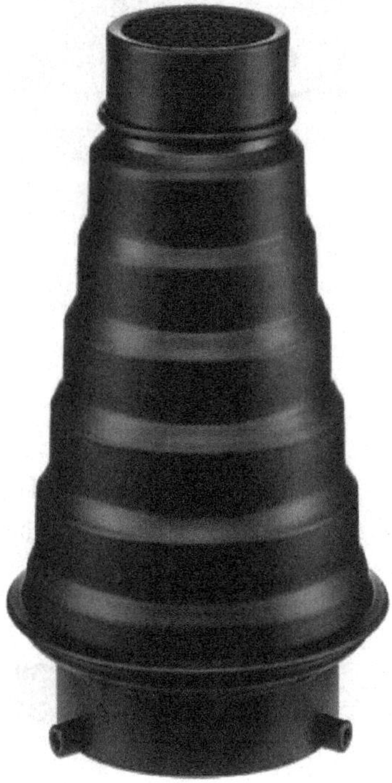

Color Gels

Transparent colored sheets may be positioned before a light or used with other modifiers like a grid. Color gels are used frequently in the studio to add depth, dimension, and atmosphere to photographs. Studio equipment would be incomplete without them; they come in every hue. They're also inexpensive, so have some fun with them. **They are about $15 on Amazon.** BUY NOW ON AMAZON Affiliate Link

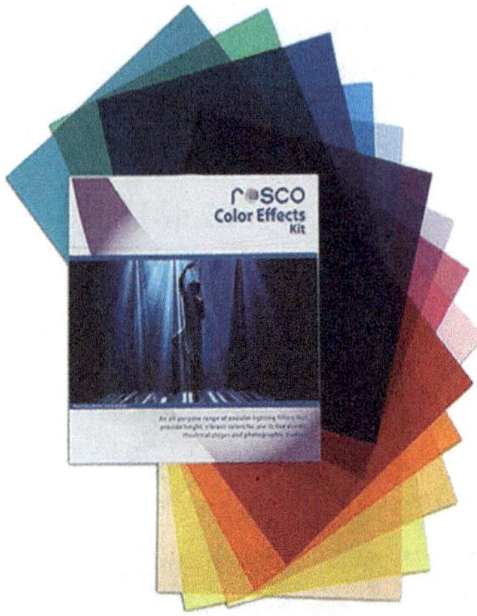

Use a Tripod

When choosing a tripod, consider where you'll use it. Indoors? Don't worry about it being as sturdy or lightweight. Outdoors? The wind is your biggest obstacle. So opt for the sturdiest, heaviest tripod you can still carry to hold your gear steady in anything more than a light breeze.

Max. Height		Max. Extended Height		Folded Length		Min. Height With Optional Short Column		Weight		Max. Load		Max. Leg Tube Diameter	
cm	inch	cm	inch	cm	inch	cm	inch	kg	lb	kg	lb	mm	inch
128	50.39	178	70.08	43	16.93	19	7.48	1.15	2.20	20	44	28	1.10

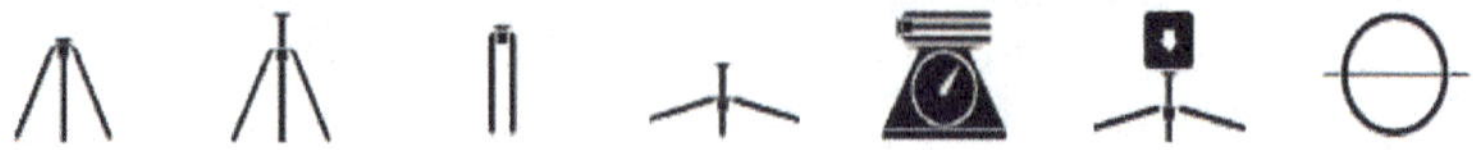

Get the right tripod for your camera by considering its weight and the maximum load of the tripods you're checking out. Don't use a heavy-duty tripod meant for a large DSLR if all you have is a compact mirrorless camera with a pancake lens. You can also get special heads for the top of the tripod.

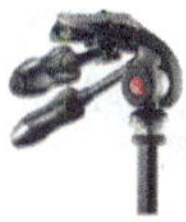
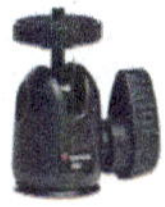
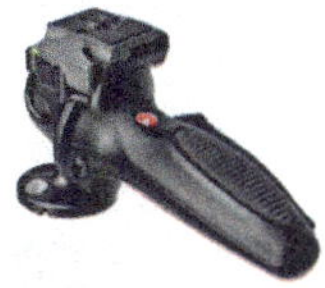

Do you want a center colom?

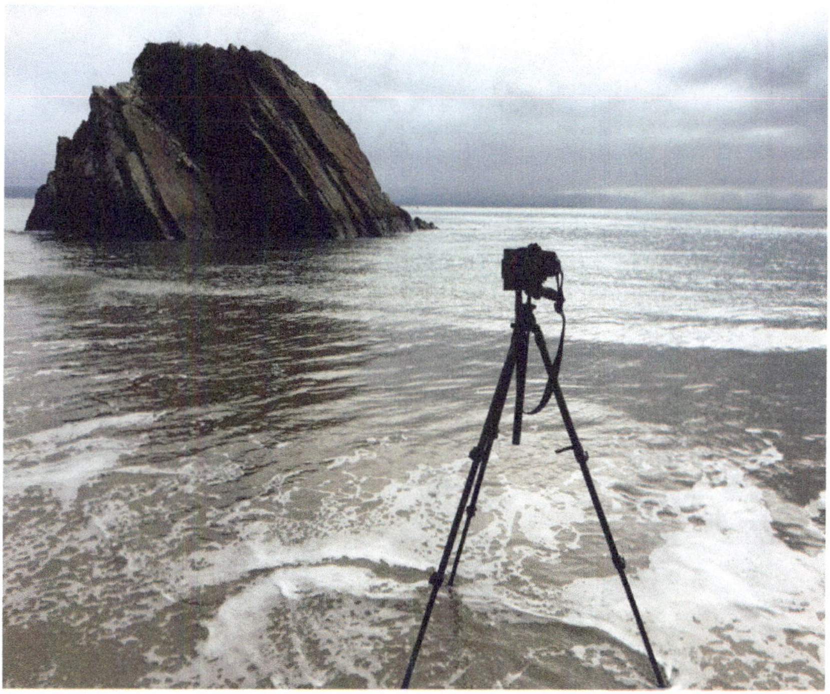

Lastly, do you want carbon fiber or not? Manfrotto Befree 3-Way Live Advanced Camera Tripod kit, Aluminium Travel Tripod, Lever Lock, with 3-Way Fluid Head, for Photo and Video, Vlogging Equipment, with Carry Bag (MKBFR-LA4BK-3WUS). **It costs $249.99 on Amazon Affiliate Link.**

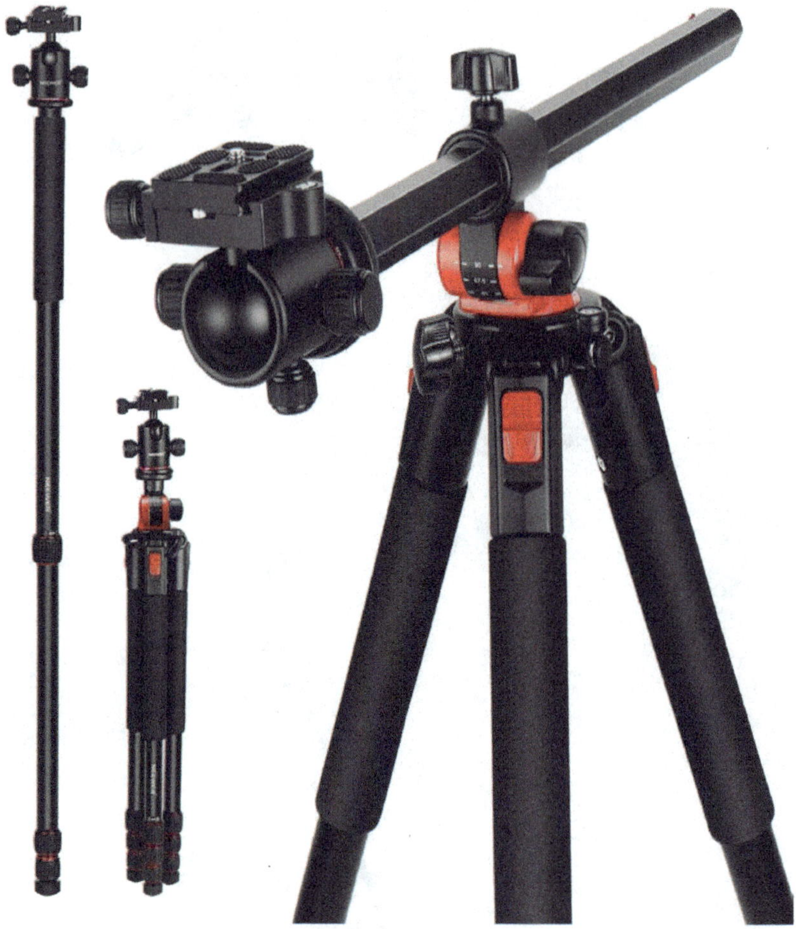

NEEWER 72 inch Camera Tripod Monopod with Center Column and Ball Head Aluminum, Arca Type QR Plate, Bag, Horizontal Tripod Overhead Camera Mount for DSLR Camera, Video Camcorder, Max Load: 33lb. **It costs only $108 on Amazon Affiliate Link.**

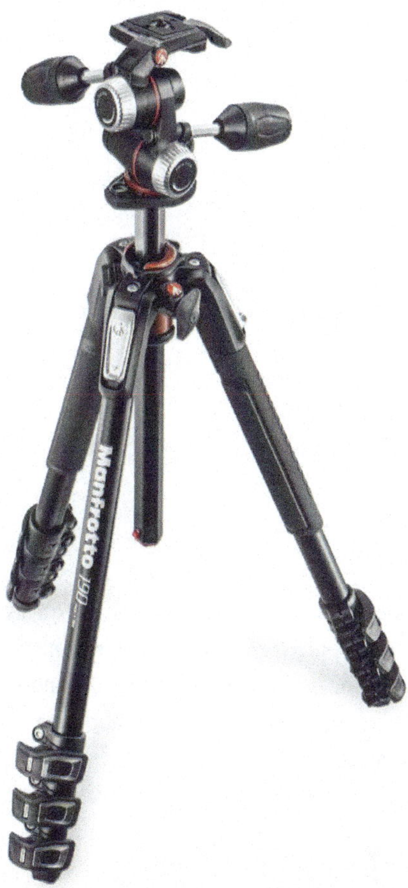

Top of the line is the Manfrotto Aluminum 4-Section Tripod Kit with 3-Way Head (MK190XPRO4-3W). It costs $325 on the Amazon Affiliate Link. This is one of my favorite tripod lines. Manfrotto has been in the business for a very long time and all of their equipment it 5 star rated.

8

POSING PEOPLE

Becoming a top-notch photographer requires an eye for detail and the ability to make people feel comfortable in front of your lens. After all, capturing beautiful portraits doesn't just depend on perfect technique - it's also down to successfully coaxing genuine emotion and connection from your subjects. From experienced models to self-conscious amateurs; with encouragement and patience, you can get amazing shots no matter who's posing for you!

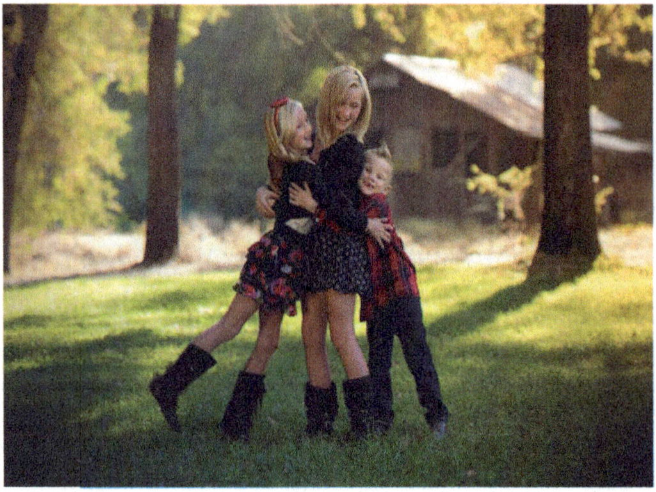

Although I have previously discussed depth of field in previous Chapters, it becomes more intricate and complex when choosing your actual poses. You can easily lose sharpness if you don't understand how to correctly pick your focal length, distance, etc.

Posing People and Depth of Field

The aperture is one of three elements that govern *exposure* and *depth of field* on your camera. It is expressed in terms of the actual opening of your lens and is measured in *f stops*.

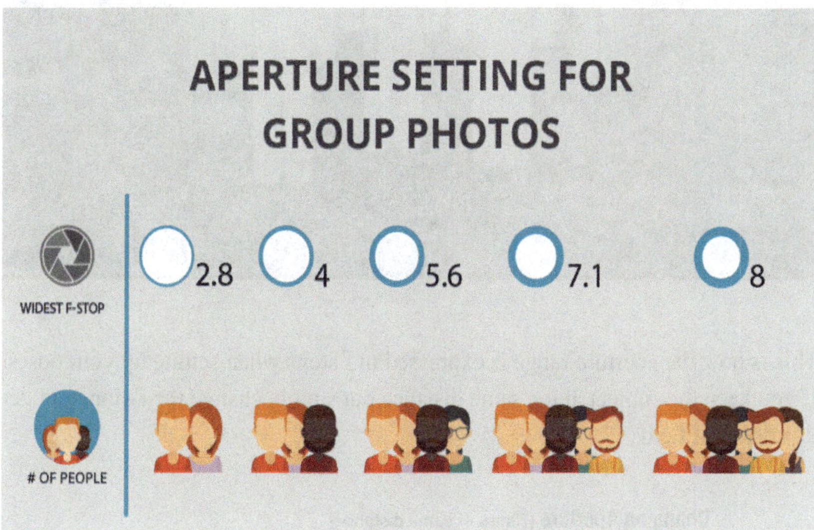

Depth of field (DOF) simply refers to the range of sharp focus in front of and behind the main subject. In this illustration, the center row is the focal plane and the primary focus. The extent of this depth of field is determined by the aperture setting you choose. While this wording can be confusing, this illustration helps explain it better.

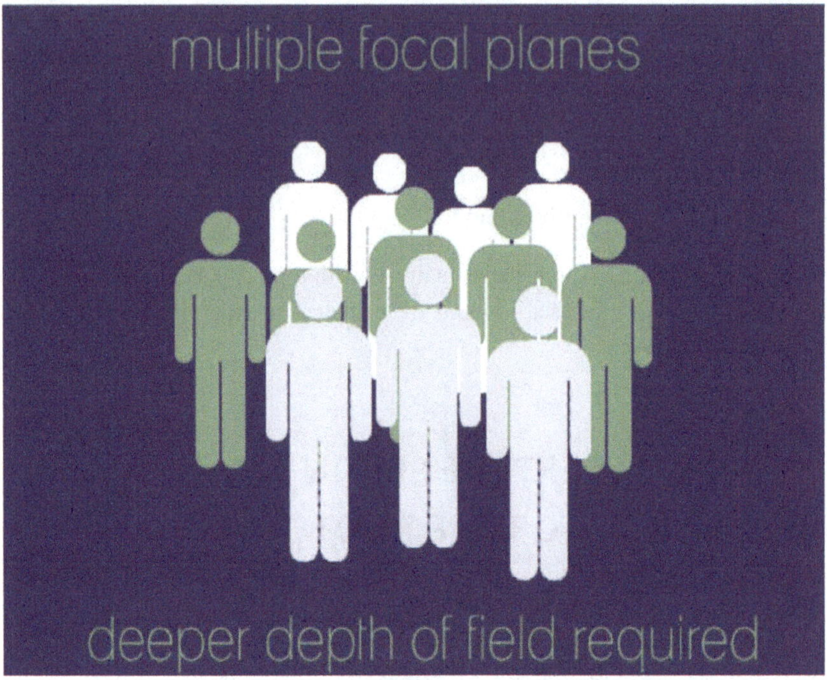

This is how the aperture range is expressed in f stops when setting up your poses. If you keep the subject at the same distance but simply change the f-stop, you get this depth of field:

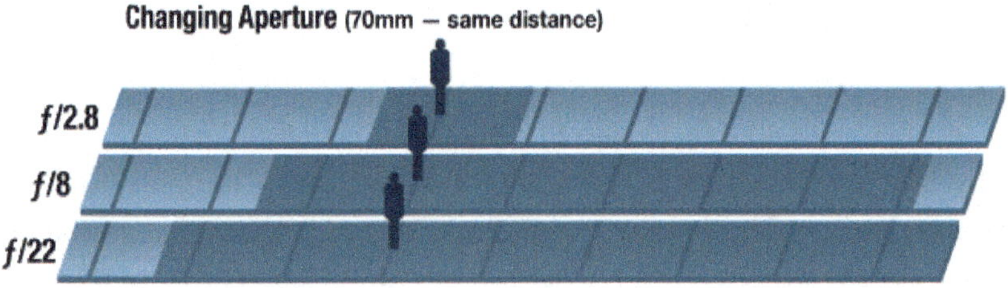

Low f stop number (e.g., f/2.8) and wide aperture result in a shallow depth of field, or a tiny region of focus in front of and behind your subject.

Wider apertures (e.g., f/32) are used when the backdrop of an image, such as one of a flower or a person, is hazy and everything else is out of focus. See example.

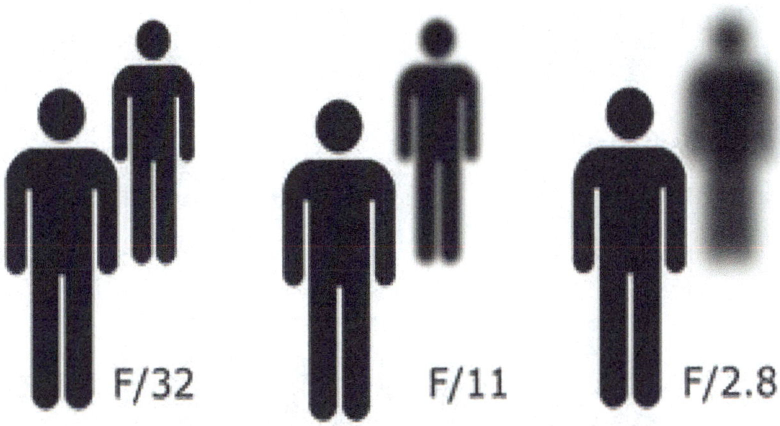

Focal Length

Your camera lens's focal length also impacts the DOF in different sizes of groups. If two lenses are focused at the same place and are both at f/4, the DOF on the 600mm lens will be smaller than on the 24mm lens. Getting that tight DOF is one of the main justifications for using longer lenses when taking portraits. See illustrations.

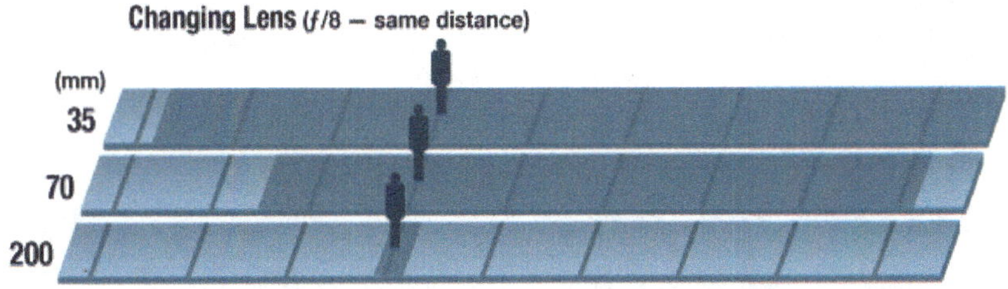

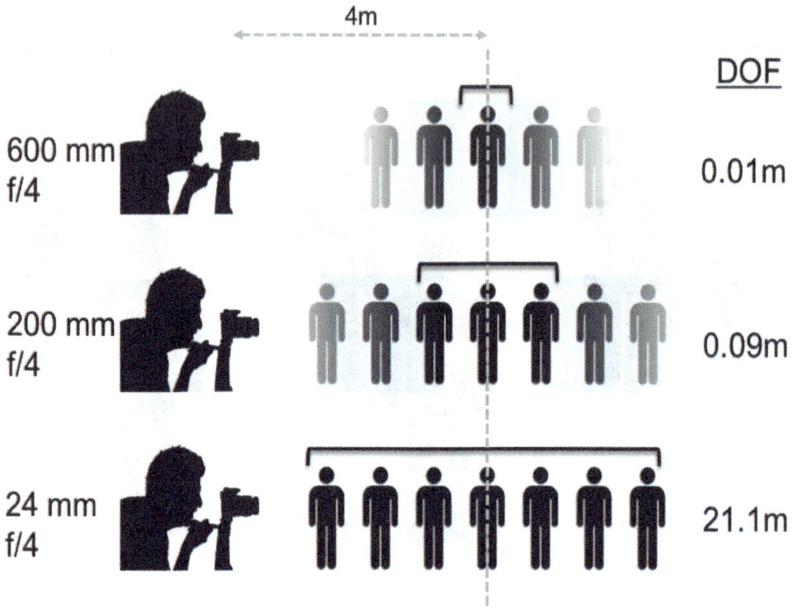

Focal Distance

Now, the depth of field also decreases with increasing distance from the subject and visa versa. As depicted in the below illustrations, a lower f-number corresponds to a narrower depth of field. A higher f-number expands the focus range, allowing for sharper details over a greater distance. If you encounter difficulties achieving accurate focus, adjusting the aperture to extend your depth of field can be a helpful strategy.

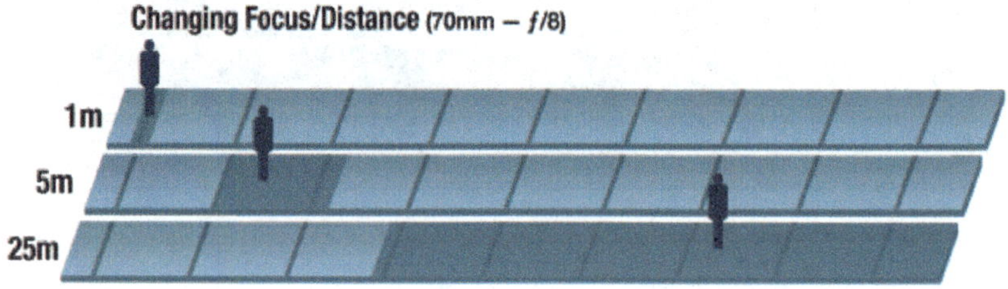

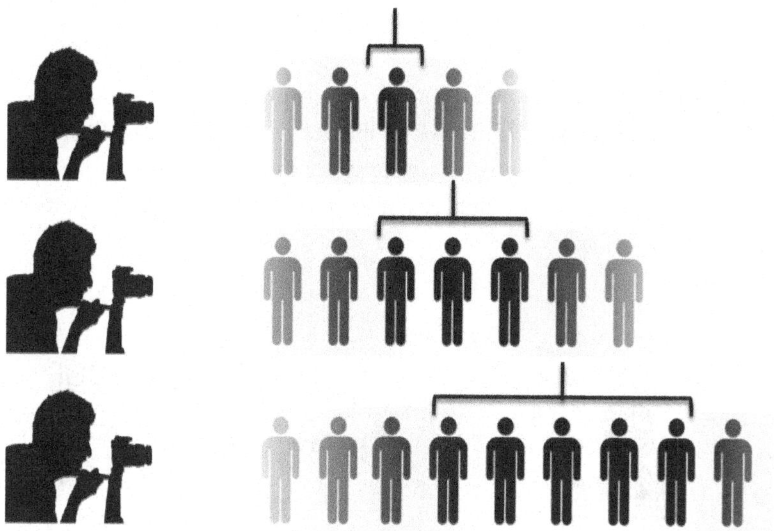

HyperFocal Distance

Essentially, this combines the above examples from before. There is a focal distance that will cause an endlessly big DOF for any focal length and aperture. You will have a DOF at this distance that extends from the point where you are in relation to the focal point all the way out to infinity. Landscape designers should be mindful of this. This number varies depending on the aperture and focal length, so make sure your lenses are in working order.

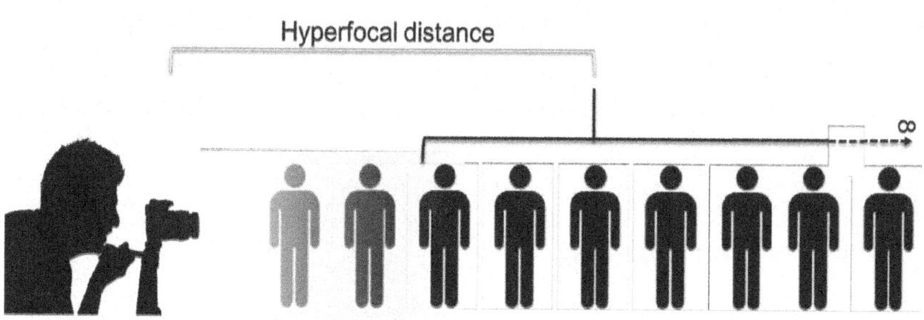

The Crop Factor

The crop factor refers to the distinction between two types of DSLR cameras: full-frame (FF) and cropped (APS-C). This differentiation is primarily based on the size of their sensors. A full-frame camera sensor matches the dimensions of a frame of "6mm film, while a cropped sensor is 1.6 times smaller (1.5 times smaller for Nikon cameras).

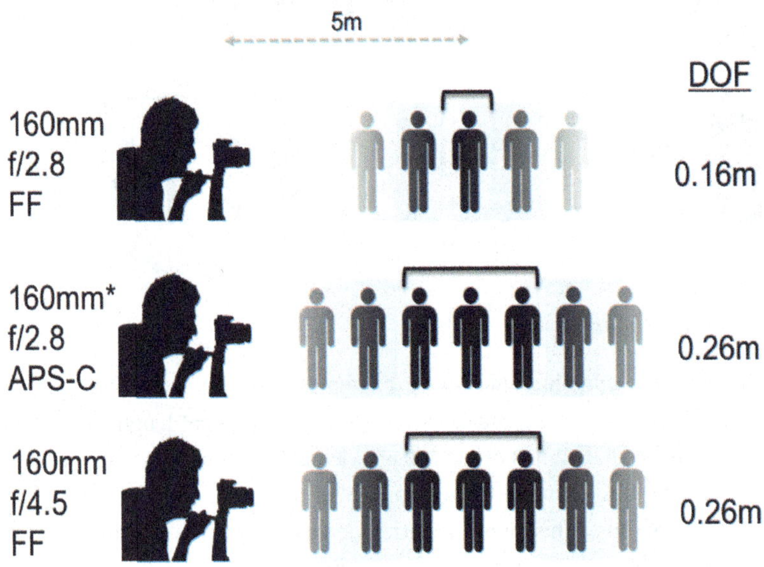

Various sensor sizes possess distinct characteristics, including those influencing depth of field (DOF). However, delving into the intricacies of sensor qualities is beyond this discussion and is covered in other Chapters. What is noteworthy is that sensor size directly impacts DOF.

Posing People and Triangles

In the next chapter, "Composition Techniques," I explore the many options that photographers have at their disposal when composing an image. However, when it comes to posing for portraits, I strongly believe that understanding how triangles can complement various poses is essential when setting them up. There are many techniques to incorporate triangles in photography composition. Let's explore five of them:

Group Triangles: Group shoots get a lot more fun with the addition of triangles. Finding a creative way to find this simple shape in your next shoot can transform it from ordinary to extraordinary. Naturally, there's no need to go on a hunt for specifically triangular objects to make your images interesting. Triangles can be simply implied and incorporated in the arrangement of the subjects' bodies and heads within an image. The triangle shape holds an appealing quality as it enables the eye to effortlessly navigate around the group, creating a pleasant visual flow. Here are several examples.

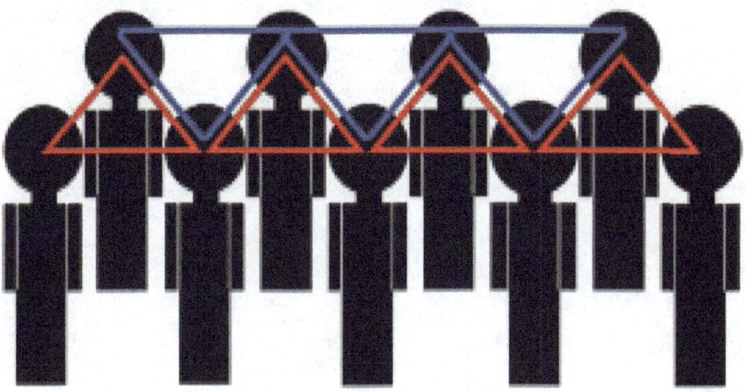

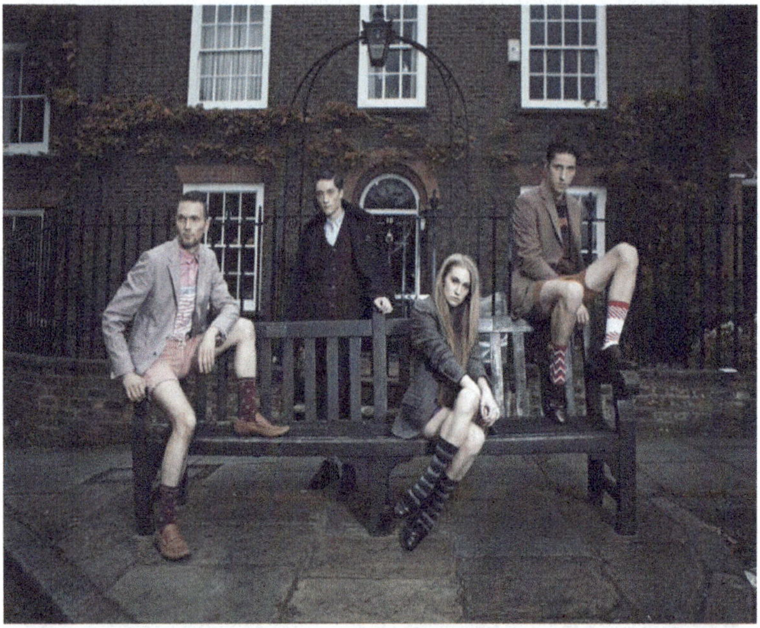

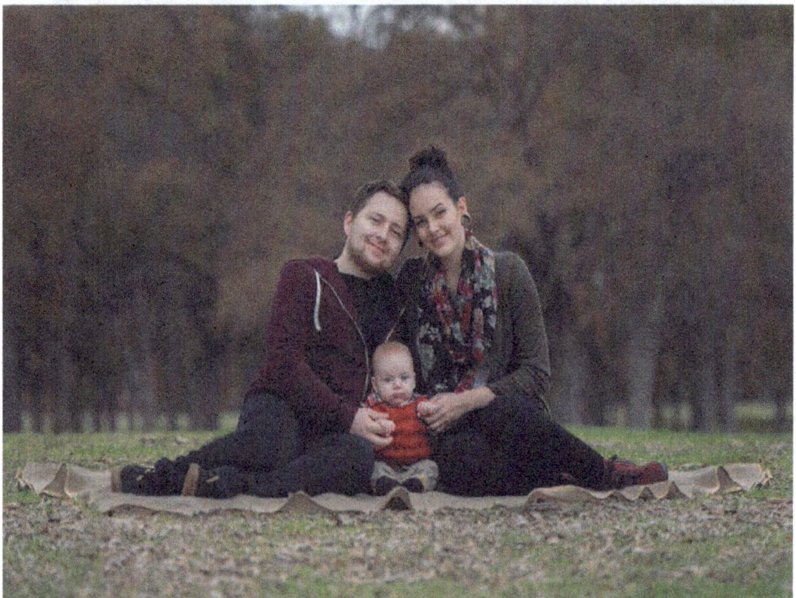

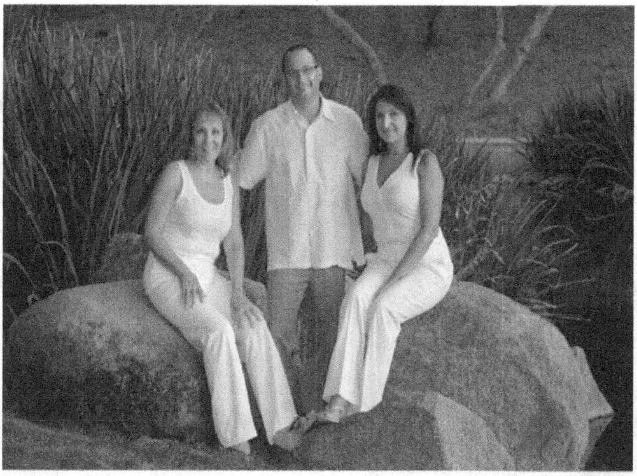

Implying Triangles: Suggesting triangles through the placement or arrangement of objects or subjects within the frame. They can be subtle, but that's what makes them fun to find and set up.

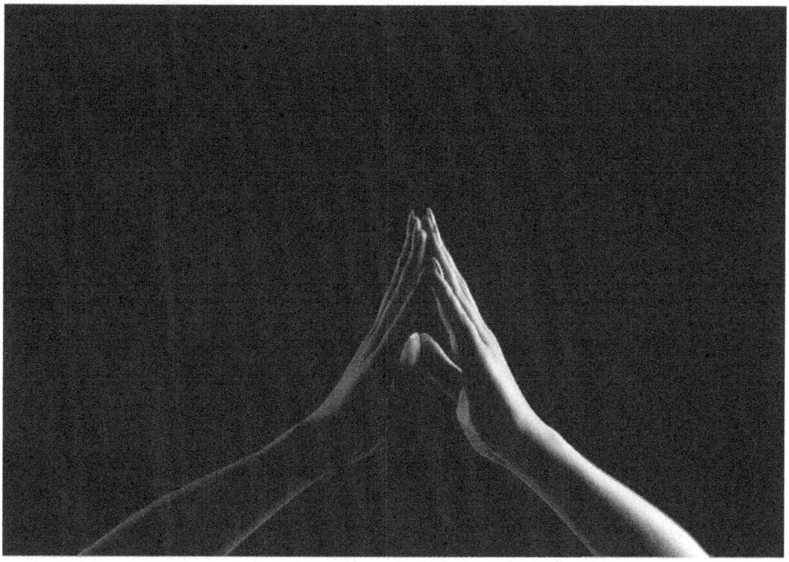

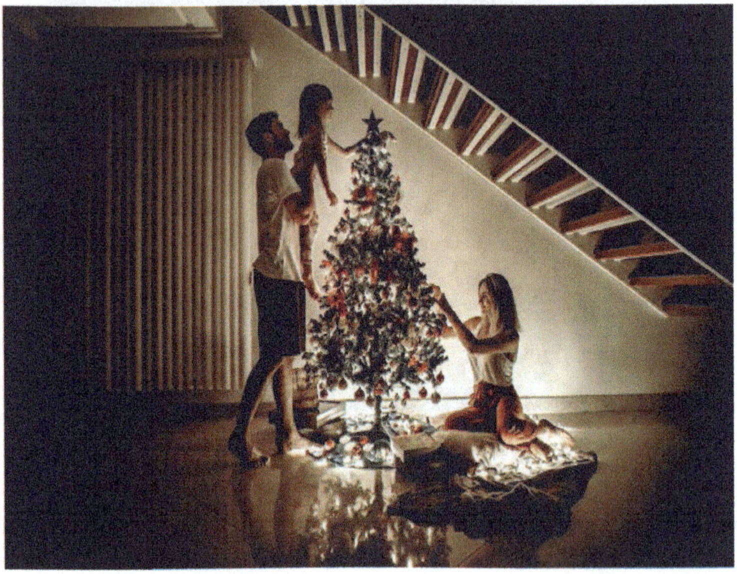

Creating Triangles with Limbs: using the positioning of limbs, such as arms or legs, to form triangular shapes within the composition.

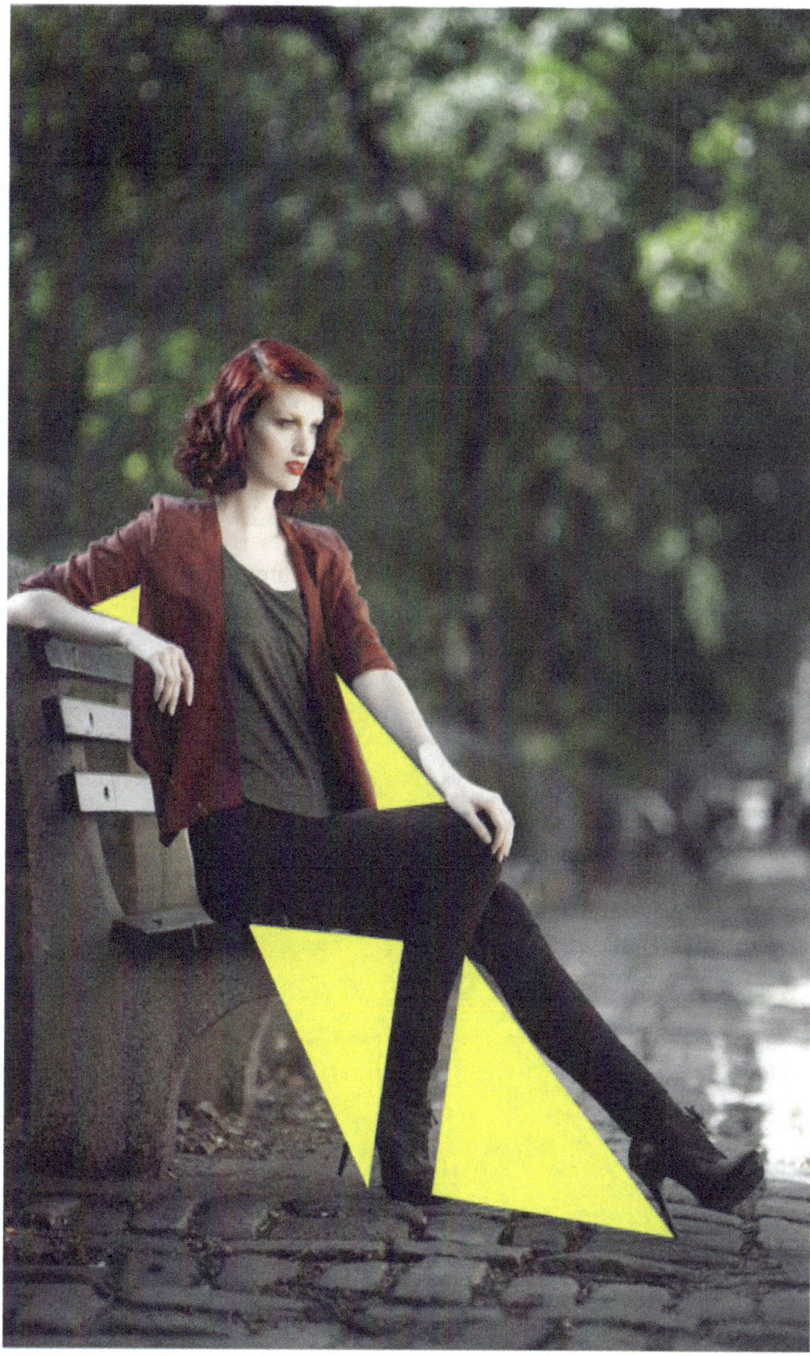

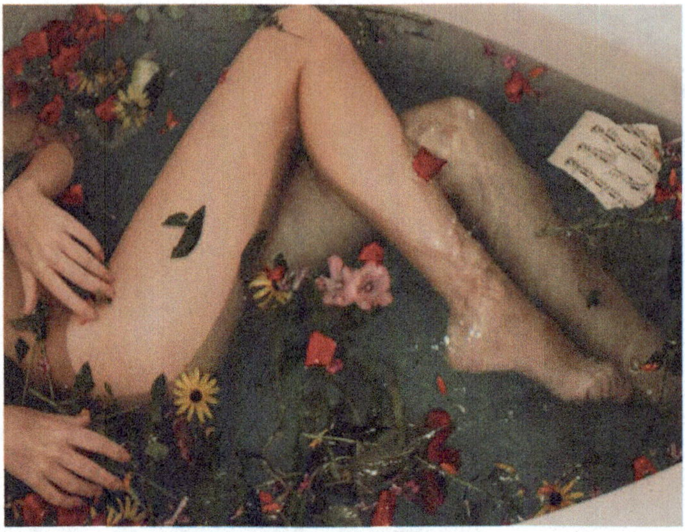

Triangles in the Landscape: Identifying naturally occurring or man-made triangular elements within the landscape and incorporating them into your composition.

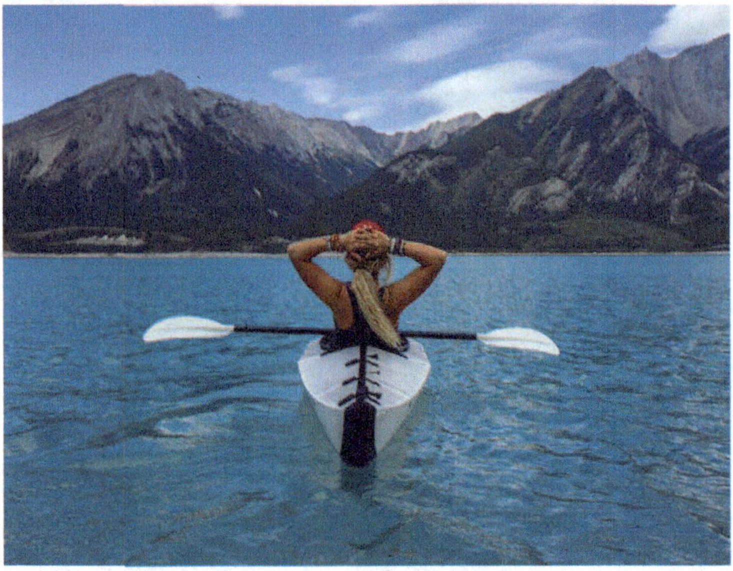

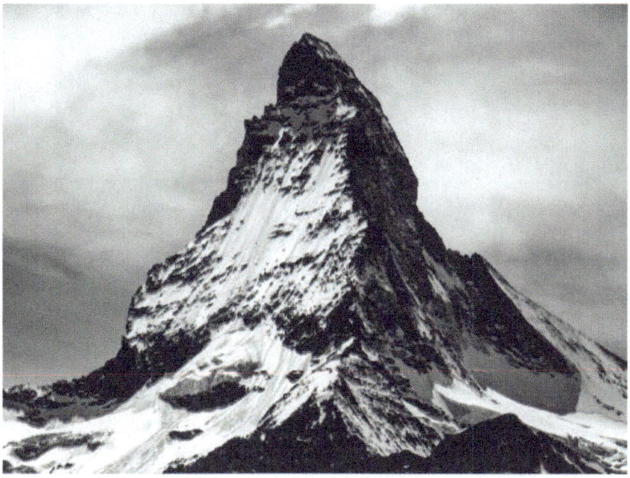

Triangles in our Surroundings: Discovering existing triangular elements in the environment and framing them within your composition.

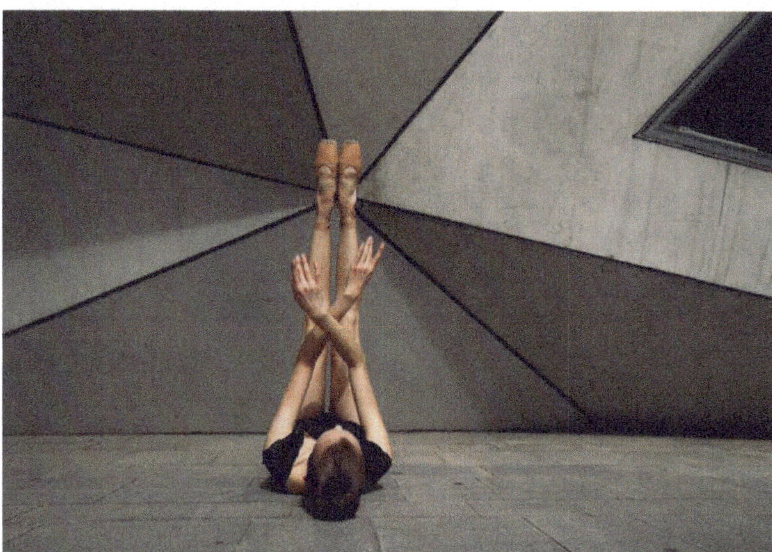

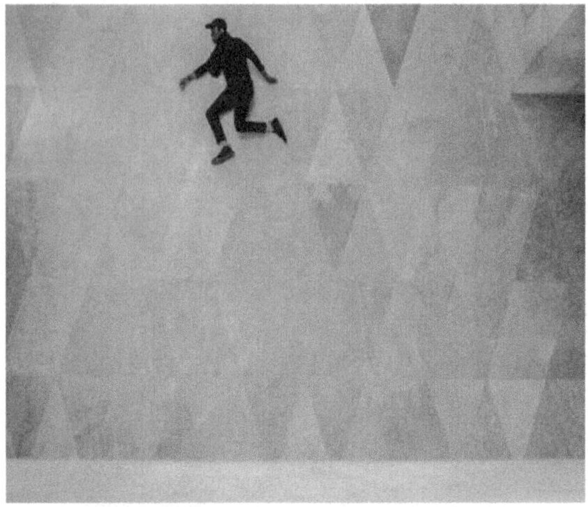

Triangles for Individuals: When a subject bends their arms and place them on their hips or head, the gap in the arms creates a triangular shape. This simple but dynamic pose adds an element of intrigue, guiding the viewer's eye to explore the image.

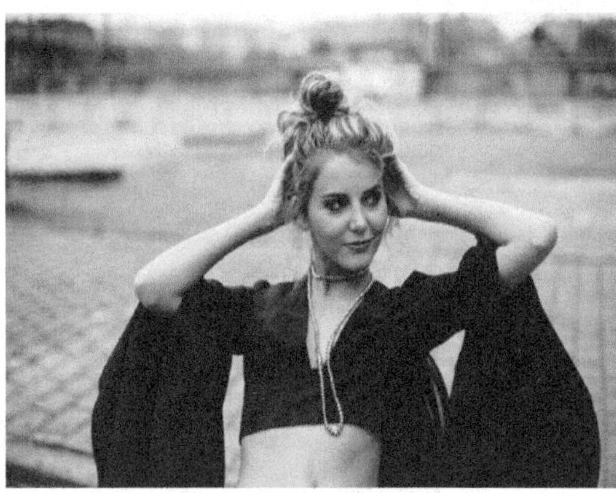

By utilizing these techniques, you can enhance the visual impact of your photographs through the strategic use of triangles in composition. Without this dynamic shape, they would simply be looking at someone standing still with nowhere else for them to look.

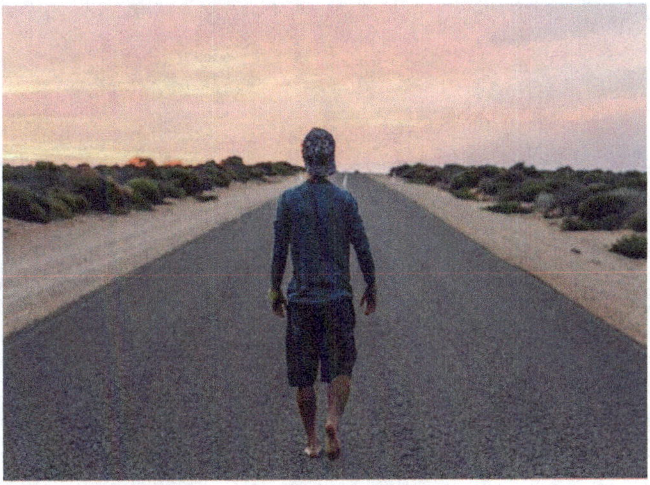

Posing Groups Ideas

Posing Groups #1: *Capture tenderness*. Capture the tenderness between two people in your next photo shoot by having them tilt their heads against each other and hold one another gently. From piggyback rides to hand-holding, a romantic date night can create memorable moments with just enough drama as they bask together in front of a sunrise or stroll down an enchanting path.

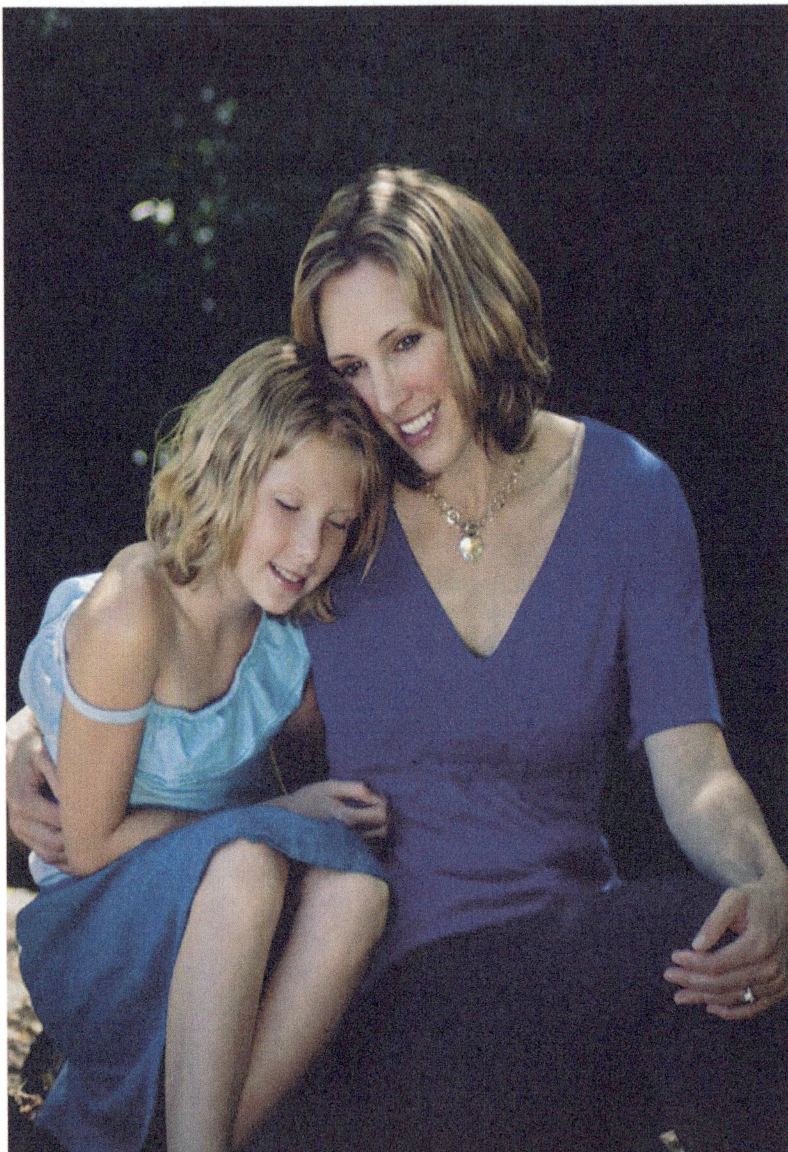

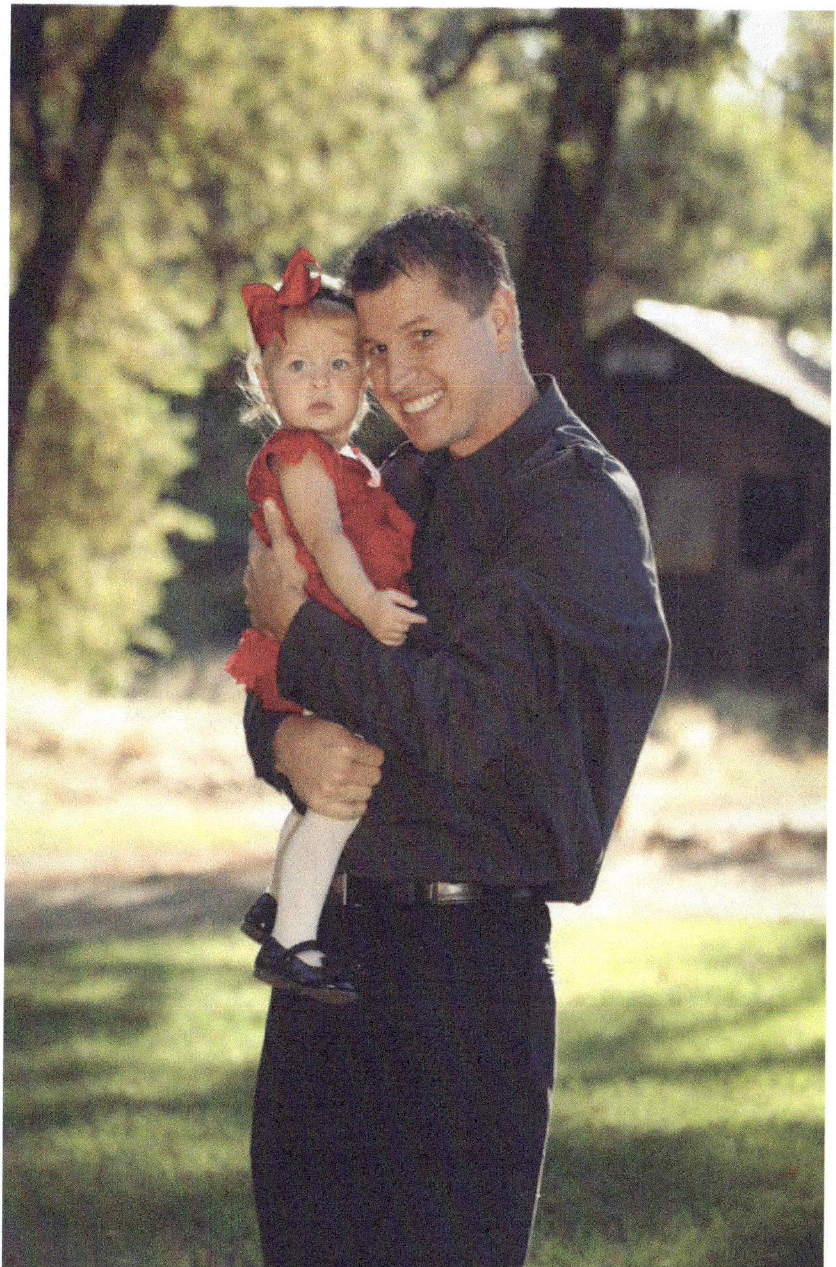

Posing Groups #3: *Jumping.* Jumping poses can be a fantastic addition to family shoots, as they often elicit laughter and create a lively atmosphere. To capture this shot, instruct the group to hold hands, look at the camera, and jump together. It's a great way to engage both parents and kids and can also work well for photographing young friends. The key is to ensure that every individual in the group is looking at the camera, regardless of the number of people involved. This creates a cohesive and engaging image that highlights the enthusiasm and joy of the moment.

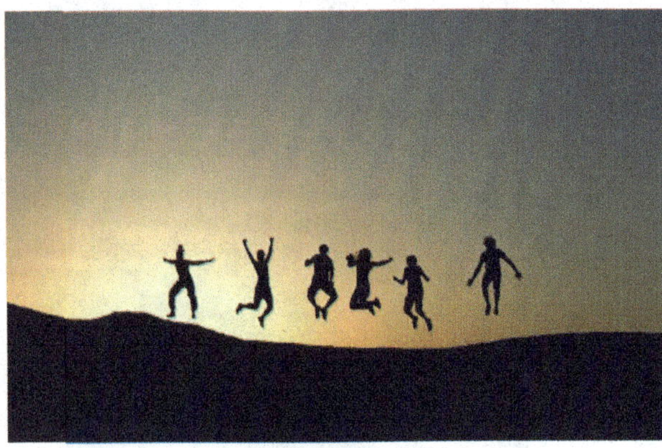

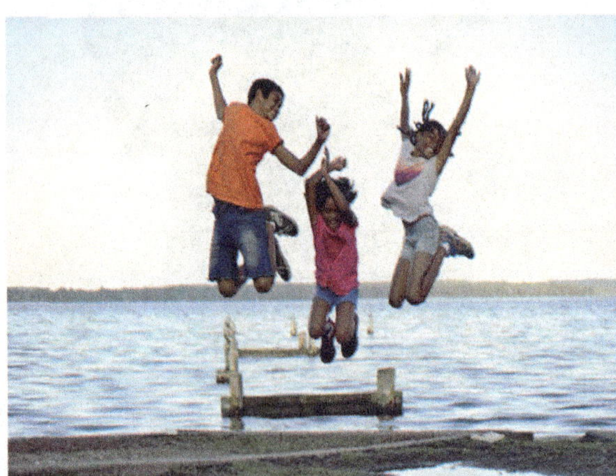

Posing Groups #4: *Having Fun.* It's important to allow families, groups of friends, kids, and even pets to have fun and pose somewhat naturally during a photoshoot. Photography should be an enjoyable experience, especially for larger groups. Encourage the kids to run toward the camera, with Mom and Dad following behind. This way, everyone is included in the shot, and it creates a more natural and dynamic composition. You can also prompt them to jump around or have them stand close together and look towards a specific point. The key is to capture genuine moments and interactions. The photo example provided above demonstrates how this approach can result in a great shot that reflects the joy and spontaneity of the moment.

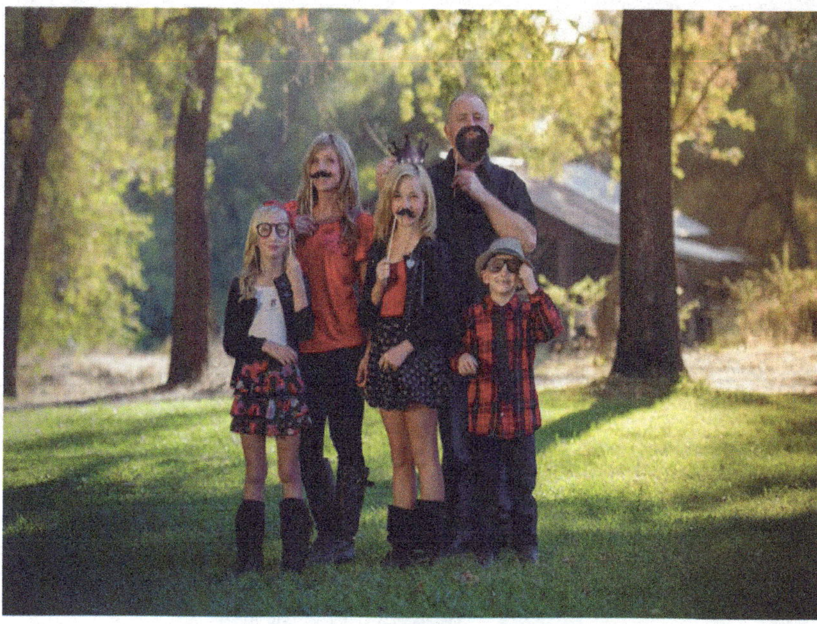

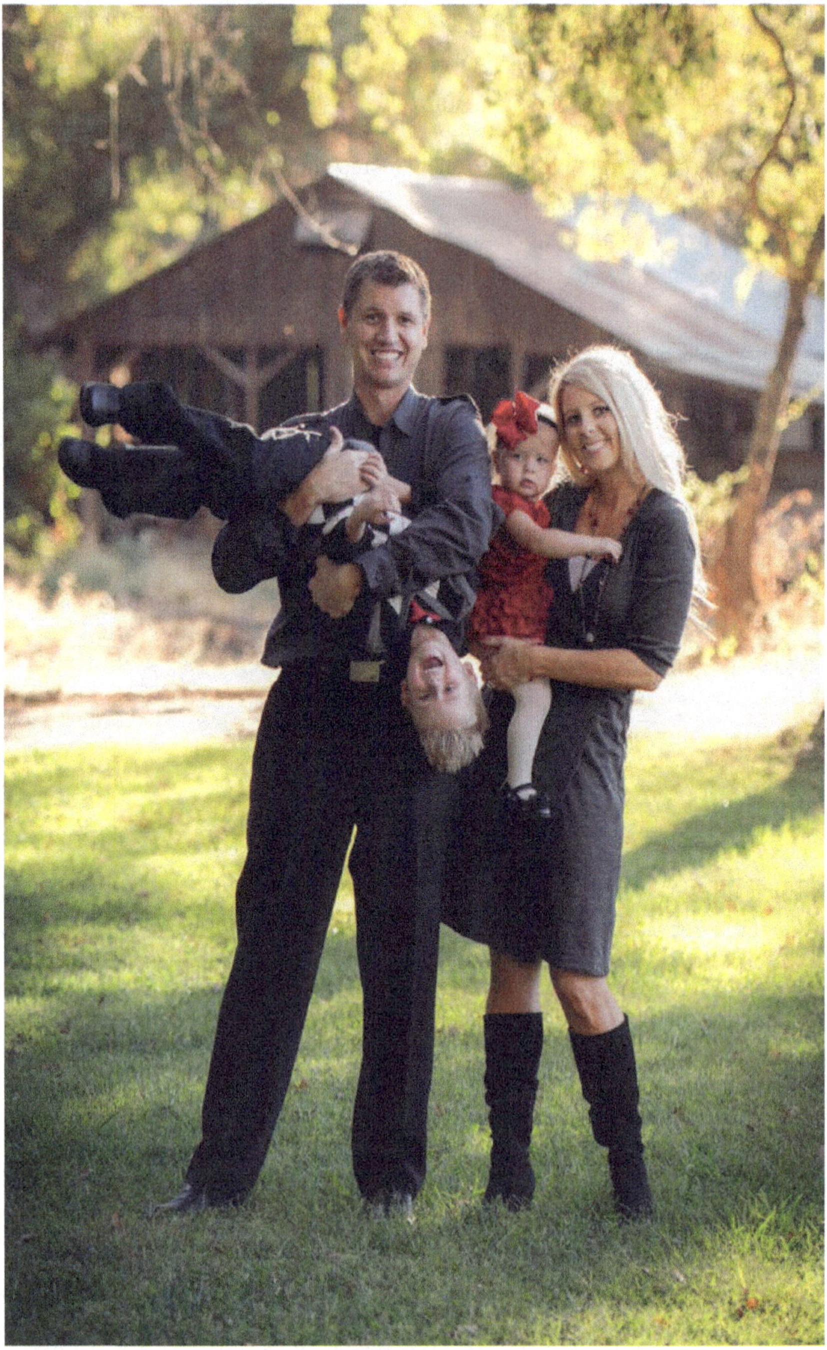

Posing Groups #5: *Head Circle on the Ground. H*ere's another friendly and effective pose, particularly suitable for outdoor photo shoots. Instruct the group to form a circle while lying on the grass and then capture the shot from an overhead perspective. Ensure that everyone is evenly spaced out, creating a sense of balance within the circle, and that all individuals are looking towards the camera. You can experiment with various angles, such as shooting directly overhead, from the side, or from a higher vantage point, to add variety to your compositions. Each angle offers a unique perspective and can bring a fresh visual appeal to the photo.

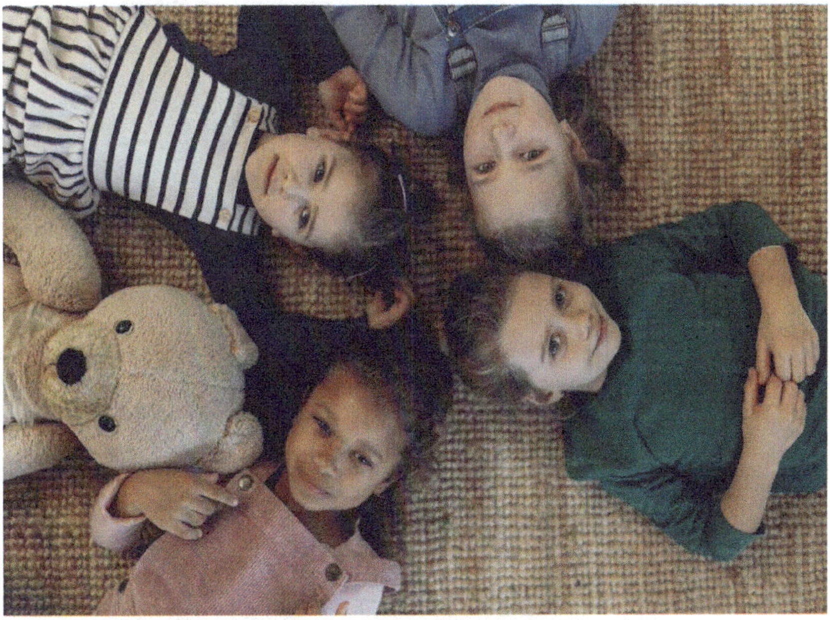

Posing Groups #2: *Walking Together.* An excellent suggestion for group poses is to encourage couples or families to hold hands and walk toward the camera. This action not only helps them maintain a close distance but also creates a natural and harmonious composition. Initially, you can ask them to walk slowly toward you, capturing their relaxed and composed demeanor. For the next shot, you can prompt them to increase their pace and run toward you, capturing a more dynamic and energetic pose. Remember, there is no single correct method to achieve this pose, and experimenting with different approaches can yield exciting results.

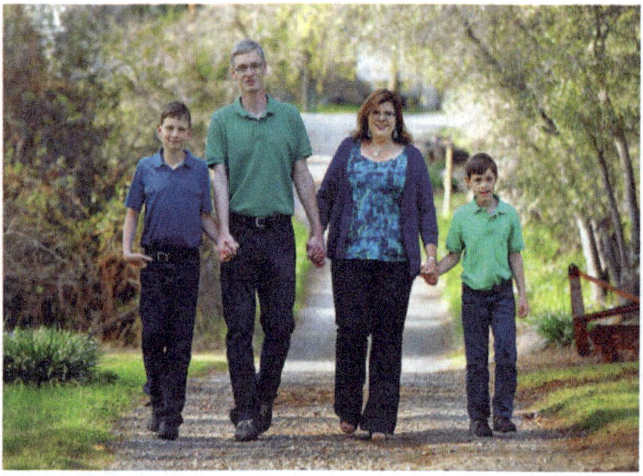

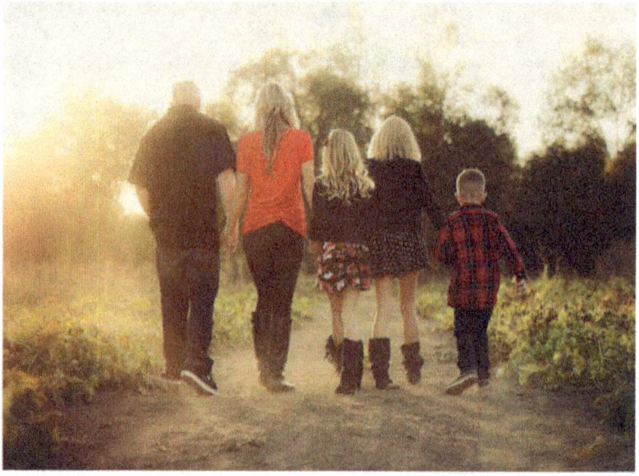

Posing Groups #7: *Family on the Lawn.* Getting outdoors for family photos is a great idea. When your subjects are sitting, it's important to adjust your position accordingly. Instead of remaining standing, get down to their eye level. By shooting from their eye level, you create a more intimate and engaging perspective, allowing viewers to connect with the subjects on a personal level. This technique helps avoid any unwanted distortions that can occur when shooting from above, resulting in more flattering and natural-looking images. So remember to lower yourself to your subjects' eye level for a more compelling composition.

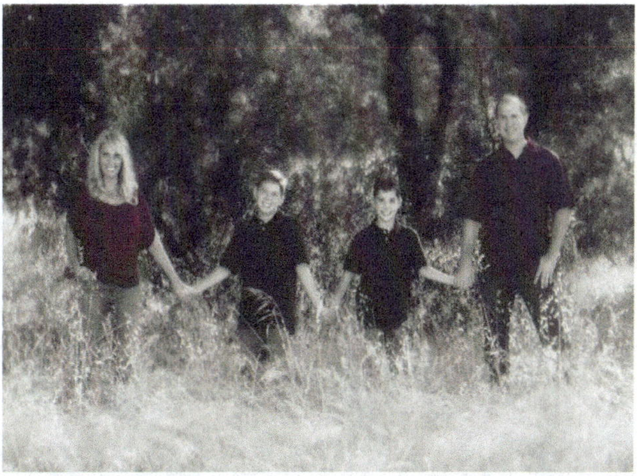

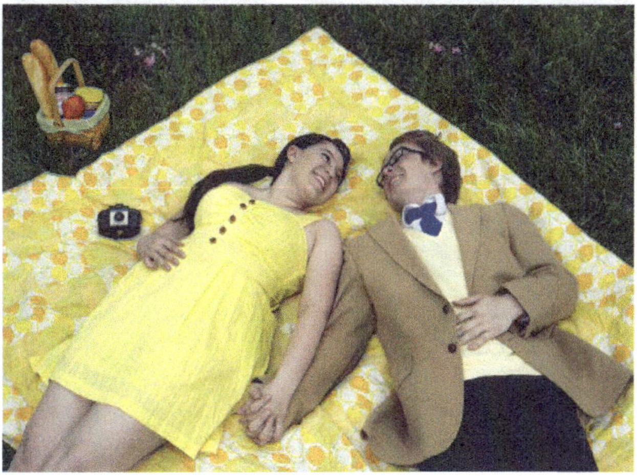

Posing Groups #8: *Family Pile Up.* Here's a beautiful and enjoyable composition for a family shot that can be done both indoors and outdoors. Select a family member to lie down on the ground or a bed, then invite the others to gently pile on top. This pose allows for a playful and intimate interaction among family members, creating a sense of closeness and affection. It works well with any number of kids, making it suitable for families of various sizes. Whether you choose to do it outside on the ground or indoors on a bed, this composition adds a touch of warmth and joy to the photo, capturing a special moment of togetherness.

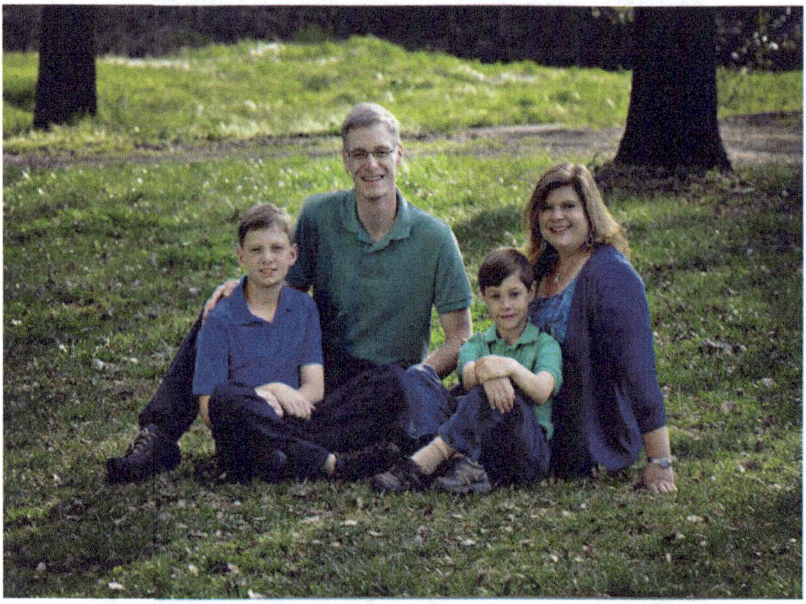

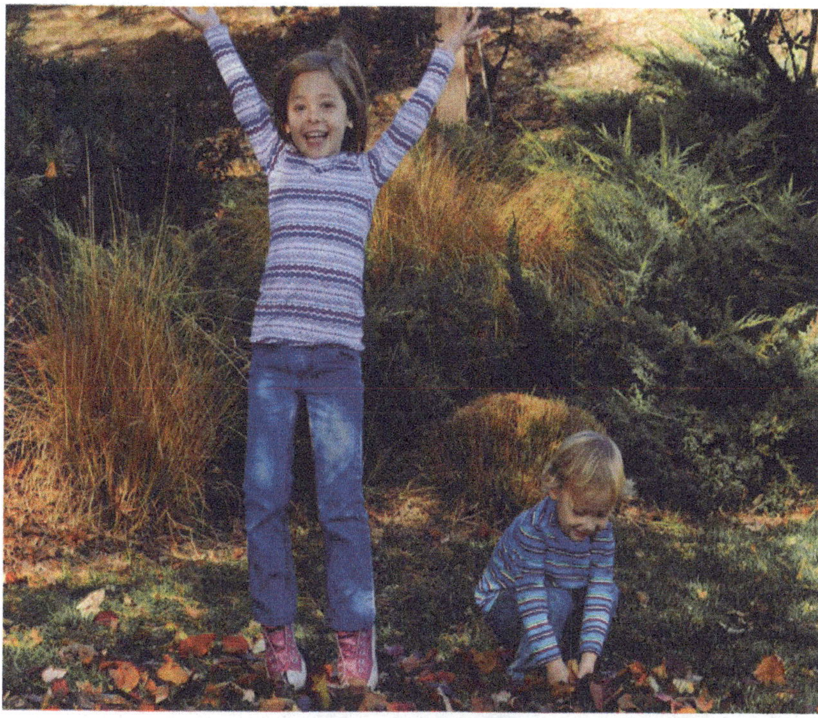

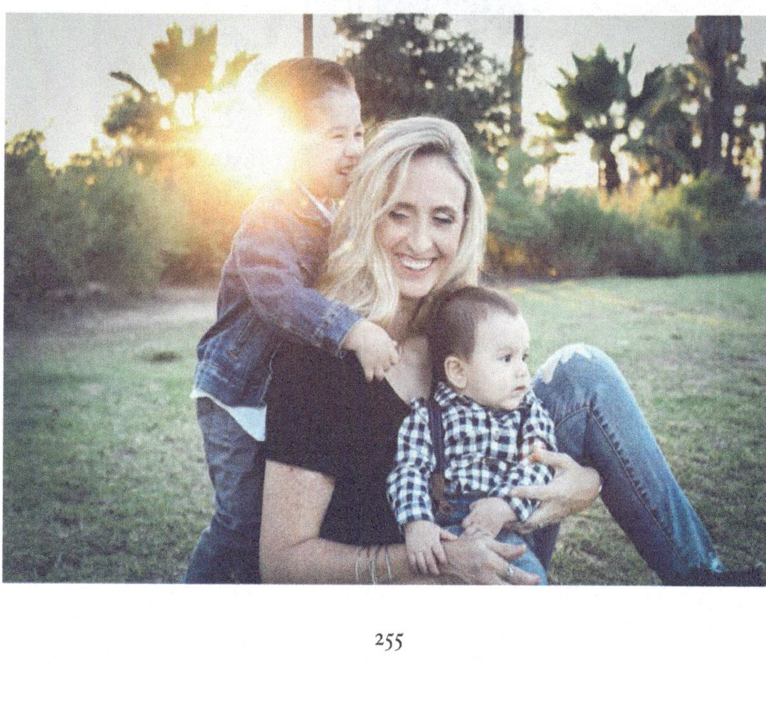

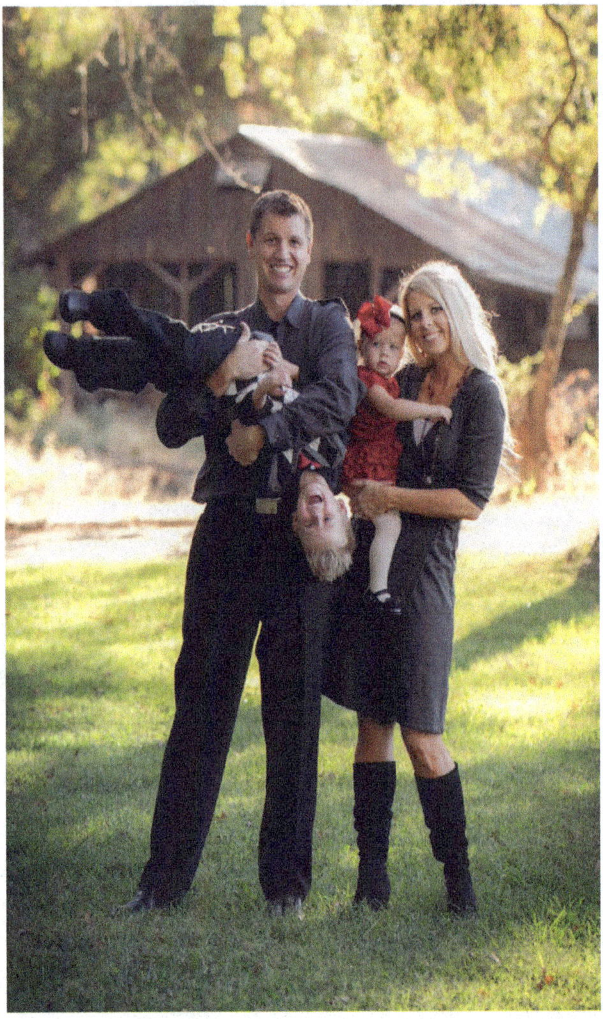

Posing Group #9: Walking around a Lake or Beach. Getting outside and utilizing natural settings like lakes or beaches can indeed create beautiful backdrops for family photos. These locations offer a serene and visually appealing environment that can enhance the overall composition. When your subjects are sitting, it's crucial to adjust your shooting position accordingly. Instead of remaining standing, get low and capture the photos from their eye level. Shooting from their eye level helps establish a more intimate connection and perspective in the images. It eliminates any potential distortions that may occur when shooting from above and ensures a more natural and flattering portrayal of the family. So, remember to lower yourself to their eye level to create engaging and visually pleasing family shots.

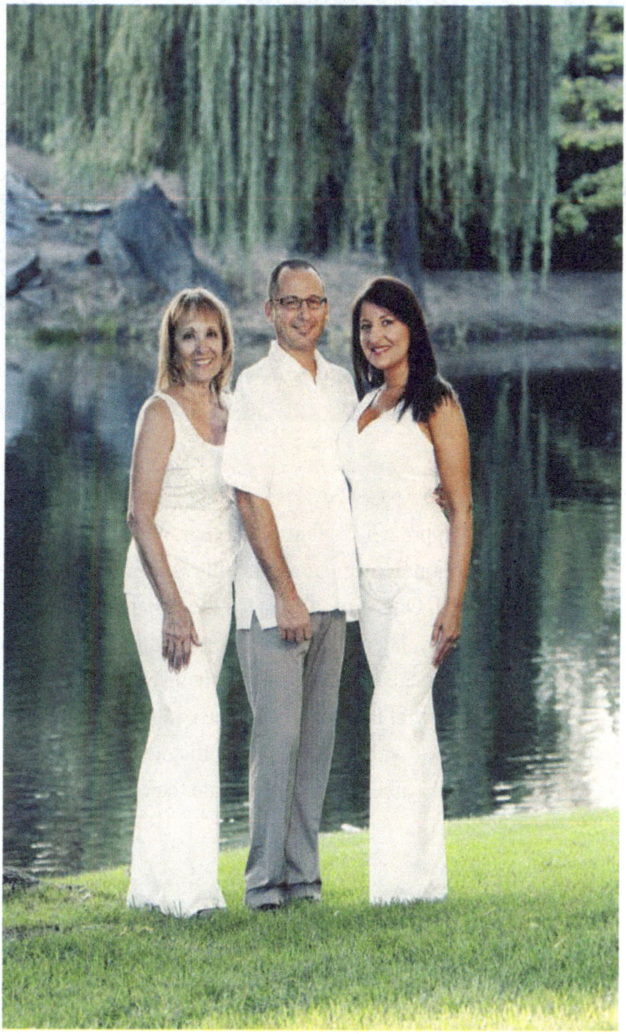

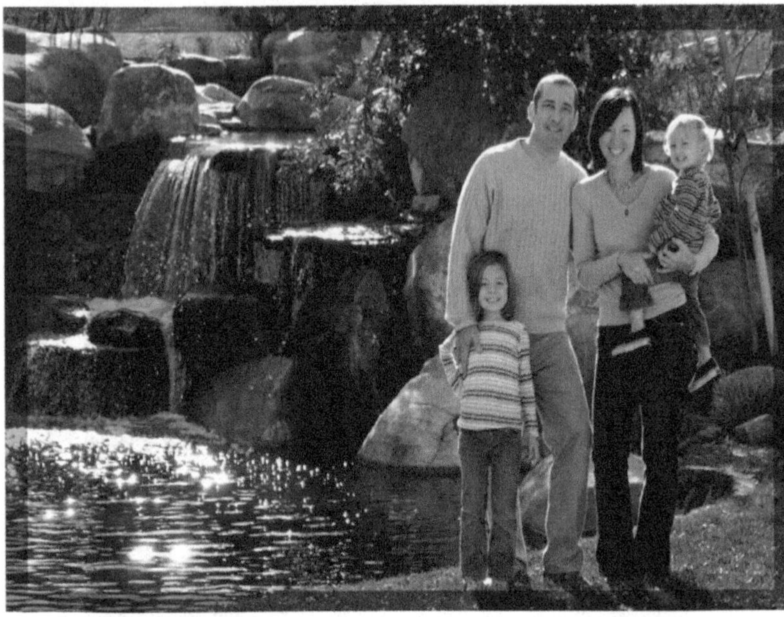

Posing Groups #10: *Sitting on a Car or Truck.* While asking a family to sit on a car or truck is a common approach for family photography, it may not be the most creatively unique option. However, it can still result in visually appealing images when executed well. One way to enhance these standard compositions is by cropping the frame tightly. By excluding the surrounding couch or room furniture, you can focus solely on the family members themselves. This tight crop allows you to fill the frame with the family, emphasizing their connection and creating a more intimate portrayal. By eliminating distractions and maximizing the presence of the family members, you can elevate the overall impact of the shot.

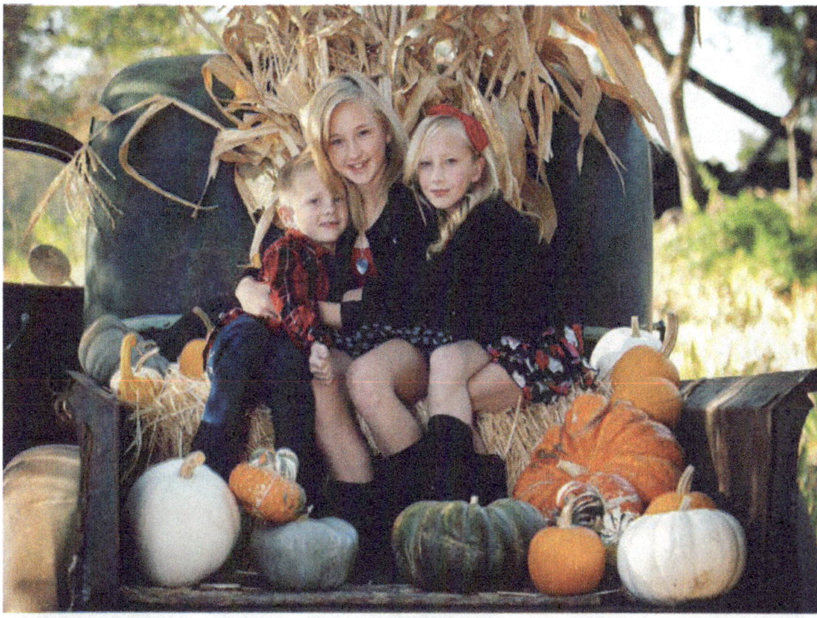

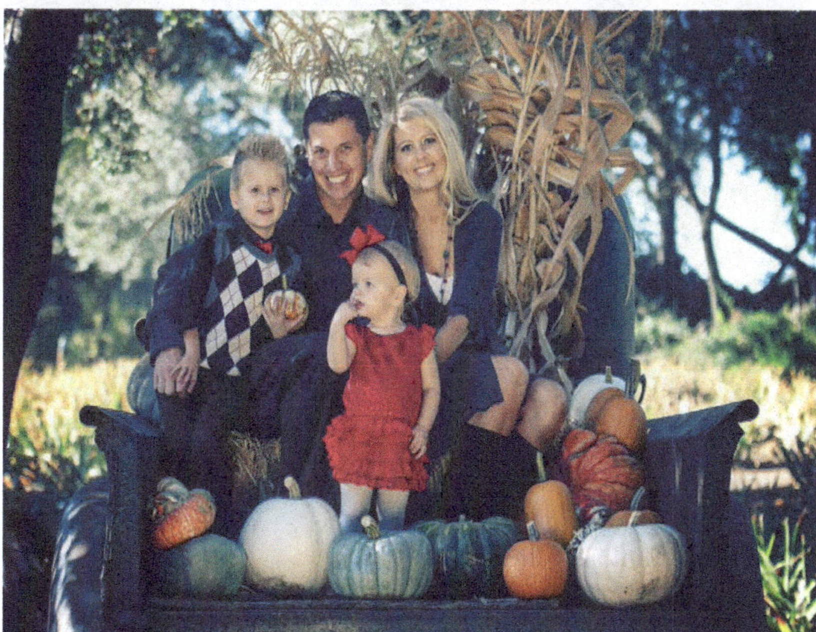

Posing Groups #11: *Everyone Facing Forward.* When dealing with a large group of individuals, it's important to recognize that you may not have complete control over each person's pose or expression. However, by focusing on the overall composition, you can still achieve a pleasing result. Start by directing everyone to stand together closely, minimizing any significant gaps between individuals. Instruct them to face forward and cross their arms over their chests. This pose helps create a sense of unity and cohesion within the group. The key aspect to keep in mind is ensuring that all people in the group are visible within the frame. Adjust your position or make any necessary arrangements to ensure that everyone is included in the photograph. By paying attention to the overall composition and making sure each person is visible, you can capture a successful group shot, even with a large number of individuals.

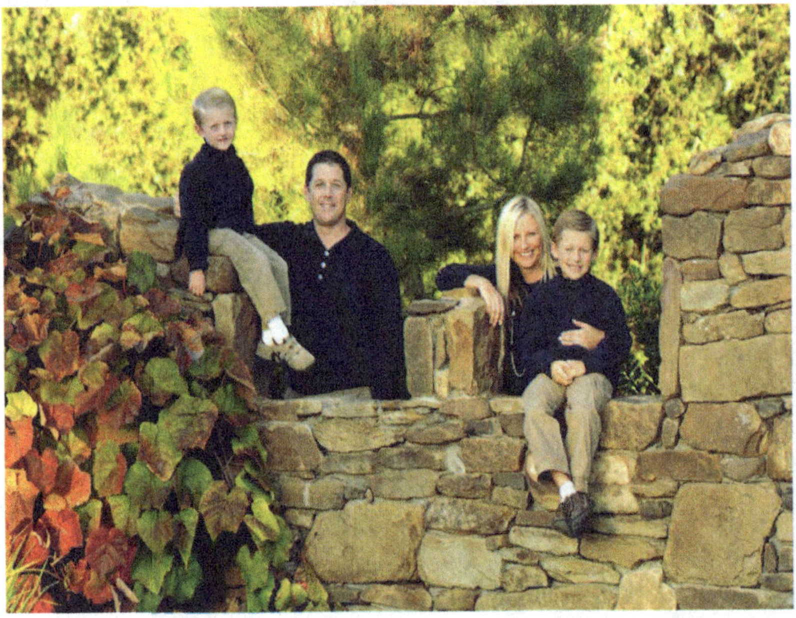

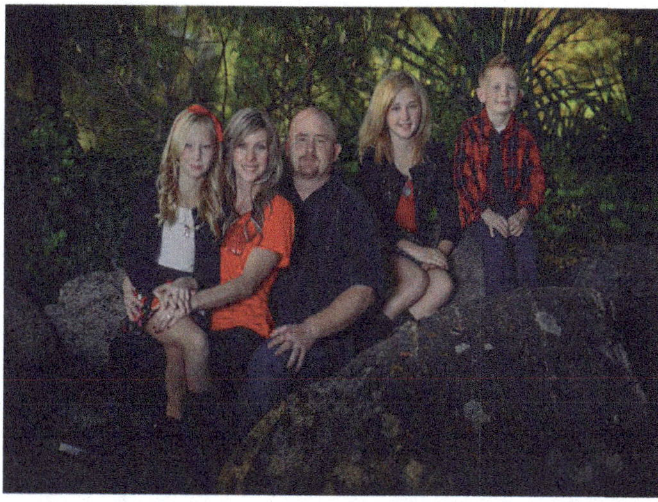

Posing Women

Posing #1: *Hands gracefully poised.* Knowing what to do with the hands is one of the most challenging aspects of learning how to posture women subjects for photographers. The size of a person's hand is approximately equal to that of their face. It's crucial to avoid having the hands directly in front of the face because of this. Instead, hold your hands out to the side, over your shoulder, in your hair, or under your chin. Women's hands should be gracefully poised, adding a touch of elegance. Vary the height for variety.

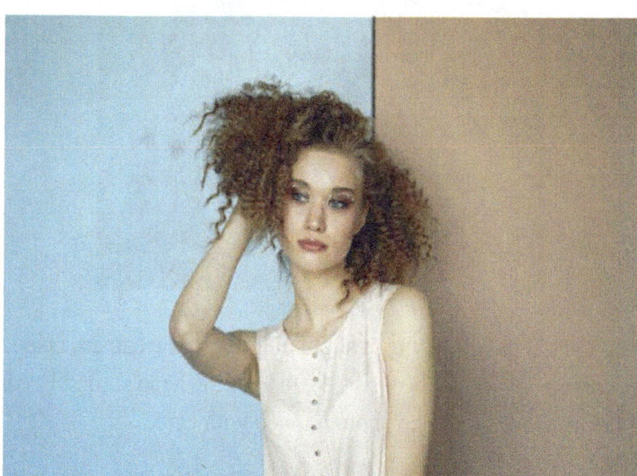

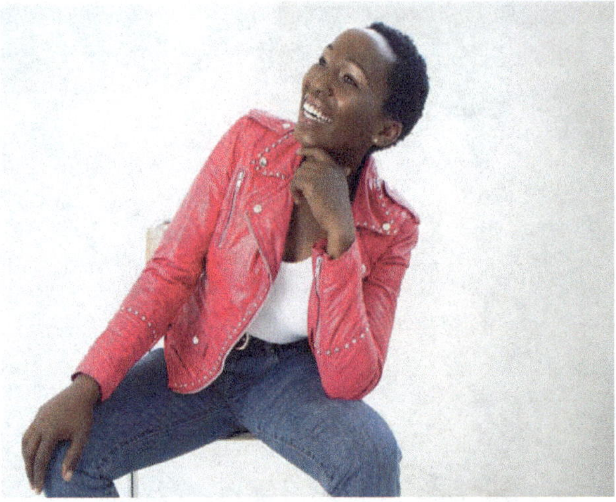

Make sure the fingers are curled, spaced slightly apart, and barely just touching the face or hair. Never show the entire palm. Most photographers still cling to this tried-and-true method.

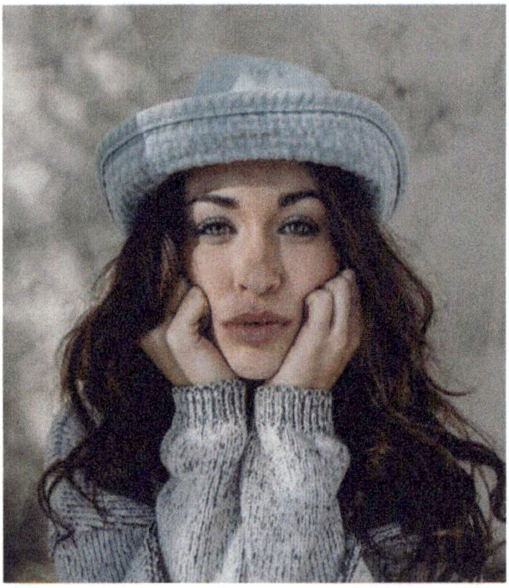

When looking at the hands, having a slight angle with the camera is ideal. When the hand is curved upward at the wrist, the side of the hand smoothly continues the line of the arm and should be photographed with care.

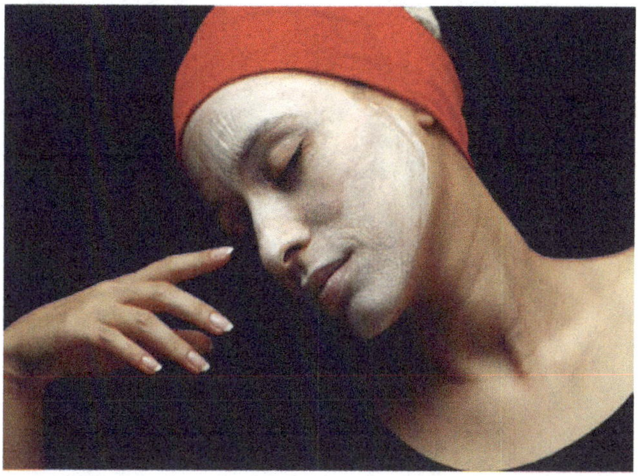

Pose 2: *Cover a Double Chin.* To flatteringly capture your subject's profile, start by pushing their chin down and forward. This subtly tightens the skin on the neck for a reduction in double chins! For an even more attractive angle, have them place their hand under their chin as they look up - it will make all the difference to any portrait shot.

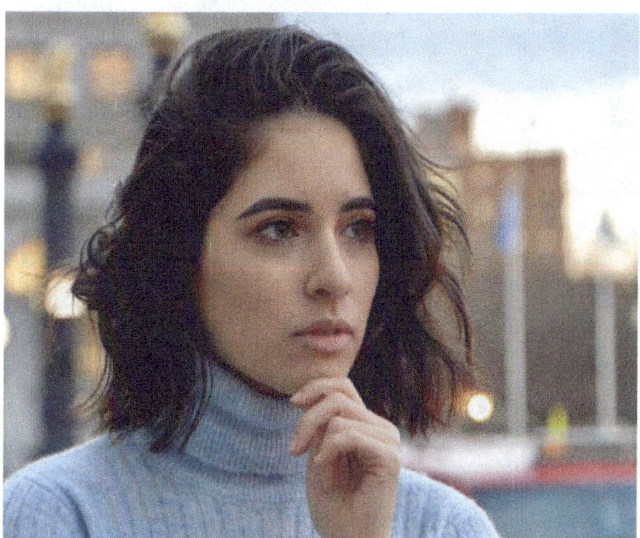

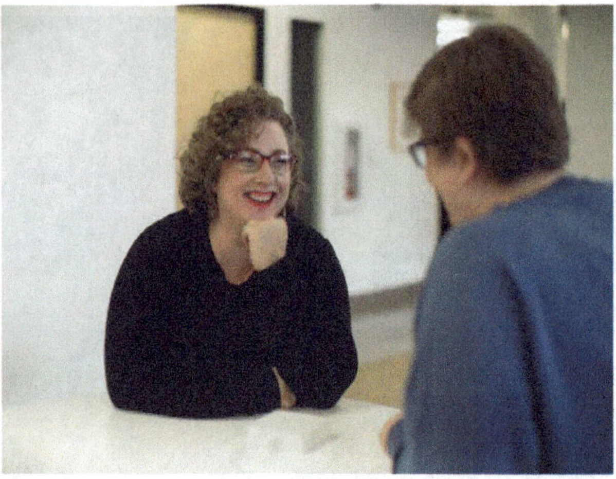

Pose 3: *Shoot from Higher Camera Angel.* Curves are vital in female portrait photography. They are what most women rely on to feel feminine. The extra advantage of emphasizing a female model's curves is that the waist seems more defined from above. Having them create "v"s and "triangles" with their body is a pleasing shape.

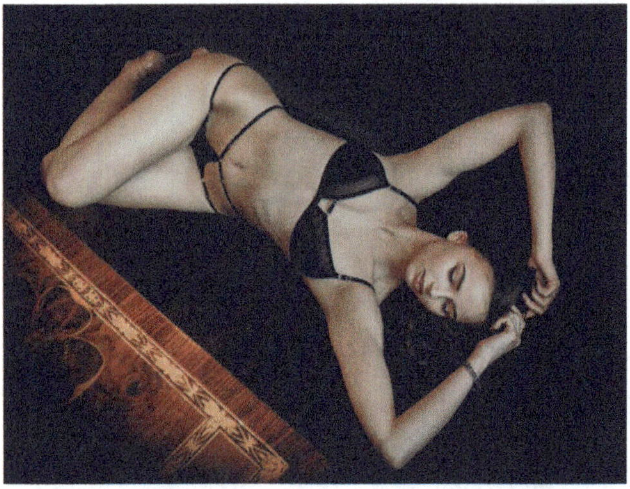

This is essential for boudoir poses, since a shirt or robe may cover up every inch of flesh. By angling closer while maintaining space with the rest of their body, you may bring attention to their face or physique and make them look much svelter than they actually are in real life. Angle their legs away or cover up the stomach area with a sheet to give them an appearance of a thinner waist.

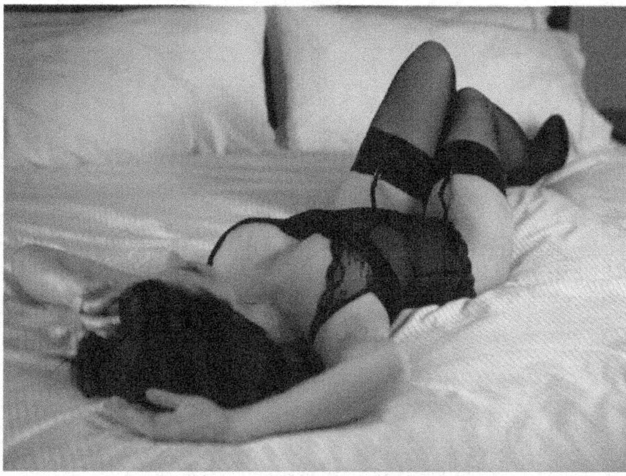

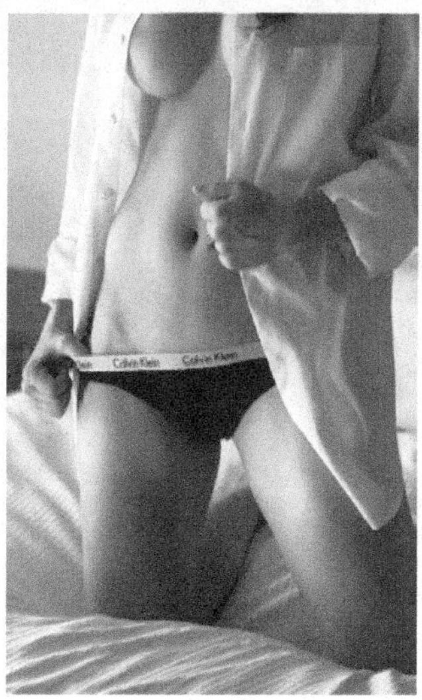

Pose #4: *Place long hair in front to narrow necklines.* Encourage them to stand at an angle or slightly lean away from the camera for added length. Avoid standing straight on with arms flat against the body, as this will make limbs appear thicker; instead, have your client bend elbows upward and into their hair for a slimming effect.

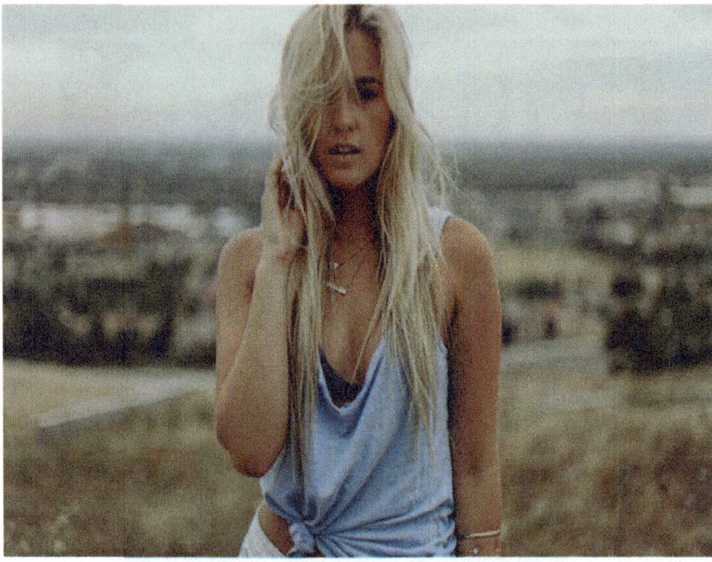

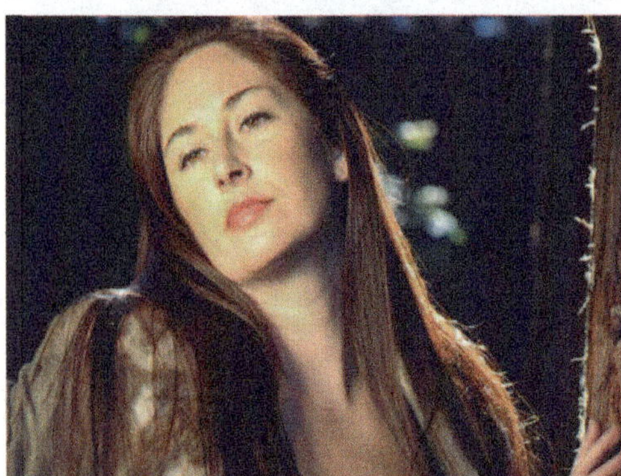

Pose #5: *Power posing.* This practice can help your subject not only feel more assertive but also create a confident business image. This also creates triangle shapes in the legs, which is a pleasing shape in photography.

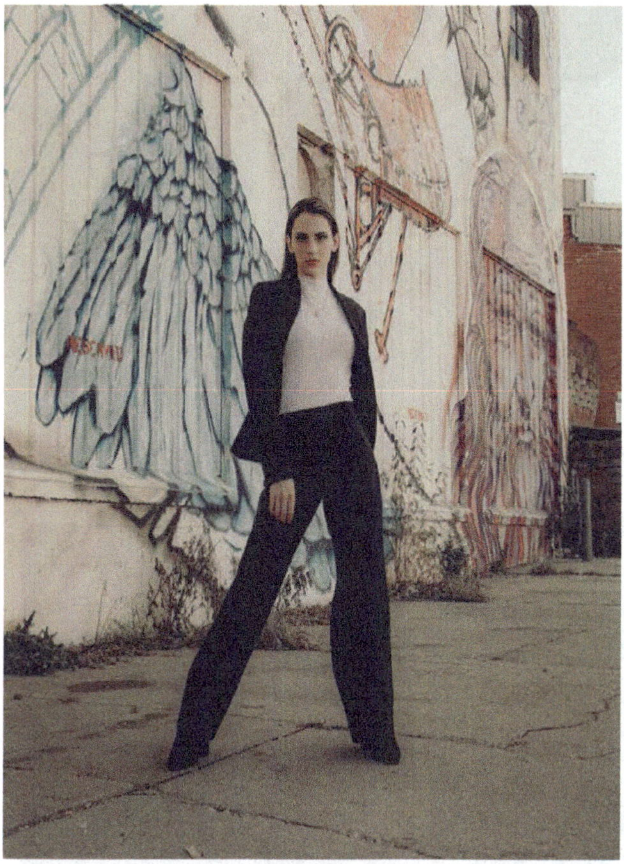

Pose #6: *Maintain a "S" form.* This can be done standing or sitting on the ground. When standing, have your subject put most of their weight on one foot with hips jutted out, which elongates their body into a graceful "S" form. When sitting, have them lean on one arm for support. Have them spread out their legs in a cross-cross pattern going in the opposite direction of their arm. This will provide the illusion of an hourglass form, regardless of your body type.

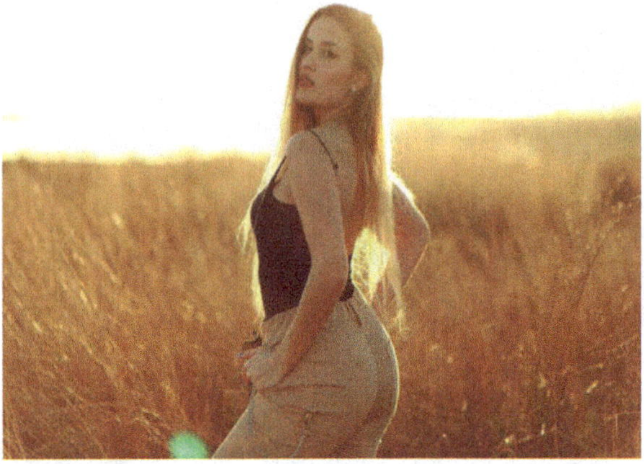

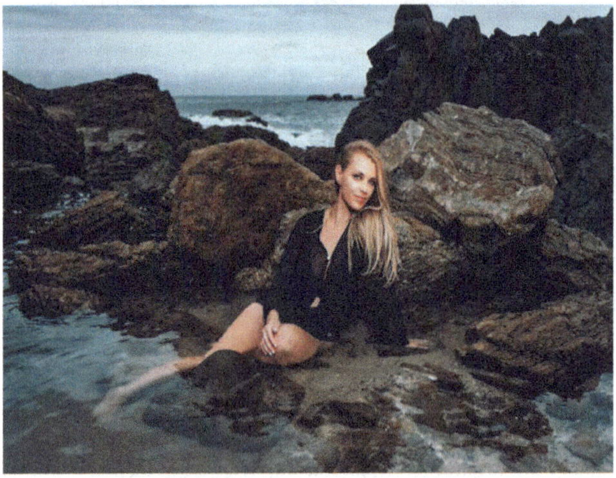

Pose #7: *Place hands on hips*. Make an artificial waist. A fake waist may be a terrific modeling tool for ladies. Try it if you want them to look slimmer and add some curves for the camera. It keeps their arms looking thinner because they are up and away from the camera. It becomes an optical illusion.

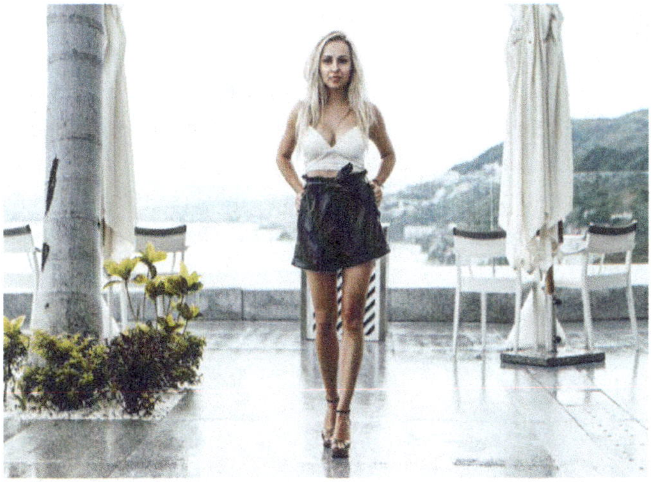

Pose #8: *Hold arms above head.* When holding your arms above their head, their arm's line is maintained, giving the impression it is longer and slimmer. Lean slightly to the side to create a curve. When done correctly, this highlights the subject's body curvature.

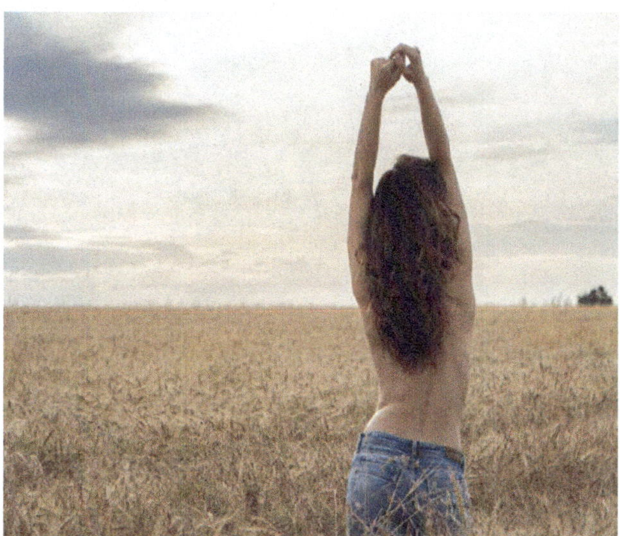

Pose #9: *Half torso look back shot.* A lot of women feel shy away from their lower bodies being photographed. You can simply do a half-shot of the subject to fix this concern. One choice is to have the subject turn away from the camera and look back over their shoulder, which creates a sensual demeanor. Although it is extremely straightforward, it has the potential to evoke strong emotions. Showing just the upper half can give the illusion of the model being shorter or thinner. It is very deceiving. Just make sure you don't accidently cut off the hands in the image. If the model has long arms, you can always have them hold both of their arms around their torso.

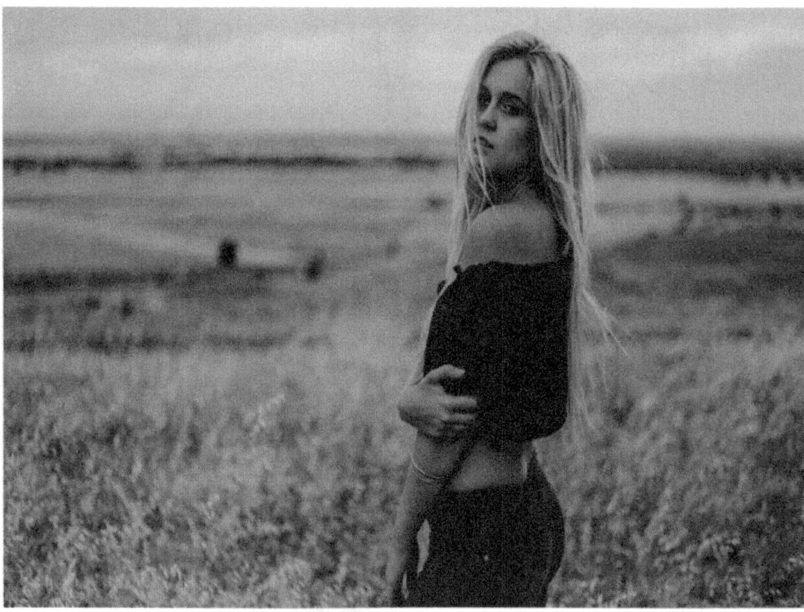

Pose #10: *Look away from the camera.* Avoid looking at the camera. A decent generalization is to have your subject follow their nose with your eyes. Their gaze will appear natural. Also, try a relaxed look by placing hands on the chin or neck for other options to this pose.

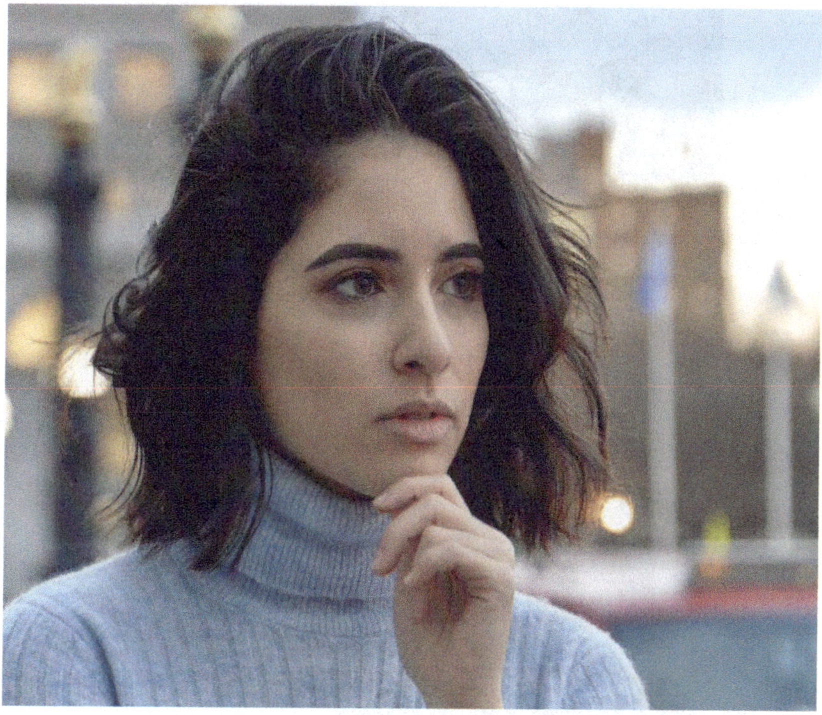

Pose 11: *Get your body and limbs apart.* This is an unusual pose, but it works because it creates great lines. Be sure to gently elevate your limbs away from your torso. Have them pull their knees up and legs out a little. This not only makes you seem smaller overall, but it also keeps your arms and legs from rubbing up against fattier areas of your body.

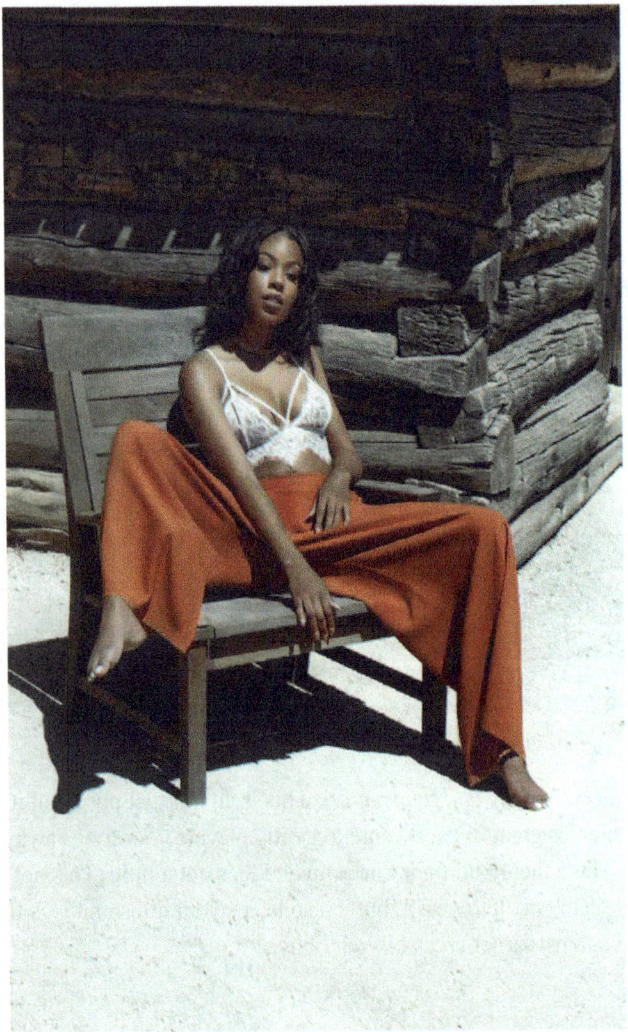

Pose #12: *Knees up and hands on feet*. A popular female portrait position. Your subject should crouch down with her knees touching or bent upward. They should also place their hands on their feet and knees. This graceful stance is perfect for dancers, too. It can be used anywhere.

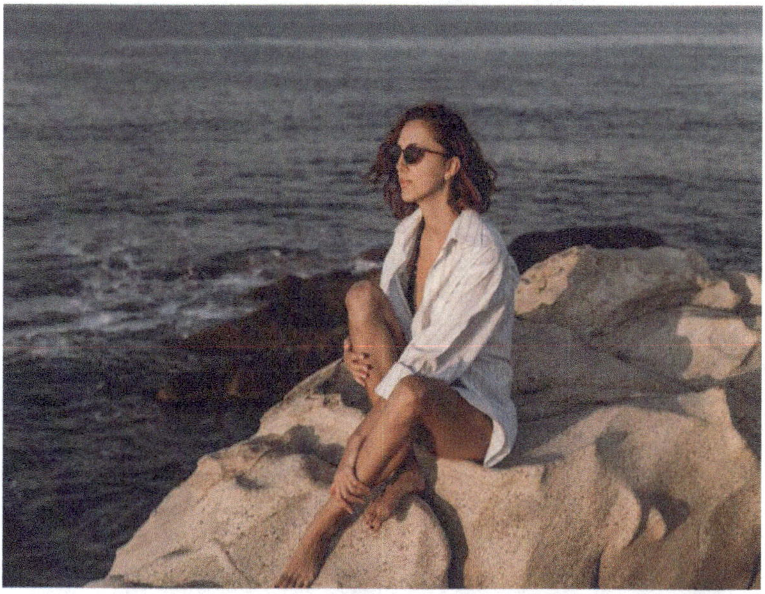

Pose #13: Squat (Baddie Pose). One of the most well-liked female positions on social media is this one. It may have appeared on Instagram by several celebrities. Your photographs may appear hip and edgy as a result. Your model only needs to squat. She should let one arm extend down. This will make your subject appear leaner and strike a balanced stance as a result. There are variations where the subject extends out one of their legs to make their body look longer.

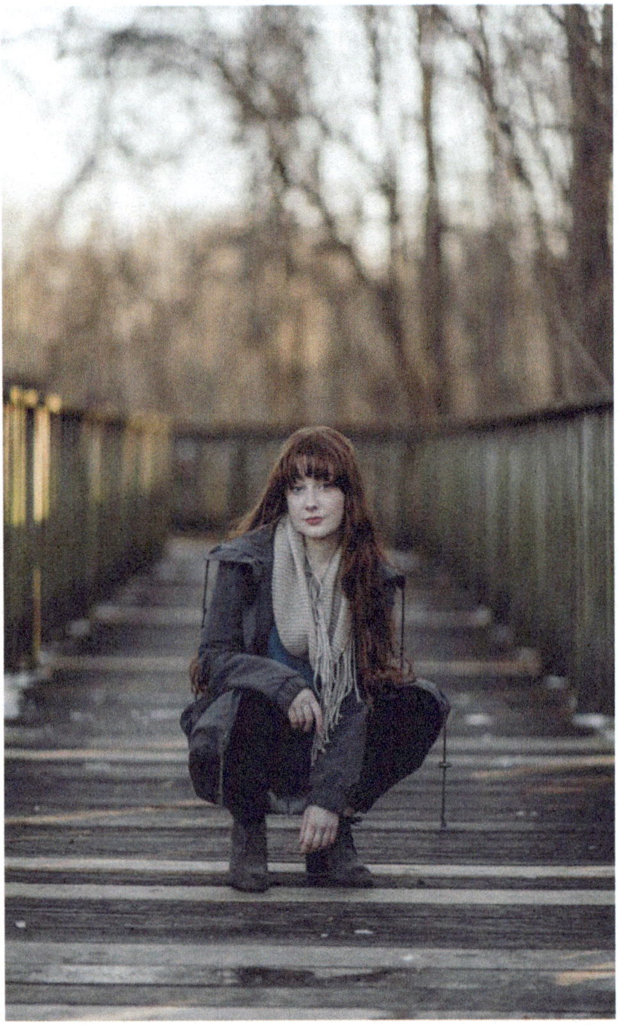

Pose #14. *The cozy pose.* The subject should appear to be embracing herself. Options are to have your subject shut her eyes to give the position a more comfortable appearance. Otherwise, she should have the subject give a peaceful glance at the camera while gently hugging herself.

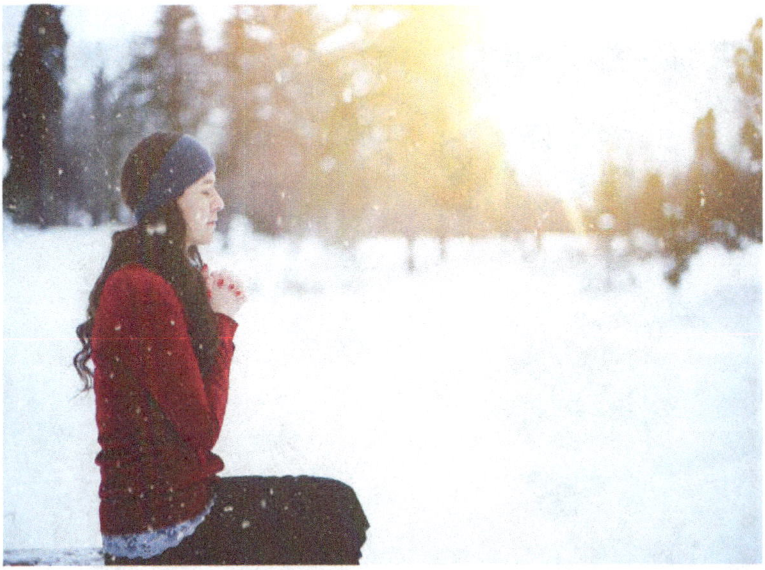

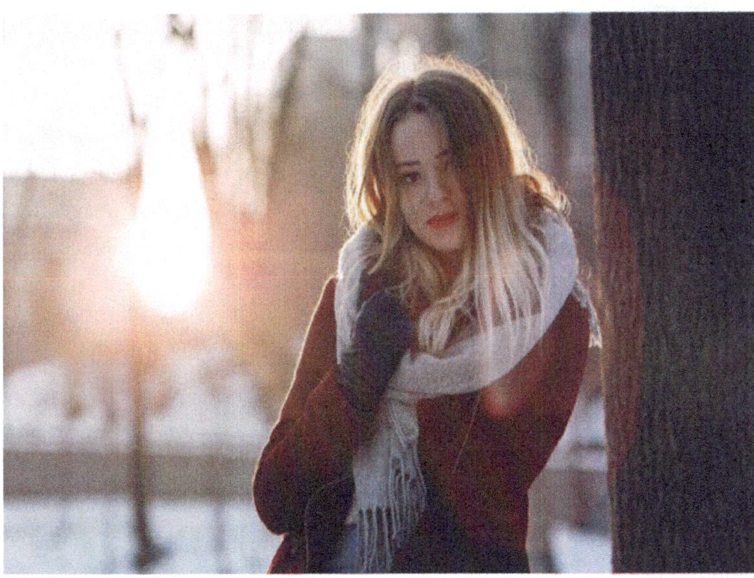

Posing Tip - Hire a Makeup Artist

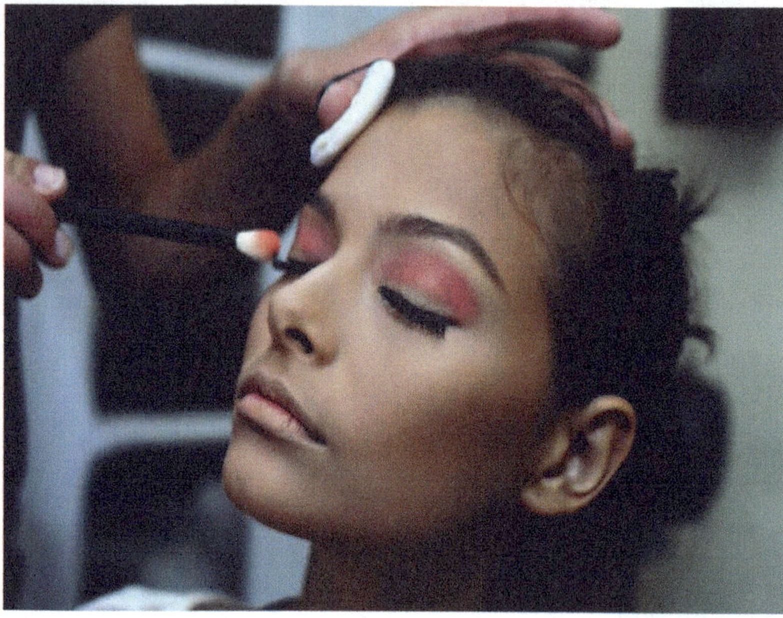

Getting behind the lens with the help of a makeup specialist is key if you want pro-level images for your own marketing, models, or even clientele who are makeup shy or inexperienced. Professional contouring techniques can enhance your photos in ways more effective than digital editing ever could—adding foundational lighting and perfectly placed shadows ideal for photo shoots. Often you can trade services with a makeup artist. You give them your images for their makeup services on your clients. They can use those images on their social media for their own marketing. It's a win-win.

Posing Men

Pose #1: *Maintain a straight back when facing the camera.* One of the standard guidelines is that men should have a wide, big build. Maintain a comfortable posture while looking forward. A nice trick is to have the subject lean forward by approximately one or two inches, putting their shoulders closer to the camera to improve the appearance of having a wider shoulder.

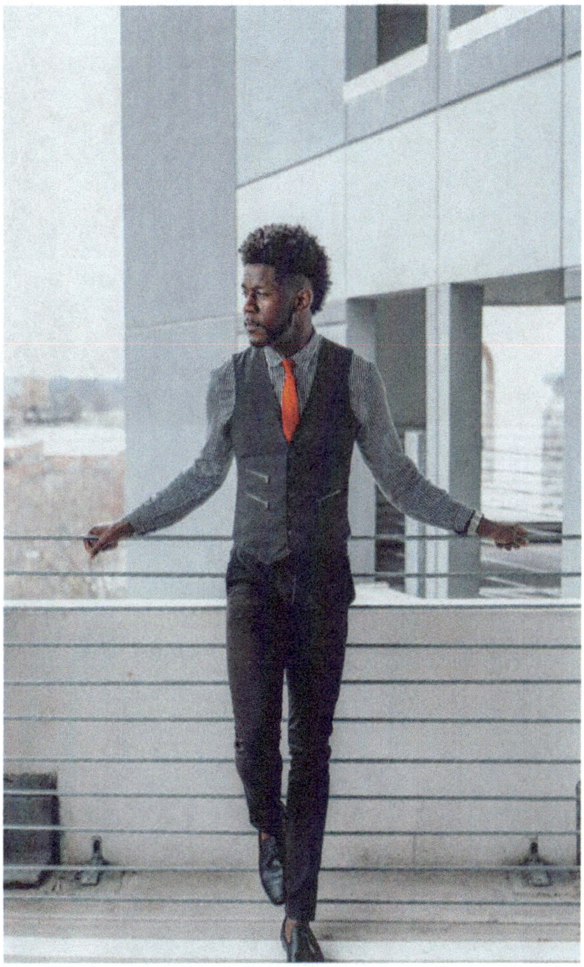

Pose #2: Put your subject's back on a wall (or tree or building). There are other types of leaning that you may choose from, including leaning with one or both shoulders on a wall. Have them bend one knee and raise their foot up against the wall. One leg should be bent, with the other slightly behind it. Keep their body straight up and down without slouching. Try the first pose with hands-free in front of them hanging down. Then try with hands in their pockets. These exude confidence and serenity.

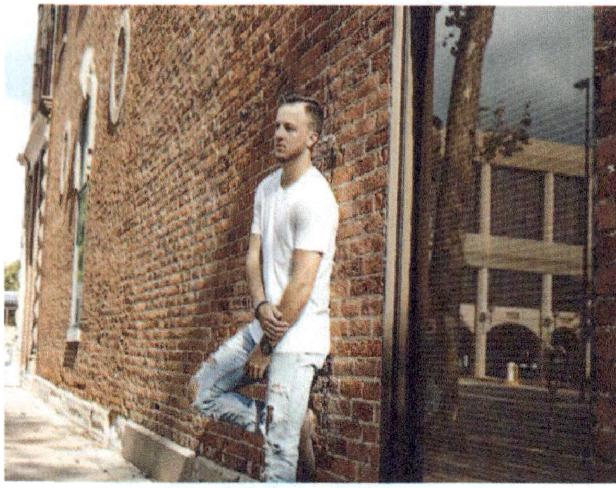

You have two choices: either put your entire hand inside your pocket, leaving the thumb out, or place roughly half of your hand inside the pocket. To change it up, wrap your thumbs around your belt loops.

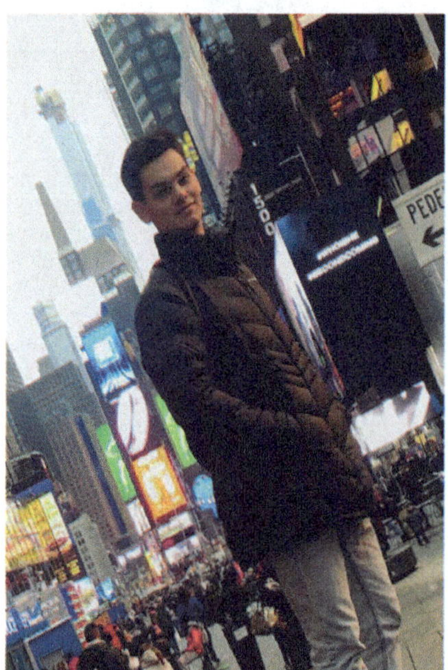

Pose #3: Run their hands through their hair. With this hand posture, it's a good idea to run your one hand through their hair. They have the option of putting their other hand in your front pocket or out of view.

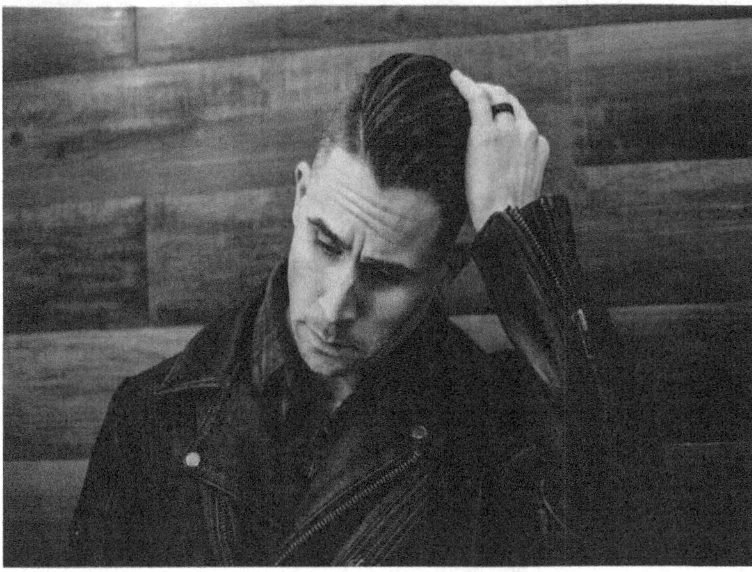

Pose #4: *Touch their face with their hand(s).* Put their hand someplace on t face to project a sense of calm or introspection. Alternatively, curl your fingers and press them up on your chin with your forefinger and thumb. You have a variety of appearances to choose from, thanks to your hand on your face. Try out several hand gestures to discover which best seems to express the message you want to send.

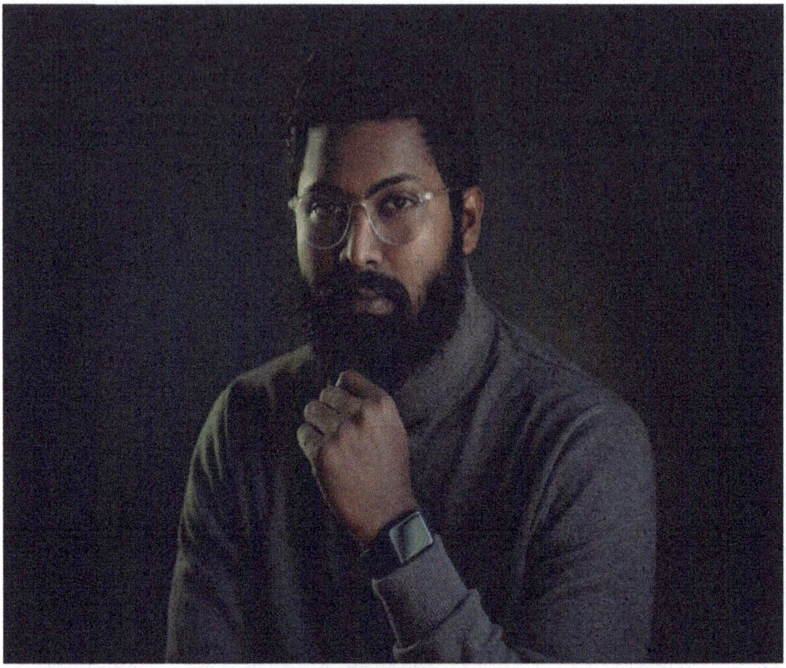

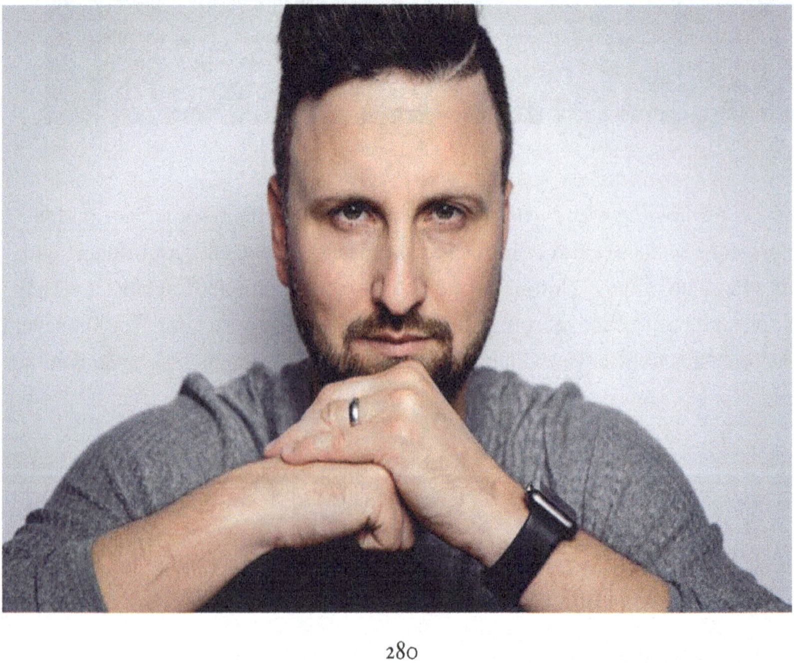

Pose #5: *Adjust their tie or cufflinks.* Placing one hand on their tie while sporting a complete suit and tie is a timeless and elegant stance. The knot doesn't even need to be moved. You may create the illusion of movement by placing your hand there. You may slightly alter this position by placing your second hand halfway down the tie. This is how you'd see if you tightened it, yet this attitude differs noticeably from the one-handed position.

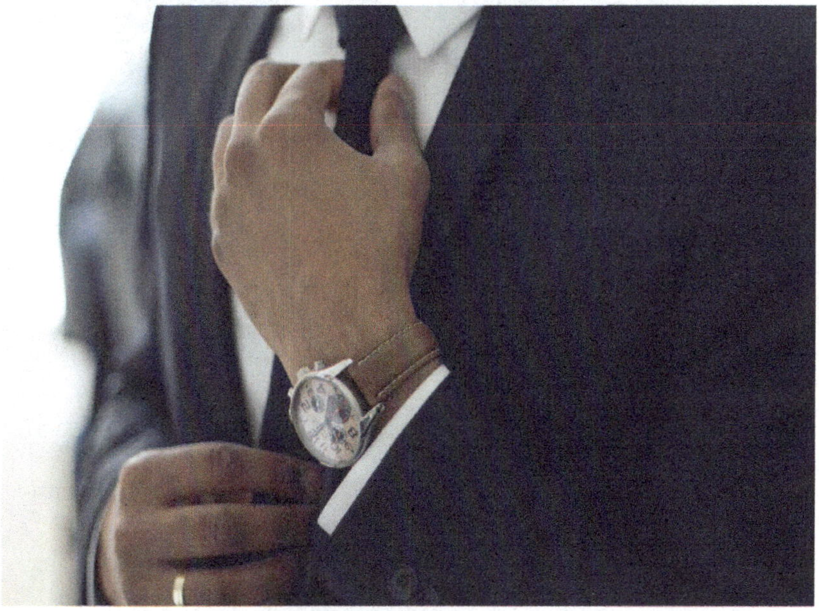

Pose #6: *Button the Jacket Closed:* Similar to tying their tie, this one is simply to have them pretend to open and close their jacket to create a sense of movement and elegance.

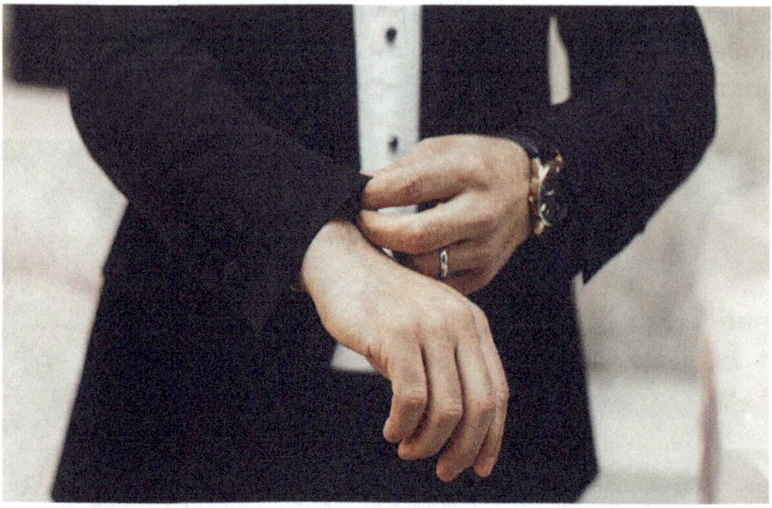

Pose #7: The subject's eyes should be slightly squinted. In a squint, lift your lower eyelids a little. This conveys a look of introspection or serious contemplation. In contrast to fear or uncertainty, it inspires confidence and composure.

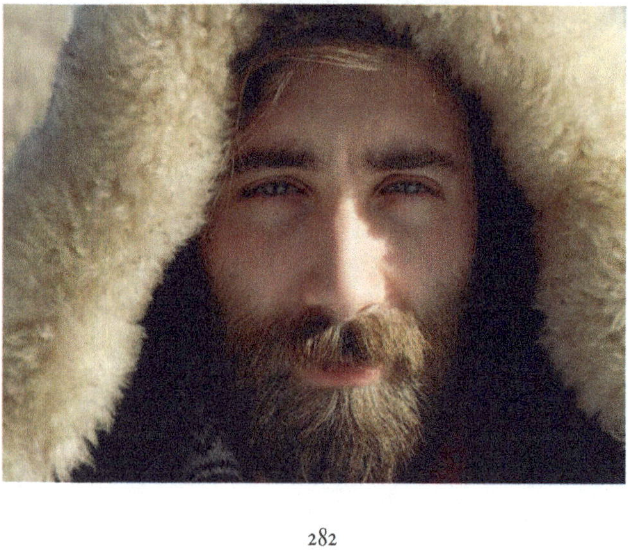

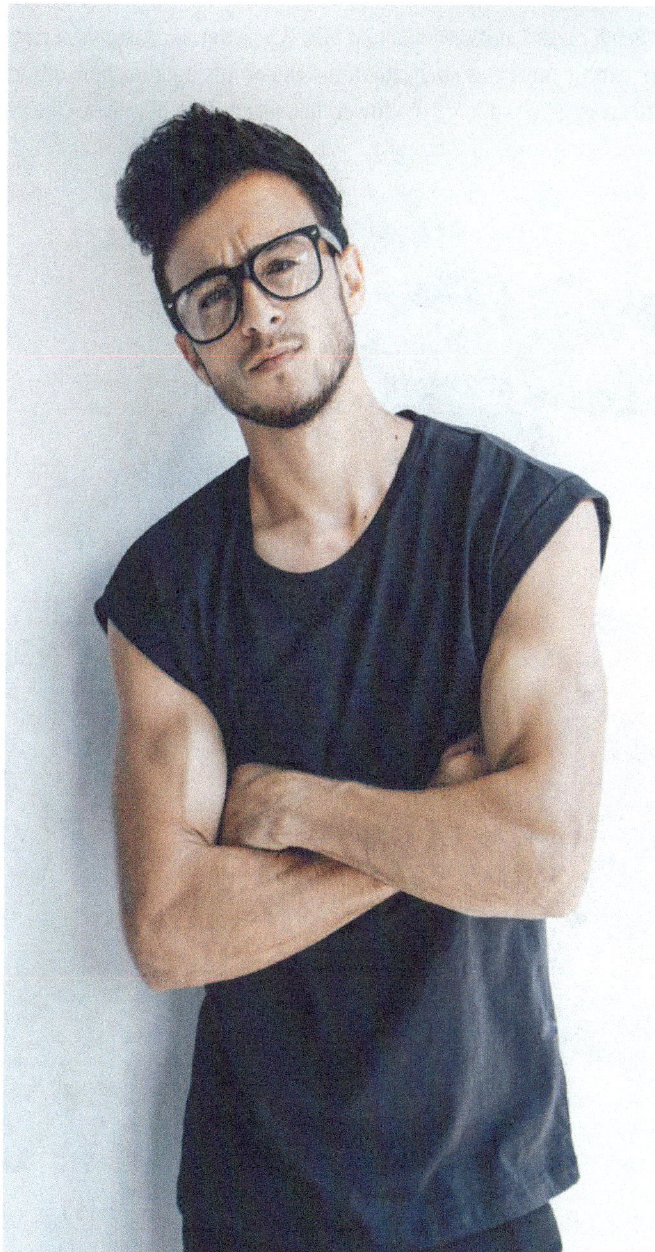

Pose #8: *Bring the subject's chin up and out.* Whenever your chin is at rest, you frequently expose more flesh beneath it. Instead of raising it to show off your nostrils, tilt your chin roughly 10% lower than usual. This eliminates the double chin by concealing some of their neck.

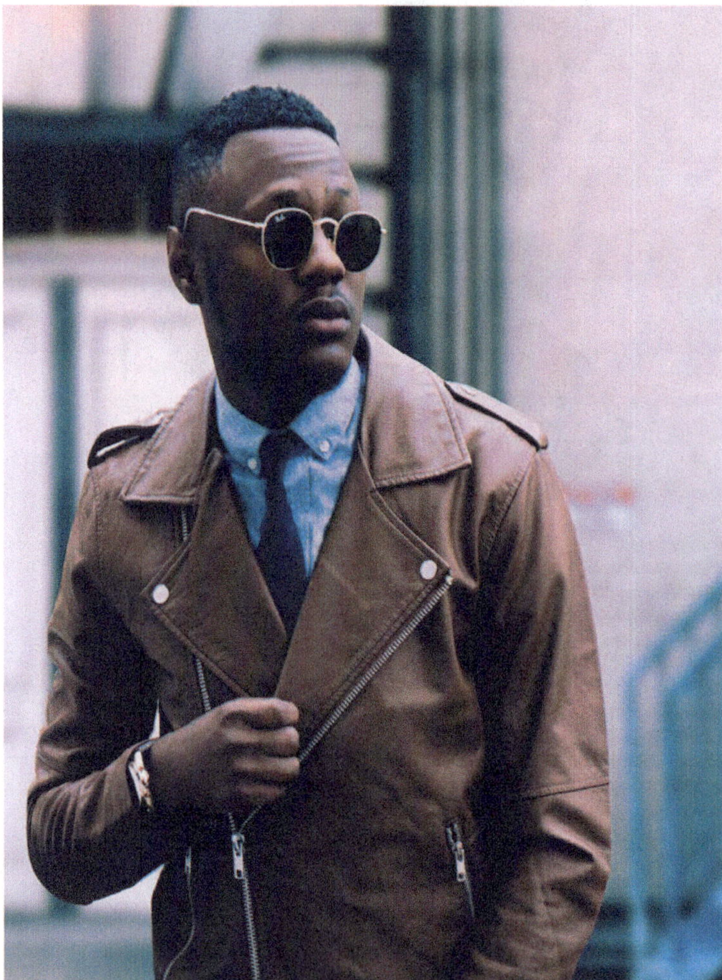

Pose #9: *When you grin, display some teeth*. Don't have them grin so broad that their mouth opens completely, just enough to keep lips still slightly pursed.

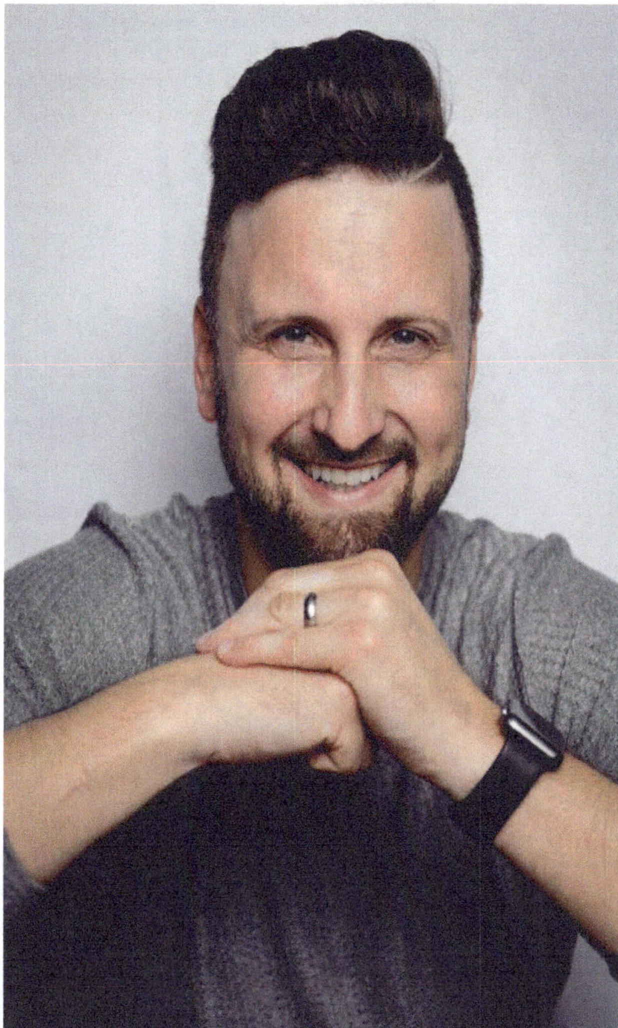

Pose #10: *Look past the camera or off into the distance.* Unless the photo specifically calls for direct eye contact with the camera, choose a point above and beyond the camera. Look at an angle toward the left or the right of the camera or look at a point just below the camera. These give the impression that you are thinking deeply. It also gives you a bit more of a natural look than if you are looking directly at the camera.

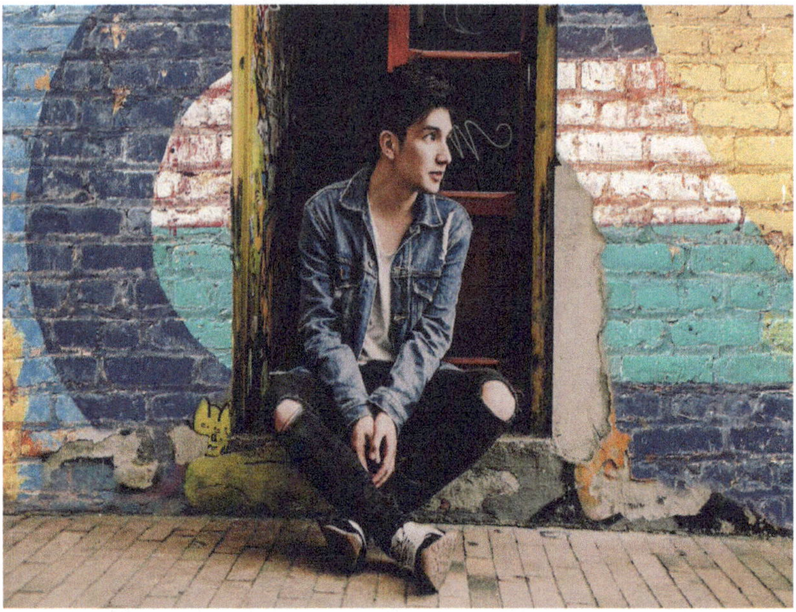

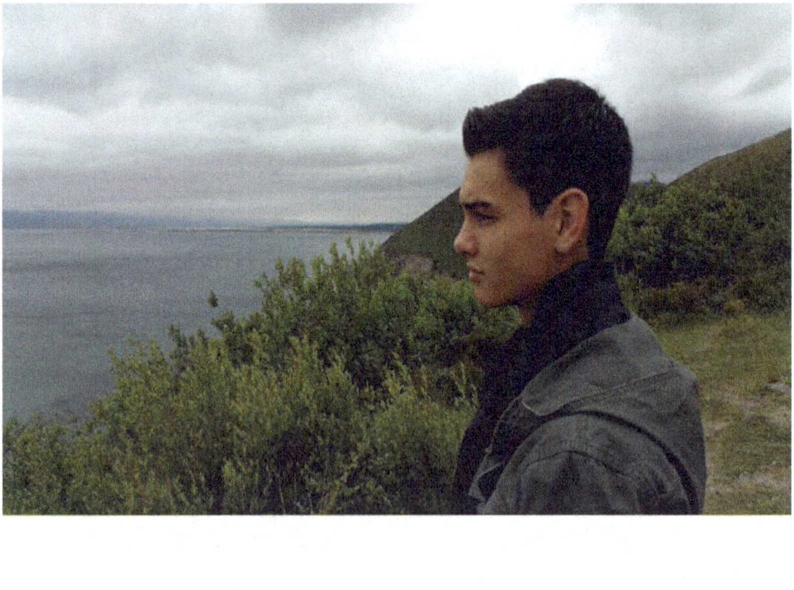

Pose #11: *Hands in Pockets:* Have your model reach inside their pockets with their hands. This guy's posture gives your image a laid-back feel. When done well, it exudes ease and confidence. When performed incorrectly, this stance may appear unnatural and inflexible. You may need to experiment with it with your model. The cut or tightness of the pants sometimes contributes to the difficulty of this stance. Your model could require a change of clothes.

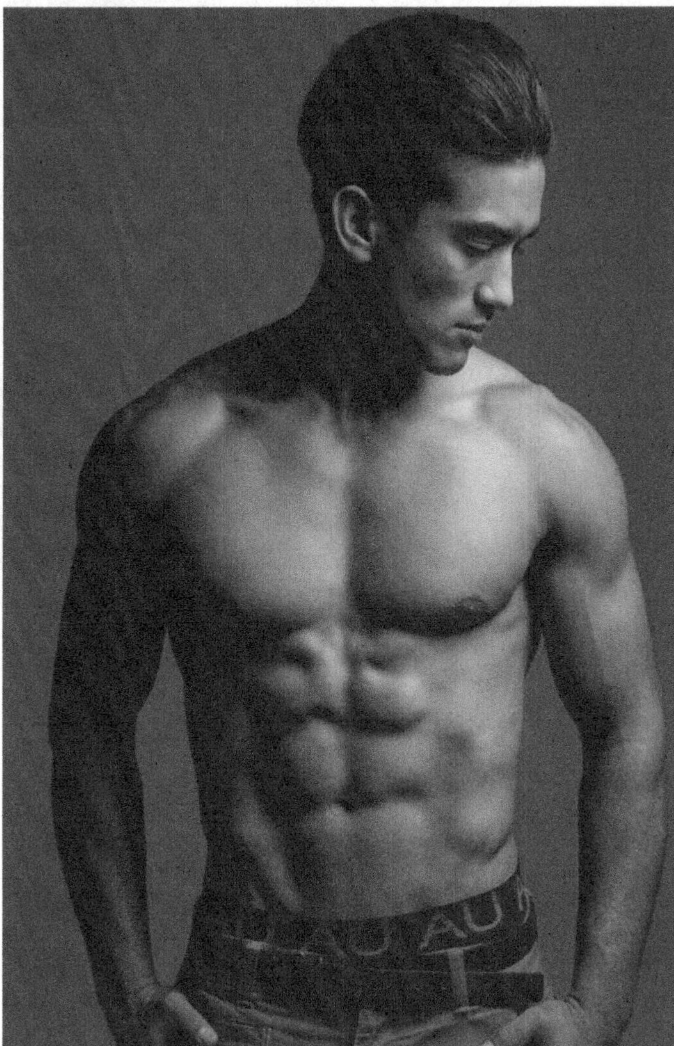

Pose #12: *Show Your Collar:* Showing their collar is another distinctive stance preferred by male models. Because it produces eye-catching lines, this stance is frequently seen in fashion publications. This position is frequently taken head-on by photographers. It's a versatile stance where the figure can sit, stand, move, or simply rest against a wall and do this pose.

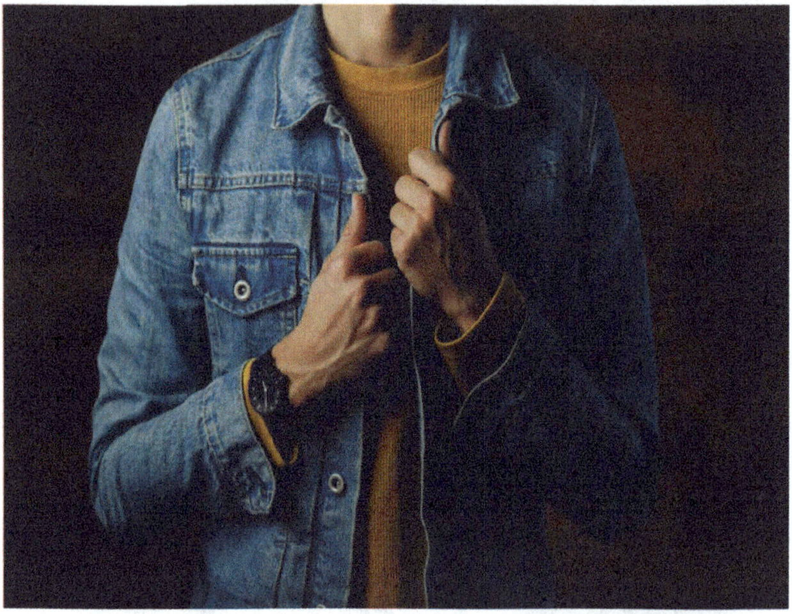

Pose #13: Squat: Young photographers or models who want to create edgy fashion photographs could use the squat position. To emphasize this, you might wish to take nighttime photos with a powerful light. Have your model kneel while holding their hands together or resting their arms on their knees. This image is suitable for urban settings or aesthetics. This stance is effective while holding your camera from various angles.

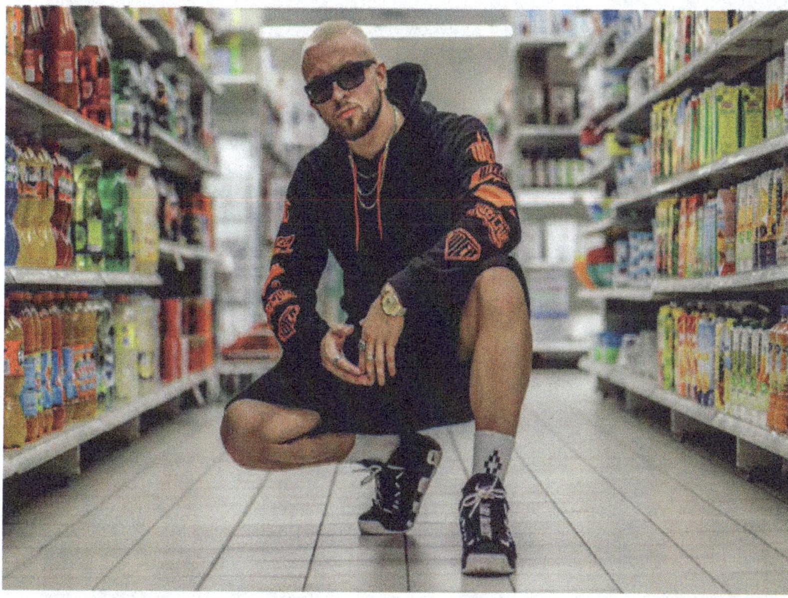

Pose #14: *The Thinking Pose.* Another sculptural position taken from Rodin's The Thinker is this one. In order to make the model appear to be lost in contemplation, you have them sit with their palm on their chin and lean forward.

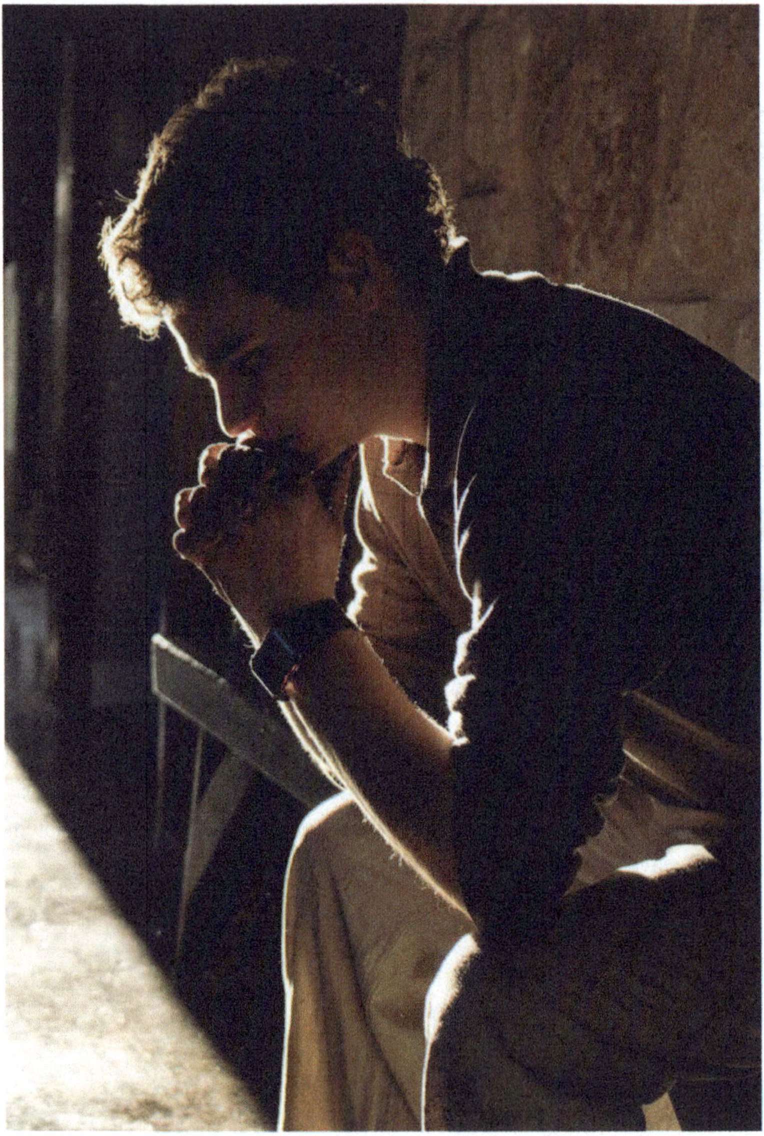

Telling your story to alter their facial expressions at this point might be wise. You're attempting to photograph someone really contemplating something. You can photograph this from a variety of angles, and it may be quite an intriguing stance to work with.

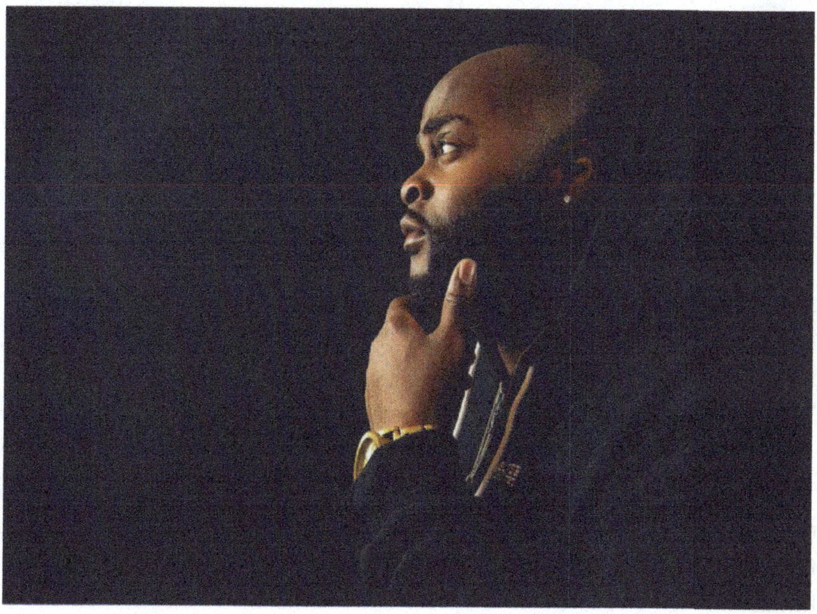

9

COMPOSITION TECHNIQUES

Whether painting images or taking photographs, composition is key. You want your images aesthetically pleasing in a landscape or thoughtfully composed in a portrait; a carefully arranged shot can make all the difference! Of course, you should still experiment with breaking these rules - but when doing so, always ensure that there's an artistic purpose behind it.

Have you ever looked at a piece of artwork and felt unimpressed, like something didn't feel right? It's possible that the artist didn't take the time to consider how each element of the scene fits into the greater whole. It's easy to get caught up in the excitement of creating something new and throw everything together hastily. Still, if you take the time to deliberate on each element, you can create genuinely captivating images. The little details can make all the difference and often add a layer of depth that elevates the piece to the next level. So next time you sit down to create something, take a breath, slow down, and give each element the attention it deserves. Your future self and your audience will thank you.

Leading Lines

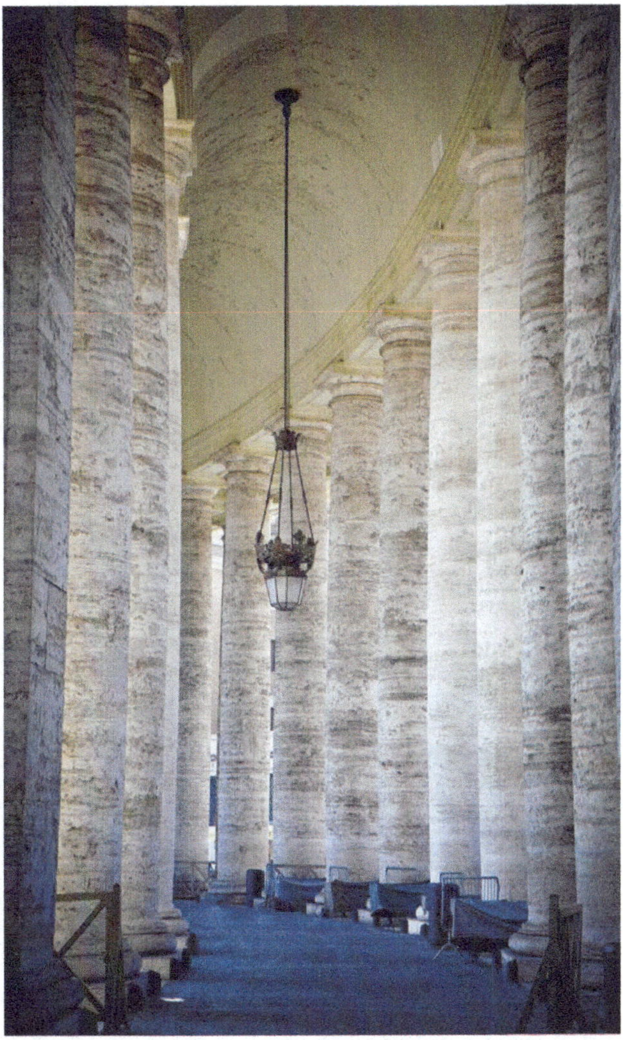

This image of Italy is for sale on my website www.tracymccrackin.com

Have you ever noticed the power of leading lines in a photograph? It's pretty remarkable how these simple elements can change the entire mood and focus of a picture. Whether it's the vertical lines of a towering skyscraper, the calming horizon line of a beach, or the winding path of a forest trail, leading lines provide a path for our eyes to follow and explore. They can add depth and energy and tell a story within a single image. Next time you're out snapping photos, keep an eye out for these powerful tools and see how they can take your compositions to the next level.

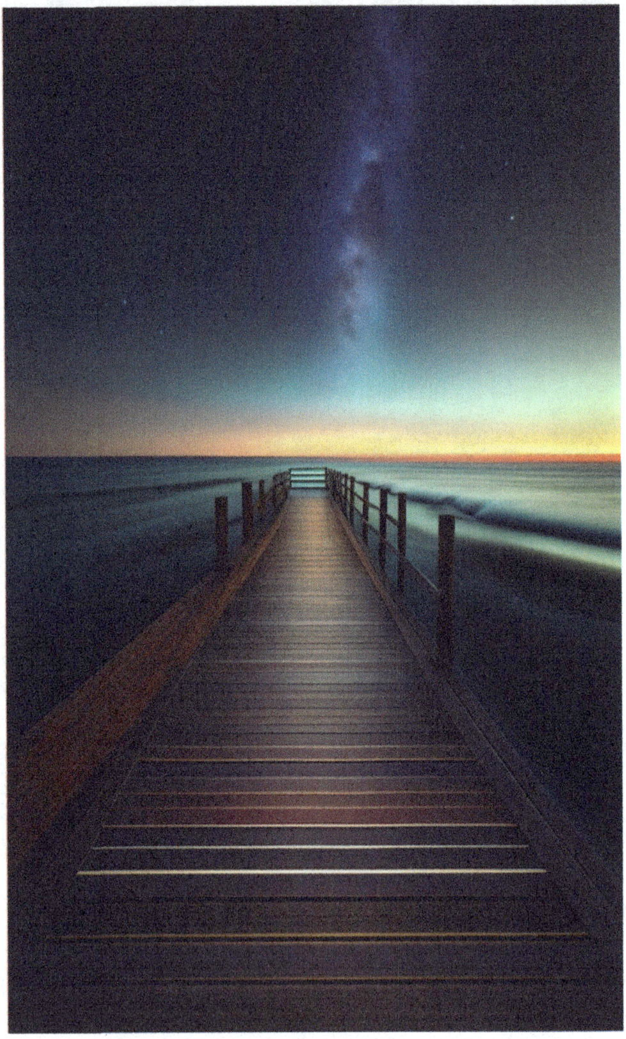

This painting image is for sale of my website www.tracymccackin.com

Perspective

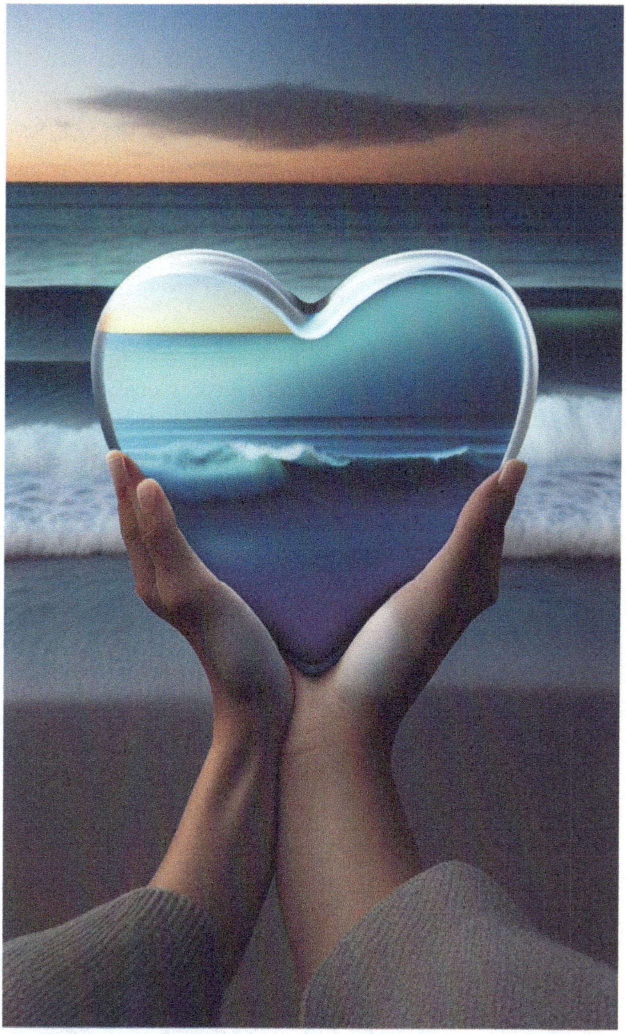

This image is for sale on my website at www.tracymccrackin.com

Have you ever wanted to change your art but didn't know where to start? Well, have you ever considered adjusting your visual focal length? It might sound technical, but it's pretty simple! By using different camera lenses, you can create many unique effects, just like the pros do. For example, if you're taking close-up shots of toy soldiers, using a wide lens from above will make them appear larger than life. And if you want to focus on their tiny facial features, use a telephoto lens instead. Plus, if you're feeling adventurous, you can even use props to hold up and photograph through to get an even more unique perspective. So get out there and experiment with your art – you never know what amazing images you'll discover!

Angles

Creating art, it's all about changing your perspective. And I mean that both literally and figuratively. Taking a fresh look at everyday objects can help you see things in a completely different way. But to spice up your artwork, try changing the physical perspective from which you shoot your photo. Try getting up high, with a bird's-eye view, or down low with a dramatic worm's-eye shot. You'd be surprised at how much impact a different angle can have on a seemingly mundane scene. So, get creative and show people something they haven't seen before!

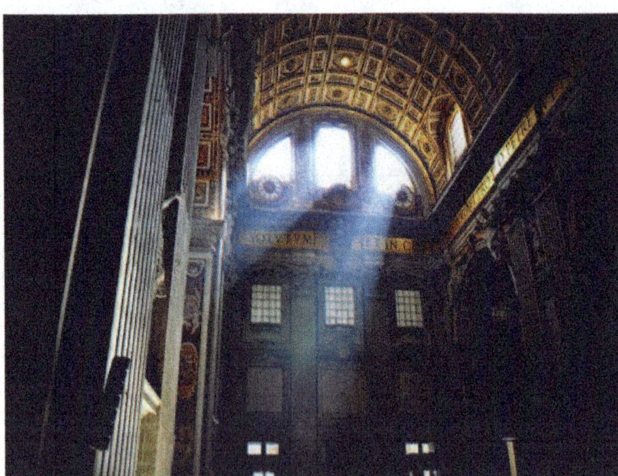

This Vatican image is for sale on my website at www.tracymccrackin.com

- **Eye-Level Shot**: Place the camera at the same height as the subject.
- **Low-Angle Shot**: Place the camera below the subject.
- **High-Angle Shot**: Place the camera above the subject.
- **Worm's-Eye Shot**: Place the camera low to the ground and close to the subject.
- **Bird's-eye Shot**: Place the camera up high and photograph downward (like a bird's view).'

Framing

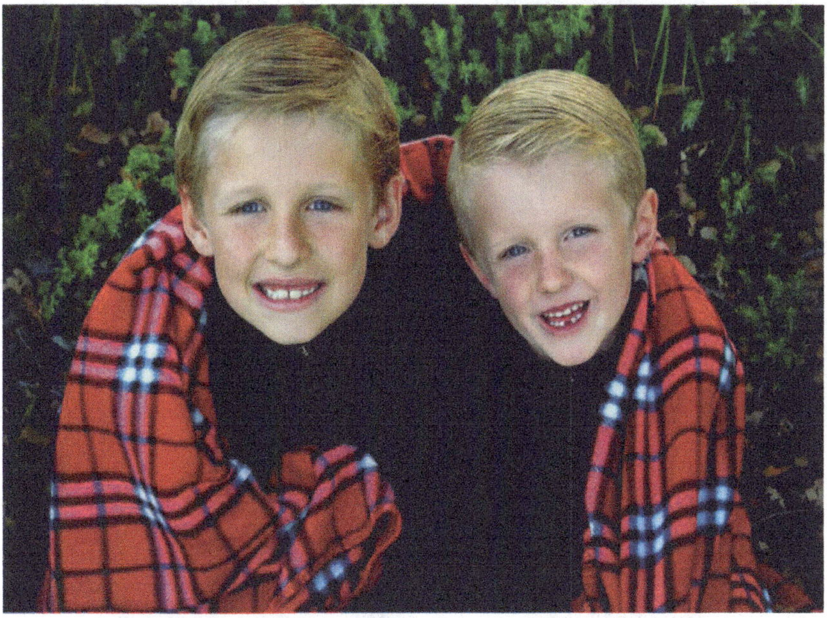

Are you tired of your artwork falling flat? Want to take your creative skills to the next level? Look no further than the magic of framing. By utilizing visual elements like doorways, windows, and prop blankets, you can draw your viewer's eye directly to your subject, creating a captivating and dynamic image. And the best part? You're not confined to traditional framing options. Experimenting with different placements and partial frames can lead to even more intriguing compositions. So go ahead, let your imagination run wild, and unlock the secrets of elevating your artwork with creative composition techniques.

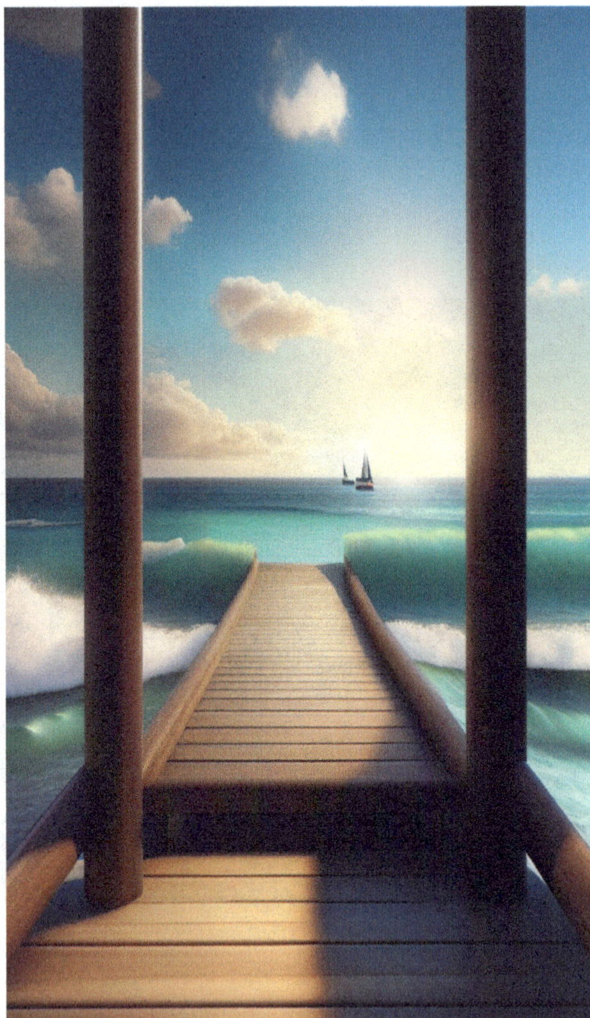

This painting is available on my website at www.tracymccrackin.com

Balancing the Elements

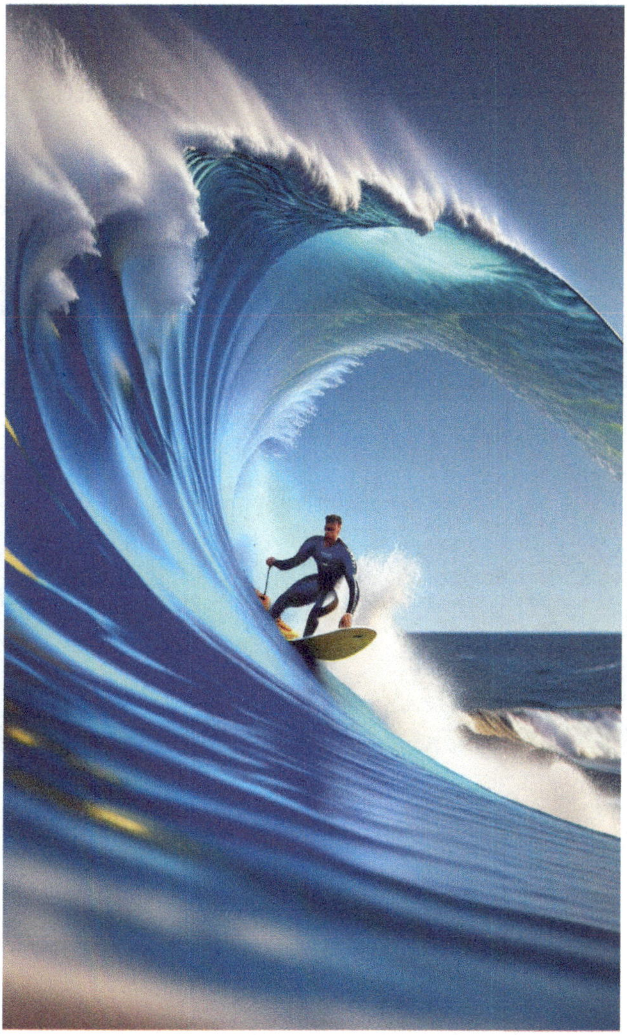

This painting image is for sale on my website www.tracymccrackin.com

Have you ever felt like your photos weren't popping out as much as they could be? Well, have no fear because the rule of thirds is here! By simply dividing your image into thirds and placing your main subject along one of those lines, you can instantly add balance and interest to your visuals. But don't forget about the power of a little anchor in the background! Whether it's a bird perched on a branch or a person walking in the distance, adding that small element can create a new level of contrast and excitement in your photo. By balancing the elements in your image, you can make it come to life and captivate your audience's attention.

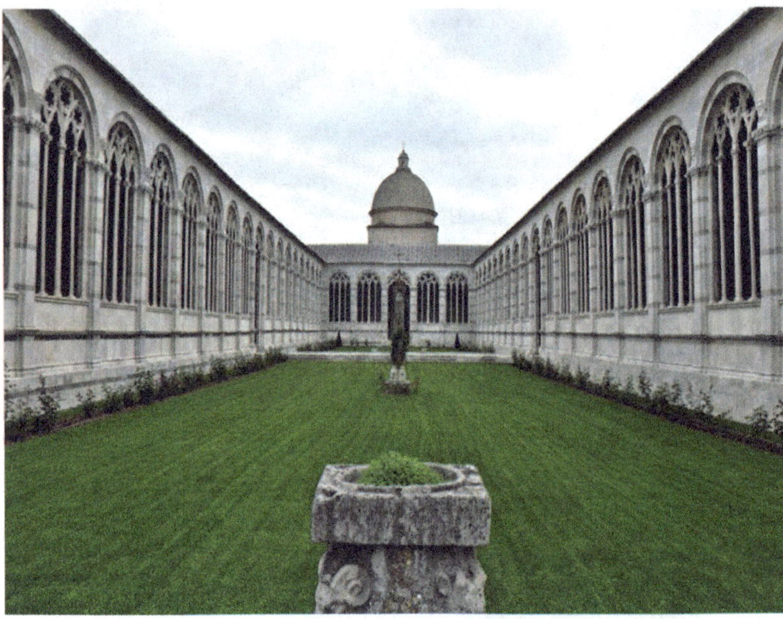

This Italy image is for sale on my website www.tracymccrackin.com

Negative Space

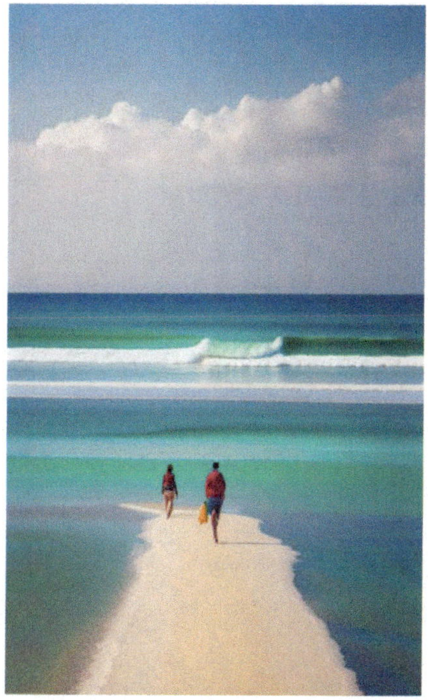

This painting image is for sale on my website www.tracymccackin.com

Have you ever looked at a photo and felt transported into the scene? That's the power of creative composition. And one technique that can make all the difference is giving your subject some breathing space. By creating a frame around your subject that gives it room to breathe, you can draw viewers in and capture their attention. This simple but effective method can create an inviting atmosphere that allows your photo to flourish truly. So the next time you're framing a shot, try giving your subject some breathing space and see how it transforms your photo.

Repetition

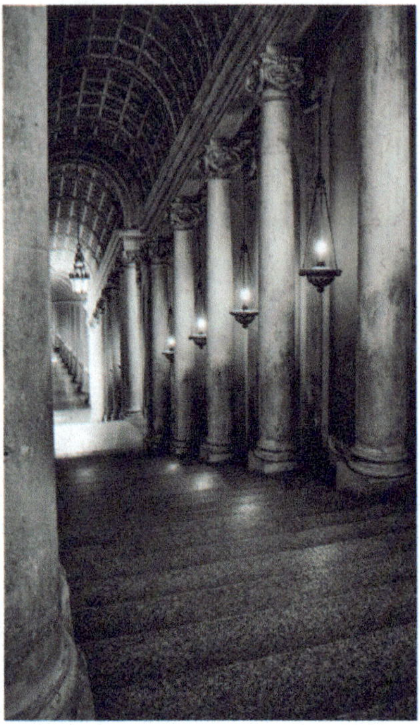

This image of the Vatican is for sale on my website www.tracymccackin.com

Have you ever stared at a photo or art, mesmerized by its intricate patterns and design? Chances are, repetition was decisive in captivating your visuals and imagination. By repeating elements like color, form, and entire items, artists and photographers can create a visual rhythm that draws your eye deeper. It's an intentional choice that can lead to maximum engagement, and while it may seem simple on the surface, the complexity lies in the details. From dynamic leading lines that guide you through the frame to unexpected variations in the repeating element, repetition can be a powerful tool to create art that leaves a lasting impression.

Selective Color

Have you ever noticed the way specific colors just seem to complement each other perfectly? From crimson and emerald to lavender and buttery yellow, these hues were practically made to be together. And that's precisely where the magic of creative photography composition comes in. By knowing which colors harmonize together and which oppose each other, a photographer can weave a visual tapestry that's downright breathtaking. There's nothing quite like the power of a vibrant image that jumps out at you from the page, and complementary colors are the secret ingredient that takes it from a good photo to a great one. Whether you're a seasoned pro or just starting, try experimenting with some unexpected color combinations and see where it takes you!

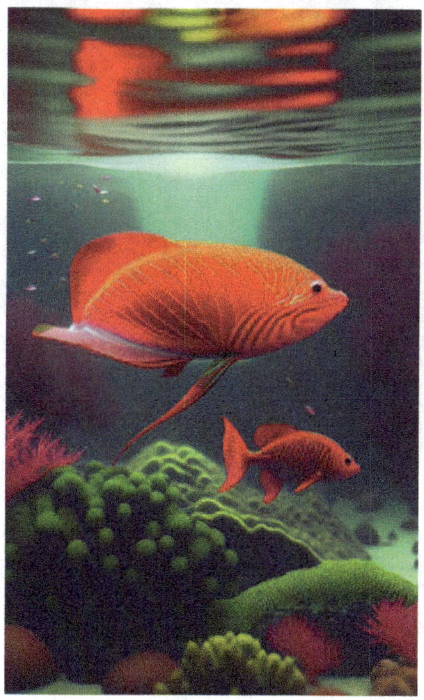

This painting is for sale of my website www.tracymccackin.com

Differential (Selective) Attention

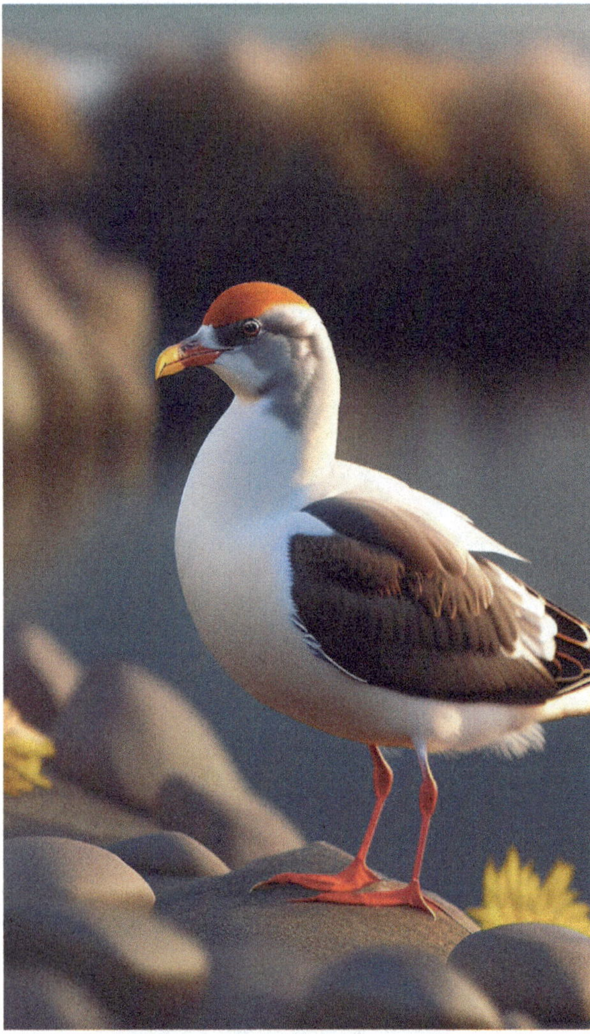

This painting image is for sale on my website at www.tracymccrackin.com

Have you ever looked at a photograph and thought, "Wow, that subject pops!"? Well, changing the focal length of a photograph is the magic trick behind that phenomenon. Photographers can guide viewers' eyes and highlight their intended subject by reducing the depth of field, which blurs out any distracting background elements. The result? Stunning portrait photographs with beautifully blurred backgrounds bring an image's focus into full view. It's incredible how a slight change can make such a significant impact, and it's one reason photography is such a captivating art form.

Depth of Field

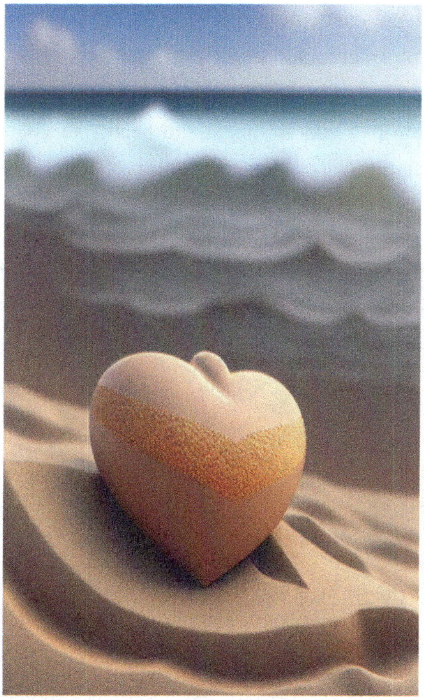

This painting is for sale on my website www.tracymccackin.com

With photography, there are many factors to consider - from the lighting to the composition. One crucial aspect that should not be overlooked is the depth of field. By manipulating this feature, you can make your subject stand out. For instance, if you're into portrait photography and want to draw all eyes to your chosen model, a shallow focus is on the way to go. This will blur out everything else in the background, focusing solely on your subject. If you're into landscapes and want to capture every detail in the frame, going for an extensive range will do wonders. Regardless of what you decide, one thing you can be sure of is that the result will be aesthetically pleasing!

Viewpoint

Have you ever tried to view something from a different perspective? Well, if not, then you should give it a go. Shifting your outlook can transform your imagery and provide new visual excitement. Take the St. Peter's Basilica in Vatican City, for instance. By simply crouching or elevating yourself above the subject, you can capture a unique and eye-catching perspective of the dome. It's amazing how a different angle can give added impact and beauty to your photos. So the next time you're out taking pictures, don't be afraid to switch things up and try out a fresh perspective!

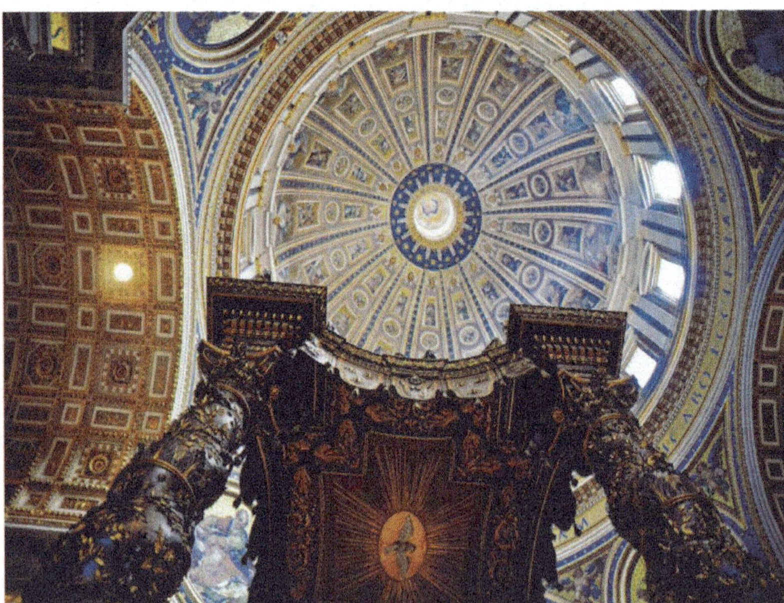

This Vatican image is for sale on my website at www.tracymccrackin.com

Symmetry

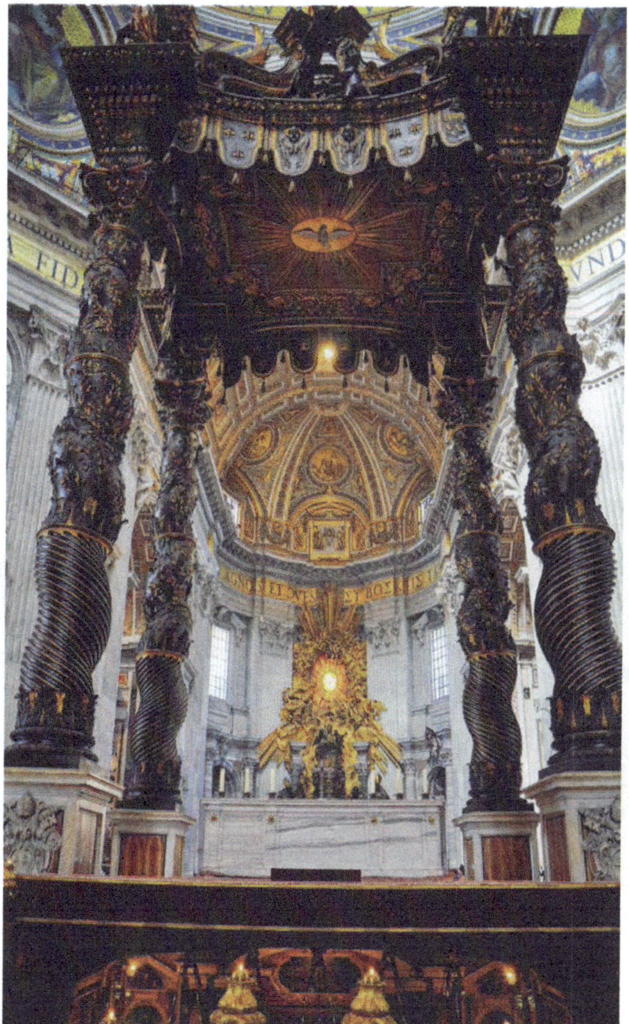

This Vatican image is for sale on my website at www.tracymccrackin.com

Symmetry can be pretty powerful, don't you think? There's just something about a perfectly balanced image that screams, "Wow!" And it's not just where this beautiful balance can be found. Check out St. Peter's Baldachin in Vatican City -

now that's a masterpiece! The thing I love most about symmetry is how it allows for some serious creativity. Breaking free from the usual design principles and experimenting with balance can cause a truly eye-catching piece of art. So next time you're snapping pics or creating your designs, give symmetry a shot. Trust me. It's worth it!

Fill The Frame

With photography, the background can sometimes be an afterthought. But trust me; it's anything but! Background manipulation can make or break an image, so it's important to curate the perfect backdrop for your shot. Whether focusing on a subject's portrait or capturing a sweeping landscape, you want your viewers' attention to be drawn to exactly what you intended - not distracted by unnecessary elements. So next time you're lining up a shot, take a moment to pause and consider what's going on behind your subject - it truly can make all the difference!

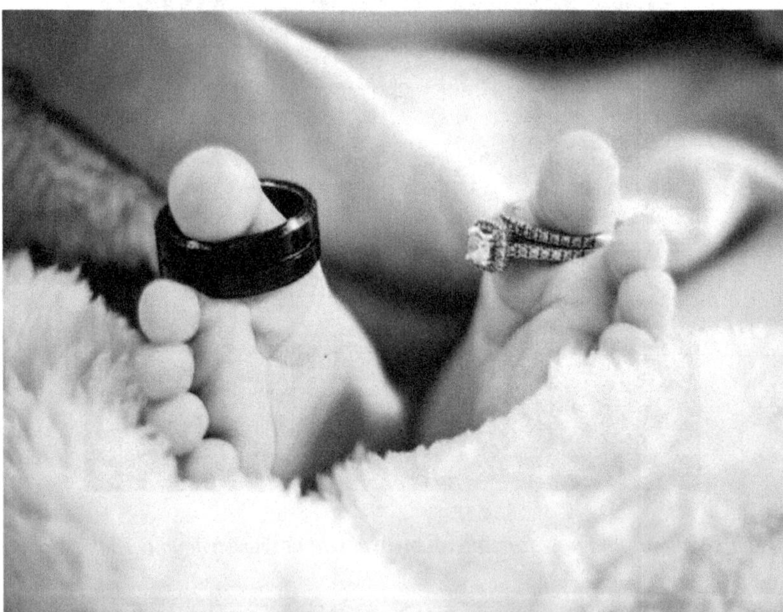

Simplicity

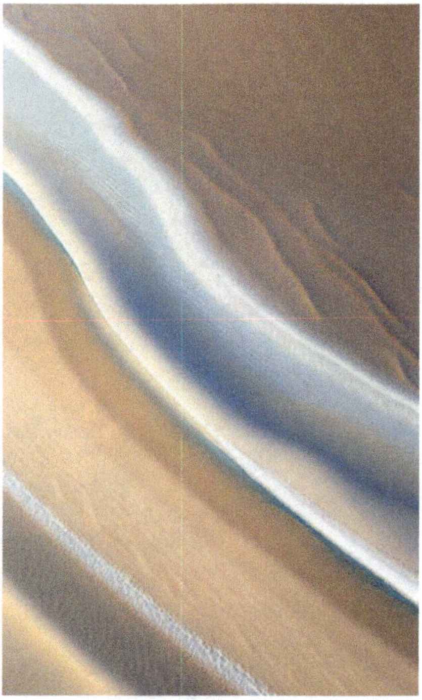

This image is for sale on my website at www.tracymccrackin.com

Have you ever found yourself overwhelmed by the excess in your surroundings? The chaos of all the objects, sounds, and images competing for your attention can be exhausting! Luckily, there is a solution: minimalism. And to master it, just focus on a tiny subject. Edward Weston was a master of this art form, and his work is truly something to behold. Looking at his pieces is like taking a deep breath of fresh air - everything else falls away, and you are left with the pure essence of the subject. It's a remarkable feeling that can only be achieved through skill and practice, but once you get there, you'll feel calmer, more centered, and more fulfilled. So give minimalism a shot - you might be surprised how much you love it!

The Left to Right Rule

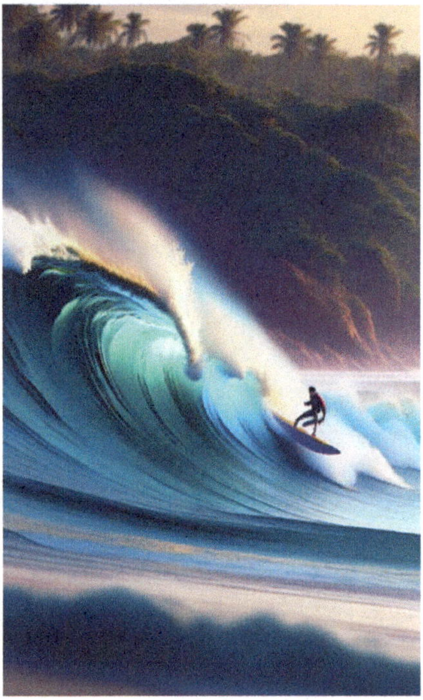

This image is for sale on my website www.tracymccrackin.com

Have you ever given much thought to the way an image is composed? Well, here's a fun fact for you - an image that reads from left to right is better for dynamic storytelling in most Western languages. It's a simple and effective compositional technique that not only respects the way we naturally read and perceive things but also serves as a reminder to consider other cultures and their storytelling traditions. We all have our unique narratives to share, and visuals are a powerful way to bring those stories to life. So next time you create an image, consider adding a slight motion that flows from left to right - like two people walking off into a sunset, a motorcycle zooming by, or a majestic bird soaring across the sky. Trust me; it'll make for an intriguing and memorable picture!

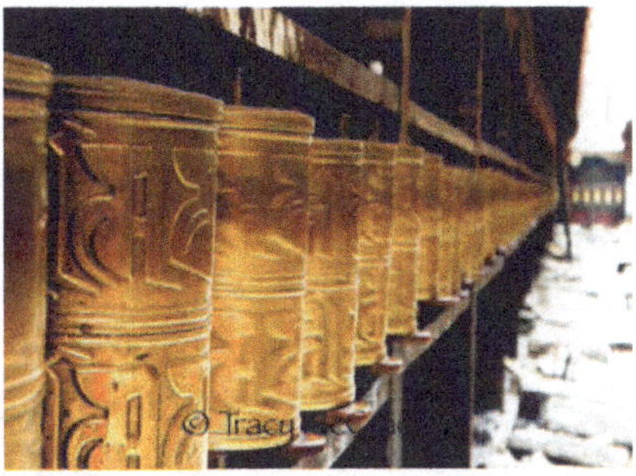

This Tibetan image is for sale on my website at www.tracymccrackin.com

Rule of Space

The Rule of Space invites the viewer to observe a captivating journey, as subjects move freely within the frame, allowing us to track their progress and feel their energy. With space allocated both ahead of them and beside them in each shot, this sense of movement is further emphasized - drawing our gaze into unknown territory with every step they take.

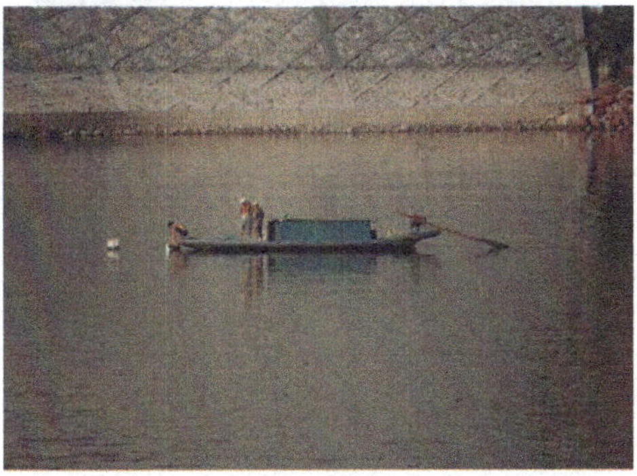

This image of Chinese fisherman is for sale on my website at www.tracymccrackin.com

Rule of Odds/Thirds

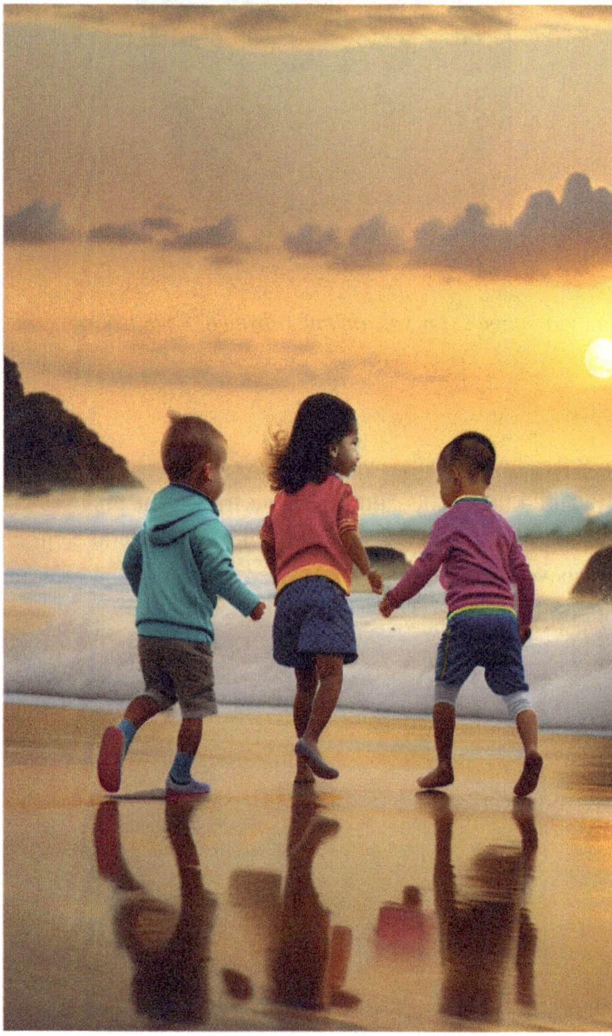

This photo realistic painting is for sale on my website at www.tracymccrackin.com

Have you ever wondered why some art pieces just seem to capture your attention more than others? Well, the secret might just lie in the ancient Greek rule of thirds. Artists have used this age-old technique for centuries to create compositions that are visually striking and engaging. And the best part? It's so simple! All you have to do is incorporate odd numbers into your composition. It makes sense when you think about it - symmetry can confuse the viewer, whereas odd numbers create a more natural flow that draws our attention in a subtle yet powerful way. So, whether you're snapping a quick photo or putting together a masterpiece, remember to keep the odd numbers in mind - it could just be the secret ingredient you've been missing all this time!

Triangles

Have you ever wondered why some paintings and drawings just catch your eye and refuse to let them go? Well, triangles might just be the secret behind those mesmerizing masterpieces. As an artist, you know the importance of composition and creating a visual journey for the viewer. And let's face it; nothing does that better than the sharp angles and lines of triangles. Whether using them line by line or grouping them to create larger shapes, triangles add movement and a sense of energy that helps create an eye-catching piece. So, next time you want to kick your art up a notch, don't be afraid to lean into the power of the triangle.

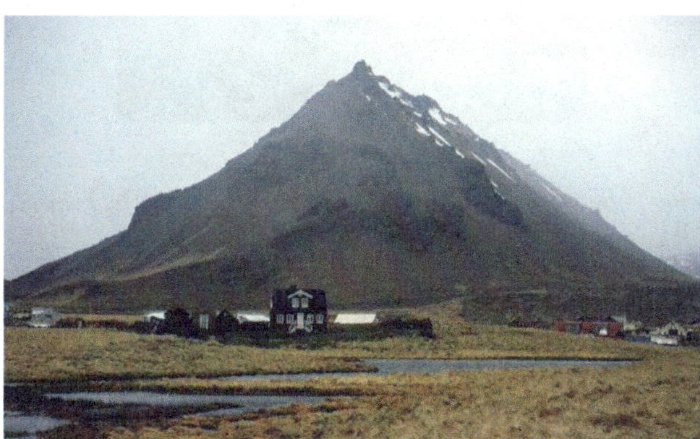

This Iceland image is for sale on my website at www.tracymccrackin.com

Have you ever taken notice of the beauty that comes from the simplistic shape of a triangle? It's an incredibly powerful shape used in artwork throughout history.

However, you don't have to search for naturally occurring triangular patterns in your artwork journey. It's just as easy, if not easier, to compose shots that feature or imply nothing but this simple yet powerful shape in paintings.

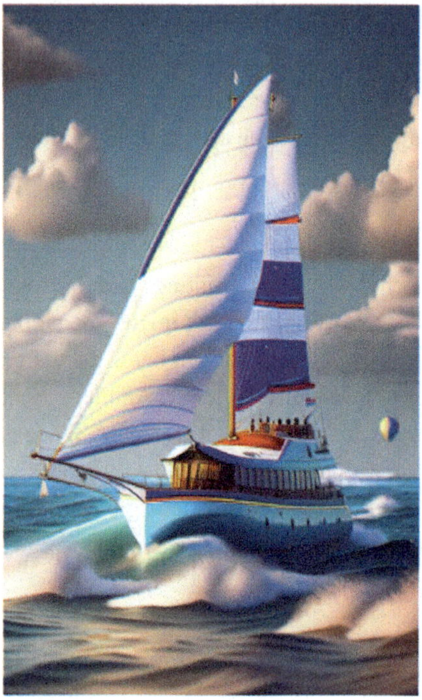

This painting image is also for sale on my website at www.tracymccrackin.com

By focusing on the shape of a triangle, you can simplify your artwork and add a dynamic element that draws the viewer's eye. It's an easy yet effective way to add dimension and depth to your art. So, why not experiment with triangles in your next piece and see how they can enhance your work?

10

METER YOUR LIGHT

Photography is all about capturing light, and if you want to take your photos to the next level, mastering the art of metering is key. It's a skill that allows you to analyze the lighting in your surroundings, whether you are outdoors basking in natural sunlight or admiring the illuminated architecture. It's not just about pointing and shooting, but taking a moment to observe your surroundings and adjust your settings accordingly. By doing so, you can capture stunning shots that showcase your skills and the world's beauty. This Mexico image is for sale on my website at www.tracymccrackin.com.

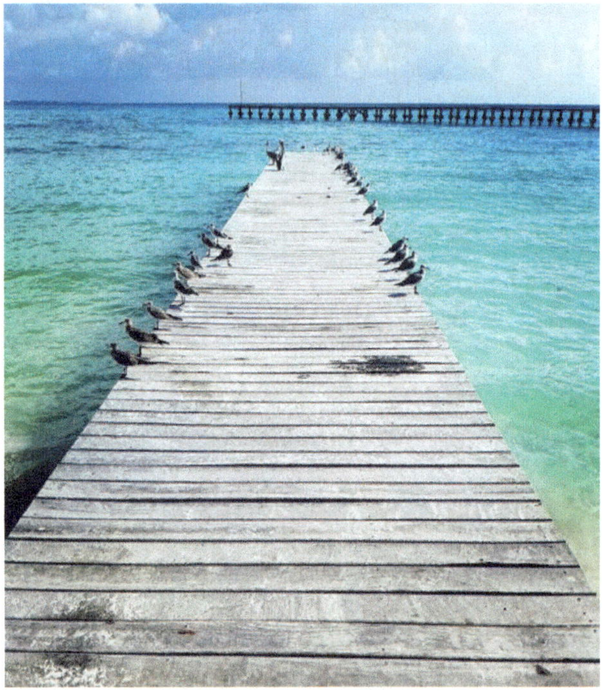

Have you ever taken a photo only to realize that the lighting was all wrong? You probably needed to adjust your exposure to get the perfect shot. That's why metering is so important - it helps your camera determine the correct amount of light needed for the perfect image. There are two main types of metering - *reflective and incident.*

Reflective Light Metering

Light is the basis of all photography—without it, capturing an image would not be possible. When light hits a subject we want to photograph, its rays bounce off and return in our direction as reflected light; this type of illumination creates both what we observe with our eyes and what cameras register when taking photographs.

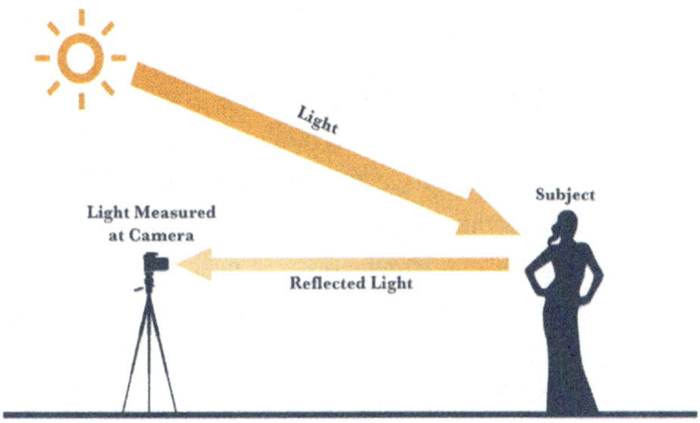

Reflective Meter Reading

To quantify these reflections accurately, photographers use integrated camera Light Meters or handheld Reflected Meters, which measure how much light bounces from the background toward their subjects. By measuring the light reflected off your subject, your camera can adjust the aperture, shutter speed, and ISO to give you a well-exposed image. It may sound technical, but it's a crucial step in getting the perfect shot!

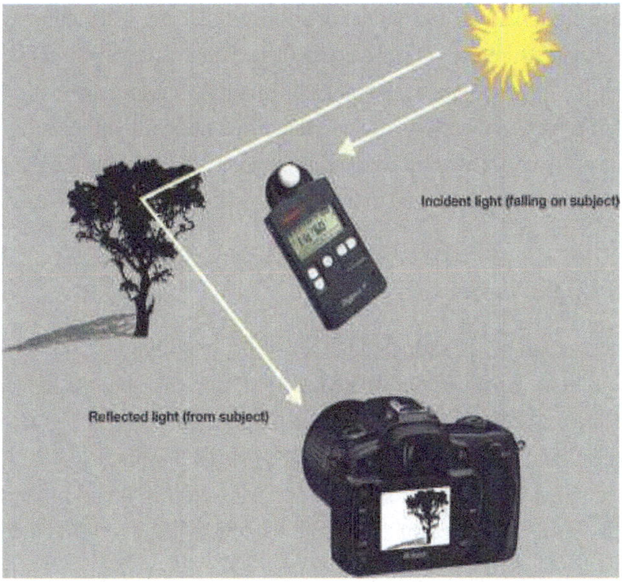

Incident Light Metering

These Meters differ because the device is measuring light *before it reflects off of a subject.* You can get a slightly more accurate reading of the total illumination because of the lumisphere. Just place the white circular disc close enough to any object you're trying to determine optimal exposure for, press go, and get pinpoint accuracy when reading these measurements – no need for estimation anymore!

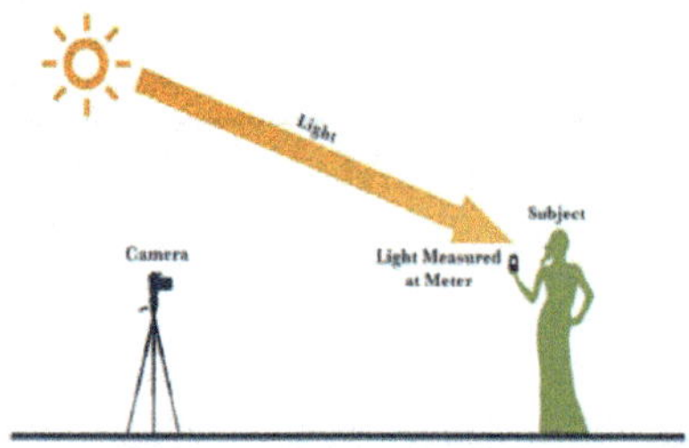

Incident Meter Reading

When capturing perfect portraits, incident metering is the way to go. Professional wedding and portrait photographers swear by it, and for a good reason. Using incident metering ensures a more accurate reading, especially for subjects that don't move around much, like studio or still-life subjects. It also allows for a more precise measurement of off-camera flash, which is excellent for those who love experimenting with manual exposure. And let's not forget about ratios! Incident metering makes it easy to measure the differences in light levels and adjust accordingly. In short, if you're serious about your photography, then incident metering is something you need to try out.

Handheld Light Meters

Have you ever struggled with getting the perfect exposure for your photographs? You're not alone. Luckily, there's a handy tool that can help - a light meter! By plugging in your ISO and letting the meter work, you can quickly determine the shutter speed and aperture combination needed for the perfect shot. And if you want to get creative with your settings, you can scroll through different pairings to find the perfect balance of light and shadow. Maybe you'll go for f/5.6 at

1/60th or f/11 at 1/15th - either way, the light meter can help you get the right amount of light for your shot.

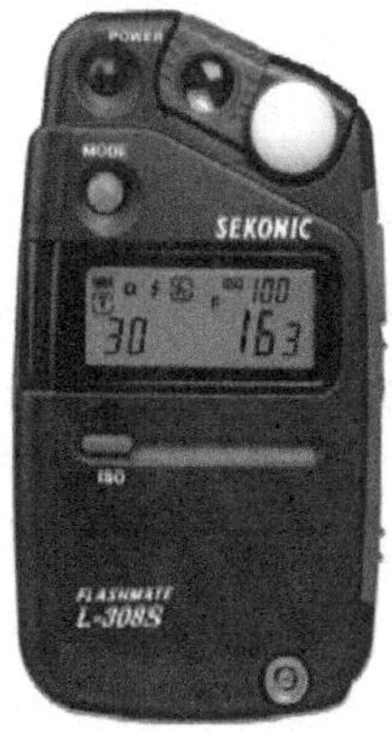

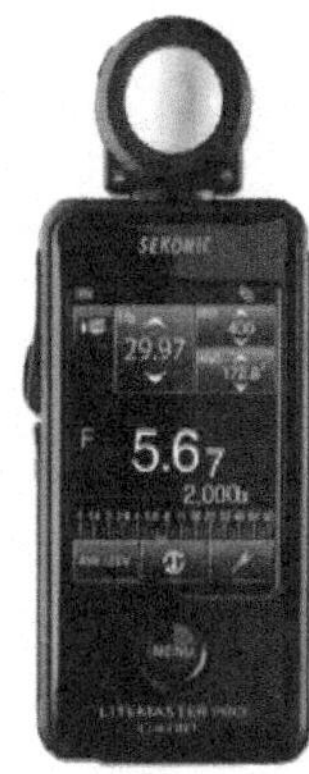

BUY ON AMAZON Affiliate Link

This 180° hemispherical dome meter below produces reliable exposure values that remain consistent, regardless of the color or brightness of an object—simply by measuring and comparing light transmitted versus reflectance.

Use a Grey Card to Meter

Have you ever found it challenging to determine the perfect exposure or white balance in your photography and can't afford a light meter? Say hello to your new best friend – the double-sided grey/white card! Using an 18% gray card as a reference in reflected-light measurement mode makes it equal to incident-light measurements for accuracy. No matter what you photograph, your exposures will be correct.

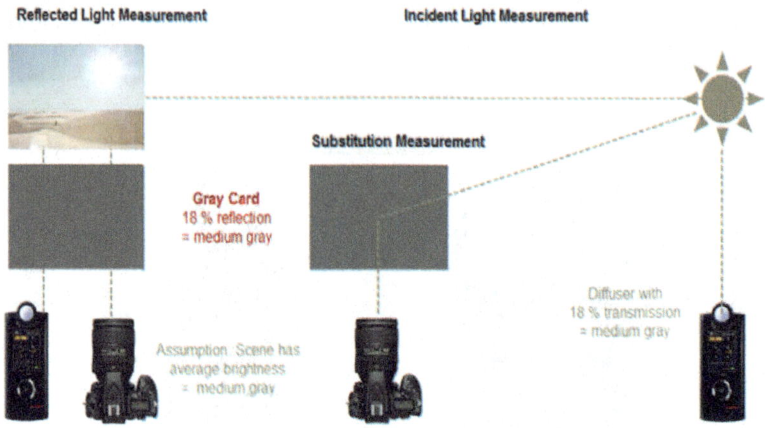

Not only does it simplify the technical issues, but it also works to correct exposure and color in varying lighting conditions. And don't worry about durability, because along with the handy reference card, you'll also receive a one-year warranty and lifetime after-service if you run into any issues. So take your photography to the next level with this must-have accessory.

Also, properly reading the exposure meter can mean all the difference between capturing an exceptional shot and a sub-par one. Light metering is integral to photography, allowing us to understand how shutter speed, ISO, and aperture interact; it helps our cameras precisely determine where—and how much of–the light is in any frame! Mastering this skill will allow you to shoot stunning images regardless of manual or automatic mode.

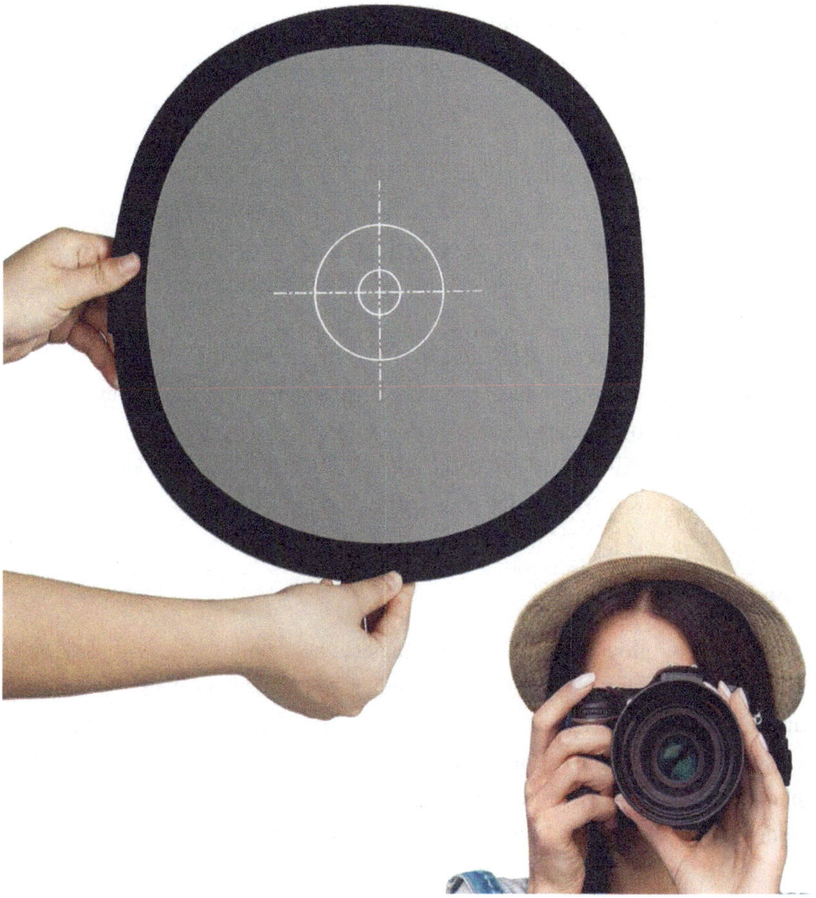

You can buy a portable one on Amazon for just $12.99. Check out my affiliate link. This is a Gray/White Balance Card,12x12 Inch (30x30cm) Portable Focus Board Two Sides Double Face 18% Grey/White Balance Reference Card with Carry Pouch for your bag.

With the help of a light meter, you can create photographs with ease and precision! Plus, seeing your work on a calibrated screen makes for an even more rewarding experience. But before that, there are still some steps involved—the films or sensors used by different companies vary widely, and so does the development/processing stage, which further affects how it appears in the end. If this sounds like something you'd enjoy learning about, take advantage of all those helpful YouTube videos meant explicitly to advise on calibrating these meters better.

Appreciating great photography requires more than an eye for composition and style. Color temperatures play a crucial role. Every location has its unique interplay of colors that can cause havoc on cameras if not adequately addressed - often resulting in unwanted yellow or blue casts to your pictures!

Thankfully, our brains can naturally adjust to differences between us ever knowing it. Still, photographers need extra help from the white balancing feature available with most modern camera models to get their shots just right. So next time you snap away at any destination, note color temperature–pros know this is vital preparation when achieving photo perfection.

Sunny 16 Rule to Meter

As technology progresses and modern cameras become more sophisticated, it's easy to overlook the old ways of doing things. But sometimes, those "old ways" are still as valid and valuable as ever. Take, for example, the Sunny 16 Rule. This classic metering rule may have originated in the film era, but it can still teach photographers valuable principles and help them take great photos. Not familiar with the rule? No worries - let's dive into the basics together!

Have you ever been out taking pictures on a bright, sunny day and struggled with the camera's meter? Well, fear not, my friend! The Sunny 16 Rule is here to save the day. This nifty little rule of thumb allows you to correctly meter for exposure during daylight without relying on your camera's meter.

The principle is simple - if it's a clear, sunny day and your aperture is at f/16, then whatever ISO you're using, your shutter speed will be the reciprocal value of that ISO. That's right, and it's that easy! And the best part? It works like a charm. So the next time you bask in the sun with your camera in tow, remember the Sunny 16 Rule and expose your shots like a pro.

SUNNY 16 RULE CHART

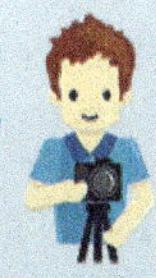

APERTURE	STRONG SUN	SUNNY	LIGHT CLOUD	CLOUDY	OVERCAST	SUNSET
	SHUTTER SPEED AT 100 ISO					
f22	1/100	1/50	1/25	1/12	1/6	1/3
f16	1/200	1/100	1/50	1/25	1/12	1/6
f11	1/400	1/200	1/100	1/50	1/25	1/12
f8	1/800	1/400	1/200	1/100	1/50	1/25
f5.6	1/1600	1/800	1/400	1/200	1/100	1/50
f4	1/3200	1/1600	1/800	1/400	1/200	1/100
f2.8	1/6400	1/3200	1/1600	1/800	1/400	1/200

www.photographyaxis.com

What about other aperture values? It can help you calculate shutter speed values with different aperture settings. As I'm sure you remember from my previous Chapter on the Exposure Triangle, the three factors determining exposure are aperture, shutter speed, and ISO. So, to keep a balanced exposure, if you change one factor, adjust another accordingly. That's where the Sunny 16 Rule comes in handy. By knowing the relationship between aperture and shutter speed, you can make quick adjustments to keep your exposure just right. It's like a mini balancing act every time you take a photo!

Have you ever found yourself when you wanted to open your aperture but couldn't figure out what to do with your shutter speed and ISO? Well, fear not, because I've got the breakdown for you. Let's say your aperture is set at f/16, and you want to go up a stop to f/11. To achieve this, you must either slow your shutter speed to 1/400 sec or lower your ISO to ISO100. But wait, there's more! If you want to go up another stop to f/8, you must change either your shutter speed or ISO. It may feel like a lot to keep track of, but with some practice and understanding, you can experiment with your settings and capture the perfect shot. Happy shooting!

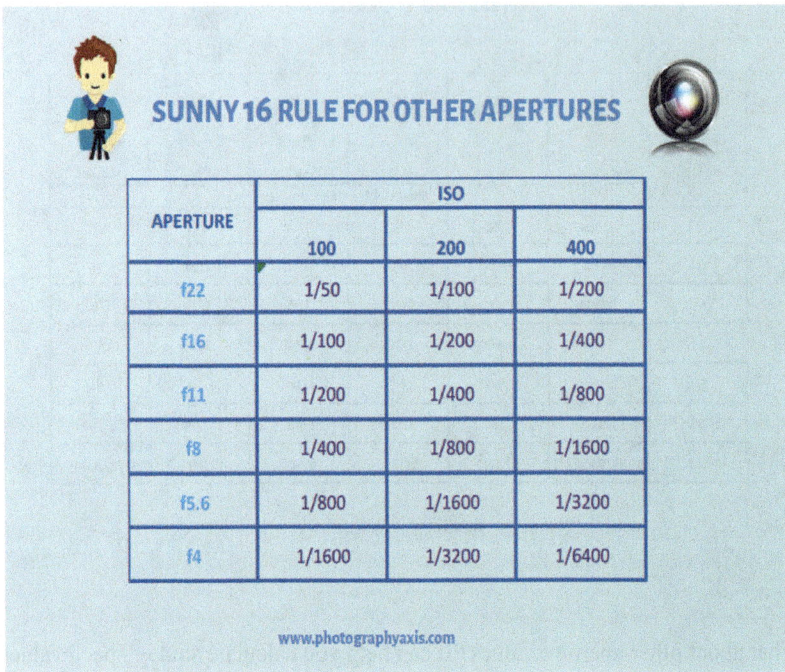

APERTURE	ISO		
	100	200	400
f22	1/50	1/100	1/200
f16	1/100	1/200	1/400
f11	1/200	1/400	1/800
f8	1/400	1/800	1/1600
f5.6	1/800	1/1600	1/3200
f4	1/1600	1/3200	1/6400

Use Your Camera's Built-In White Balance Meter

With wedding and event photography, proper exposure is essential to capturing the perfect moment. Hidden behind your camera are potent tools like light meters, which can gauge how much air and shutter speed should be used for each frame - helping you avoid wasting precious film or missing an important shot altogether!

Every good photograph starts with the right colors, and that's why your camera has a white balance setting. This sophisticated feature adjusts shades to create images that more accurately reflect reality — no matter what light source you're using! From warm daylight hues to deep twilight blues, tweaking the settings can help you capture exactly what it felt like at any given moment, so anyone who looks at the photo gets an authentic experience.

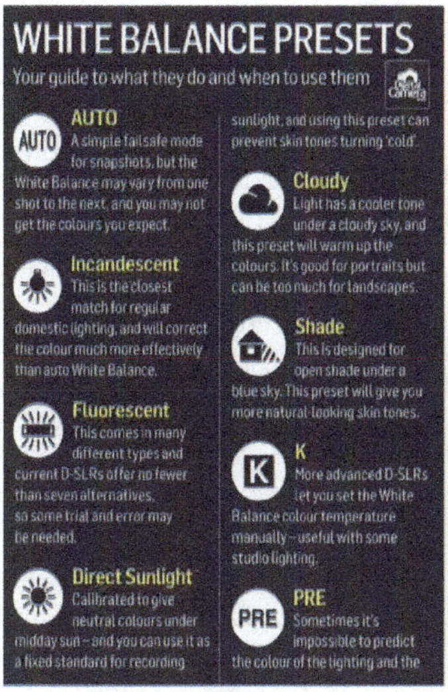

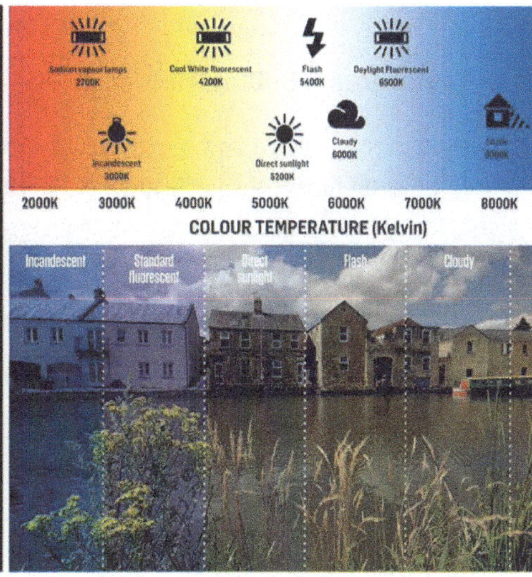

- **Auto**: The camera will pick the white balance for you when you use this option. This option is excellent on modern DSLRs and works well most of the time.
- **Flash**: This white balance setting ensures correct color reproduction when shooting with flash as a significant light source.
- **Daylight**: In bright sunlight, this is the ideal backdrop for outdoor photography.
- **Cloudy**: To take a picture in the shadows, use this mode.
- **Shade**: When taking a photograph in the shade, choose this setting.
- **Tungsten**: This white balance option might be employed when tungsten lighting dominates.
- **Fluorescent**: In rooms with mostly fluorescent illumination, this setting is appropriate.
- **Kelvin**: Color temperature may be controlled by selecting a Kelvin color temperature.
- **Custom White Balance**: A calibration target or a gray card may take a shot to select the white balance in this mode.

Experiment with how different light sources can transform your subject and create unique visual effects - from creating stark contrasts to making soft, subtle shadows.

Use Your Camera's Built-In Histogram

Have you ever wondered how to represent the colors and tones in an image accurately? Look no further than a histogram. This handy visual tool breaks down the highlights, shadows, and mid-tones of an image into easy-to-read graphs. It's like a treasure map for photographers and designers, showing them where the peak tones are and where there may be gaps in the color distribution. With a histogram, you can ensure that your images are correctly balanced and your tone is accurately represented.

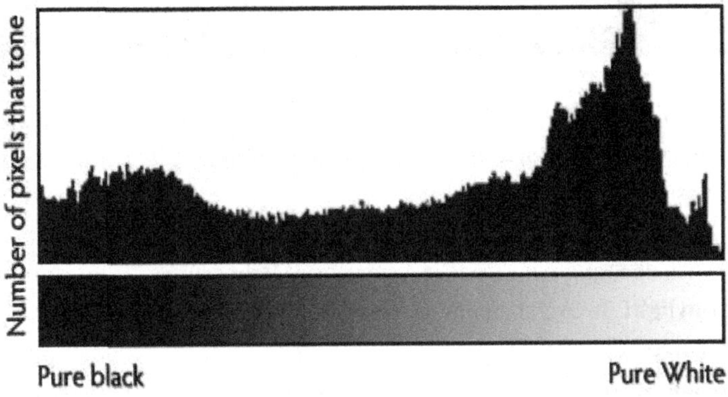

For photography, capturing a scene with well-rendered shadows, highlights, and mid-tones is a significant goal. But how can you determine if you've achieved that level of detail in your photo? You could check it out on your camera's LCD screen or a computer. However, if you want a more objective method of evaluating tones, the histogram is your go-to. This nifty tool can reveal blown-out highlights, clipped shadows, and whether your photo is too dark or too light. So, let the histogram be your guiding light the next time you aim to capture the perfect exposure.

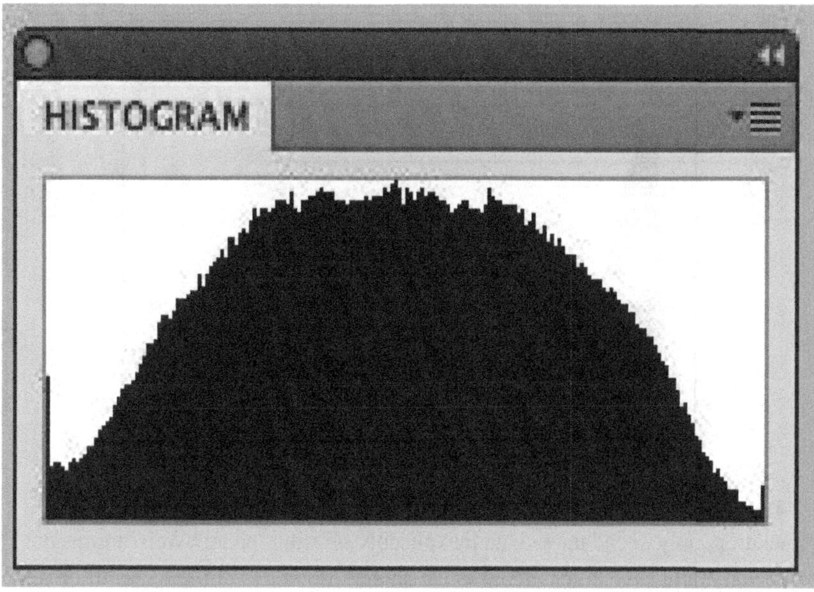

If it's skewed to the left, you might have some underexposure going on, which means you've got a lot of dark pixels. If it's skewed to the right, overexposure is likely the culprit, leaving you with many light pixels. But fear not, because if your histogram is well-balanced and centered, you've got nothing to worry about! This shows a beautifully detailed, well-exposed image because you've got many mid-tones happening. So next time you check out your histogram, take a moment to appreciate its helpful insight into your photo's exposure.

Your scene may be naturally darker or lighter than middle gray. Have you ever taken a photo of a black rock against a starry night sky and been disappointed with the histogram? Don't worry; you're not alone. Even if you've captured all the details correctly, this type of image can often result in a skewed histogram. While a well-balanced, unskewed histogram is ideal for images with mid-tones, it's not always possible to achieve in every scene. So, don't be afraid to experiment and capture unique shots, even if they don't fit the mold of a standard histogram. The beauty of photography is in capturing the essence of a moment, regardless of the technicalities.

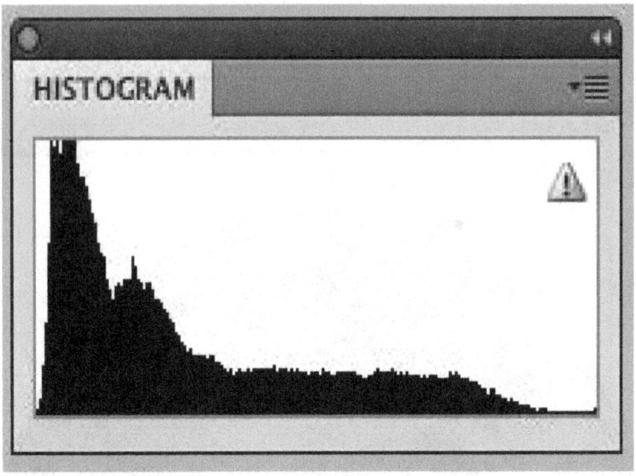

Have you ever tried to capture the perfect shot of a white tree against a snowy backdrop, only to end up with an inexplicably off-kilter photo? Well, it turns out that you might have fallen victim to the natural brightness of the scene, throwing off your camera's exposure. With such a naturally light and bright scene, it's easy to accidentally skew your photo in the wrong direction and miss out on capturing the true beauty of the moment. Next time you're out in the snow, keep this tip in mind and optimize your exposure settings accordingly!

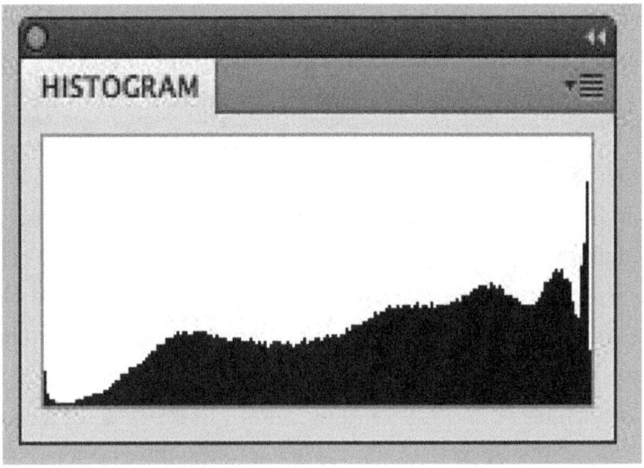

When analyzing your image's histogram, it's essential to take a step back and ask yourself a few questions before diving in. First, consider whether your scene should average out to a middle gray tone or if it should have a more obvious skew. This will give you some excellent guidance on how you should approach the editing process. By understanding the overall tone of your scene, you can make adjustments that highlight the details and bring out the best in your image. Don't rush into editing before taking the time to consider your scene's unique characteristics!

11

CAMERA LENSES

While any camera can take good portraits, these items will take your images to the next level. As a beginner, it's easy to get overwhelmed, which is why I've curated a list of must-have photography lenses. With my tips and recommendations, you'll have everything you need to nail your next shoot and take stunning images. While I already covered camera focal lengths in previous Chapters, I dig deeper here on how focal length determines your camera lens choices.

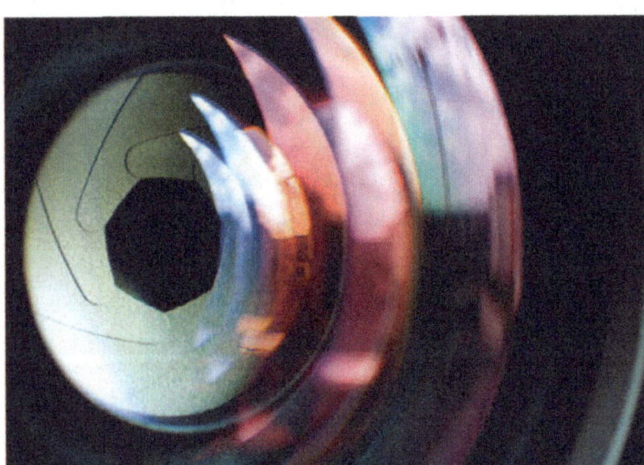

How Does Focal Length Determine Your Lens

Discover the secret behind the perfect angle of view! Focal length is a vital technical aspect of lenses that measures the distance between the optical center and the image sensor. By measuring in millimeters and focusing to infinity, it determines the angle of view, regardless of the manufacturer or camera format. Check out the diagram below to see how focal length and angle of view work hand-in-hand.

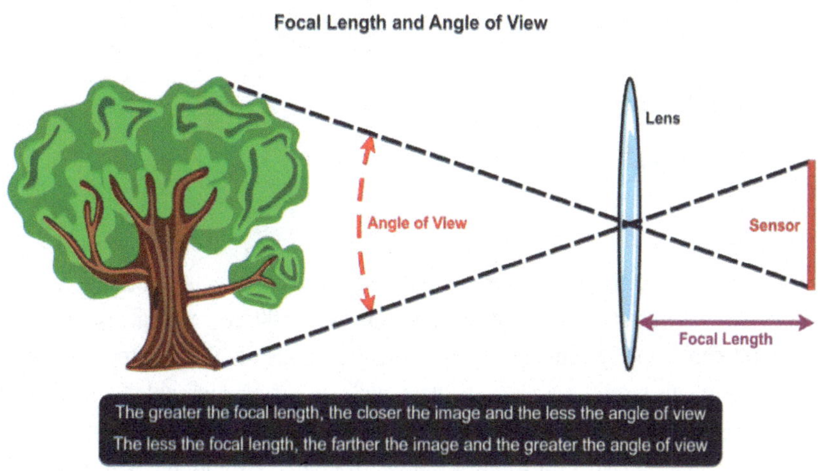

Get ready to capture the perfect shot with the right lens! The focal length of your lens determines how much of the scene your camera captures. Short focal lengths, like a 24 mm lens, provide a wide angle of view, showing a large area but with small subjects.

Long focal lengths, such as a telephoto lens, give a narrow angle of view but with larger subjects. Plus, they compress the image, making the background seem closer and larger. Now you can choose the perfect lens for your next photo adventure!

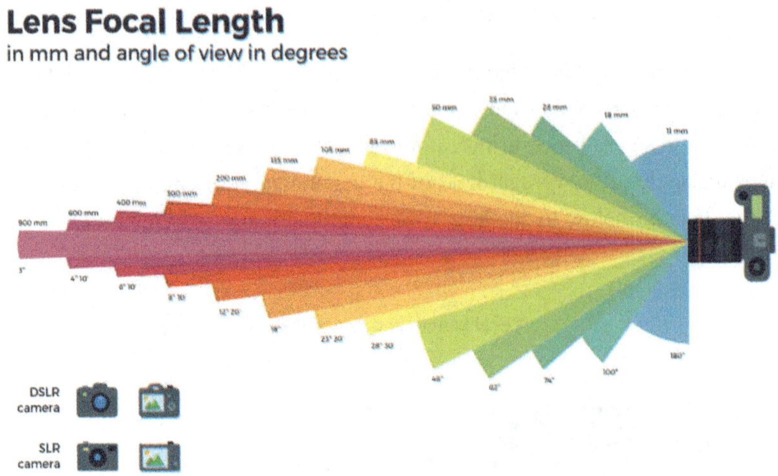

Discover the wide array of lenses and their capabilities for your photography needs. The 11 mm fisheye lens offers an impressive 180-degree angle of view. For landscapes, the 28 mm lens with a 74-degree angle of view is a top choice. The 50 mm lens provides a more realistic angle of view comparable to the human eye at 46 degrees. And finally, the extreme 900 mm lens brings the angle of view to just 3 degrees, perfect for capturing shots from afar. Explore the world of photography with these lenses!

Discover the ideal focal length and unlock your artistic potential! Explore how various focal lengths impact your photography and capture stunning images that truly express your vision. Check out our photo comparisons below.

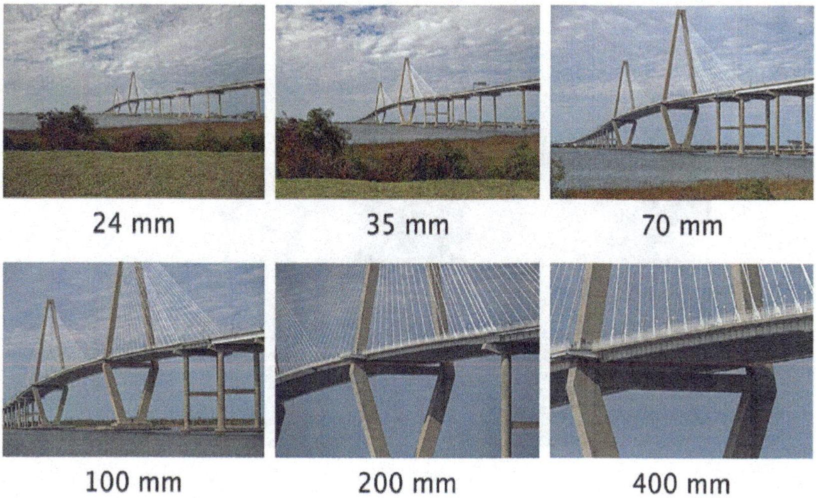

Discover the Perfect Lens Focal Length for Your Photos! Explore the spectrum of focal lengths to pinpoint the ideal one for your shooting needs. Whether you're capturing landscapes, portraits, or action shots, we'll guide you to the perfect focal length for stunning results. Say goodbye to blurry or dull photos and hello to crystal-clear images!

Prime Lenses

A fixed lens is an excellent choice for photography enthusiasts looking to get the most out of their images. *Its key feature - it can't zoom!* Instead, its focal length remains constant and stays at one specific setting; this means that with a 50mm prime lens, you only capture photos with the same field of view no matter how much you adjust your angle or framing. When compared to more expensive zooms, primes make up in quality what they lose in flexibility: they are "faster" when taking pictures due to increased maximum aperture, which makes them especially suited for low light conditions as well as creating stunning bokeh effects in your images.

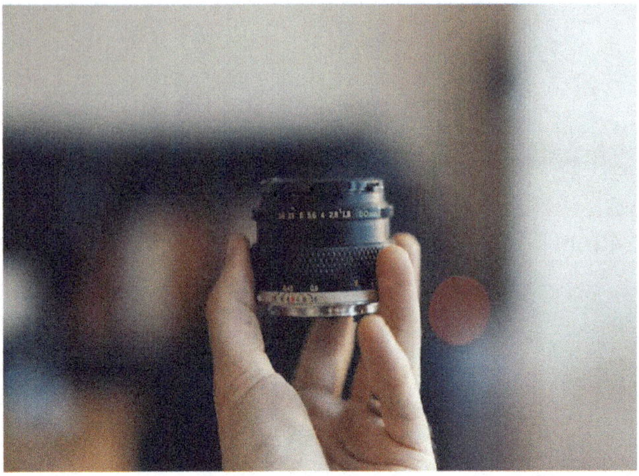

Standard Lens

Discover the lens everyone raves about - the standard lens. With a focal length of around 50mm or anything between 35mm and 85mm, it mimics what the human eye sees, perfect for capturing real-life perspectives. It's also popular for its sharp images and minimal distortions, making it suitable for various types of photography. A must-have for any aspiring photographer!

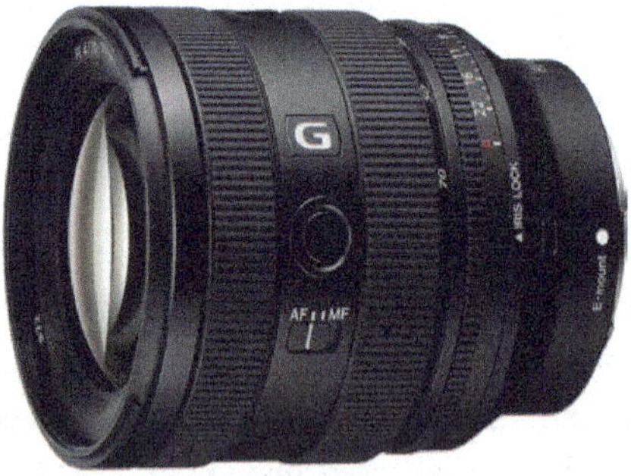

Perfect for travel, street, floral, and portrait photography, these lenses can also achieve stunning landscape shots. And if you're looking for one for all your photography needs, look no further than the "nifty fifty" 50 mm lens - renowned for its impressive performance in multiple roles. This is the best first camera lens you should start working with until you can add other lenses to your repertoire.

Fisheye Lens

Looking for a way to capture a full 100 – 280 degree view? Consider fisheye lenses with short focal lengths in the 8-15 mm range. They offer an incredibly wide angle and some specialized options can even expand up to 280 degrees. There are two categories to choose from: the diagonal fisheye, which fills the entire frame with a horizontal view, and specialized fisheye lenses that offer even wider angles. Capture stunning photos and take your photography to the next level with fisheye lenses.

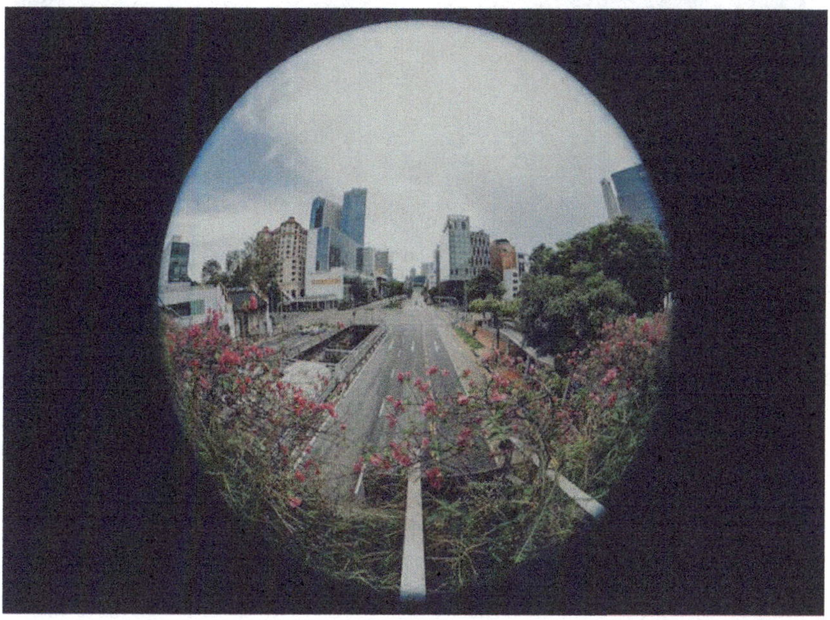

Macro Lenses

Macro lenses capture stunningly detailed closeup photos of even the tiniest subjects. Specialized optics and a minimum focus distance of 30cm make it possible - at 1:1 magnification ratio, you can get an image on your sensor plane with equal or greater detail compared to real life! Whether bugs, coins, or flowers, these lenses are ideal for marveling over little details that would otherwise be impossible to admire and envy.

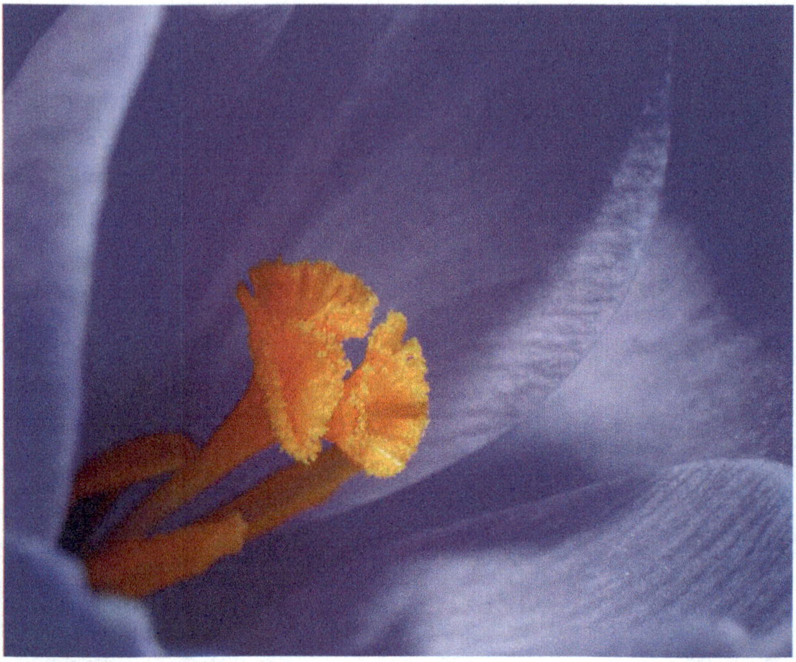

Wide-Angle Lenses

Capture stunning landscapes and explore beyond the limits of the human eye with wide-angle lenses. Typically, any lens with a focal length of less than 50mm is considered a wide-angle lens. Specifically, lenses with a focal length of 16-24mm are classified as wide-angle, while those from 24-35mm are standard wide-angle lenses. With their excellent depth of field, these lenses are a must-have for landscape photographers looking to immerse viewers in the beauty of the natural world. The wider angle of the lens contributes to minor distortions, causing parallel lines to converge. However, experienced photographers know how to embrace distortion and use it creatively. Discover the techniques to make the most of your wide-angle lens.

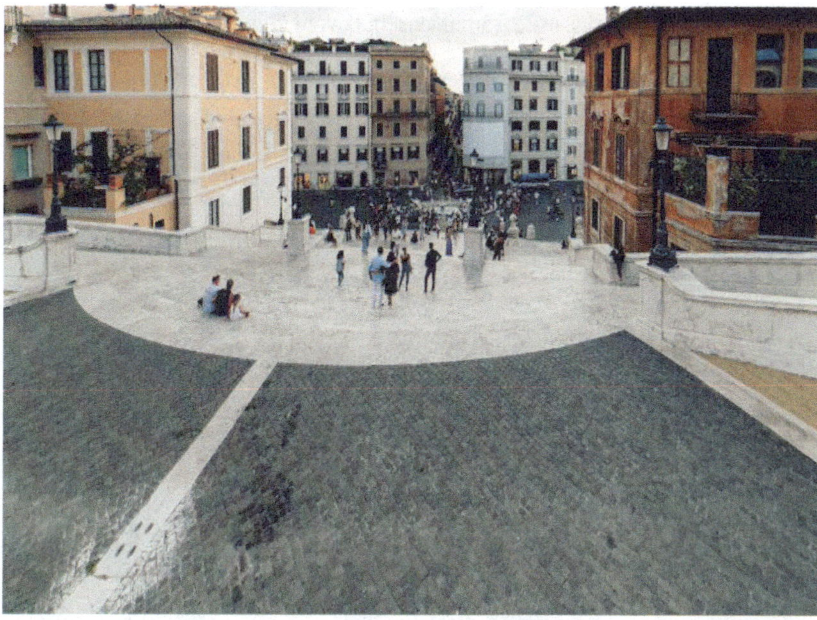

Zoom Lenses

Expand your photography possibilities with a standard zoom lens. This versatile tool enables you to capture everything from full-body shots to unique environmental portraits and group photos, without needing to switch lenses. With a range of 24-70mm, you have the flexibility to shoot solo and group portraits without missing a beat. This flexibility is beneficial when shooting in a location where it would be challenging to switch lenses quickly, all while achieving picture quality that rivals prime lenses!

Want to take stunning portraits? Invest in a 24-70 mm zoom lens on a full-frame camera. Versatile yet consistently beautiful, this lens is a must-have for photography enthusiasts. For dreamy background blurs, aim for a wide maximum aperture of f/2.8. Capturing stunning photos can be challenging without an f/2.8 lens; however, this doesn't mean you cannot achieve the same effect at f/4, f/5.6, or f/6.3. Though it may take more effort, beautiful photos can still be captured.

Be cautious when shooting wide-angle portraits - close-up shots can cause distortion. For full-body shots, use a 35mm lens, but avoid going even wider unless you want a unique creative effect.

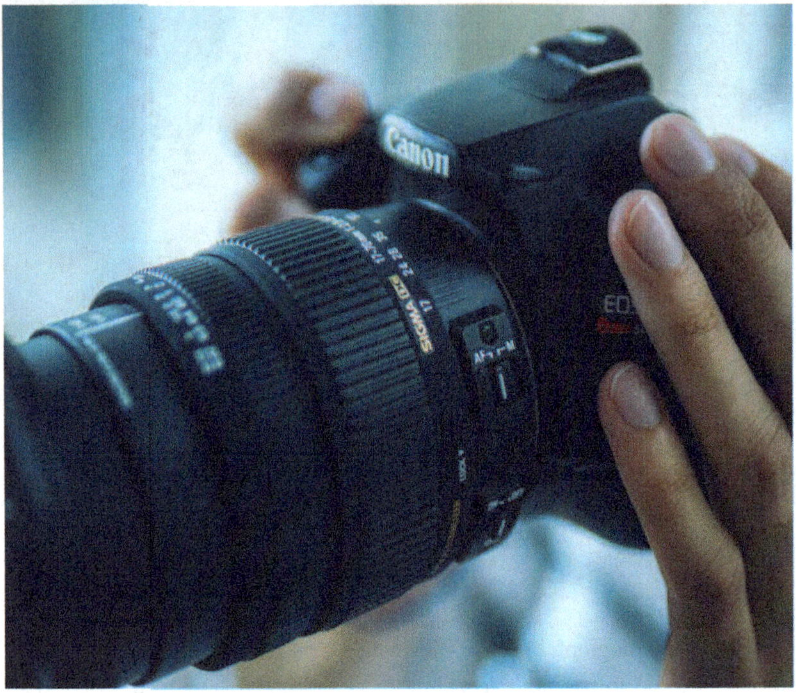

Telephoto Lenses

Discover the world of telephoto lenses, the secret weapon for stunning shots. A telephoto lens magnifies your subject beyond your lens's diagonal size, providing crystal-clear detail and magnificent shots. Many photographers define telephoto lenses differently, with some insisting on a minimum focal length of 70mm, others preferring 80 or 85mm, and some arguing that the mid-telephoto range must exceed 135mm. Whether you're a pro or an amateur, a telephoto lens can capture breathtaking images that take your breath away. The camera settings that worked wonders with your wide-angle lens might not be the right fix for your telephoto lens. Find out the reason your telephoto lens is more prone to camera shake and how to take tack-sharp shots every time. This image is for sale on my website: www.tracymccrackin.com.

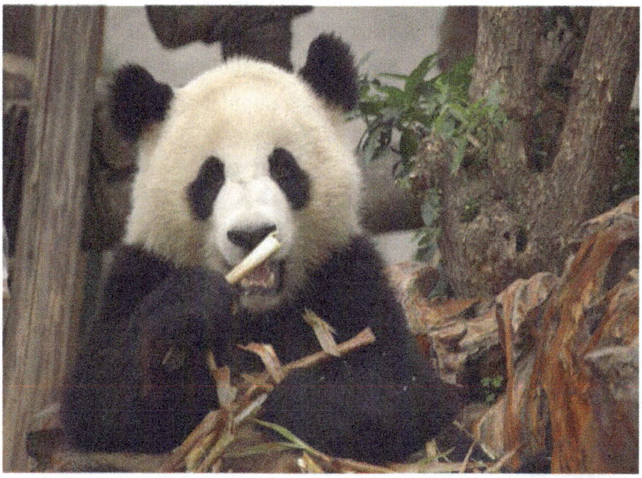

Medium Telephoto Lens

Discover the diverse sub-categories of telephoto lenses, based on their focal length. Optimal for capturing close-up shots, short telephotos (ranging from 85-135mm) offer stunning background separation for portrait, product, and event photography, without needing lengthy distances between photographer and subject. While longer focal lengths offer even more dramatic results, short telephotos are a popular choice for their versatility and ability to elevate any shot.

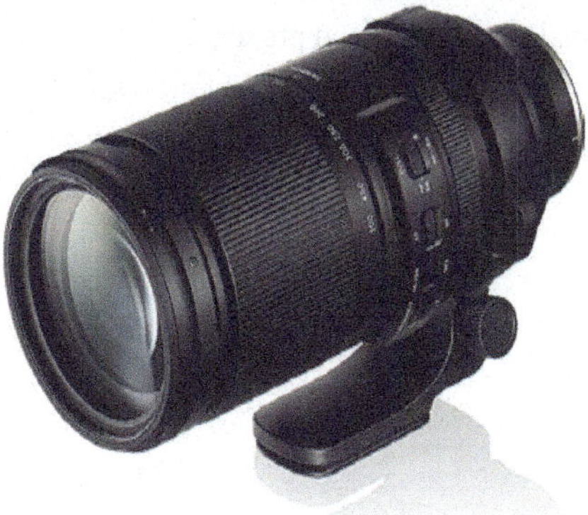

Get the best of both worlds with a medium telephoto lens! At 135 to 300mm, this lens provides great reach for capturing stunning shots without breaking the bank. It's no wonder why these focal lengths are so popular among photographers.

Super Telephoto Lens

Get closer to the action with super-telephoto lenses - typically anything above 300mm. With the ability to reach up to 1000mm on a crop sensor, these lenses offer the most reach for capturing sports, wildlife, or the night sky. Keep in mind that they have a narrow field of view, ranging from 1 to 8 degrees, but the pros know that this high-quality gear is worth the investment.

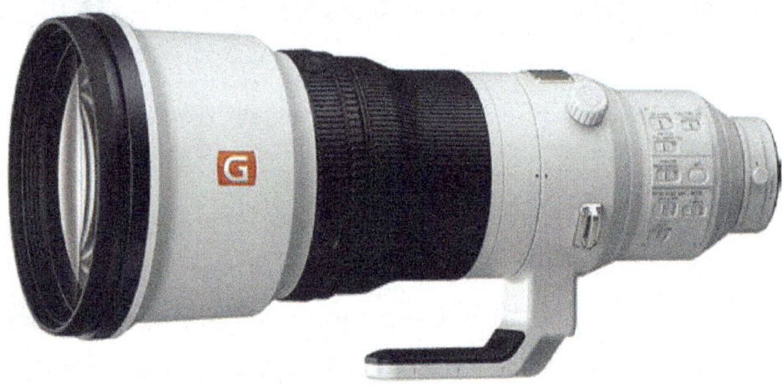

Super-telephoto lenses may offer impressive focal length, but their hulking size is not meant to be handheld. Even with in-lens image stabilization, you'll need a reliable tripod to steady your shots and prevent blurs. Fortunately, most of these lenses come with a tripod collar for added support. Don't compromise on your photo quality - always bring a tripod when shooting with super-telephoto lenses!

12

AI & PHOTO MANIPULATION

History of Photo Manipulation

The history of photo manipulation is quite interesting. It can be traced back to the early days of photography itself. As soon as photography emerged in the 19th century, photographers and artists began experimenting with various techniques to alter and manipulate images. Below, I summarize the history of photo manipulation.

Early Manual Techniques

In the early years of photography, before digital technology, photo manipulation was primarily done through manual and analog methods. Artists and photographers would physically manipulate the photographic prints or negatives using techniques such as retouching, scratching, or painting to alter or enhance the images.

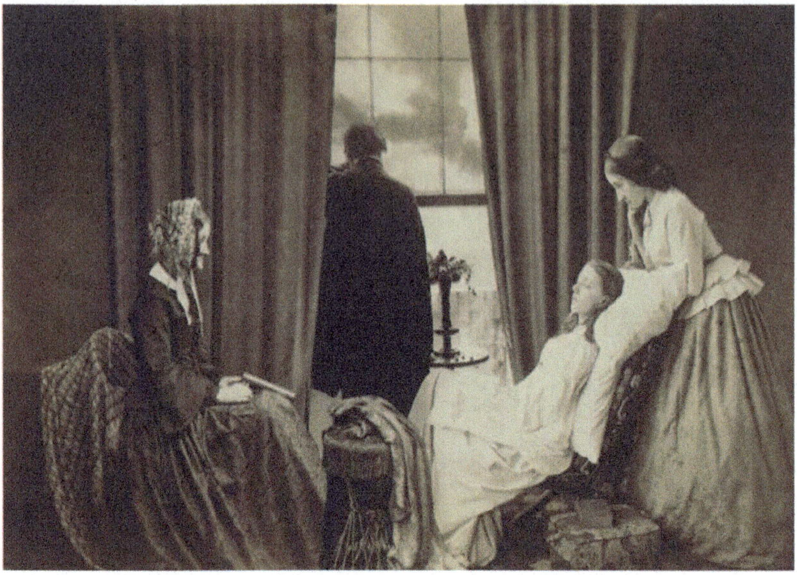

"Fading Away" is a notable photograph created by Henry Peach Robinson in 1858. It is considered one of the earliest examples of composite photography, where multiple negatives were combined to create a single image. The photograph depicts a scene of a young girl on her deathbed surrounded by her grieving family.

Robinson was a prominent photographer and advocate for artistic photography during the Victorian era. "Fading Away" was highly regarded for its emotional and narrative qualities, capturing a poignant moment of loss and mourning. The image resonated with Victorian sentimentality and was well-received by the public. The photograph gained particular attention when Prince Albert, the husband of Queen Victoria, purchased a print and showed great interest in Robinson's composite images. This led to Albert placing a standing order for all future composite works produced by Robinson.

Combination Printing

Combination printing is indeed a photographic technique that involves using the negatives of multiple images to create a single composite image. It allows photographers to combine different elements from separate negatives to create unique and imaginative compositions.

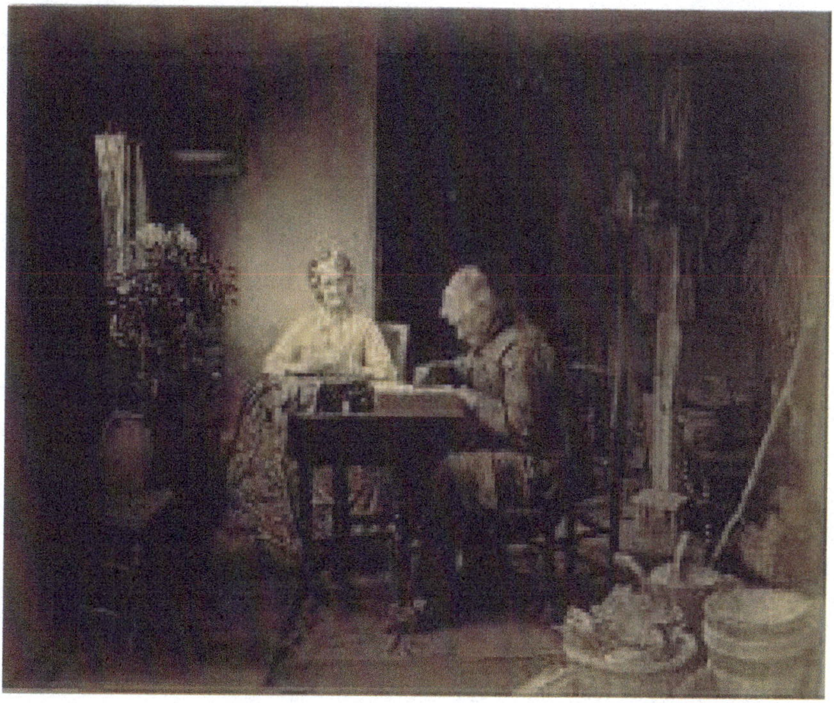

The process of combination printing can be technically complex, requiring precise alignment and exposure control. Here's a general overview of how combination printing is typically done:

1. Selection of Negatives: The photographer chooses two or more negatives that contain the desired elements to be combined in the final image. These negatives may have been taken at different times or locations.

2. Contact Printing: Each negative is individual contact printed on a sheet of photosensitive paper. This creates a positive image in the paper, which will later be combined with other positive prints.

3. Trimming and Aligning: The positive prints are carefully trimmed to remove

any unwanted edges or parts. The prints are then aligned and positioned in the desired arrangement, ensuring that they fit together seamlessly.

4. Exposure and Development: The aligned positive prints are placed together onto a new sheet of photosensitive paper. The entire arrangement is exposed to light, using appropriate exposure times for each positive print to achieve a balanced overall exposure.

5. Development and Finishing: The exposed paper is developed, fixed, and washed to produce the final composite image. Additional adjustments and enhancements, such as dodging and burning, can be made during the printing and development process to fine-tune the image's tonal range and details.

Combination printing allows photographers to create images that may not be possible to capture in a single exposure. It offers artistic freedom and the ability to create unique compositions by combining elements from different negatives. While technically more complex than traditional single-exposure printing, combination printing provides photographers with a creative tool to express their vision and create visually striking images.

Photomontage and Surrealism

The photomontage is indeed an artistic practice that has been prevalent since the early days of photography. It involves combining multiple photographs or images to create a new composite image that often carries a unique artistic expression or narrative. The photomontage is a versatile and expressive technique that has been embraced by artists throughout the history of photography. It continues to evolve and adapt to the changing artistic landscape, offering endless possibilities for creative exploration and visual storytelling.

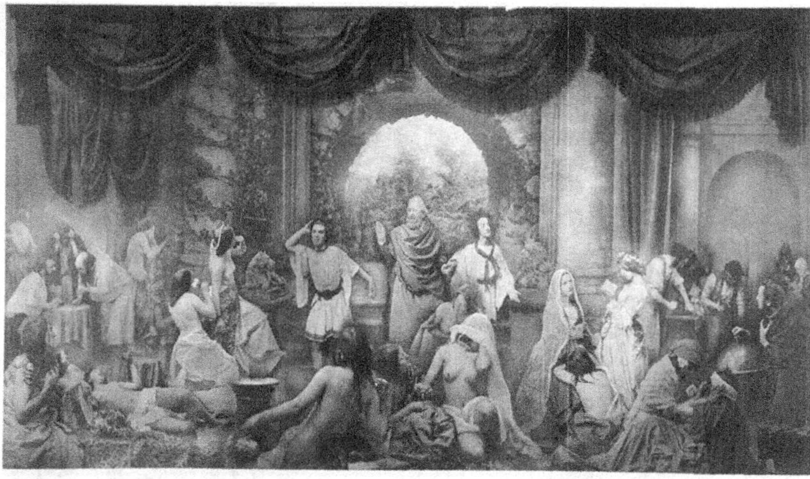

Oscar Gustave Rejlander's "Two Ways of Life" is a significant artwork in the history of photography, particularly in the Victorian era. Created in 1857, it is considered the first example of photomontage during that time. "Two Ways of Life" is a composite photograph consisting of over thirty individual negatives meticulously combined to create a single large-scale image. The artwork measures approximately 40 by 28 inches (101.6 by 71.1 cm). Rejlander meticulously arranged the different negatives to construct a complex narrative scene. The photomontage features a central tableau depicting two contrasting paths in life. On the left side, a scene of virtue and domestic bliss is portrayed, with a family engaged in various wholesome activities. In contrast, the right side illustrates a more morally ambiguous and decadent lifestyle, with figures engaged in activities associated with vices and temptation.

Rejlander's "Two Ways of Life" explores themes of morality, virtue, and choice. The composition prompts viewers to contemplate the consequences of the choices made in life and the potential divergent paths one might follow. The artwork serves as a visual allegory, contrasting the rewards of virtuous living with the potential pitfalls of a morally compromised existence. His innovative use of photomontage had a significant impact on the development of photography as an art form. The artwork showcased the potential of combining multiple negatives to create a cohesive and narrative-driven image, foreshadowing the later development of photomontage techniques by artists such as Hannah Höch and John Heartfield. It was well-received during its time, garnering critical acclaim and catching the attention of Queen Victoria and her husband, Prince Albert. The royal couple purchased a copy of the artwork and became patrons of Rejlander's work, leading to increased recognition and popularity for the artist.

Darkroom Manipulations

In the analog era of photography, darkroom techniques played a vital role in manipulating and enhancing photographs. Here are some of the key darkroom techniques that photographers and artists employed both then and now:

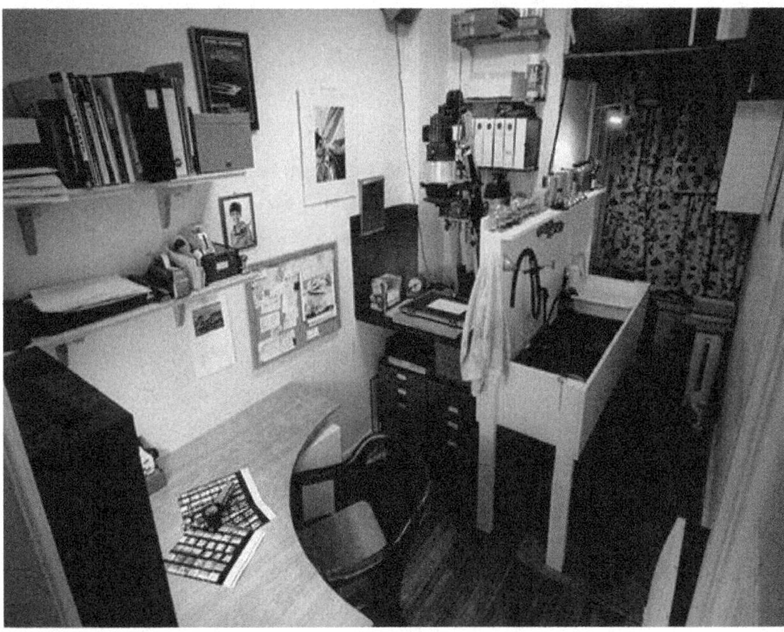

1. Dodging and Burning: Dodging involves selectively blocking light during the printing process to lighten specific areas of the image. Burning involves selectively exposing certain areas of the image to increase their darkness or contrast. These techniques allowed photographers to control the brightness and contrast of different parts of the image, emphasizing or de-emphasizing specific elements.

2. Solarization: Solarization, also known as the Sabattier effect, involved briefly

exposing a partially developed print to light during the darkroom process. This resulted in a partial reversal of tonal values, creating a distinct and surreal effect where areas of the image appear as negative or exhibit a halo-like glow. Solarization added an element of unpredictability and uniqueness to the final print.

3. Multiple Exposures: Multiple exposures involved exposing the same photographic paper or film multiple times, either in camera or during the printing process. By superimposing multiple images onto a single print, photographers could create dreamy and ethereal compositions. This technique allowed for the blending of different subjects or perspectives, resulting in abstract or layered visuals.

4. Collage and Montage: Artists often employed collage and montage techniques in the darkroom, combining multiple photographic prints or cutouts to create a new composition. By physically layering or juxtaposing images, they could create surreal or narrative-driven artworks that extended beyond the boundaries of a single photograph.

Although digital photography and editing software have largely replaced traditional darkroom techniques, the analog era's legacy lives on. Many of these techniques still inspire and influence contemporary photographers and artists who seek to recreate the aesthetic and creative possibilities of the darkroom in a digital realm.

Digital Revolution

Digital photography and the rise of computer technology revolutionized the field of photo manipulation. With the introduction of image editing software like Adobe Photoshop in the late 1980s and early 1990s, artists and photographers gained access to powerful digital tools that enabled them to manipulate images in ways previously unimaginable.

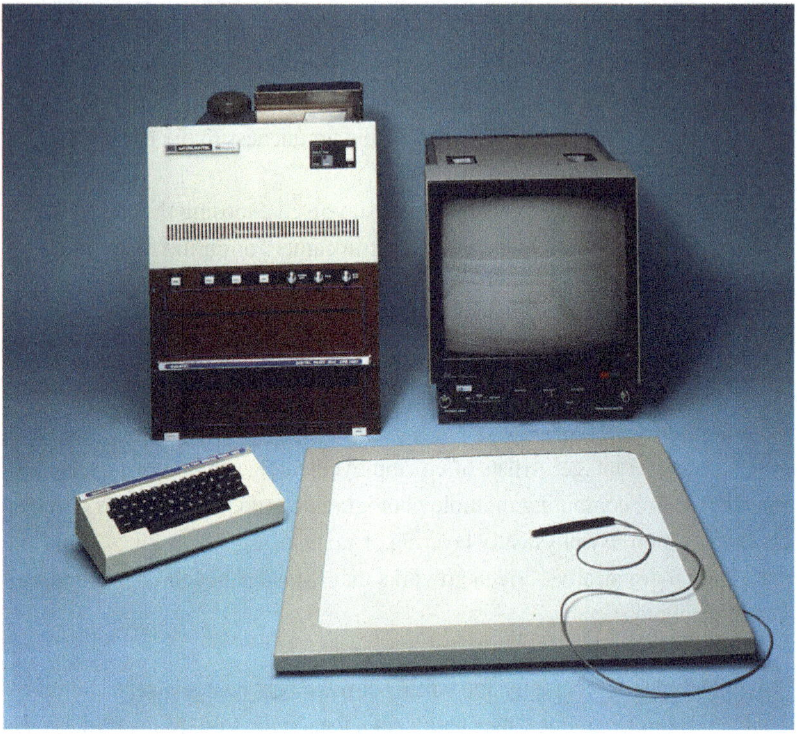

The Quantel Paintbox, is a virtual machine in the history of television. (Mel GX/ Flickr)

The Quantel Paintbox is widely recognized as one of the first digital workstations used in the field of graphics and image manipulation. The British company Quantel developed it in the 1980s, primarily for the television and film industries.

The Quantel Paintbox revolutionized the way images and graphics were created, edited, and manipulated. It combined a dedicated computer system, specialized hardware, and software, providing a powerful tool for digital image processing and compositing. It allowed artists and designers to work on high-resolution images in real-time, providing greater control and efficiency compared to traditional analog methods. The history of photo manipulation showcases the evolution of techniques and technologies that have enabled photographers and artists to alter and transform images creatively. From early analog methods to the digital era, photo manipulation has become an essential aspect of visual storytelling and artistic exploration.

Digital Photo manipulation

Digital photo manipulation allows for precise and seamless alterations to images. Artists and photographers can use software tools to retouch, composite, and transform images, creating unique and imaginative compositions. With the advancement of technology and the proliferation of digital cameras and editing software, photo manipulation has become more accessible to a wider audience.

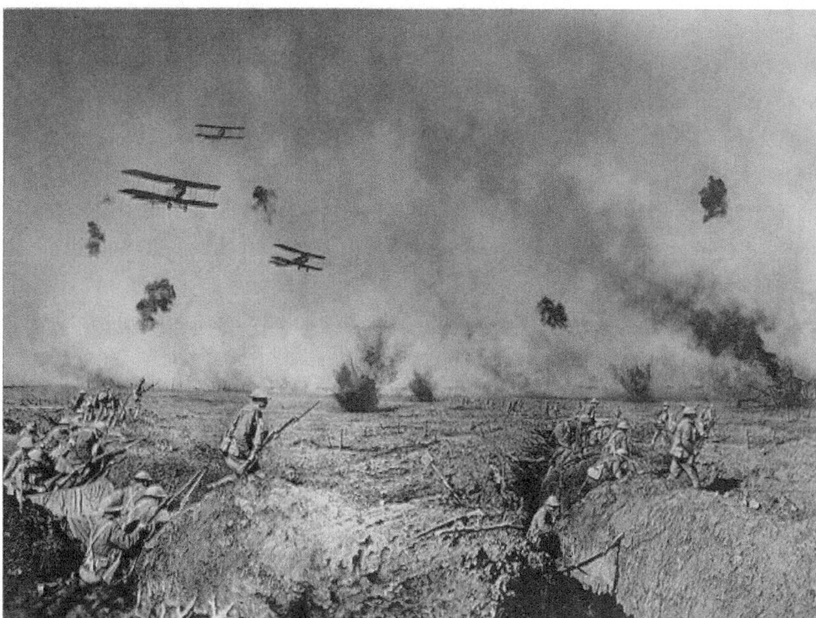

Frank Hurley's World War I - Combined 3 Negatives

Frank Hurley, an Australian photographer, was known for his pioneering work in documenting the realities of war, particularly during World War I. One of his notable photographs, formed from three original negatives, captures the essence of the war in Belgium. Here's some further information on this composite photograph and Hurley's views on compositing photos:

Hurley's composite photograph aimed to convey the scale and impact of war by combining multiple images into a single composition. He believed that a single negative could not adequately capture the vastness and complexity of the war experience. By using multiple negatives, Hurley sought to create a more comprehensive representation of the war's reality. Hurley faced ethical concerns and debates with his superiors regarding the use of composite photographs. Some believed that compositing photos compromised the authenticity and integrity of documentary photography. However, Hurley argued that the magnitude of the war demanded a different approach. He believed that composite images could convey a more truthful representation of the war's chaotic and overwhelming nature.

Hurley's work challenged traditional notions of photographic objectivity and pushed the boundaries of documentary photography. His composite photographs aimed to communicate the emotional and visceral impact of war, rather than merely capturing straightforward documentation. Hurley's views on compositing photos reflected his understanding of the limitations of a single image in capturing the complexity of war. His composite photographs sought to evoke a deeper emotional response from viewers and provide a more comprehensive visual narrative. Frank Hurley's contributions to war photography and his innovative use of composite photographs have had a lasting impact on the field. His work continues to be recognized for its artistic and documentary significance, shedding light on the realities of war and the evolving nature of photographic storytelling.

Contemporary Photomanipulation

Contemporary photomanipulation refers to the practice of digitally altering and manipulating photographs using various software and techniques available in the digital era. With advanced digital editing tools and software like Adobe Photoshop, photographers and artists have expanded the possibilities of creating visually stunning and imaginative compositions. Here are some key aspects of contemporary photomanipulation:

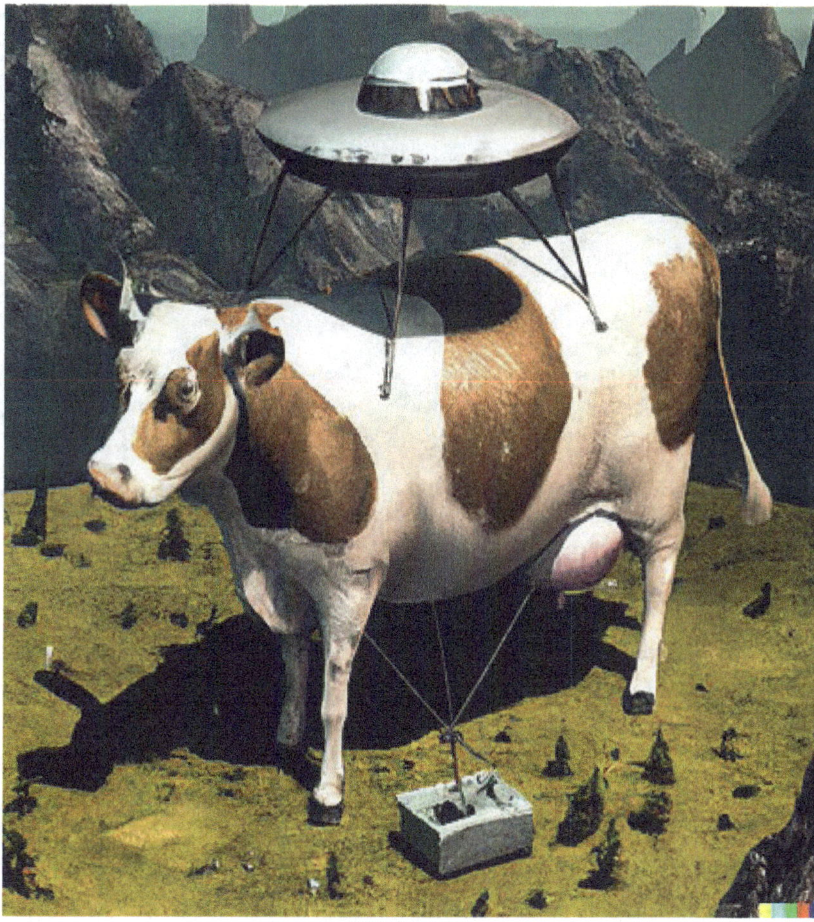

This image was created by DALL-E

Contemporary photomanipulation is a dynamic and evolving field, driven by advancements in technology and the creative vision of artists. It continues to push the boundaries of what is possible in terms of image manipulation, allowing for innovative and visually captivating compositions. This image was created byDALL-E 2, an AI model developed by OpenAI to generate an image based on the text prompt "1960's art of cow getting abducted by a UFO in the Midwest," it might create a surreal and imaginative depiction. This image I created in Adobe Photoshop, it is for sale on my website at www.tracymccrackin.com.

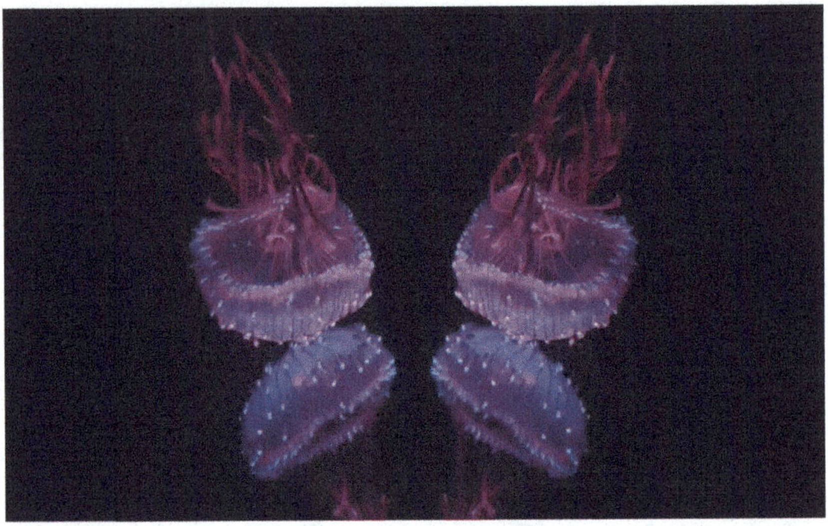

How To Choose A Photo Editor

The history of AI photo generators is relatively recent, but their development has rapidly advanced in the past decade. They are now at the heart of almost all photo editors. AI photo generators have continued to evolve and produce increasingly realistic and sophisticated images. They have found applications in various domains, including art, design, entertainment, and even generating human-like faces and scenes. Continued research and advancements in AI algorithms and models are expected to further enhance the capabilities and creative possibilities of AI photo generators in the future. This image was created in DALL-E.

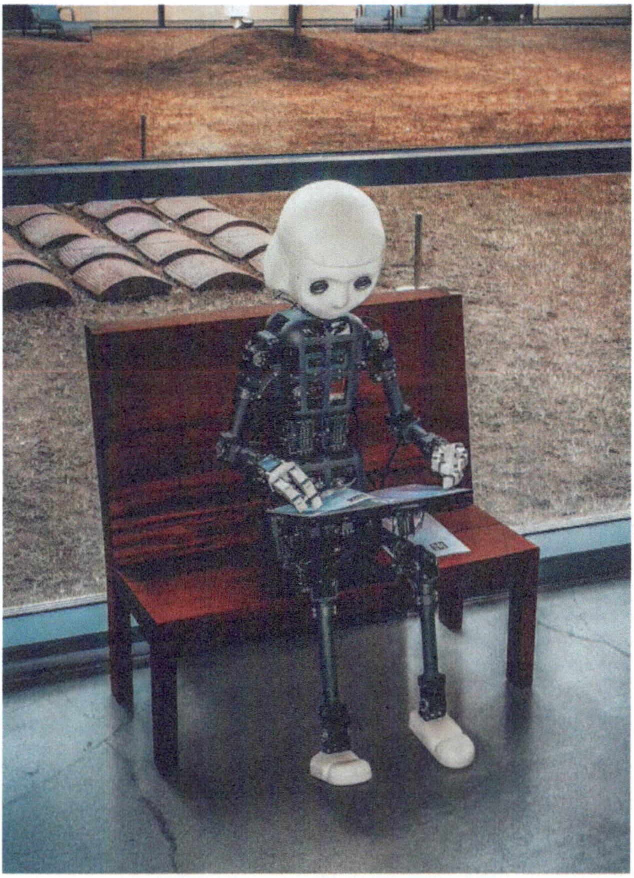

There are now hundreds of AI-powered photo editing tools available, such as Adobe Photoshop with its AI-enhanced features, or online platforms like Pixlr, Fotor, or Canva that offer AI-based editing capabilities. Select the tool that best suits your needs and familiarity.

As someone who has spent countless hours editing and revising images, I always seek new and innovative editing tools. I am not affiliated with any of these companies, so these are just my personal favorites with samples from several:

1. Dream by WOMBO
2. Midjourney

3. MyHeritage's AI Time Machine
4. Runway Gen 2
5. Stable Fusion
6. DALL-E
7. Deep AI
8. Shutterstock AI
9. StarryAI
10. Canva

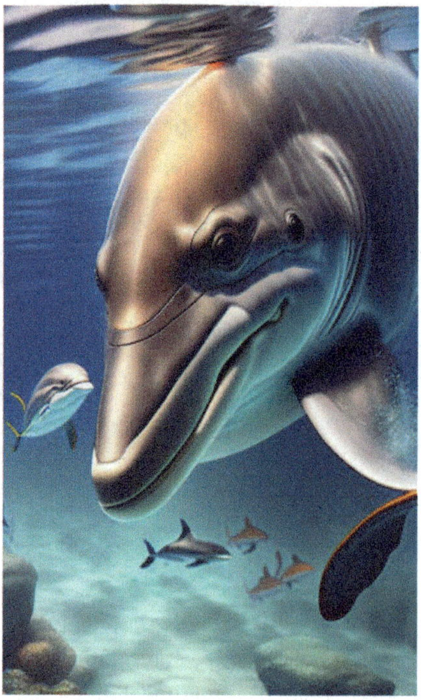

This Midjourney Image can be purchased on my website at www. tracymccrackin.com

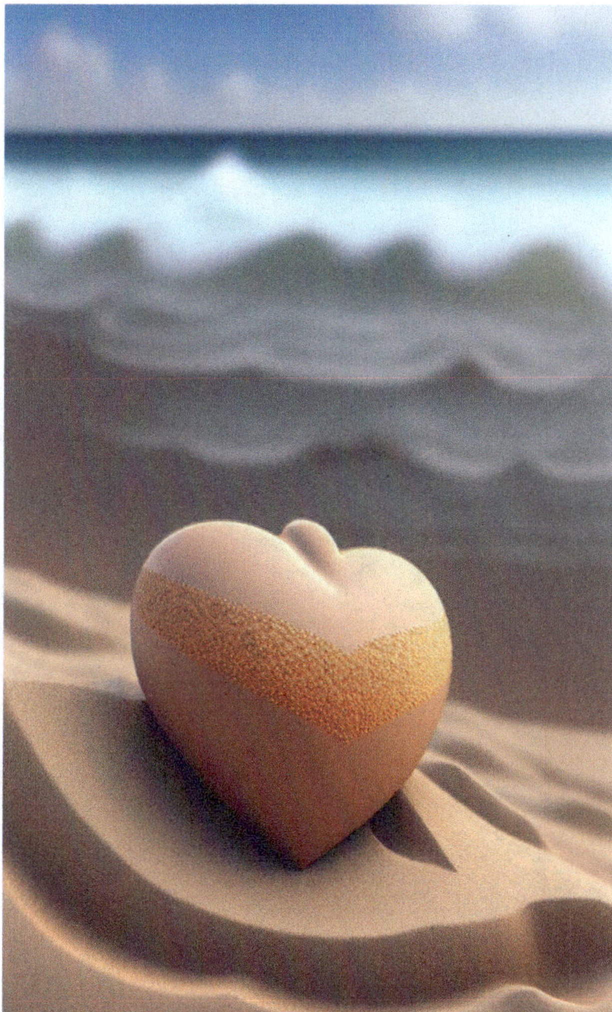

This DALL-E can be purchased on my website www.tracymccrackin.com

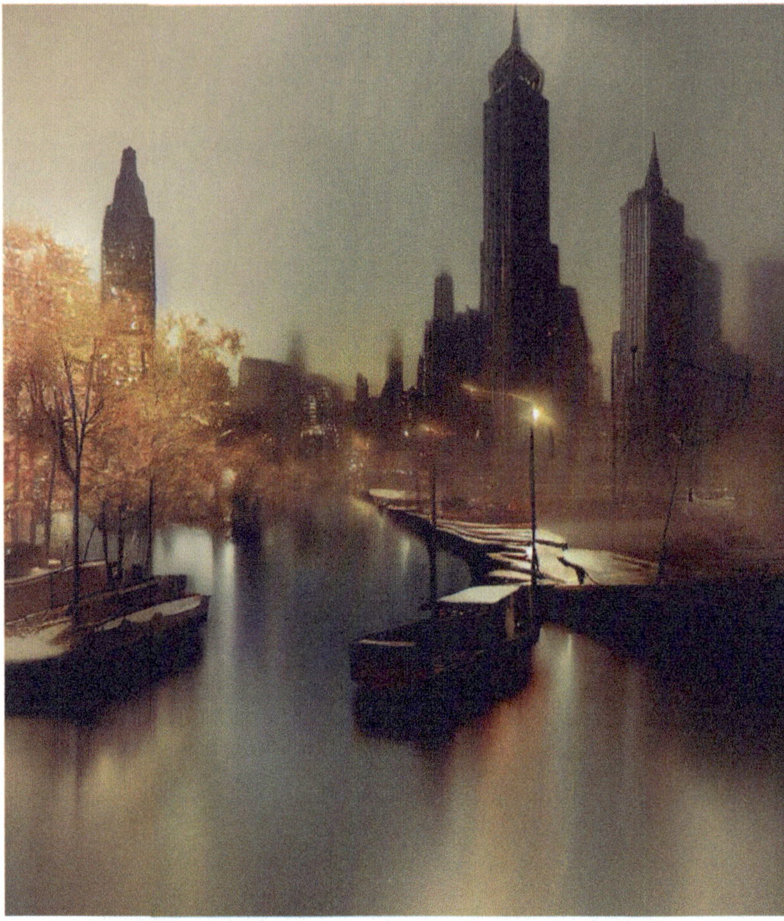

This Stable Fusion image can be purchased on my website www. tracymccrackin.com

Remember, while AI-powered photo manipulation tools offer convenience and creative possibilities, it's important to exercise artistic judgment and avoid over editing. Strive to achieve a balance between enhancing your images and maintaining a natural and appealing visual aesthetic.

13

SAVING YOUR FILES

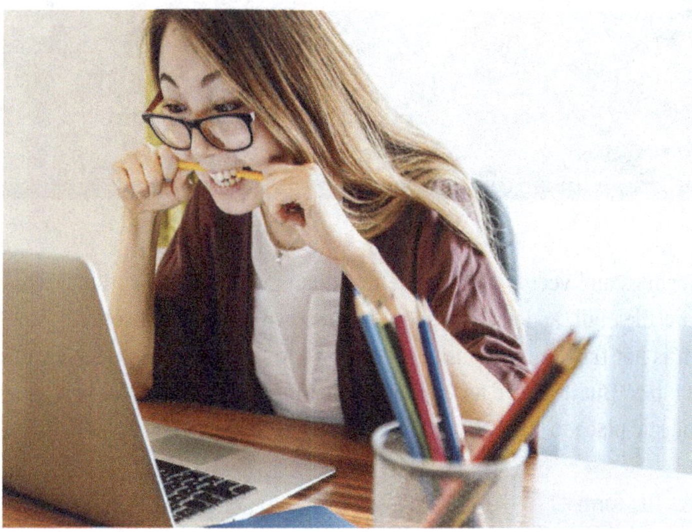

Struggling to decide which file format and color mode are best for your images? We have the solution! This handy guide will help you make informed decisions, giving you the confidence that comes from knowing your choices were correct.

Different Types of Image Formats

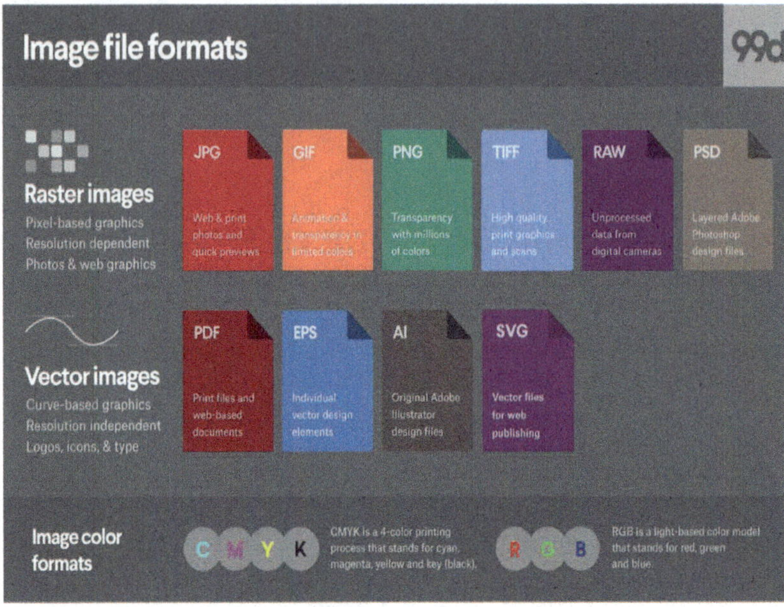

Raster files and vector files are the two main graphic categories into which most picture files fall, and each category has its own unique applications. This breakdown is not flawless. For instance, certain formats really allow for incorporating both types. But if you're unsure about what format to use for your projects, this is a fantastic place to start.

Raster file formats

- JPEG
- GIF
- PNG
- TIFF
- RAW
- PSD

Vector file formats

- PDF
- EPS
- SVG
- AI

Raster Files Defined

Each pixel in a raster picture is given a specific color and is composed of a grid of dots known as pixels. Raster pictures, in contrast to vector images, are resolution-dependent, which means they only exist at one size. Raster images can become "pixelated" or fuzzy when they are transformed since doing so stretches the pixels inside the picture. Your program basically makes an educated estimate about what picture data is missing when you magnify an image based on the surrounding pixels. The outcomes are typically not fantastic.

Photographs, digital art, and online graphics (such as banner advertisements, social networking posts, and email graphics) are frequently created using raster images. The industry-standard image editor, Adobe Photoshop, is used to generate, design, and edit raster pictures and to enhance already-existing designs with textures, shadows, and effects.

Both CMYK and RGB are the two basic color models that may store raster pictures.

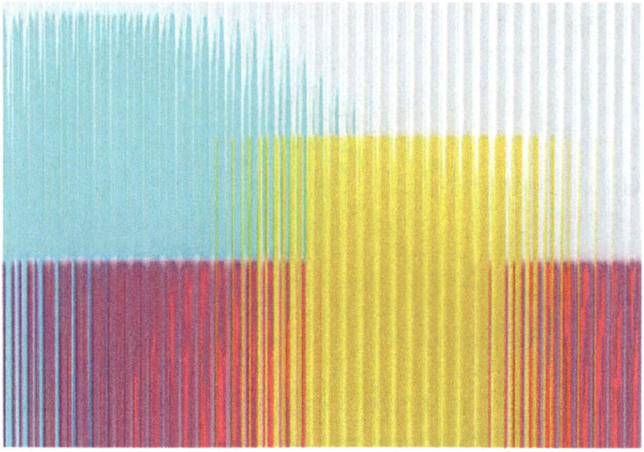

CMYK: which stands for cyan, magenta, yellow, and key (black), is a four-color printing technique. These hues represented the four inks that will mix throughout the printing process. The files you save in this format will be ready for actual printing.

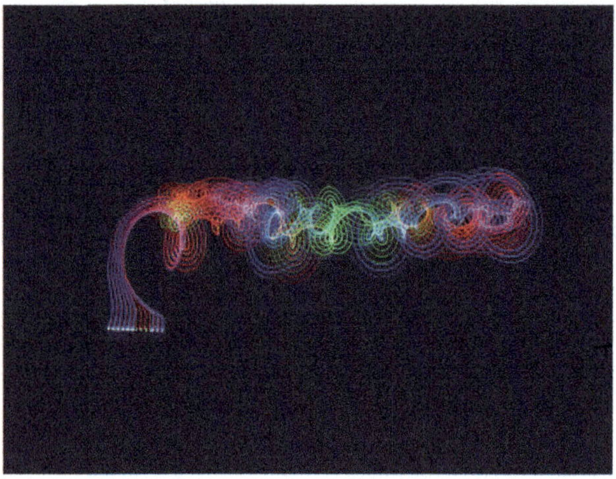

RBG: which stands for Red, Green, and Blue, is a color model based on light. These are the main light colors that may be combined to create additional colors. All screen-based media, including the web, mobile devices, movies, and videos, will benefit from files saved in this format.

Vector Files Defined

Vector files are typically illustrations composed of paths (think lines and shapes), not pixels. They are scalable. Vector files are essential for large format graphics because they will not get blurry or lose their print quality matter how large you scale them up.

Lossy vs. Lossless

Depending on how the format handles your picture data, each raster image file is either lossless or lossy.

Lossless picture formats preserve every bit of the original file's information. The phrase "lossless" refers to the fact that nothing from the original file, picture, or work of art is lost. Even if the file is still compressed, all lossless formats may restore your image to its original condition.

Lossy picture formats simulate your original image as closely as possible. For instance, a lossy picture can scale back the number of colors in your image or scan it for extraneous information. Even though they could lower the quality of your photograph, these ingenious technological tactics will often minimize the file size. Lossy files are often substantially smaller than lossless files.

14

PRINT OPTIONS

Home Printing

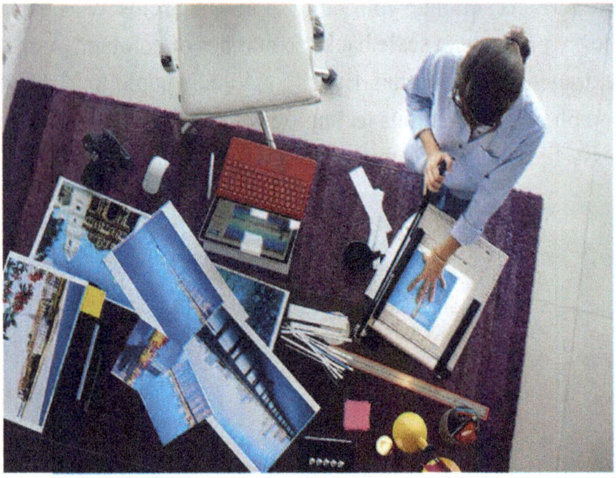

With printing for your enjoyment, there's no need to overspend at a fancy printing company. Thanks to technological advancements and more affordable solutions in the market today, you can now get top-notch quality from home printers without breaking the bank! For those looking for semi-pro or professional photography prints, though - that's when splashing out on a high-end printer is worthwhile.

Regarding printing images, the cost is only one factor–quality depends on carefully selecting the correct printer and materials. Don't make the mistake of rushing into a purchase without considering what kind of paper and ink you'll need to get your desired results! To ensure that your digital images stand the test of time, archival paper is essential: made from more expensive acid-free material, durable prints can be produced with a lifespan lasting up to 100 years. The exact duration depends on factors such as the quality of materials and storage conditions–but no matter what you opt for, it will keep memories alive far into the future.

Inkjet vs. Laser Printers - Basics

The fundamental differences between inkjet and laser printers come down to how each technology produces. This influences what a printer can do effectively, how much it costs to print papers and images, and how much you'll spend upfront.

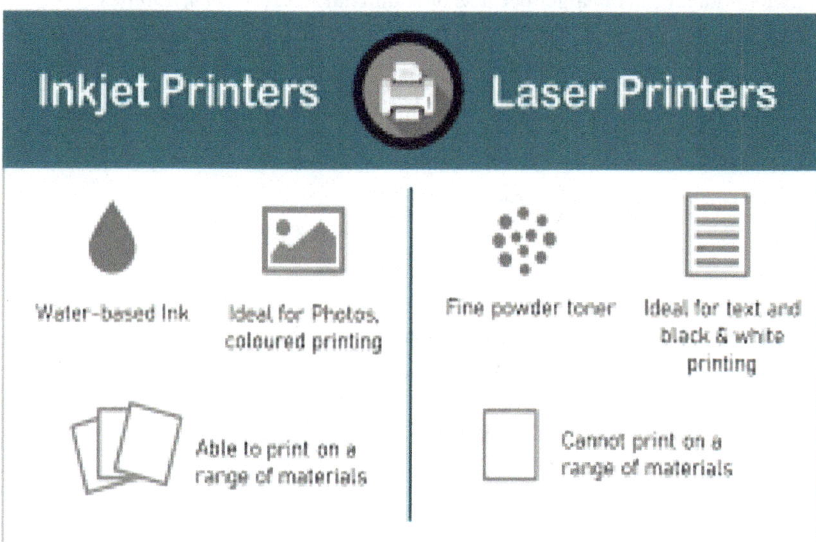

Inkjet printers are less expensive to purchase. If you don't print often, a low-cost inkjet printer may be gained for $100 or less. However, keep in mind that ink costs may make even the most economical inkjet printers more costly to run. They often run into 5-8 color cartridges per unit. So inkjet printers are superior in printing photographs.

Inkjet printers are smaller compared to laser printers. One reason for their compact design is that inkjet printers do not require multiple internal drums and rollers like laser printers do.

Inkjet printers work by spraying tiny droplets of ink onto the paper to create an image or text. They typically have a simpler internal mechanism that allows for a more compact size. Laser printers use a complex system of internal drums, rollers, and a laser beam to transfer toner onto the paper. This system requires more internal components and, therefore, results in larger printer sizes. The smaller footprint of inkjet printers makes them a popular choice for home users, small offices, or environments where space is limited. They can easily fit on a desk or a small workspace without occupying too much room. However, there are variations in size among different inkjet printer models, and some high-end inkjet printers can be larger because of additional features or capabilities.

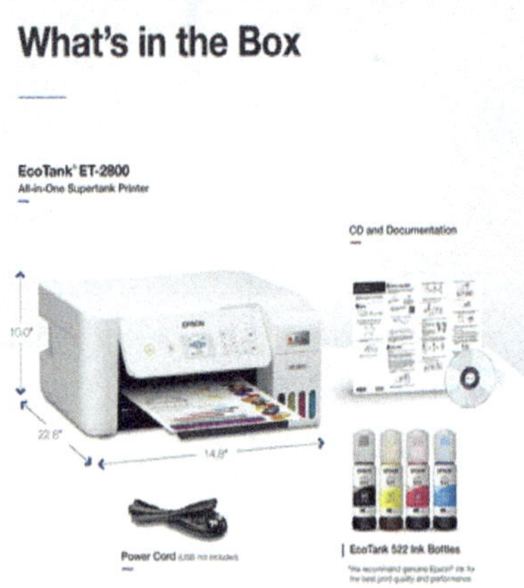

This Epson EcoTank ET-2800 Wireless Color All-in-One Cartridge-Free Supertank Printer with Scan and Copy and is only $199 at the Amazon Affiliate Link.

Laser printers are preferable for text and documents. If you're printing a lot of basic documents, a laser printer - even a monochrome laser printer - can produce page after page of high-quality output than an inkjet.

Laser printers often have the lowest page cost. Toner is very inexpensive per page and will not dry up like old ink cartridges. However, more and more inkjet printers with refillable tanks are being produced, which may give comparably economical printing if you are ready to spend more ahead.

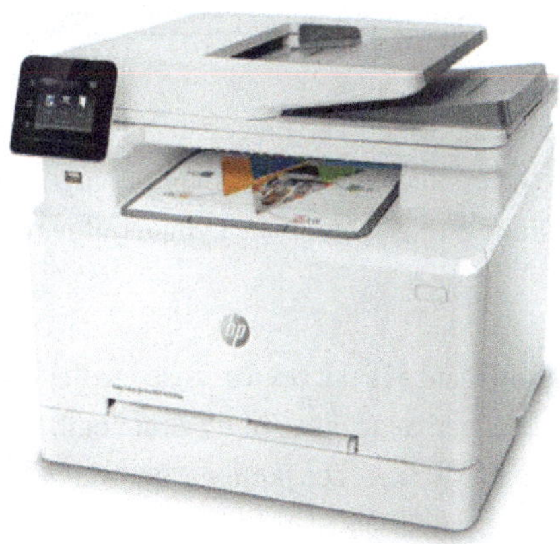

HP Color LaserJet Pro M283fdw Wireless All-in-One Laser Printer, Remote Mobile Print, Scan & Copy, Duplex Printing, Works with Alexa. It's $499 at the Amazon Affiliate Link.

Inkjet vs. Laser Printers - Printing Technologies

While the most fundamental concept of printing is the same for both inkjet and laser printers – placing letters and pictures on paper – the two systems accomplish this in quite different ways.

Inkjet printers employ liquid ink that is deposited onto the paper by a print head with hundreds of micro-nozzles. It prints by depositing small droplets of ink onto paper. Depending on whether the ink is dye-based or pigment-based, it may affect the color of the paper or merely dry as a deposit on the paper's surface.

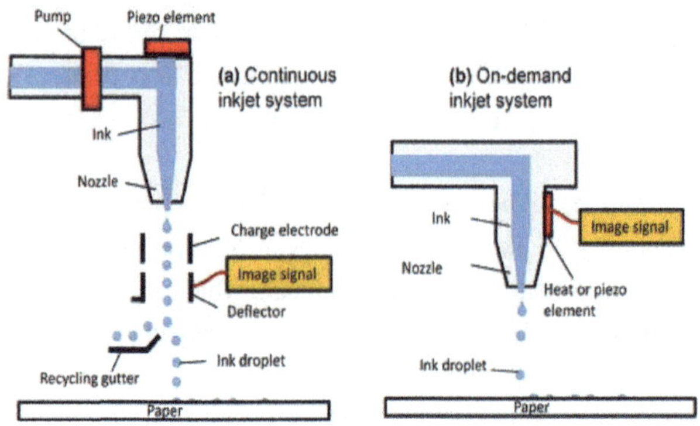

Laser printers use toner, a powder. The process begins with a laser beam that projects the image to be printed onto an electrically charged cylinder known as a "Drum Unit." The Drum Unit is a revolving cylinder of photoconductive selenium.

The regions of the drum that have not been exposed to the laser become conductive due to the photoconductive qualities of the drum unit. This is when the toner (powdered ink) comes into action. The portions that were not affected by the laser beam now attract the toner powder, whilst the laser-charged areas repel it. This is how the needed picture is created at first.

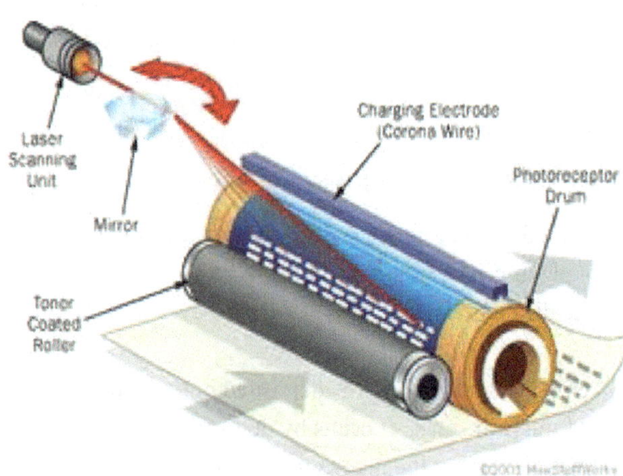

The "Fuser" is the final stage of laser printing, which warms up the toner powder on the paper at extremely high temperatures and then binds it to the paper. Most people have probably felt the warmth of the sheets that come out of a laser printer, and now you'll understand why. These two techniques will impact everything from the size of a printer to the cost of a single printed page. Both technologies are available in single-function or all-in-one printers, together with scanning, copying, and faxing. Either may be an excellent match as long as you recognize their respective strengths and shortcomings.

Inkjet vs. Laser Printers - Print Quality

Inkjet printers, with their dye and pigment-based inks, do exceptionally well with color, especially for photographs and photos that contain nuanced shades of color. Because of liquid ink, certain mixes are simpler to duplicate on an inkjet printer rather than a laser printer.

Laser printers are not necessarily designed to print photos, instead depending on halftone dots to generate certain colors on paper. Even laser printers that can print higher-quality color photos require specialist laser-printer-ready photo paper, making it significantly less practical than using normal photo paper on an inkjet.

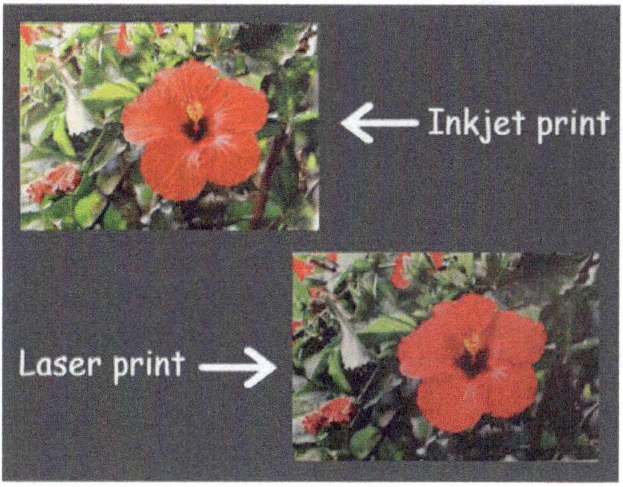

Inkjet printers are great for printing family photos at home. The secret lies in understanding DPI–dots per inch - the measure of printer resolution. While some super-high resolutions promise better quality prints than expensive models offer, all you need is an excellent introductory model with 1200 x 1440 dpi; anything higher won't give much extra benefit if your photo's not bigger than 5x7 inches! That way, you'll get what counts most: gorgeous prints of treasured memories without breaking the bank. If you want to go big with poster-sized prints of your photography, invest in one of today's top professional photo printers like Epson Expression Photo, where resolutions reach up to 5760 x 1440 dpi – now that's detailed printing!

Inject vs. Laser Printers - Maintenance Cost

With the money spent on a laser or inkjet printer, there are two categories of charges to consider. The first is the printer's initial cost, sometimes known as its retail price. The second is the expense of upkeep, which is a considerably more involved issue. Inkjet printers are less expensive to purchase since the printing technique is basic.

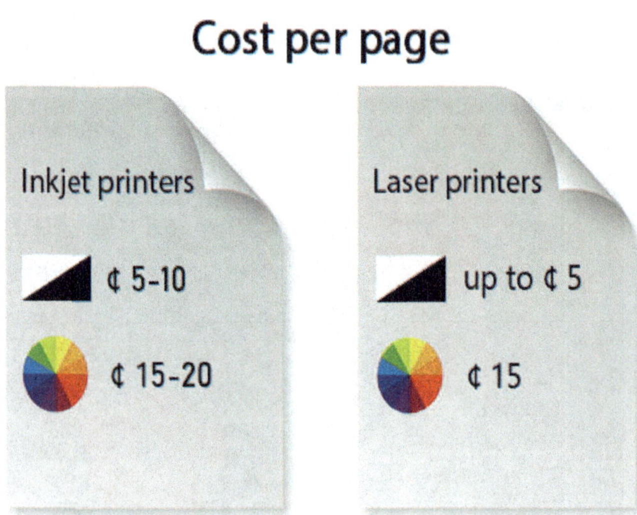

Laser printers are more expensive to purchase since they are more difficult to manufacture. They are usually priced at least $200 for each piece, which is pretty high.

With maintenance costs, toner, and ink cartridges are the most expensive. And inkjet printers are losing the war. Because liquid ink is so costly, black-and-white prints will cost roughly 5-10 cents per page, depending on the printer type. Meanwhile, color printing will set you back an additional 15-25 cents for each page.

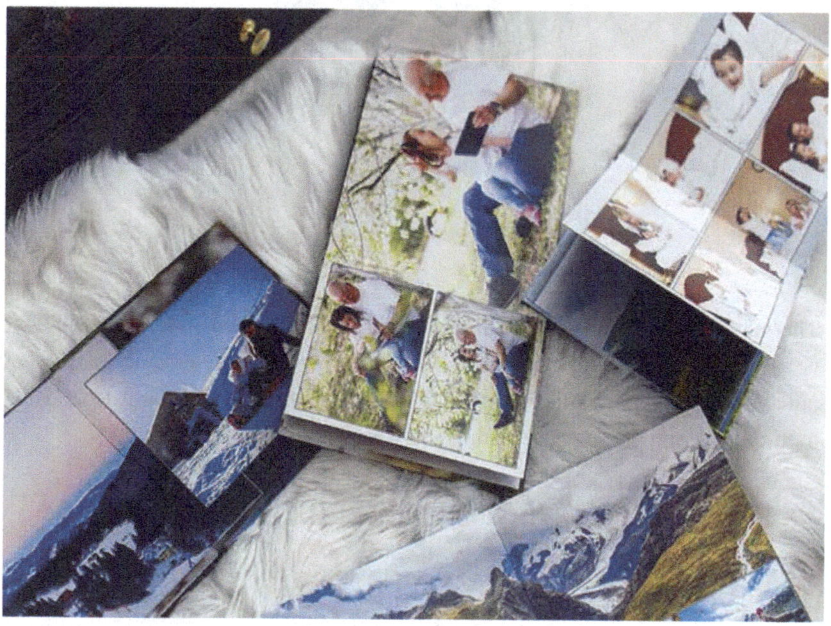

New Technology in Inkjet Printing

The "Thermal Inkjet" (TIJ) technique is a form of inkjet printing in which a print image is transferred to the carrier media utilizing small drops of ink in a contact-free and accurate manner. Thermal inkjet printers heat the ink droplets to 300°C before firing them out of the print nozzle. The "piezo inkjet" technique, in which the droplets are moved mechanically, is another option. Thermal printers, unlike inkjet printers, do not generate pictures by spraying liquid ink via a nozzle.

Thermal printers, such as the DuraLabel Toro Max, instead employ small heating elements to activate or transfer pigments.

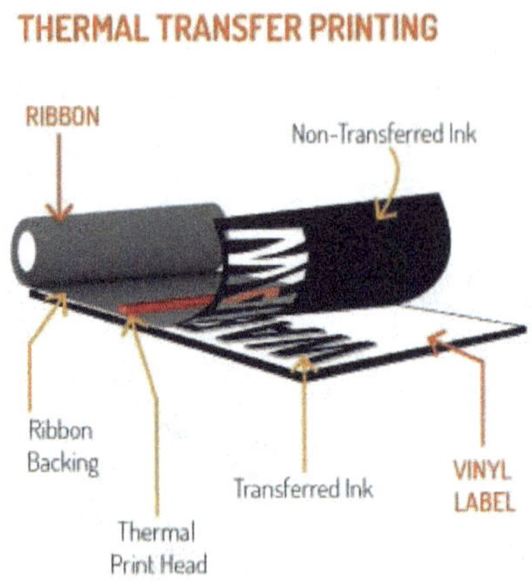

Thermal inkjet has been the industry standard since its inception in the 1980s. It is a well-established technology because it allows for low-cost, versatile, and quick product identification. Our TJ500 and TJ1000 versions are dependable, high-quality, and precise. Both printers are simple to set up and use.

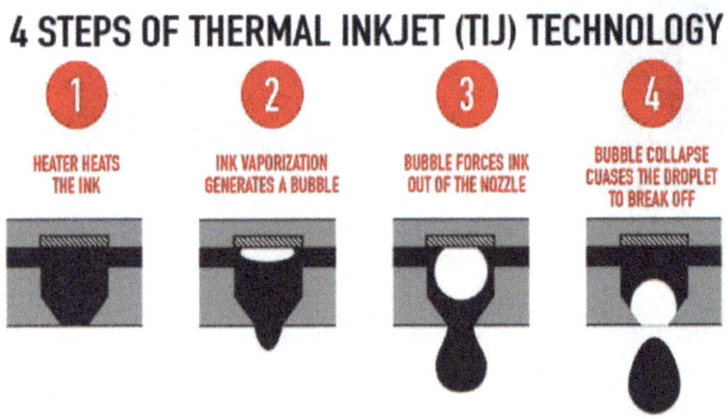

Thermal inkjet printer ink cartridges have heating components that create high temperatures of up to 300°C, heating the ink over its boiling point. The volume of the printing ink grows because of the temperature-induced change in physical state from liquid to gas, resulting in the formation of a vapor bubble. This creates a lot of pressure, which pushes the droplets needed for the printing process out of the nozzle. They are supplied to the carrier material with precise accuracy. The ink then swiftly cools and returns to its liquid form. The ensuing negative pressure forces fresh ink through the nozzle. Specialized inks for thermal inkjet printers are used for this technique, which is designed to create high-quality prints on a range of surfaces.

Continuous Inkjet printers and Drop-on-Demand printers are well-established and dependable options in the industrial arena. Both solutions are classified as inkjet printers. However, the technological concept of the printing process differs in both circumstances. Both systems are contactless, with ink droplets traveling through the air to the object. As for costs, the specialized materials needed in thermal printing are far more expensive than those used in inkjet printing; even the most basic thermal printer can cost hundreds of dollars.

What is a Wide Format Inkjet Plotter?

More photographers are discovering the necessity for various types of wide-format printers. These specialty printers are used by huge organizations and photographers who need to print many marketing materials and wall-size artwork. In reality, many people will require print jobs that are larger than the conventional 8.5 x 11-inch paper size occasionally.

It is a lot better than outsourcing it to big labs that can charge a fortune to print work. To see a buying guide, click this link.

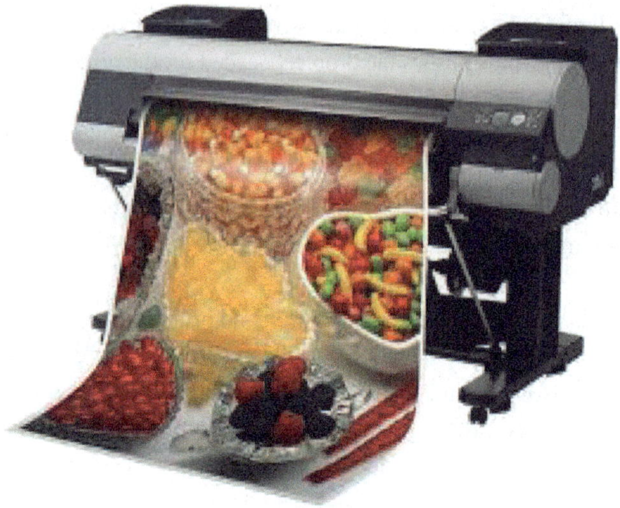

You must first choose which sort of big format printer is most suited to your requirements. I am going to assist you by guiding you through the many sorts of wide format printers, including size and printing style. cartridges.

Oversized Tabloid Sizes

When most people think of a wide-format printer, they imagine a massive machine that can handle professional printing jobs like poster-sized media or engineering/architectural papers. Over-sized, tabloid, and super-tabloid printers, on the other hand, are types of wide-format printers that may help with a wide range of common printing needs.

Over-sized, tabloid and super-tabloid printers may use wide-format sheets such as 11 x 17-inch tabloid or 13 x 19-inch super-tabloid paper. They are commonly referred to as "oversized multi-function printers," however, because they can also handle smaller paper sizes. Furthermore, they usually scan, copy, and fax all in one machine, making them a fantastic alternative for businesses with a wide range of printing needs.

Common Uses:

They can be expensive, but if you want to print from home wall size artwork, this is one of your better options. HP, Canon, and a few other manufacturers make these types of "large format" printers. This one is what I have at home. They range from 600-4,000 per unit. This is what I have purchased for my business. It prints up to 24 inches wide.

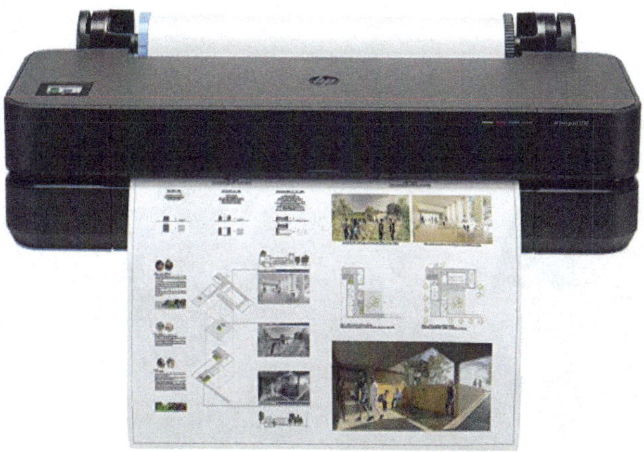

This HP DesignJet T210 Large Format 24-inch Plotter Color Printer prints sizes up to 24-inch wide media rolls and up to 13 by 19 sheets. It's $699 through the Affiliate Link on Amazon.

- Big spreadsheets
- Little fliers and posters
- Brochures - Reports
- Books
- Pictures
- Regular sheet paper is utilized. Specialty paper rolls are not necessary to buy.
- Accepts paper up to twice the size of a regular letter
- Capabilities that are versatile and multifaceted

Wide and Super-Wide

Hundreds of square feet may be printed in less than an hour using more conventional wide-format printers. A super-wide printer, sometimes known as a "grand large format printer," can print on rolls that are over 100 inches wide. When it comes to professional wide-format printers, there are three standard alternatives.

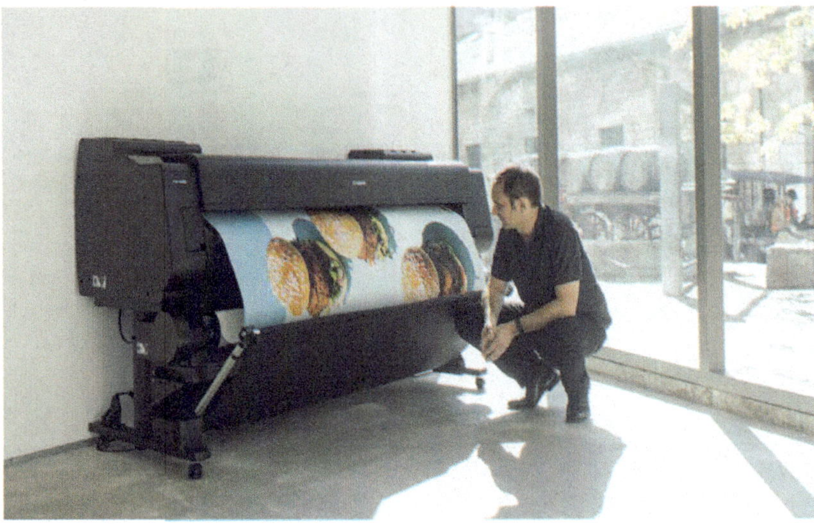

This one is the top of the line. CES IMAGING ImagePROGRAF PRO-6100 60" Professional Photographic Large-Format Inkjet Printer. It is $11,550 on the Amazon Affiliate Link.

- Roll-fed means that the machine is fed by a roll of paper or another flexible medium.
- Flatbed printing uses single sheets or boards.
- Hybrid: capable of handling both rolled and sheet materials.

These are commonly used for the following:

- Banners
- Posters
- Trade show graphics

- Wallpaper
- Murals
- Back lit film
- Vehicle wraps
- Architectural drawings
- Construction plans
- Large artwork
- Signage

Budget-Friendly Printing Online

Printers may require a bigger upfront investment, but in the long run, they'll save you money. They offer fast print rates and have a lower cost per page compared to inkjet models - which can be especially beneficial if you need high-quality color prints for everyday use! Plus, with prices starting at just $50, laser printing has never been more accessible or economical.

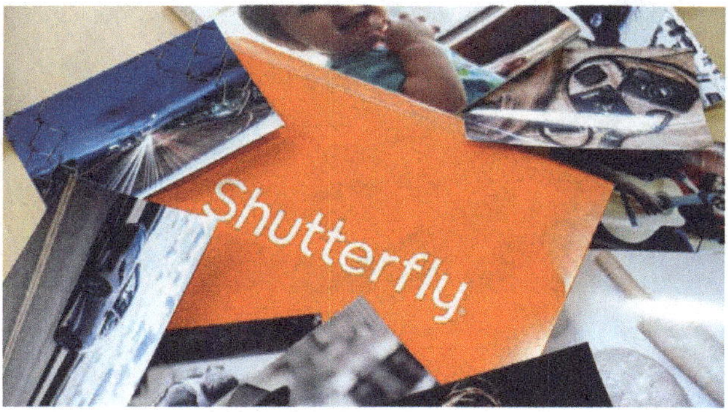

But if you don't want to invest in a printer and hire a company online to print your work, here are the top budget-friendly options. I don't have any affiliation with any of these companies, this is just the list of the most common photography labs.

- www.walmart.com (Wal-Mart)
- www.target.com (Target)
- www.kmart.com (K-Mart)

- www.CVS.com (CVS Drugs)
- www.walgreens.com (Walgreens)
- www.snapfish.com (Snapfish)
- www.shutterfly.com (Shutterfly)

Professional Printers Online

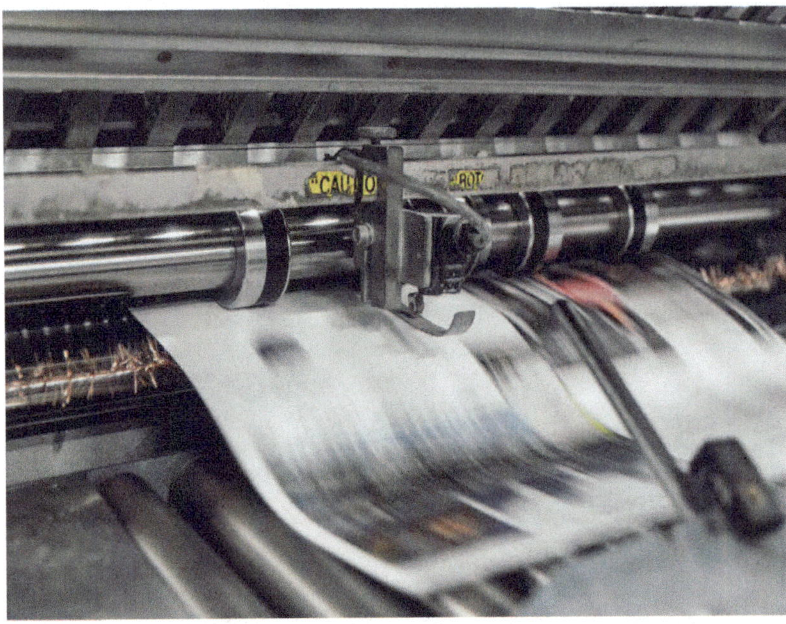

Now, if you don't want to sacrifice the quality of your images by using budget-friendly labs, these pro labs are a great choice! Whether you need to print an image 24 inches wide or blow it up into a vast 60-inch masterpiece, there's sure to be something available in this expansive selection that fits your desires and budget.

- Nations Photo Lab
- Printique by Adorama
- Saal Digital
- ProDPI
- Mpix

- Bay Photo
- Miller's Professional Imaging

Need your photos to last? Professional printing companies will preserve your precious memories for generations! Pick from my favorite, trusted sources, and you can expect 50-100 years or more of vibrant prints on high-quality paper. No matter the maker, quality, or conditions in which they're stored - your treasured images are secure with these qualified professionals who'll ship them right to you after receiving the files.

15

CAREERS

Commercial Photographer

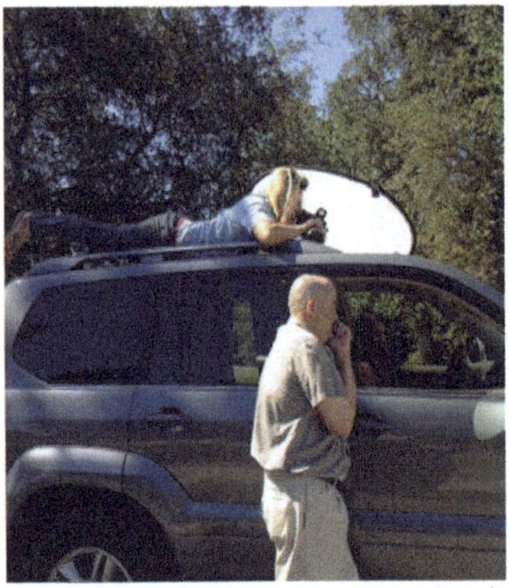

Here is a numbered list highlighting key aspects of being a commercial photographer:

1. Develop strong technical skills in photography equipment, lighting, composition, and image editing software.
2. Cultivate creativity and a keen eye for aesthetics to bring unique and compelling visuals to commercial projects.
3. Adapt to various shooting environments, such as studios, on location, or specialized settings, based on project requirements.
4. Communicate effectively with clients, art directors, and creative teams to understand their needs and deliver successful results.
5. Collaborate with clients, models, stylists, and other professionals to achieve the desired outcome and create impactful visuals.
6. Understand the business aspects of photography, including pricing, contracts, licensing, and client management.
7. Develop a strong personal brand and effectively market your services to attract clients and stand out in the competitive industry.
8. Pay close attention to detail in lighting, props, styling, and post-processing to ensure high-quality and professional images.
9. Maintain professionalism, and reliability, and deliver projects on time to build a strong reputation.
10. Continuously learn and stay updated with the latest trends, techniques, and equipment in the field of commercial photography.

This numbered list provides a concise breakdown of key elements to consider when pursuing a career as a commercial photographer. Each point represents a crucial aspect that contributes to success in the industry.

Fashion Photographer

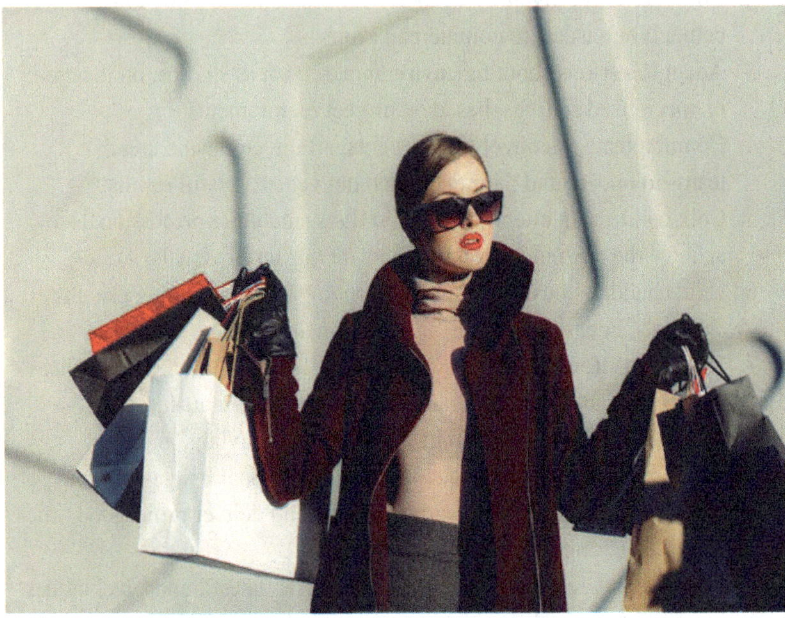

Fashion photography is a genre of photography that focuses on capturing clothing, accessories, and fashion trends in a visually appealing and artistic manner. It is often used for advertising campaigns, editorial spreads in magazines, catalogs, and other fashion-related publications. Fashion photographers work closely with models, stylists, makeup artists, and art directors to create visually stunning images that showcase the clothing and accessories in the best possible way.

Here are some key aspects of fashion photography:

1. Concept Development: Fashion photographers collaborate with a team to develop a concept or theme for the photo shoot. This includes deciding on the location, styling, mood, and overall aesthetic of the images.
2. Model Selection: Models play a crucial role in fashion photography, as they are the ones who showcase the clothing and accessories. Photographers work with modeling agencies or directly with models

to select individuals who fit the desired look and can bring the concept to life.

3. Styling and Wardrobe: Fashion photographers work closely with stylists to curate outfits and select the appropriate wardrobe for the shoot. They may also collaborate with fashion designers or brands to feature specific clothing or accessories.
4. Lighting and Composition: Creating striking images requires careful attention to lighting and composition. Fashion photographers use various lighting techniques, both natural and artificial, to enhance the mood and highlight the clothing and accessories. Composition and framing are important to create visually pleasing and balanced images.
5. Location and Set Design: Fashion shoots can take place in a studio or on location. Photographers often scout for unique and visually interesting locations that complement the concept or theme. They may also collaborate with set designers to create custom sets and backgrounds.
6. Posing and Directing: Fashion photographers direct models during the shoot to achieve the desired poses, expressions, and body language. They provide guidance on how to showcase the clothing and accessories effectively.
7. Post-Processing: After the photo shoot, fashion photographers retouch and edit the images to enhance their quality, correct imperfections, and achieve the desired aesthetic. This may involve adjusting colors, contrast, and overall image composition.

Fashion photography is an ever-evolving field that reflects current fashion trends, cultural influences, and artistic visions. It requires creativity, attention to detail, and effective collaboration with a team to produce captivating images that inspire and evoke emotions.

Industrial Photographer

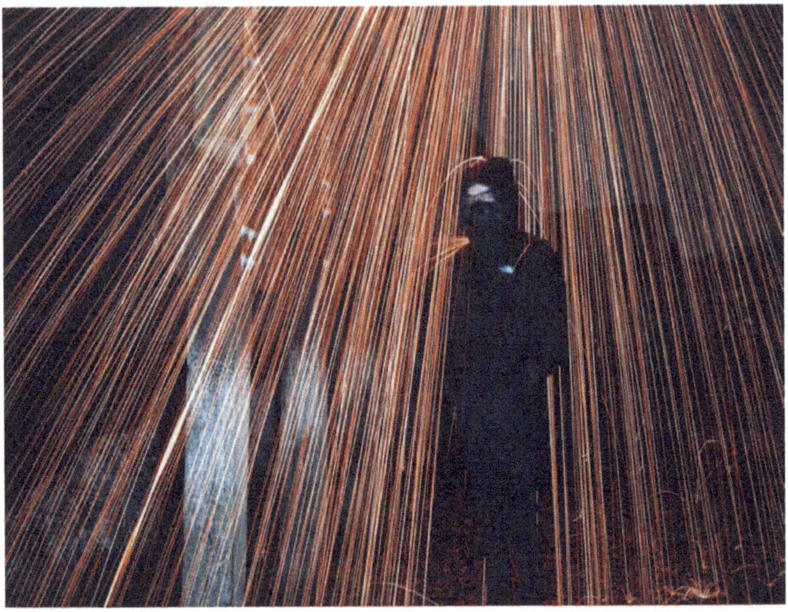

Industrial photography is a specialized genre of photography that focuses on capturing images related to industries, manufacturing processes, and industrial environments. It is often used for commercial and promotional purposes by companies in sectors such as manufacturing, construction, energy, transportation, and engineering. Industrial photographers aim to showcase the scale, intricacies, and technical aspects of industrial operations through their images. Here are some key aspects of industrial photography:

1. Documentation: Industrial photographers document various aspects of industrial processes, including manufacturing, construction, machinery, infrastructure, and production lines. They capture images that depict the equipment, facilities, and people involved in these operations.
2. Safety and Regulations: Industrial photography requires adherence to safety protocols and regulations. Photographers must be aware of

potential hazards and follow safety guidelines to ensure their own safety and the safety of others in the industrial environment.

3. Equipment and Machinery: Industrial photographers capture images of complex machinery, equipment, and tools used in industrial processes. They focus on highlighting the functionality, precision, and scale of these elements.
4. Architectural and Structural Photography: Industrial photographers may also document industrial architecture and structures, such as factories, power plants, refineries, bridges, and construction sites. They aim to showcase the design, engineering, and scale of these structures.
5. Environmental Considerations: Some industrial photography may involve capturing images related to environmental sustainability, pollution control, or renewable energy sources. Photographers may showcase efforts to minimize the environmental impact of industrial activities.
6. People and Portraits: Industrial photography often includes photographs of workers, engineers, technicians, and other individuals involved in industrial operations. These images can convey the human aspect of the industry and showcase the expertise and dedication of the people working in these environments.
7. Lighting and Composition: Lighting is crucial in industrial photography, as it helps highlight specific details, textures, and shapes. Photographers may use a combination of natural light and artificial lighting techniques to create visually appealing images. Composition plays a vital role in capturing the scale, perspective, and overall aesthetics of the industrial subjects.
8. Post-Processing: Industrial photographers may perform post-processing on their images to enhance their visual impact. This can involve adjustments to color, contrast, and sharpness, as well as removing distractions or imperfections.

Industrial photography requires a good understanding of industrial processes, technical expertise, and the ability to capture images that convey the desired message or story. It often involves working in challenging environments and requires effective communication and coordination with clients and subjects in the industrial sector.

Military Photographer

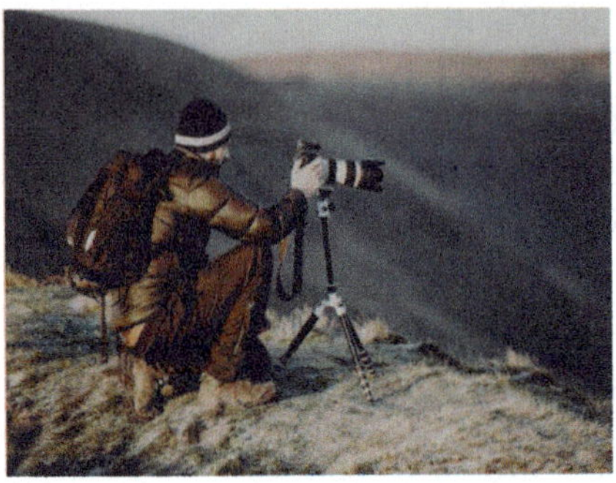

Military photography, also known as military combat photography or military photojournalism, involves documenting military operations, personnel, equipment, and events related to the armed forces. Military photographers are typically embedded with military units to capture images that depict the reality and experiences of military life. Here are some key aspects of military photography:

1. Embedded Photography: Military photographers often work closely with military units, gaining access to combat zones, training exercises, and other military activities. They document the experiences of soldiers, capturing their daily routines, training, missions, and deployments.
2. Operational Photography: Military photographers document military operations, including combat missions, humanitarian efforts, peacekeeping missions, and training exercises. They capture the action, emotions, and challenges faced by military personnel in various situations.
3. Equipment and Technology: Military photographers showcase the equipment, weapons, vehicles, and technology used by the military. They capture images that highlight the capabilities, functionality, and impact of these resources.

4. Portraits and Personnel: Military photographers often capture portraits and candid shots of military personnel, both on and off duty. These images provide a human perspective, showcasing the individuals who serve in the armed forces and their personal experiences.
5. Training and Exercises: Military photographers document training sessions and exercises, capturing the intensity, teamwork, and skill development involved. These images can also be used for educational or promotional purposes.
6. Military Events and Ceremonies: Military photographers cover official military events, ceremonies, and commemorations. This includes parades, medal ceremonies, change of command ceremonies, and other significant military gatherings.
7. Risk and Safety: Military photography can involve significant risks, especially in combat zones or during dangerous operations. Photographers must follow military protocols and safety guidelines to ensure their own safety and the safety of those around them.
8. Photojournalism and Storytelling: Military photographers aim to tell compelling visual stories through their images. They strive to capture the reality, emotions, and unique experiences of military personnel, allowing viewers to gain insight into military life.
9. Ethics and Security: Military photographers must adhere to ethical standards and respect operational security. They often undergo training to understand the boundaries of what can be photographed and published to ensure sensitive information is not compromised.

Military photography plays a crucial role in documenting history, informing the public, and preserving the experiences of military personnel. It requires technical skills, adaptability, resilience, and the ability to capture powerful images in challenging and dynamic environments.

Nature/Wildlife Photographer

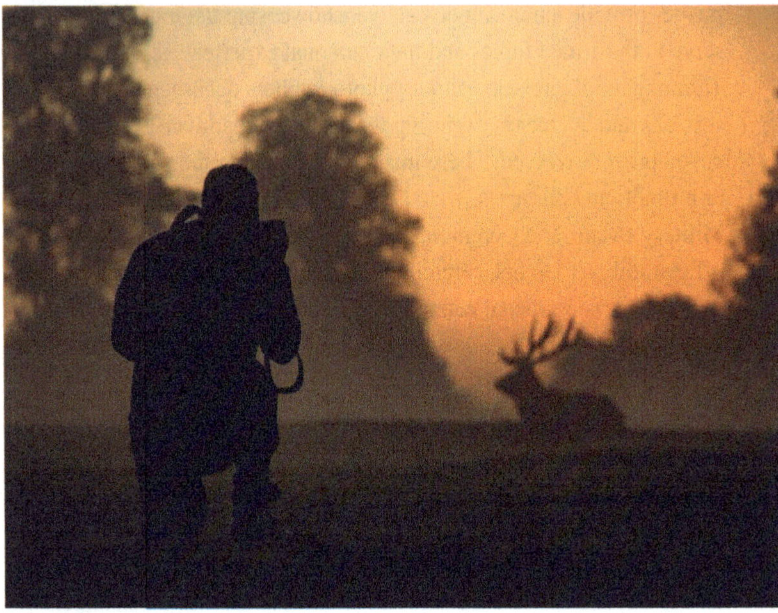

Wildlife and nature photography is a genre that focuses on capturing images of animals, plants, landscapes, and natural environments. Wildlife photographers strive to document the beauty, behavior, and diversity of the natural world, while nature photographers often emphasize the grandeur and serenity of landscapes. Here are some key aspects of wildlife and nature photography:

1. Fieldcraft and Patience: Wildlife photographers need a good understanding of animal behavior and habitats. They spend time researching their subjects and locations, observing wildlife patterns, and positioning themselves to capture the best shots. Patience is crucial as it may take hours or even days to capture the desired image.
2. Equipment: Wildlife and nature photographers typically use specialized camera equipment and lenses to capture distant or elusive subjects. Long telephoto lenses, tripods, and other accessories are commonly employed to maintain stability and capture detailed images.

3. Composition and Lighting: Composition plays a vital role in wildlife and nature photography. Photographers strive to create visually pleasing and balanced compositions, using techniques such as the rule of thirds, leading lines, and framing. Understanding and utilizing natural lighting conditions is crucial for capturing captivating images.
4. Conservation and Ethics: Wildlife and nature photographers often have a strong conservation mindset and aim to raise awareness about environmental issues. They follow ethical guidelines, respect wildlife and their habitats, and avoid disturbing or altering natural behaviors for the sake of a photograph.
5. Research and Preparation: Successful wildlife and nature photographers conduct thorough research on the subjects they intend to photograph. This includes learning about the species, their habitats, migration patterns, and best times for observation. They also prepare for the challenges of working in remote locations and extreme weather conditions.
6. Wildlife Behavior and Action: Capturing unique and engaging moments of wildlife behavior is a key objective for wildlife photographers. This may include interactions between animals, hunting, feeding, courtship displays, or other noteworthy actions that reveal the essence of the species.
7. Landscapes and Environmental Context: Nature photographers often incorporate landscapes to provide context and emphasize the natural beauty of the environment. They capture wide-angle shots of mountains, forests, deserts, or other scenic locations to showcase the grandeur and diversity of the natural world.
8. Post-Processing: After capturing images, wildlife and nature photographers engage in post-processing to enhance their photos. This can include adjustments to colors, contrast, sharpness, and cropping. The goal is to present the images in a way that reflects the photographer's artistic vision while maintaining the authenticity of the natural subject.

Wildlife and nature photography offers opportunities to connect with nature, appreciate biodiversity, and inspire conservation efforts. It requires a deep appreciation for the natural world, technical skills, fieldcraft knowledge, and an artistic eye to capture stunning images that tell stories and evoke emotions.

Landscape photographers

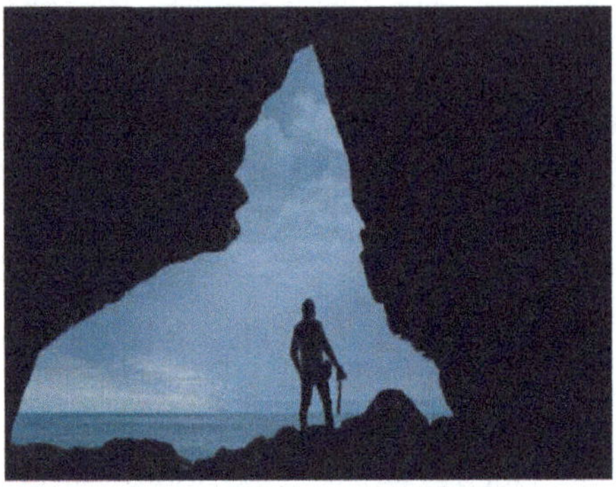

Landscape photography is a genre that focuses on capturing images of natural scenery, such as mountains, seascapes, forests, deserts, and other natural environments. Landscape photographers aim to convey the beauty, serenity, and grandeur of the landscapes they capture. Here are some key aspects of landscape photography:

1. Composition: Composition is a fundamental aspect of landscape photography. Photographers carefully frame their shots to create visually appealing compositions, utilizing techniques such as the rule of thirds, leading lines, foreground interest, and balanced elements.
2. Lighting: Lighting is crucial in landscape photography. Photographers often seek out the best lighting conditions, such as the soft light of early morning or late afternoon, to enhance the mood and atmosphere of the scene. The direction and quality of light can dramatically impact the final image.
3. Foreground and Depth: Creating a sense of depth and scale is important in landscape photography. Photographers often incorporate a strong foreground element to draw viewers into the image and create a sense of perspective. They also work with different focal lengths and depths of field to emphasize the layers and distance in the landscape.

4. Timing and Patience: Landscape photographers often need to be patient and wait for the right moment to capture their desired shot. This may involve waiting for the perfect light, the right weather conditions, or waiting for elements in the scene to align harmoniously.
5. Equipment: Landscape photographers typically use a variety of equipment to capture their images. This may include wide-angle lenses to capture expansive scenes, tripods for stability, filters to control light and enhance colors, and remote shutter releases to minimize camera shake.
6. Planning and Research: Successful landscape photographers often research their locations in advance. They study maps, weather patterns, and seasonal variations to determine the best time and conditions for photographing a particular landscape. This preparation helps them anticipate the optimal moments for capturing their desired shots.
7. Post-Processing: After capturing the images, landscape photographers engage in post-processing to enhance and refine their photos. This may involve adjusting colors, contrast, and sharpness, as well as removing distractions or imperfections. The goal is to present the landscape in a way that reflects the photographer's artistic vision while maintaining the natural beauty of the scene.
8. Environmental Considerations: Landscape photographers often have a deep appreciation for the environment and strive to minimize their impact on natural landscapes. They follow ethical guidelines, respect protected areas, and avoid actions that could harm or disturb the environment or wildlife.

Landscape photography offers a way to connect with nature, appreciate the beauty of the world, and convey a sense of awe and wonder through images. It requires a combination of technical skills, artistic vision, and an appreciation for the natural world to capture stunning landscape photographs that evoke emotions and inspire viewers.

News/event photographer (or Photojournalist)

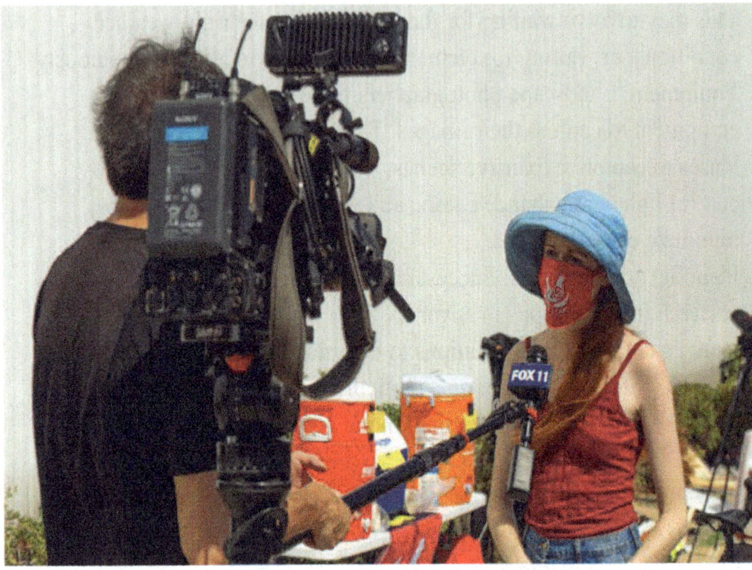

A news photographer, also known as a photojournalist, is a professional who captures images to visually document news events, current affairs, and stories of public interest. News photographers work for newspapers, news agencies, online publications, and other media outlets to provide visual coverage and support news articles. Here are some key aspects of news photography:

1. News Gathering: News photographers are assigned to cover a wide range of events, including political rallies, protests, sports events, natural disasters, crime scenes, cultural events, and more. They are responsible for capturing compelling and informative images that help tell the story and provide visual context to the news articles.
2. Timeliness: News photographers work under tight deadlines and must capture and deliver images quickly. They are often required to transmit their photographs promptly to the newsroom or upload them to digital platforms for immediate publication.
3. Visual Storytelling: News photographers aim to tell a story through their images. They capture key moments, emotions, and impactful scenes that convey the essence of the news event or story. They strive

to create images that engage viewers and provide them with a deeper understanding of the subject matter.

4. Ethics and Accuracy: News photographers adhere to ethical guidelines and professional standards. They maintain accuracy and fairness in their visual representation of events, avoiding manipulation or distortion that could alter the truthfulness of the images.
5. Adaptability and Versatility: News photographers must be adaptable and ready to cover various types of assignments. They may need to quickly switch between different subjects and environments, adjusting their approach to suit the specific news event or story.
6. Equipment and Technical Skills: News photographers use professional camera equipment and lenses to capture high-quality images in different lighting conditions and environments. They need to be proficient in operating their equipment and have a solid understanding of exposure, composition, and other technical aspects of photography.
7. Safety Considerations: News photographers often work in challenging and potentially hazardous situations. They must prioritize personal safety and follow safety protocols while covering events like protests, conflicts, or natural disasters. They may also need to be sensitive to the privacy and emotions of individuals involved in sensitive news stories.
8. Captioning and Metadata: News photographers provide accurate and detailed captions, including names, locations, and context, along with their images. This information helps provide accurate and informative captions for news articles and ensures proper credit for their work.

News photographers play a vital role in journalism, providing powerful visual documentation of important events and stories. They work alongside journalists, editors, and other news professionals to convey information and engage audiences through their images. Their work contributes to the overall storytelling and impact of news articles and publications.

Portrait Photographer

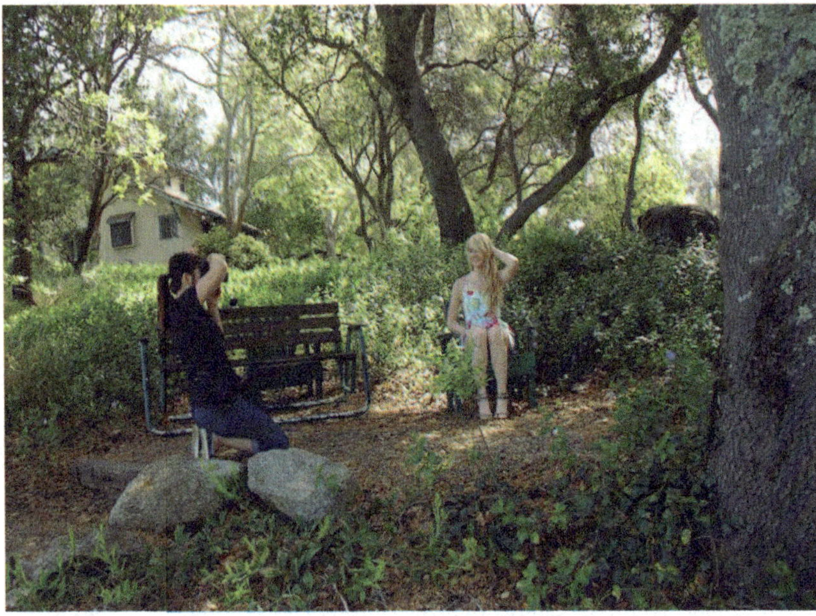

A portrait photographer specializes in capturing images that showcase the personality, expression, and essence of an individual or a group of people. Portrait photography is often used for personal, professional, or artistic purposes, including family portraits, headshots, senior portraits, corporate portraits, and editorial portraits. Here are some key aspects of portrait photography:

1. Communication and Connection: Portrait photographers work closely with their subjects to establish a comfortable and trusting environment. They communicate with their clients to understand their preferences, goals, and the desired outcome of the portrait session. Building a rapport with the subjects helps create a relaxed atmosphere and enables the photographer to capture authentic and meaningful expressions.
2. Posing and Expression: Portrait photographers guide their subjects in posing and capturing natural expressions. They provide direction on body positioning, facial expressions, and the use of props or settings

to enhance the visual impact of the portrait. They strive to capture the unique qualities and emotions of the individuals being photographed.

3. Lighting and Composition: Portrait photographers use various lighting techniques to flatter their subjects and create the desired mood or style. They may work with natural light, studio lighting, or a combination of both. Composition is essential in portrait photography to create visually pleasing and balanced images, utilizing elements such as framing, rule of thirds, and leading lines.
4. Location and Background: Portrait photographers can work in a studio or on location, depending on the desired aesthetic and client preferences. They may utilize various backdrops, props, or settings to create an environment that enhances the subject's character or complements their profession or personality.
5. Retouching and Post-Processing: After the photo session, portrait photographers often engage in post-processing to enhance and refine the images. This may involve adjusting colors, retouching skin imperfections, enhancing details, and overall image composition. The goal is to create polished and visually appealing portraits while maintaining the natural look of the subject.
6. Specialized Portrait Types: Portrait photographers may specialize in specific types of portraits. For example, family photographers capture images that convey the relationships and connections within a family. Corporate photographers focus on professional headshots or portraits for business purposes. Senior portrait photographers specialize in capturing the personalities and milestones of high school seniors. Each type of portrait requires a unique approach and understanding of the subject matter.
7. Creative Expression: Portrait photography also allows for artistic expression. Portrait photographers may experiment with different styles, techniques, and post-processing effects to create unique and captivating portraits that convey their artistic vision.

Portrait photography is a highly personal and creative field that requires strong interpersonal skills, technical expertise, and an ability to capture the essence of an individual or group. It aims to create images that evoke emotions, tell stories, and preserve memories for years to come.

Sports Photographer

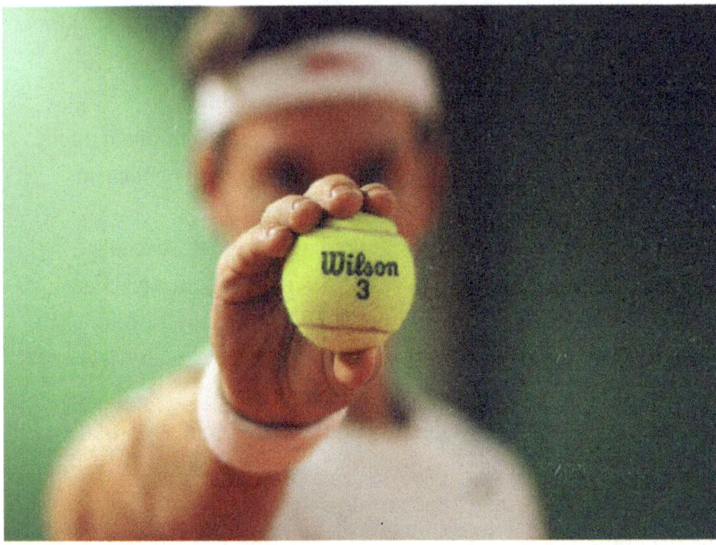

Sports photography is a specialized genre that focuses on capturing dynamic and impactful images of sports events and athletes in action. Sports photographers work in a fast-paced environment, often in challenging lighting conditions, to document the excitement, athleticism, and emotions of sports competitions. Here are some key aspects of sports photography:

1. Timing and Anticipation: Sports photographers must have excellent timing and anticipation skills to capture the decisive moments in a sports event. They need to anticipate actions such as a winning goal, a dramatic dive, or a key moment in the game to capture images that convey the intensity and passion of the sport.
2. Fast Autofocus and Burst Mode: Sports photographers use fast cameras with advanced autofocus capabilities to track and capture moving subjects. Burst mode allows them to shoot multiple frames per second, increasing the chances of capturing the perfect moment.
3. Telephoto Lenses: Sports photographers rely on telephoto lenses to bring distant subjects closer and capture the action from the sidelines or stands. These lenses provide the reach and compression needed to

capture tight shots of athletes, isolating them from the background and emphasizing their movements.

4. Understanding Sports: Sports photographers need a good understanding of the sport they are capturing to anticipate the action and choose the right angles. They familiarize themselves with the rules, strategies, and player positions to position themselves for the best shots.
5. Composition and Visual Impact: Sports photographers aim to create visually compelling images that tell a story and engage viewers. They utilize composition techniques such as leading lines, framing, and rule of thirds to create dynamic and visually pleasing photographs.
6. Lighting and Venue Considerations: Sports events can take place in various lighting conditions, from outdoor daylight to indoor arenas with artificial lighting. Sports photographers adapt to different lighting situations and adjust their camera settings accordingly to capture well-exposed images. They also consider the venue layout and positioning to capture the best angles and perspectives.
7. Post-Processing: After capturing the images, sports photographers engage in post-processing to enhance and refine the photographs. They may adjust exposure, color balance, sharpness, and crop the images to highlight the key elements and bring out the action and emotions captured.
8. Editorial Deadlines: Sports photographers often work on tight deadlines, especially when covering live events for newspapers, magazines, or online publications. They need to quickly select and edit their best shots to meet publication deadlines.

Sports photography requires technical skills, knowledge of the sport, and the ability to react quickly to capture the fleeting moments that define a game. It also demands the ability to tell a story through images and convey the energy and excitement of the sports event.

Wedding Photographer

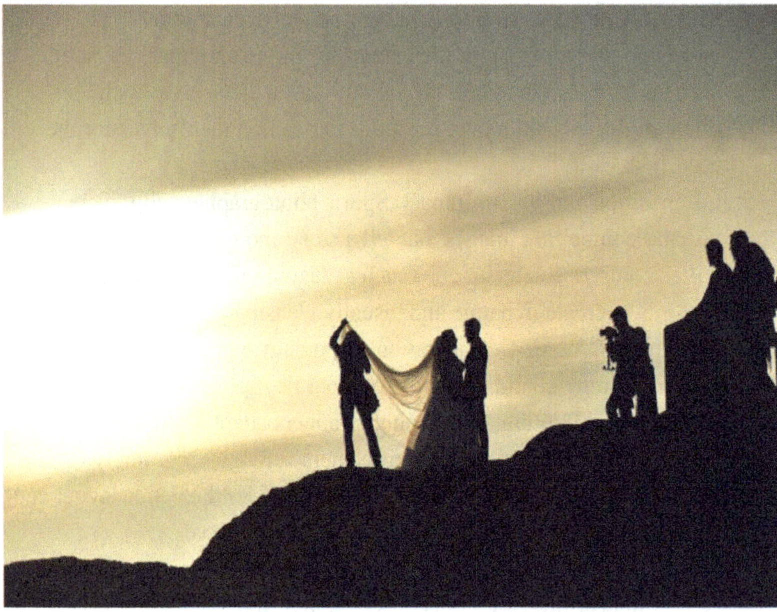

Wedding photography is a specialized field that focuses on capturing the special moments and emotions of a wedding day. Wedding photographers play a crucial role in documenting the joy, love, and celebration of this significant event in people's lives. They work closely with couples to create a collection of images that tell the story of their wedding day. Here are some key aspects of wedding photography:

1. Pre-wedding Consultation: Wedding photographers typically meet with the couple before the wedding day to discuss their vision, preferences, and specific moments they want to capture. This consultation helps the photographer understand the couple's style, the wedding theme, and any specific cultural or religious traditions that need to be considered.
2. Coverage of Key Moments: Wedding photographers are responsible for capturing the key moments of the wedding day, including the

ceremony, exchanging of vows, ring exchange, first kiss, first dance, cake cutting, and more. They also document candid moments, emotional interactions, and the overall atmosphere of the day.

3. Candid and Posed Shots: Wedding photographers aim to capture a mix of candid and posed shots. Candid photos capture spontaneous moments and genuine emotions, while posed shots involve carefully directed poses and compositions. They work to strike a balance between capturing authentic moments and creating beautifully composed images.
4. Attention to Details: Wedding photographers pay attention to the small details that make each wedding unique. They capture shots of the wedding rings, bouquet, table settings, wedding décor, and other elements that contribute to the overall ambiance of the day.
5. Lighting and Composition: Wedding photographers work with different lighting conditions, both natural and artificial. They utilize their skills in lighting and composition to create visually stunning images. They consider factors such as the venue, available light, and the desired mood to capture images that are well-exposed, balanced, and visually pleasing.
6. Portrait Sessions: Wedding photographers typically conduct portrait sessions with the couple, family members, and wedding party. These sessions involve capturing formal portraits, as well as more relaxed and creative shots. They guide the subjects in posing and provide direction to create images that reflect the personalities and emotions of the individuals.
7. Post-Processing and Album Design: After the wedding day, wedding photographers engage in post-processing to enhance and refine the images. They may adjust colors, exposure, and crop the images for optimal results. Additionally, they may offer services for album design, selecting and arranging the best images to tell the story of the wedding day.
8. Professionalism and Organization: Wedding photographers need to be highly organized, punctual, and professional. They should be able to work efficiently under pressure, as weddings often have a tight schedule and many moving parts. Good communication and

interpersonal skills are also important, as they interact with the couple, family members, and guests throughout the day.

Wedding photography is a significant investment for couples, as it allows them to cherish and relive the memories of their special day. Wedding photographers have the privilege of capturing moments that will be treasured for a lifetime, and they strive to create a collection of images that reflect the love, joy, and emotions of the couple and their loved ones.

Forensic Photographer

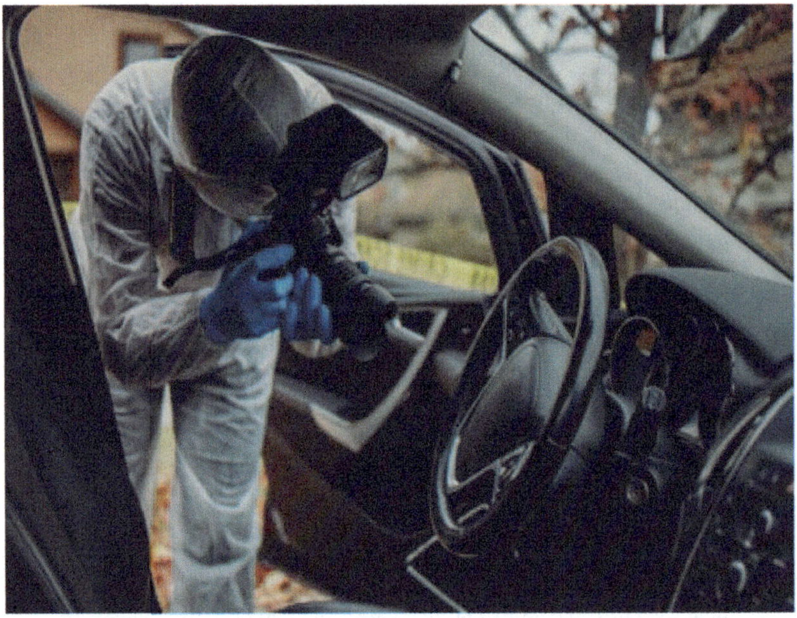

As a forensic photographer, you play a vital role in the criminal justice system. Your work helps document and preserve crucial evidence that can be used in investigations and court proceedings, ultimately contributing to the pursuit of justice and ensuring the guilty are held accountable. By accurately documenting crime scenes and collecting visual evidence, you assist law enforcement agencies in solving crimes and ensuring public safety. Your work directly impacts society by helping to identify and apprehend criminals, potentially preventing further harm. Forensic photography requires a combination of technical skills, knowledge of forensic procedures, and an understanding of legal requirements. Pursuing a career in this field allows you to continually develop and enhance your expertise, which can lead to professional growth and advancement opportunities. Here is a numbered list highlighting key aspects of being a forensic photographer:

1. Technical Skills: Develop expertise in photography equipment, including cameras, lenses, and lighting, to capture high-quality and accurate images at crime scenes.
2. Attention to Detail: Pay meticulous attention to detail when documenting evidence, ensuring that every relevant aspect is captured accurately.
3. Knowledge of Forensic Procedures: Understand forensic protocols and procedures to effectively document and preserve evidence while adhering to legal requirements and chain of custody.
4. Forensic Photography Techniques: Learn specialized techniques such as scale photography, close-up/macro photography, and alternate light sources for capturing specific types of evidence.
5. Documentation and Organization: Maintain thorough and organized documentation of each photograph, including metadata, location, time, and case details.
6. Collaboration: Work closely with law enforcement, forensic experts, and other professionals involved in crime scene investigations to ensure accurate and comprehensive photographic documentation.
7. Confidentiality and Integrity: Uphold strict ethical standards, ensuring the confidentiality and integrity of the evidence and maintaining professionalism in all aspects of the job.
8. Understanding of Legal Proceedings: Familiarize yourself with legal processes and requirements for presenting photographic evidence in court, and be prepared to testify as an expert witness if necessary.
9. Continuous Learning: Stay updated with advancements in forensic photography techniques, equipment, and industry best practices through training and professional development.

10. Emotional Resilience: Possess the ability to handle emotionally challenging and graphic scenes while maintaining composure and professionalism.

This numbered list provides a concise overview of key aspects to consider when pursuing a career as a forensic photographer. Each point represents an important element that contributes to success in this specialized field.

ABOUT THE AUTHOR

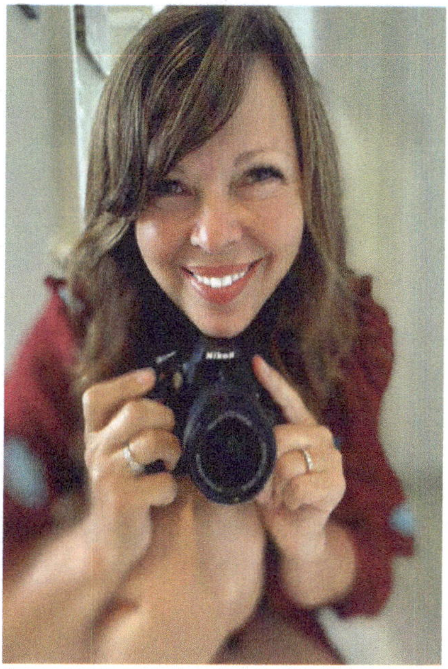

Tracy Heschong-McCrackin is an award-winning writer and photographer with her work recognized across the country. As a former winner of the Sacramento Film Festival and past Miss Rocklin & Miss Placer County, Tracy has gained extensive experience in both theater and the arts. Her IMBD filmology can be found at IMBD.com.

She started her photography studio 20 years ago and specialized in portraits, landscapes, and commercial photography. She has also acted in several TV commercials and now resides in Southern California with her husband of 30 years. Tracy has two grown children and four grandchildren. The Editor has acknowledged several of Tracy's images at National Geographic YourShots.

Her ability to capture the true essence of her subjects makes her artwork so compelling. Each photograph tells a story and immortalizes a moment that would have otherwise been lost. Tracy draws much of her inspiration from her travels. She has a passion for investigating off-the-beaten-path locations, cultures, and individuals. In those moments of exploration, her creativity is ignited, and much of her artwork is born.

Tracy's love for people is further shown in her commitment to being a Red Cross volunteer. Yet, despite all her professional and humanitarian credits, her two grown children and four grandchildren remain Tracy's greatest accomplishments. Tracy was recently honored as a Distinguished Past Alumni with their "Excellence in Creative Arts Award."

Her gallery work can be seen and purchased at www.tracymccrackin.com. She maintains active travel and guest blogs on other travel websites. She is currently working on other books, which can be purchased on her website.

http://www.tracymccrackin.com
https://twitter.com/tracymccrackin
https://www.facebook.com/tracymccrackinphotography

ALSO BY TRACY MCCRACKIN

Please check out my other photography work at www.tracymccrackin.com that are in the works…

Make Money As An Empty-Nester By Blogging!

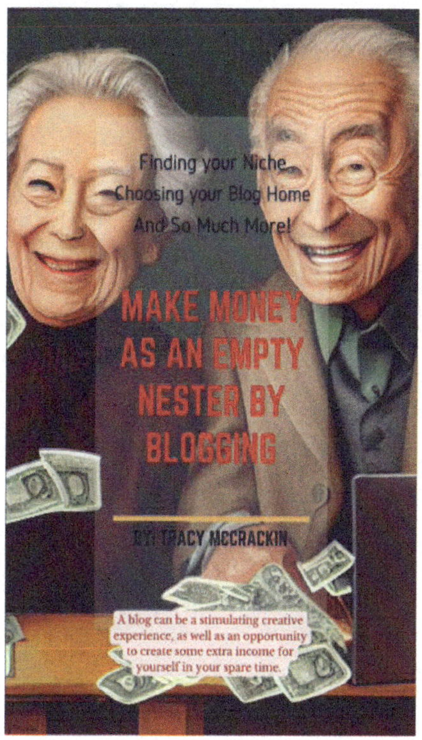

Now that your children have flown the coop, you may find yourself with some extra time on your hands. And what better way to spend that time than by generating some extra income for yourself? Whether you're looking for a little extra spending money or need to contribute to your family's financial bottom line, there are plenty of ways to start earning some serious cash. With my help, you can turn your hobbies and passions into a money-making venture. From selling homemade crafts online to renting out your unused space, there are countless opportunities to earn money in the "empty nest" phase of life. So why wait? Let's get started on your journey to financial independence today!

Made in United States
North Haven, CT
09 February 2025

65604057R00225